Essential Software
for Writers

A COMPLETE GUIDE FOR EVERYONE
WHO WRITES WITH A PC

HY BENDER

WRITER'S DIGEST BOOKS
CINCINNATI, OH

98 97 96 95 94   5 4 3 2 1

Library of Congress Cataloging in Publication Data

Bender, Hy.
    Essential software for writers/Hy Bender.
      p. cm.
    Includes index.
    ISBN 0-89879-667-9
    1. Authorship—Data processing. I. Title
    PN171.D37B46 1994   93-40898
    808'.02'0285—dc20   CIP

Cover illustration © 1993 Ken Coffelt/SIS

Essential Software for Writers

for Writers

**A COMPLETE GUIDE FOR EVERYONE
WHO WRITES WITH A PC**

To my father

Acknowledgments

First and foremost, my thanks go to my editor, William Brohaugh, for his belief in this book. My thanks also go to Lynn Perrigo, Mert Ransdell, Michael Mellin, Tom Dillon, Mia McKrosky, Elizabeth Gehrman, Julie O'Leary, Carol Barth, and Greg Reynolds for their editorial and production work.

I'm very grateful to Elena Andrews for helping me cull hundreds of drawings out of Dover clip art books and matching them to writing quotations. Thanks for coming to my rescue as the deadlines started closing in, Elena.

I also appreciate the efforts of the many people who provided me with the products and information that form the foundation of this book. There are way too many to mention here, but those who went above and beyond the call include Alex Gross, Mark McBride, Alan Melby, Christine Miller, and Christy Heinen.

Lastly, I offer my heartfelt thanks to Tracey Siesser and Stefan Petrucha for their constant friendship; and to the members of my biweekly writer's workshop—Elena Andrews, Ed Bungert, Adam-Troy Castro, Jennie Grey, Sharon Gumerove, Ken Houghton, Rory Metcalf, NancyKay Shapiro, Janna Silverstein, and Susan Solan—for their advice, support, and bad jokes. Thanks, pals; I love you all.

About the Author

Hy Bender has been involved with virtually every area of the personal computer field. He's worked as a programmer, a software designer, and a trainer who's helped thousands of new PC owners get up and running.

He's written several computer books for Que and Osborne/McGraw-Hill, as well as numerous software training manuals and videotapes, and articles for the respected technical publications *PC Magazine, PC World,* and *PC Week.*

When not playing with computers, Bender has taken on such diverse tasks as editing a newsletter on journalistic ethics, scripting comedy skits for cable television, and writing for magazines like *Mad, Spy, Advertising Age,* and *American Film.* He lives in New York.

CONTENTS

Part V   Handling Specialized Writing Tasks   207

Chapter 11   Tools for Newspaper, Magazine, and Book Writers   209

Chapter 12   Tools for Movie, Television, and Theatre Writers   225

Chapter 13   Tools for Poets   259

INTRODUCTION

The tools I need for my work are paper, tobacco, food, and a little whisky.

—William Faulkner

I think the same situation is involved as painting and sculpture. If you use the best materials you can afford, somehow you have more respect for what you do with them.

—John MacDonald

I love being a writer. What I can't stand is the paperwork.

—Peter De Vries

I have everything I need to begin my writing career—pens, paper, and the illusion that I have talent.

—Broomhilda

Whatever your job is, I'll bet a significant part of it depends on using your PC for some kind of writing. The writing may be directed at a magazine article, or an office memo, or a sales report, or a legal brief. But regardless of the type of prose you produce, you are a *writer*, and have the same basic needs as any full-time writer for instruction and support.

There are many books on specific word processors (such as *WordPerfect: The Complete Reference* and *Mastering Microsoft Word*) that teach the mechanics of entering and editing text. However, these works don't help with the complex processes involved in pulling words from the air and making them sing.

At the same time, there are lots of books that address the mental writing process (such as William Zinsser's *On Writing Well* and John Gardner's *The Art of Fiction*), but these fail to discuss the slew of down-to-earth tools available to writers working with modern technology.

For example, if you're grappling with a blank screen, you may benefit from electronic idea generators and writing coaches. If you're seeking help with editing, you can get it from disk-based spelling checkers, thesauruses, dictionaries, grammar checkers, and style checkers. And if you're conducting research, you can obtain information quickly and easily from electronic encyclopedias, quotation collections, atlases, almanacs, and thousands of other reference works available on disk or CD-ROM, or through a modem.

While such products can be invaluable aids to your writing process, they're often produced by relatively small companies and receive little press coverage. Until now, no one has comprehensively covered the numerous tools available for writing with a PC.

That's where this book comes in. *Essential Software for Writers* touches on every significant aspect of researching, composing, editing, laying out, and printing documents with your computer.

The book begins by describing and comparing the most popular word processing programs. It then discusses the wide range of other software you can buy to help with your writing.

The book also attempts to hone in on your *specialized* writing needs via chapters for newspaper, magazine, and book writers; movie, television, and theatre scripters; poets; businesspeople; lawyers; physicians; scientists and engineers; multilingual writers; and students and academics.

It then examines programs that help your PC operate more efficiently, translate file formats, produce attractive layouts, and print your final-draft documents. Lastly, it provides appendices that explain common PC terms, list additional information resources, and offer over $2,000 worth of discount coupons.

I've designed this book to be modular, which means you don't have to read Part II before you read Part III. You can skip around all you like, and read only the sections that most interest you. If a topic is mentioned in more than one chapter, I include a cross-reference to let you know which chapter provides the fullest discussion of it.

In addition to being informative, I'm hoping you find the book to be, well, *fun*. To that end, I've sprinkled amidst the product reviews over 170 illustrations matched with scores of classic quotations about writing.

Oh, and if you're wondering who I am: On the computer side, I'm a writer who's produced thousands of pages of classroom and video PC training materials for corporate and government audiences. I've also done time as a programmer, a software support techie, a co-designer of a top-rated spelling checker, and the author of three previous books on PC software. On the non-computer side, I've tackled such roles as journalist, short story writer, TV scripter, and newsletter editor, and been published by such magazines as *Mad*, *Spy*, *American Film*, and *Advertising Age*. In brief, I understand software, and I'm familiar with the needs of a wide range of writers.

What You Need to Know

First, I'm assuming that you have some basic PC knowledge. If you don't, you'll still find it useful to read through this book, as it'll give you a sense of what's currently available. However, you may want to reread certain chapters after you've picked up some computer experience.

I'm also assuming that you're currently using some kind of word processor. If you aren't, don't sweat it; Chapter 1 was made for you, and Chapter 2 will also prove helpful. However, you may find that certain sections of the book make more sense after you've developed a solid feel for how a word processor works, and what it can and can't do for you.

I've attempted to avoid PC jargon as much as possible, but the use of some standard terms is unavoidable. If you run across a computer word that baffles you (such as *disk*, *CD-ROM*, or *modem* in this Introduction), try looking it up in Appendix A, which is a glossary of PC terms. If you find yourself still struggling, you might consider buying a computer dictionary or the electronic equivalent (see Chapter 5, *Electronic Dictionaries and Thesauruses*).

Also, because PC programs now come in two "flavors," you need to know the difference between DOS and Windows.

DOS versus Windows

Before the PC could be born in 1981, IBM had to hire Microsoft to create a program that would run in the background and in effect act as the machine's brain. This special program, called an *operating system*, was DOS, and it hasn't changed a whole lot in the past decade. DOS is *character-based*, which means it's centered around a somewhat rigid display of letters and numbers. DOS programs are typically fast and efficient, but don't offer much visual pizzazz.

In 1990, Microsoft created a more modern operating system, called Windows 3.0, which runs in conjunction with DOS and takes over many of DOS' functions. Windows provides a *graphical user interface*, which roughly means that it's based around dynamic images rather than static text. Windows makes it easy for programs to draw anything anywhere on the screen, and so allows for a more flexible and colorful display (which is especially useful for desktop publishing). In addition, Windows provides such technical advantages as better management of your PC's memory and the ability to run multiple programs at the same time.

Because it does so much, however, Windows places heavy demands on your PC's brainpower, and so tends to encumber the operation of the programs you're using. In fact, if your PC is slower than a 12 megahertz 286 or has less than four megabytes of memory, don't even bother trying to run Windows, because it will make everything run so sluggishly that you won't be able to stand it.

Despite its speed drawbacks, Windows is extremely popular. As a result, many programs now come in two versions: one for DOS, and one for Windows. In most instances the two versions will be virtually identical (with the qualification that the Windows version will be more attractive), though occasionally the dual versions will have vast differences (and this book will let you know when that's the case). For now, the important thing is to be aware that both types of operating environments exist, and that when you're ready to purchase a product you may need to choose whether you want the DOS version or the Windows one. (For more information about this, see Chapter 1.)

There *are* still many products that work exclusively under DOS, though. Therefore, unless I explicitly say that a program works under Windows, you can assume that it's a DOS program.

By the way, just to confuse you, there are other operating systems available for the PC, such as Unix and OS/2. If your needs are typical, though, you can ignore these others. For the foreseeable future, the only two systems that count (that is, that are supported by tens of millions of users, and thus by most software publishers) are DOS and Windows.

Copy Protection

In the early days of the PC industry, publishers were afraid that their customers would freely make copies of their software and give them away to friends, neighbors, and passers-by. As a result, these publishers "protected" their products with software routines that allowed only one or two installations; or with a plastic device, called a *dongle*, that had to be placed on a PC's parallel printer port for the program to run.

As the field matured, the vast majority of publishers came to realize that it didn't make good business sense to treat their customers like thieves. Besides, software copy protection often caused hard-to-anticipate installation and hard disk maintenance problems; and dongles were a pain for a customer with several products that required them, or for someone who used a laptop PC. Nowadays, with the exception of games companies, very few publishers still employ copy protection.

However, a small number still do. I've actually cut certain borderline programs from this book when I discovered they were copy protected. But some packages are so unique that I felt they deserved to be included despite their anti-customer safeguards. In these rare cases, I always clearly state that the product is copy protected, and whether it's protected by software or by a dongle. If you decide to buy any of these programs, complain long and often to the publisher taking your money until the copy protection is dropped.

Conventions, Typographical and Otherwise

This book has a few conventions that you may find helpful to know about.

For starters, when referring to the name of a key on the PC keyboard, the book capitalizes only the first letter, and sets the key's name in the same typeface as the rest of the text. Therefore, you'll see Enter instead of EN-TER, Shift rather than *Shift*, and so on.

An instruction to press two keys at the same time is represented by a plus (+) sign. For example, if you're supposed to hold down both the Ctrl key and the number 1 key simultaneously, you'll be told to press Ctrl+1.

On the other hand, if you're supposed to press one key, release it, and then press a second key, the sequence is represented by a comma (,). For example, the two separate keypresses of Esc and 1 are represented by Esc,1.

Moving on from typography, another convention you should understand is how product information is handled.

For every program discussed in this book, you're provided with the publisher's name, address, 800 number, local number, and fax number. In addition, you're given the product's version number; its list price, which is set by the publisher; and its approximate street price, which is a much lower price that's offered by quality mail order vendors such as PC Connection (800/800-0004) and MicroWAREHOUSE (800/367-7080).

(Actually, there are three exceptions to the "street price" rule. If a product is sold exclusively through its publisher, I use the phrase "generally not discounted." If I believe a product *is* sold through other channels but simply haven't been able to locate a vendor who discounts it, I use the phrase "Street Price N/A." And if this book contains a discount coupon for a product, I say so and supply the coupon price instead of the street price, since the coupon price is always lower.)

All this data appears at the end of each chapter under a section titled "Product Information," which is organized alphabetically by company name. Therefore, the first time a chapter mentions a program, the name of the product's company is also provided (unless the software and company names are virtually identical), so that you can quickly locate the product's contact information at the end of the chapter.

Finally, one caveat: Things change quickly in this industry. Therefore, it's a good idea to call a program's publisher to verify version numbers and prices before ordering.

That's all you need to know for now, so let's get started!

PART I

GETTING THE MOST FROM YOUR WORD PROCESSOR

The machine has several virtues....One may lean back in his chair and work it. It piles an awful stack of words on one page. It don't muss things or scatter ink blots around.

—Mark Twain, writing his first letter on a typewriter

CHAPTER

1

CHOOSING A WORD PROCESSOR

Twiddle-twiddle away at my softly clicky keyboard for a while, making twiddly adjustments all along—and then print what I have twiddled. Glare at the printout and snarl and curse and scribble almost illegibly all over it with a ballpoint pen. Go back to the machine and enter the scribbles. Repeat this procedure until I hate the very meaning of every word I know.

—Roy Blount, Jr.

If you've ever gotten trapped in a discussion about "which word processor is best?", you know it can get as passionate as a debate over religion or sex. It's no wonder, really. We spend an awful lot of time in our word processors; and the way that time is spent ranges from telling the program our inner-most thoughts to laboriously honing how we present ourselves to our peers.

So if you're firmly convinced the word processor you're now using is the greatest thing this side of creation, don't let anyone tell you different; because of the attachments you've developed to it, that program probably *is* the best one for you.

If you haven't yet selected a WP program, though, or if you think you might be interested in checking out the competition, read on. Word processing is the liveliest and most competitive software market, so there are a number of outstanding products to choose from.

The Contenders

In the early days of the PC, there were hundreds of word processing programs, and using *any* of them was vastly superior to banging away on a typewriter. For example, each program let you:

- Enter text in a continuous flow, instead of making you press a carriage return at the end of every line and change paper at the end of every page.

- Revise text on-screen, instead of via white-out.

- Delete, copy, and move sections of text with ease.

- Find words in a document instantly, and optionally replace them with different words.

- Print out new drafts at a keystroke.

On the other hand, a lot of the packages didn't do well beyond these basics; and they *all* left something to be desired.

Things have changed. There are now fewer than a dozen serious contenders in the word processing market, and they're all versatile and feature-packed.

For most people, the ones worth considering are, in order of popularity:

- WordPerfect for DOS
- Microsoft Word for DOS
- Microsoft Word for Windows
- WordPerfect for Windows
- Lotus Ami Pro (for Windows)
- XyWrite/Nota Bene (for DOS)

However, if you're a beginner or want to save some money, you might also consider:

- PC-Write Advanced Level (for DOS)
- Textra (for DOS)
- Lotus Write (for Windows)
- PFS:WindowWorks (integrated program for Windows)
- Microsoft Works (integrated program for DOS or Windows)
- Q&A (integrated program for DOS)

This chapter covers all of these programs, as well as a few others.

DOS versus Windows, Round II

Probably the first thing you noticed about the word processors just listed is that they come in two flavors: DOS and Windows. As explained in the Introduction, DOS programs tend to be fast and efficient, while Windows programs tend to be flexible and powerful.

If you don't have a machine capable of running Windows effectively (technically speaking, at *minimum* a 12MHz 286 with 4MB of memory and a 40MB hard disk), then your choice is simple: stick with DOS. If you have a fast machine with plenty of memory, though, your choice will depend on what your primary goals are.

The Case for DOS

If your main concern is composing and editing text (for example, if you're a journalist or fiction writer), you're probably better off with DOS. A DOS program will take your text as fast as you can type it, while a Windows program may force you to pause or suffer through a lot of on-screen blinking as it struggles to digest your words. Other operations, such as printing, will also typically go faster under DOS.

Something else to consider is that a DOS program is keyboard-intensive, meaning that once you learn how it works, you can do anything in the program fairly quickly via a few keystrokes. To operate a Windows program, however, you'll generally want to use a mouse, which forces you to periodically take a hand off the keyboard, breaking the flow of your typing. Windows programs also provide ways of getting at commands via keystrokes, but often do so grudgingly, requiring cumbersome keystroke sequences for even simple tasks.

Take a simple operation like highlighting a section of text that you want to copy or move to another location. In a typical DOS program, you press a single keystroke to mark the beginning of the text, and then use movement keys (such as the arrow keys, or a search command) to get to the end of the text. In a Windows program, if you don't use the mouse, you have to hold down the Shift key as you move. It's cumbersome to press both the Shift key and movement keys at the same time; and if you accidentally let go of Shift at any point, all the highlighting you've done is lost, forcing you to start from scratch. Further, using a search command to mark the end of your highlighting isn't even an option in a Windows program.

I revel in the prospect of being able to torture a phrase once more.

—S.J. Perelman

Another consideration is that, surprisingly, DOS screens are typically easier to read. A DOS word processor gives you large letters that are mono-spaced—that is, of the same size and shape. A Windows word processor, in contrast, proportionally spaces letters, so an *i* or *l* appears much thinner than an *n* or *m*. Proportional spacing is stylish on a printed page, but can give you eyestrain when you're trying to make out thin letters on your screen. (This problem is even worse when you're working in the small font sizes generally used for typeset manuscripts.)

A second visual advantage of DOS word processors is that they let you easily adjust the color of your letters and screen background—for example, you can set sharp white letters against a blue background, or soothing green letters against a black background. Windows programs, on the other hand, use black letters against a white background, which most closely resembles the look of a printed page, but may not happen to be the screen color combination that best suits your taste or your eyes. (You can change Windows colors, but only through the Windows Control Panel, which is rather tricky to operate, and which applies any color change to *all* your Windows programs, an effect you may not care for.)

At least as important, though, is the difference in philosophy. DOS word processors concentrate on displaying your bare text, shunning the flash and elegance of their Windows counterparts. While not as much fun, this spareness can help you to concentrate on content, instead of glittery formatting features that have nothing to do with the job of writing. Once you've grown accustomed to a solid DOS word processor, you can almost forget it's there and just let the words flow directly from your brain to your fingers.

Bottom line: If your main interest is fast, transparent text entry, and editing that never forces you to remove your hands from the keyboard, go with DOS.

The Case for Windows

On the other hand...if you make heavy use of such desktop publishing elements as fonts, graphics, and multi-column layouts; or if you use other Windows programs, and so are comfortable with the Windows way of doing things; or if you simply find using a mouse to be intuitive and fun, then Windows is for you. A DOS word processor can provide powerful desktop publishing features, and can even offer a Windows-style screen centered around mouse commands; but the way those features are implemented is downright clunky compared to the way they work in Windows.

Also, a Windows program is easier to learn because it organizes all its commands into a few *menus*. For example, a File menu will list commands for opening, saving, and printing document files; an Edit menu will list commands for copying, moving, and deleting text; and so on. You can view, or *pull down*, a menu with your mouse simply by clicking on the menu's name at the top of the program's window; you can then select any listed command by, again, just clicking on it. If the command leads to further options, they are presented in a rectangular *dialog box*, which typically lets you check off the choices you want by clicking to the left of them.

This visual system not only makes it a snap to get acquainted with a program's basic features, it also allows you to quickly access fancy features you might otherwise overlook. Further, when you *do* select a fancy feature —such as multiple columns or assorted fonts—you see the results of your choice immediately on screen, and can adjust the way things look to your heart's content. (In contrast, DOS programs force you to select a Print Preview command to see how your document will look, and won't allow you to revise anything while in Preview mode.)

All Windows programs look and feel pretty much alike, which means that once you learn how to work a Windows word processor such as Ami Pro, you've already learned a lot about how to use a Windows spreadsheet such as Microsoft Excel, or a Windows illustration package such as Corel Draw. This makes it easy to become fluent in several different programs, which is handy if you have to perform a number of diverse chores.

On top of that, Windows lets you keep many programs open at the same time, and quickly switch from program to program by pressing Alt+Tab or by just clicking on the program window you want. You can also easily move data between programs; and even set up links that automatically update, for instance, by changing a chart in your word processor whenever you revise the chart's data in your spreadsheet.

In a nutshell, Microsoft Windows is the current state-of-the-art. If you have use for its fancy features, it's clearly the way to go.

Those who can, write. Those who can't, write.

        —Duns Scotus

We are all apprentices in a craft where no one ever becomes a master.

        —Ernest Hemingway

All good writing is swimming under water and holding your breath.

        —F. Scott Fitzgerald

Then Again...

There's really no right or wrong here. Some people swear that WordPerfect for DOS has everything you could ever want in a word processor, while other fine folk contend that anyone who doesn't use Word for Windows or Ami Pro is brain-damaged. Truth is, a lot of it boils down to personal taste.

Then again, you could always do what *I* do: create and edit your text in a DOS word processor, and then import the polished document into a Windows word processor—or Windows desktop publishing program—to create your layout and final printout. Vive la différence.

The DOS Word Processors

The DOS word processing market is dominated by two giants: Word-Perfect and Microsoft Word. Some professional writers, however, prefer XyWrite/Nota Bene. Let's briefly review each of these packages.

WordPerfect for DOS

Simply put, WordPerfect is king. With a customer base exceeding 13 million, WordPerfect for DOS is one of the most ubiquitous and well-supported programs ever. This means that if you have a WordPerfect problem, you probably won't have much trouble finding someone nearby who can help. You'll also find scores of books, cassettes, videos, add-on programs, and other materials to aid you in exploiting the package's features to their fullest. On top of all that, the quality of WordPerfect's 800-number toll-free tech support is legendary.

WordPerfect's popularity is deserved. If you can stand wading through its hundreds of Windows-like menu options and dialog boxes, you'll find there isn't much the program can't do. And if you master its unintuitive 48-command function key structure (corresponding to the 12 function keys alone and in combination with Shift, Alt, and Ctrl), you'll whiz through complex operations with a few select keystrokes. The program has its quirks—for example, pressing PgDn actually moves you down a full page, while in virtually every other program PgDn moves you down by a screen—but if you can't grow accustomed to them, you have the option of redefining the keyboard so critical keys do what you think they should. You can also easily create macros—that is, collections of keystroke sequences you use frequently—and assign them Alt+letter keystrokes, such as Alt+S to save your document, or Alt+P to print it.

When you get stuck, you can get instant pop-up help by pressing a function key. Another nice, though lesser-known, feature is that if you press the

Help key twice, you get a display of all 48 of the commands assigned to the function keys.

WordPerfect gives you more options than you know what to do with, from numbering lines to numbering pages with Roman numerals to redlining. It also offers an editable graphics screen that lets you perform powerful desktop publishing operations (though not with the ease that a Windows program provides). Its ability to take advantage of the individual features of over 500 types of printers is easily the best in the industry. And WordPerfect even incorporates several products that you'd ordinarily have to purchase separately, such as a fully functional spreadsheet, fax software that lets you send and receive faxes without exiting your document, a program that prints your personalized logo along with your return address on your envelopes, and a topnotch grammar checker.

WordPerfect for DOS isn't perfect; it's a bit idiosyncratic, takes up an enormous amount of disk space, and isn't as strong in some areas as its competitors. But overall, you won't go wrong with WordPerfect; it's a safe choice and, for most people, even the right choice.

If you would not be forgotten as soon as you are dead, either write things worth reading or do things worth writing.

—Benjamin Franklin

History will be kind to me, for I intend to write it.

—Winston Churchill

Microsoft Word for DOS

Like WordPerfect, Microsoft Word for DOS tries to mix the advantages of character-based word processing with those of Windows packages. WordPerfect manages to pull off this difficult feat by providing full support for the DOS way of doing things (that is, quick and keystroke -intensive). Word is more grudging about its DOS side, emphasizing the use of menus and a mouse, and sometimes makes you feel like it really wishes it were in Windows.

However, Word is a solid program, and it's reasonably popular, with about 30 percent of the market to WordPerfect's 55 to 60 percent. Among Word's users are people who desire a Windows-style program, but either own an old PC that can't run Windows, or simply don't want to be saddled by the slowness of Windows.

Aside from its different look and feel, Word is notable for a few features that it implements more effectively than WordPerfect. One example is in its smooth ability to handle your document as an outline, letting you collapse and expand selected text sections as you need them. This is great when you want to switch rapidly between the "big picture" and the small details it encompasses.

Most significant, however, is Word's approach to formatting, which is based on a great idea called style sheets. A *style sheet* is a collection of formatting elements such as underlining, boldfacing, and type size that can be applied uniformly to sections of text. Style sheets are a powerful tool for making formatting changes quickly and consistently.

For example, let's say you created a document that set the first letter of selected paragraphs in 16-point type, and emphasized certain text sections with underlining. If you later decided to start your selected paragraphs with 18-point type and to emphasize using italics, you'd ordinarily have the tedious chore of revising your entire document manually. If you had applied your formatting using a style sheet, however, you could make all of the changes in two simple steps: change the definition of your paragraph-starting style from 16-point to 18-point, and your emphasis style from underline to italic.

A style sheet can do more than set character formatting, however; it also lets you define styles for the way entire paragraphs, and even entire pages, are handled. When dealing with long, complex documents, the flexibility and forced consistency provided by a style sheet becomes indispensable. Other word processors, such as WordPerfect, also let you use style sheets, but Microsoft Word was the pioneer of this feature and still provides the best implementation of it in the DOS world.

Word offers reasonable speed, though it doesn't have the quick feel of WordPerfect, let alone XyWrite (which is covered next). And as I've indicated, while you can work the program from the keyboard alone, doing so is a bit clunky; the package is really designed for use with a mouse. Like I said, it represents a compromise. Still, Word for DOS is faster than a typical Windows program; and if a feature such as style sheets is right for your needs, or you simply would like a program that's easy to learn, Word may be perfect for you.

Why do writers write? Because it isn't there.
> —Thomas Berger

We write to taste life twice: in the moment, and in retrospection.
> —Anais Nin

Great writers leave us not just their works, but a way of looking at things.
> —Elizabeth Janeway

Writing is putting one's obsessions in order.
> —Jean Grenier

XyWrite/Nota Bene

Let's get it out up front: *I* use XyWrite.

At the same time, saying XyWrite isn't for everybody is an understatement.

XyWrite is a speed demon. Text entry is smooth as can be, and the program responds so instantly to commands it can make your jaw drop. Programs that are normally considered fast, like WordPerfect, feel leaden next to XyWrite. A few seconds here and there may not seem like much, but they really count when you're in a hurry to get your words down and need your word processor to be as invisible as possible. Even if you're using an older, slower machine, Xywrite will fly on it.

XyWrite is also super-flexible. You can redefine the keyboard to your heart's content, easily fiddle with printer codes, perform complex operations using XyWrite's powerful programming language, work with up to nine documents at the same time, recover deleted text up to 30 levels deep, and generally make the thing jump through hoops.

A blessing/curse feature is that, in its most effective configuration, XyWrite's functions are command-driven, requiring you to type only two letters and press Enter. This is a major reason that XyWrite has less than 2 percent of the market; it can take a while to learn. However, once you've memorized the two-letter commands you'll regularly need (or assigned them to a keystroke you'll easily remember, such as Alt+P for printing), you'll find using XyWrite enormously faster than trudging through menus and dialog boxes. (Also, if you work at a newspaper or magazine that uses the popular Atex system, your learning curve will be minimal, because XyWrite is patterned after Atex.)

On top of all that, XyWrite document files are in *ASCII*, which is a universal format that can be read by any other PC program. This is especially convenient if you're creating electronic mail, or program code, or performing any of the other activities that require ASCII. Other word processors can generate ASCII files, but only when you explicitly tell them to; XyWrite saves you that extra step.

Because of its raw speed, flexibility, and ASCII format, XyWrite is a favorite among journalists and other professional writers. Indeed, the program is used at many newspapers and magazines, including *The New York Times*, *PC Magazine*, *PC Computing*, and *PC Week*. However, again, many people find the program tough to learn. Also, because it's never been very popular, it doesn't have the third-party support (in the form of books, training tapes, add-on software, and so on) enjoyed by WordPerfect or Microsoft Word.

Another interesting choice is Nota Bene, which uses XyWrite as its "engine," but has been customized to address the needs of academic writers. Nota Bene is stronger than XyWrite in certain features, such as style sheets and outlining, and employs a more intuitive menu system. It also works with a suite of add-on products, including a foreign language processor (N.B. Lingua), a text search and retrieval engine (N.B. Orbis), a bibliographic reference manager (N.B. Ibid), and a concordance builder (due out by the time you read this). On the other hand, Nota Bene lacks some XyWrite features that aren't considered critical for academics, such as mouse support, an editable graphics mode, and translation filters that let you read in and write out files in various word processor formats. Still, nothing approaches Nota Bene for academic work. (For more information, see Chapter 18, *Tools for Multilingual Writers*, and Chapter 19, *Tools for Students and Academics*.)

Despite all their advantages, it takes a certain "rugged individual" sensibility to enjoy using XyWrite or Nota Bene. While full-featured, they refrain from the everything-but-the-kitchen-sink approach of WordPerfect, preferring to be lean and mean. They also lack the security of WordPerfect, if only because there are so few other people out there who use them. This latter situation may improve because the programs—which were previously published by two small, competing companies—were both recently acquired by The Technology Group, which has the resources to aggressively sell the products; but it will take time for TTG to grab market share.

Therefore, if you're in a corporate environment, WordPerfect is probably a better choice. If you're a professional or academic writer, however, both XyWrite and Nota Bene merit a very close look.

The Windows Word Processors

At first glance, it may not seem to matter much which Windows program you pick, since they all look alike and operate in a similar way. The truth is, beneath the surface of menu bars and scroll bars, there can be *many* differences, including speed, number of features, consistency, and convenience.

At the same time, the two best programs—Lotus's Ami Pro and Microsoft's Word for Windows—are updated with ferocity, and regularly "borrow" each other's best features and implementations along the way, so these two giants actually do have at least as many similiarities as differences. Indeed, which program is better is often determined by which has come out with the most recent upgrade.

When I face the desolate impossibility of writing 500 pages, a sick sense of failure falls on me and I know I can never do it. Then gradually I write one page and then another. One day's work is all I can permit myself to contemplate.

—John Steinbeck

As for WordPerfect, the word processor that dominates the DOS market, its Windows version is selling fine—at the time of this writing, Microsoft Word for Windows has about 55 percent of the market, WordPerfect for Windows has about 36 percent, and Lotus Ami Pro has a mere 6 percent. However, the sales of WordPerfect 5.2 for Windows have been largely due to the inertia of customer loyalty to the DOS product; it's just not in the same league as Ami Pro and Word. One reason is that for a long time WordPerfect Corporation refused to believe that Windows would take off, and so ended up jumping into the market very late. As a result, it's several upgrades behind the fiercely competitive Lotus and Microsoft products, and has to play catch-up. Another problem is that WordPerfect Corporation, in trying to cater to its installed base of DOS users, has hobbled its Windows product with character-based features that really aren't appropriate for Windows, in effect creating the worst of both worlds. WordPerfect for Windows may ultimately achieve the elegance of its competition, but there's no need to hold your breath waiting for that to happen; both Ami Pro and Word are spectacular achievements, and are two of the best programs of *any* kind ever written for the PC.

Lotus Ami Pro

Ami Pro does just about everything you could imagine a word processor doing, and quite a bit more, besides. It's currently the most comprehensive and powerful word processor for the PC. The wonder is, thanks to its thoughtful and consistent design, Ami Pro may also be the easiest to learn.

The program can read and write files in a variety of popular word processing formats, and can even let you preview a file's contents before opening it. Its editing features include a spelling checker, a grammar checker, a thesaurus, flexible outlining, footnote and endnote capabilities, and table of contents and index generators. Also included are group editing features; for example, it allows multiple readers to annotate sections of a document, lets you set any revision to a document to be automatically marked, enables you to run a comparison between two versions of a document and print a composite document reflecting the differences between them, and offers quick electronic mail transmission via links to the popular corporate packages Lotus cc:Mail and Lotus Notes.

Where Ami Pro really shines, however, is in making your documents look great. The program provides several ways to easily change font styles and sizes, and delivers a more accurate display on your editing screen of what your printed document will look like than any other word processor. It also includes powerful style sheets, plus a unique "fast formatting" feature that lets you apply a selected text's formatting to other text.

Ami Pro supports a variety of graphic formats, and makes it easy to resize and rotate images. Even more impressive, it includes a versatile built-in drawing program, which is especially useful for circling titles, drawing arrows to important paragraphs, and otherwise jazzing up documents. The program also furnishes elegant chart-building software, a scientific equation editor that lets you insert math and Greek symbols with a few mouse clicks, and the ability to create tables that contain text and/or numbers (and that can handle simple math formulas).

You can even create boxes called *frames* to hold either text or graphics, and then move the frames around anywhere in your document; your existing text will automatically flow around the frames. This invaluable feature allows you to freely experiment with various design elements on a page.

You can also examine your page from a variety of perspectives, since Ami Pro lets you go anywhere from a 10 percent view (to see the forest) to a 400 percent view (to see the trees—or, more accurately for that size view, the veins in the leaves). And when you're ready to get your work on paper, Ami's superb background printing program lets you return to your editing screen quickly, a marked contrast to many other Windows programs which freeze up your machine for long minutes during printing.

Writing is the hardest work in the world not involving heavy lifting.

—Pete Hamill

Despite all these features (and many more I'm skipping over), Ami Pro is very easy to learn and use. This is partly thanks to its electronic tutorials, and its context-sensitive help that instantly explains the feature you're currently trying to access. It's also due to clever conveniences, such as alternative pop-*up* menus you can access from the bottom of the window to quickly revise fonts and type sizes, or get information about the status of the document. An even better example is Lotus's pioneering SmartIcons, which are small images that each represent a particular command sequence. Clicking on a SmartIcon with your right mouse button displays a message about what it does, while clicking on it with your left mouse button activates the feature (often a great alternative to slogging through menu options). You can select among a number of pre-existing SmartIcons, as well as create your own; and organize different sets of SmartIcons for different types of documents (one set for business reports, another for newsletters, another for brochures, and so on). You can also move a set of SmartIcons anywhere you want—even outside of your document.

Aside from any specific feature, though, Ami Pro is a pleasure to use because it's been carefully designed to be intuitive and consistent. For example, you can insert a header by just clicking near the top of your window and typing. Frames work the same way for text as they do for graphics; you can edit charts with the same tools you use for drawing; and the drawing program has a similar feel to the equation editor. Even a traditionally difficult feature such as mail merge (which combines a list of addresses with a master document to produce form letters or mailing labels) is made almost fun by Ami Pro's friendly step-by-step prompting. On the other hand, if you don't like the way something is done, you have enormous freedom to change things around to suit your needs using Ami Pro's amazing macro language, which can string commands together and link them to a Smart-Icon, or make them part of a style sheet, or even use them to create a new menu display or dialog box. In fact, Ami Pro provides the most powerful macro language ever seen in a PC word processor.

Of course, no program is perfect for everyone. For one thing, Ami Pro is page-oriented rather than document-oriented; that is, when you go past the end of a page, your screen jumps to the top of the next page, instead of allowing you to see portions of both pages at once. This is fine—often even preferable—if you tend to create individual text and graphic frames that you frequently move around on a page, say, for a flyer or newsletter. However, it can be a pain if you're working with a long document that consists mostly of text, such as a book. You can get around Ami Pro's page orientation by selecting Draft view instead of Layout view; but what you see on-screen in Draft mode won't accurately represent what your document will look like when printed. (Word for Windows, by contrast, is document-oriented, and so can be better suited for long documents.)

Another potential problem is that Ami Pro's style sheets aren't hierarchical; in other words, you can't make one style a subset of another style. This can be a nuisance if you've decided to change, say, your main font, and you've already defined dozens of styles that each individually specify that font. (Word for Windows, by contrast, provides hierarchical style sheets, and so can be better suited for style-heavy documents.) On the other hand, Ami Pro is unique in letting you connect multiple documents to a single style sheet (called a "global" style sheet), so that when you change a style, all the associated documents are automatically updated; if you work with many related files, you may find this a more critical feature.

Finally, because currently it has such a small share of the market, Ami Pro doesn't attract nearly as many books, training tapes, add-on software, and other third-party products as Word and WordPerfect. For example, there are several screenwriting programs written in the macro languages of

WordPerfect for DOS, Word for DOS, and Word for Windows (see Chapter 12, *Tools for Movie, Television, and Theatre Writers*); but there are none for Ami Pro, because the customer base simply isn't large enough yet.

Aside from these caveats, however, no word processor beats Ami Pro for power combined with ease of use, or for convenient low-end desktop publishing features.

Microsoft Word for Windows

Word for Windows is the *other* best Windows word processor.

Word goes head-to-head with Ami Pro on almost all features. At the time of this writing, Ami Pro has a few things Word for Windows doesn't (such as background printing, moveable SmartIcons, and gray-scale image control), and does a few key things better (such as providing a layout view that more accurately represents what the document will look like when printed, and a Clean Screen option that instantly clears away all menus and status lines). However, given the intense competition between the two programs, it won't be long before Word for Windows matches most of Ami Pro's extras, and also throws some new nifty features into the game. (And then, of course, another release of Ami Pro will come out to raise the stakes again....It's a continuing battle, with all of us as the winners.)

Something else to consider is that Word for Windows has a more stolid "look" to it. While Ami Pro feels playful and artistic, Word for Windows makes you think of financial reports and corporate offices. However, this doesn't affect functionality: both programs are beautifully designed, easy to learn, and amazingly powerful.

As mentioned above, while Ami Pro shines at single-page layout, Word for Windows can be preferable for long, text-intensive documents. In addition, Word offers a number of convenient Ctrl-keystroke shortcuts that let you skip accessing menus for popular commands, thus making it easier to keep both hands on the keyboard as you enter and edit text.

Word for Windows is also a great choice if you're looking to switch from WordPerfect for DOS. For one thing, like Ami Pro, Word can transparently read in and write out files in any popular WordPerfect format. Word can also redefine your function keys and cursor keys to accept WordPerfect keystrokes, allowing you to be productive with it right away and learn its menu commands at your leisure. And Word offers superb disk-based help centered on smoothing the transition from WordPerfect for DOS to a Windows-based program—better help, in fact, than WordPerfect for Windows provides.

Ultimately, though, a choice between Ami Pro and Word for Windows boils down to subtle factors such as personal taste. It's therefore a good idea to try out both packages before you make a purchase decision. However, you really won't go wrong with either of them.

WordPerfect for Windows

Microsoft is sometimes charged with having an unfair advantage over other software companies because, in addition to publishing Windows application programs, it publishes Windows itself. Chairman Bill Gates responds that the main advantage was when he said "everyone should commit wholeheartedly to writing programs for Windows," there was no hesitation in *his* company about following that sound advice.

One of the companies that did hesitate is WordPerfect Corporation. The folks at WordPerfect apparently refused to believe Windows would amount to anything, and so lost years of development time while competing programmers created and honed Microsoft Word for Windows and Lotus Ami Pro. WordPerfect for Windows did finally came out, in late 1991, and it sold spectacularly thanks to the enormous number of loyal WordPerfect for DOS users. Sales aside, though, the program has problems.

WordPerfect for Windows release 5.2 (which is the current version at the time of this writing) lacks certain key features, such as an accurate, editable view of what a document will look like when printed, and solid drawing and charting programs. Also, many of the features it *does* have are significantly less powerful than Word's or Ami Pro's, such as its macro language and its outliner; or much harder to use, such as its mail merge. Even more importantly, WordPerfect doesn't tend to execute as quickly, as smoothly, or as flawlessly as its competition. (One disgruntled letter writer in *PC Computing*, who switched from WordPerfect for Windows to Word, likened the move to "stepping from a Yugo to a Mercedes.")

WordPerfect Corporation's resistance to Windows is also evident in the design of its program. While Ami Pro and Word provide menus that are well-organized and consistent with Windows conventions, WordPerfect for Windows menus have an arbitrary feel to them. Dialog boxes are also a bit chaotic, varying unexpectedly in size and placement on the screen. More generally, the program lacks the flash and glitz one has come to expect from topnotch Windows programs—it carries with it much of the clunky look and nonvisual procedures of DOS (for example, formatting by using inserted codes rather than the Windows convention of "applying" formats to selected text). This may make some writers coming directly from DOS feel more at home; but once they orient themselves and start looking at other Windows programs, it's questionable whether they'll stay satisfied with WordPerfect for Windows' conservative design choices.

WordPerfect 6.0 for Windows, due out by the time you read this, is bound to be a major improvement, and is worth investigating. However, if history is any guide, it may take an additional upgrade or two before WordPerfect matches the excellence and elegance of Ami Pro and Word for Windows.

Low-Priced WP Alternatives

Top-of-the-line word processors are great if you require the many powerful features they provide. However, if your writing needs are modest, you can save both money and disk space by going with a simpler package.

PC-Write Advanced Level

For example, if you're just starting out and are wary of spending around $270 for WordPerfect, you might first try a shareware word processor. *Shareware* is a category of software that you're encouraged to obtain from your friends or from an electronic bulletin board (see Chapter 10, *Online References*). After a trial period (say, 30 days) during which you use the program for free, you may decide that you really don't care for it and delete it from your hard disk. On the other hand, if you want to keep using it, you are honor-bound to mail the publisher a check for the cost of the software —which is typically much lower than that of a retail program. Once you do so, you become an official registered user, and are entitled to such extras as technical support and notification of new releases. Shareware is based entirely on the honor system; the nice thing is, it works.

As it happens, there are no truly outstanding shareware word processors. However, Quicksoft's PC-Write Advanced Level for DOS is probably the best of a less-than-exciting lot. Its menus provide more than enough options to get basic writing work done and, if you're a beginner, will give you a good feel for how word processing works. Even if you later decide PC-Write isn't for you, the experience of using the program can provide you with a better basis for choosing which word processor you *really* want to invest in. The only feature the shareware version lacks is an electronic thesaurus; that's provided only after you pay the program's $69 price.

Textra

A word processor doesn't have to be shareware to be inexpensive, though. The best example in the DOS world is Textra from Ann Arbor Software, which costs only $95 but is in many ways as versatile as its most expensive competitors. Like XyWrite, this program is extremely fast, and makes it easy to redefine keyboard functions. And like Microsoft Word, Textra lets you open up to eight document windows, and will instantly duplicate any change you make in one window of a document to all other windows containing the same document.

Textra works through easy-to-learn menu options. If you prefer using shortcut keystrokes, though, Textra also gives you the option of issuing commands via the function keys, alone or in combination with Shift, Alt, and Ctrl. If you request it, the program will make it easy to learn these keys by displaying their initial definitions at the bottom of the screen, and letting you cycle through their other three sets of meanings at any time via the F1 key.

If you're going to write, don't pretend to write down. It's going to be the best that you can do; and it's the fact that it's the best that kills you!

—Dorothy Parker

Other nice Textra features are a punctuation/style guide you can access at a keystroke; the ability to read in and write out files in other popular formats, such as WordPerfect and Microsoft Word; the ability to list and retrieve any of the last 10 documents you've opened; support for over 250 different printers; a dBASE-compatible "address book" that simplifies the process of printing mailing labels and envelopes; and solid graphics handling, superb font support, and one of the best page previews around.

Of course, Textra also has some flaws. For example, its spelling checker often gets stumped if you mistype a word's first letter; and the program doesn't let you apply underlining or boldface to text until *after* you've typed the text, and it doesn't let you view and directly edit such codes. Textra also lacks a few features, such as the ability to generate footnotes (though it *does* support endnotes). However, the full program requires only 2MB of disk space and can be configured to take up even less room, so it's handy for laptop use. In a nutshell, if you're looking to save some money and don't mind using a product that most of your colleagues have never heard of, you'll find Textra to be a very good buy.

Lotus Write, Competitive Upgrades, and Windows Write

On the Windows side, one choice stands out high above the rest: Lotus Write. This program is a gem, and if you don't have heavy-duty formatting needs, you may actually prefer it to a word processor with more overhead. Lotus Write is a scaled-down version of Lotus Ami Pro, and so duplicates most of Ami's features. What it lacks are Ami's built-in drawing program (though it can resize and rotate any graphic you import); table generation (though it will let you link in spreadsheet data via the Microsoft Windows technical features DDE and OLE); table of contents and index generation; master documents, which contain multiple files; background print formatting; grammar checking; and a few other high-end features. In return for what you give up, you get less-cluttered menus (since they offer fewer "glitz" options), a smaller program (5MB versus 13MB for Ami Pro), and a somewhat lower cost—at the time of this writing, a street price of about $139 versus about $299 for Ami Pro. In addition, if you later outgrow Lotus Write, you'll find it easy to switch to Ami Pro; since the programs look and feel very similar, your files will be in the same format as Ami files, and Lotus will probably let you buy Ami Pro for a low upgrade charge instead of the full price.

At the same time, you should be aware that Lotus, Microsoft, and Word-Perfect often run "competitive upgrade" offers which let you buy their high-end Windows WP programs for as little as $95, as long as you can offer some proof that you own (or, it sometimes seems, once came within five feet of) a competing word processor. These competitive upgrades provide tremendous bargains, so check around before making your purchase decision.

Lastly, if you're a beginner, an even cheaper alternative is Windows Write, the word processor that's provided free with every copy of Windows. Windows Write isn't great, but you can easily churn out letters and small documents with it, and get a solid feel for word processing under Windows (including the ability to play around with a variety of fonts).

PFS:WindowWorks, Microsoft Works, LotusWorks, and Q&A

Of course, you may do a lot more with your PC than write. If spreadsheets and/or databases are also part of your job, you could be better off with a program that integrates several functions. The best such program is PFS: WindowWorks from Spinnaker Software, which contains a very strong entry-level word processor, as well as solid spreadsheet, charting, database, address book, mailing label, telecommunications, and fax programs. All the components operate in a similar manner, and WindowWorks lets you easily switch among them and move data between them. The spreadsheet isn't as versatile as Borland's Quattro Pro or Microsoft's Excel, and the database isn't as powerful as Borland's Paradox or Microsoft's FoxPro; but if you're running a small business, you may find PFS:WindowWorks provides just the right mix of features. The package, at a street price of around $50, is also a whole lot cheaper than even a single high-end program.

Keep a diary and one day it'll keep you.
—Mae West

On the other hand, if you'd prefer to stick with DOS, your best bet is Microsoft Works, which provides strong word processing, spreadsheet, database, and telecommunications components, as well as a super-automation program that sets up various standard tasks for you. There's also an excellent Windows version of MS Works, which offers all the features just mentioned except for telecommunications (and for the latter, you can use the free Terminal program that's included with Windows). MS Works is also a fine choice if you want both DOS and Windows versions of the same program, which can be useful if, for example, you want to perform your data entry in the DOS version, and the final layout and printing in the Windows version. You may even already own Microsoft Works, because it's often bundled in for free with new PCs.

Another program often bundled with PCs is LotusWorks. It isn't as elegant as its competition, but if you already have it, you'll find it also does the job. One note of caution, though: if you're even an occasional Windows user, LotusWorks for DOS' insistence that you press F10, not Alt, to activate the menu bar will quickly drive you up the wall.

Finally, if you don't care about spreadsheets but love databases, check out Symantec's Q&A. This popular package provides a fine entry-level word processor (long lauded by science fiction writer and *Byte* columnist Jerry Pournelle), and a sophisticated database that's easy to use. The name of the program stems from the database's emphasis on making it easy to search, or query, for the information you need using everyday language instead of computerese.

Product Information

Note: Version numbers and prices may have changed by the time you read this.

Ann Arbor Software
345 S. Division
Ann Arbor, MI 48104
(313) 769-9088
Fax: (313) 769-4907

Textra 7.0: List Price, $95; generally not discounted

Lotus Development Corporation
55 Cambridge Parkway
Cambridge, MA 02142
(800) 343-5414; (617) 577-8500
Fax: (617) 253-9150

Lotus Ami Pro 3.0: List Price, $495; Street Price, about $249;
Competitive Upgrade (when offered), about $95

LotusWorks 3.0 (for DOS): List Price, $149; Street Price, about $95

Lotus Write 2.0: List Price, $199; Street Price, about $139

Microsoft Corporation
One Microsoft Way
Redmond, WA 98052
(800) 426-9400; (206) 882-8080
Fax: No generic sales or information fax number

Microsoft Word 6.0 for DOS: List Price, $495; Street Price, about $209

Microsoft Word 2.0 for Windows: List Price, $495; Street Price, about $299; Competitive Upgrade (when offered), about $129

Microsoft Works 3.0 for DOS: List Price, $149; Street Price, about $95

Microsoft Works 2.0 for Windows: List Price, $199; Street Price, about $129

Microsoft Works 2.0 (CD-ROM version): List Price, $199; Street Price, N/A

Quicksoft, Inc.
219 First Avenue N. #224
Seattle, WA 98109
(800) 888-8088; (206) 282-0452
Fax: (206) 286-8802

PC-Write Advanced Level 4.1: List Price, $69; generally not discounted

Spinnaker Software Corporation
201 Broadway
Cambridge, MA 02139-1901
(800) 826-0706; (617) 494-1200
Fax: (617) 494-1219

PFS:WindowWorks 2.0: List Price, $109.99; Street Price, around $50

Symantec Corporation
10201 Torre Avenue
Cupertino, CA 95014-2132
(800) 441-7234; (408) 252-3570
Fax: (800) 554-4403

Q&A 4.0 for DOS: List Price, $399; Street Price, about $249
Q&A 4.0 for Windows: List Price, $249.95; Street Price, about $150

The Technology Group
36 South Charles Street
Suite 2200
Baltimore, MD 21201
(410) 576-2040
Fax: (410) 576-1968

XyWrite 4.0 for DOS: List Price, $495; via coupon near the back of this book, $149

Nota Bene 4.1: List Price, $449; via coupon near the back of this book, $179

WordPerfect Corporation
1555 N. Technology Way
Orem, UT 84057
(800) 321-4566; (801) 225-5000
Fax: (801) 228-5377

WordPerfect 6.0 for DOS: List Price, $495; Street Price, about $269

WordPerfect 6.0 for Windows: List Price, $495; Street Price, about $279; Competitive Upgrade (when offered), about $129

CHAPTER

2

WHAT YOUR WORD PROCESSOR CAN AND CAN'T DO

The sheer joy of moving handwritten words around on a large pad of paper; of relying on my own hard-won memory (hours of spelling drills as a child); of looking up words in a vast Webster's Unabridged Dictionary, *where I frequently lose myself to the glory of the language; or thumbing through a well-used thesaurus for shadings and variations of word meanings makes any key pressed on a computer by those zealots pale by comparison.*

—Rachel Pollack

In the old days—like, nine years ago—a word processor's features were pretty basic. Specifically, it let you enter text, edit it, and print it...and carried an aura of "you should be darn grateful I do *that* much." At the time, we PC owners not only stood for that; we actually *were* grateful. We didn't want to go back to our (shudder) typewriters.

As time went on, though, word processing became the most competitive arena in the computer industry, and companies fiercely piled feature after feature into their products. As a result, a lot of program categories that were once hot in their own right have virtually disappeared as separate products, and instead are provided "free" within most high-end word processors.

Therefore, before we start covering all the great supplementary programs available to help you write, let's briefly consider what you've already got in your word processing program.

Spell-Checking

Virtually all word processors now include a spelling checker. Among them are the WordPerfect checker, which was created and is used exclusively by WordPerfect, and is probably the best at coming up with appropriate suggestions; the fine Houghton Mifflin checker, which is used by such programs as Ami Pro and Word for Windows; and the Microlytics checker, which is licensed out to such programs as XyWrite and Nota Bene (where it's actually the fastest checker around, thanks to The Technology Group's lightning-fast implementation).

A spelling checker can initially be a pain, since it stops at lots of words that *you* know are perfectly fine but *it* is too stupid to recognize. After you spend some time "training" the thing by adding appropriate words to its electronic dictionary, though, it becomes an invaluable tool. Very few people are so eagle-eyed and objective about their work that they don't let at least a few typos slip by, and there's nothing that so easily deflates the credibility of one's prose as misspelled words. (If you aren't convinced about that, remember Dan Quayle and "potatoe.") That's why you should always have the dumb-but-thorough checker go over your documents before you let anyone else see them.

There are, of course, other benefits to spelling checkers. For example, I like using the one-word check to correctly insert words I'm too lazy to spell properly—y'know, like "Mississippi." And it's sometimes fun to throw non-dictionary words at the checker to see what strange alternatives it comes up with. ("Hy" gets the XyWrite checker to start off sweetly with "shy," then move to the poetic with "thy" and "why," and then trail off into Disneyland with "ha, he, hi, ho"—and off to work we go.)

By the way, if you ever want to check your checker, give it a word like "sykology," or even "sychology." If it can't come up with "psychology," it's doing a poor job of phonetic guessing, and you should consider running your spell-checks in a less frustrating program.

Thesauruses

Virtually all word processors also include a thesaurus. Among them are the proprietary WordPerfect thesaurus, which also offers antonyms; the fine Proximity thesaurus, which is used by such programs as Ami Pro, and also provides definitions; and the terrific Soft-Art thesaurus, which is used by Word for Windows, and gives you both antonyms and definitions.

If you don't like the thesaurus in your word processor, or if you want to be able to pop up a thesaurus at any time (say, while you're creating titles in a spreadsheet or composing mail in your telecommunications program), you have the option of buying one. For example, Microlytics sells Word Finder as a separate product; and several companies sell thesauruses in combination with other utilities, such as dictionaries (see Chapter 5, *Electronic Dictionaries and Thesauruses*).

To work a thesaurus, simply position your cursor on the word you'd like to change, and press the appropriate keystroke or click the appropriate menu option. You're then presented with a list of synonyms to choose from. You can highlight the synonym you want and press Enter to have the word replace the one that's in your document. In addition, most thesauruses give you the option of selecting a synonym and bringing up a list of *its* synonyms, and repeating that cycle endlessly, until you find the perfect word for your sentence.

When considering thesauruses, we should keep in mind the words of Mark Twain: "The difference between the right word and the nearly right word is the same as that between lightning and the lightning bug."

And we might also consider the words of Alexander Smith: "It is not of so much consequence what you say, as how you say it. Memorable sentences are memorable on account of some single irradiating word." And what, do you suppose, are the odds that "irradiating" came to Smith off the top of his head?

That's why thesauruses are great. And it's why they've become a standard feature in word processing.

Grammar Checking

While a spelling checker is great at finding typos, it won't help you detect errors in punctuation, usage, or style. That's why word processors are beginning to also include grammar checkers, which scan for mechanical problems such as misplaced commas, incomplete sentences, and tense shifts, as well as subtler problems such as passive voice, redundancy, and clichés.

I can't write five words but that I change seven.
—Dorothy Parker

There are days when the result is so bad that no fewer than five revisions are required. In contrast, when I'm greatly inspired, only four revisions are needed.
—John Kenneth Galbraith

Interviewer:
How many drafts of a story do you do?

S. J. Perelman:
Thirty-seven. I once tried doing 33, but something was lacking, a certain—how shall I say?—je ne sais quoi. On another occasion, I tried 42 versions, but the final effect was too lapidary—you know what I mean, Jack? What the hell are you trying to extort—my trade secrets?

Nothing you write, if you hope to be any good, will ever come out as you first hoped.
—Lillian Hellman

Word for Windows and Ami Pro now both include the Houghton Mifflin checker CorrecText, which is the same software "engine" used in the popular standalone program Correct Grammar. The implementation differs slightly in each product, though. For example, the Word for Windows grammar checker also spell-checks your document as it goes along, conveniently allowing you to proof for everything in one pass. Ami Pro, on the other hand, allows you to select a document category (such as Business, Legal, Technical, or Fiction) and choose which grammar rules you want enforced before you begin, thus cutting down on irrelevant error messages and making the checking go faster. At the same time, neither word processor version offers the customization options of Correct Grammar itself, which lets you choose, for example, whether or not to spell-check as you go along, and allows you to create highly personalized style guides.

As for WordPerfect, it didn't offer any kind of grammar checking until recently; but it then made up for lost time by incorporating the top-of-the-line program Grammatik 5 (and buying the program's publisher, Reference Software, in the bargain!). The only Grammatik features not included are the Rule Designer, which lets you program your own rules; the Help Designer, which lets you create your own help screens; and support for a variety of other word processing formats. Therefore, if you own the latest version of WordPerfect and don't require sophisticated customization features, look no further; you already have the best grammar checker on the market.

Most other word processors currently don't provide grammar checking. However, it's only a matter of time until they do, just to stay competitive.

Grammar checking is a very complicated task, and so far no PC program exists that does it nearly as well as a skilled human proofreader. However, if you're nervous about your writing skills, a grammar checker can definitely help. For more information, and a discussion of the full-featured standalone programs available, see Chapter 6, *Grammar and Style Checkers*.

File Translation

There are many things in the PC world that are standardized. Unfortunately, the word processing file format isn't one of them.

WordPerfect saves its files in a significantly different format than Microsoft Word, and Word uses a different format than Ami Pro, and on and on; it's a Tower of Babel. It used to be that the only way to exchange documents between word processors was to save them in ASCII (American Standard Code for Information Exchange), which is a universal format for PC data, but which leaves out formatting information such as underlining, boldface, fonts, and margins.

Nowadays, as the word processing market reaches saturation, software companies are concentrating on getting people who already own a word processor to switch to another brand. As a result, programs are increasingly offering the capability of importing files in other formats, and even exporting files in those other formats. For example, if you want to use Ami Pro but your colleagues all use WordPerfect, no problem; Ami Pro will automatically detect when a file is in WordPerfect format and read it in seamlessly. Further, Ami Pro gives you the option of saving any document in WordPerfect format, ensuring that you can readily share files with your co-workers.

All this is done by built-in translation software that contains extensive information on a variety of word processing formats. Of course, just as with human language, there's always a chance that something will get lost or garbled in the translation; but modern format translators usually do a good job.

Ironically enough, however, file translation has not yet become a standard feature; and even word processors that provide it do so only for the most popular programs. Therefore, if your word processor doesn't perform translations, or if you need support for less popular formats, you may want to turn to one of several excellent standalone translation programs. For more information, see Chapter 21, *Converting File Formats*.

Outlining

When I hear the word "outline," a reflexive shudder goes through me dating back to childhood. In school, I *hated* doing outlines. My attitude was, "I'm not a baby, y'know; why don't you trust me to just go ahead and *write* the thing?"

Well, I'm still not a baby (except occasionally, like when my hard disk crashes), but the projects I now work on are considerably more complex than school assignments. Sometimes the only sane way to tackle a job is to organize it into components, and sub-components, until each piece is small enough to be manageable.

One of the best ways to keep track of the pieces and how they relate to one another is to place them into outline form. Doing so lets you keep the scope of what you're doing in front of you, even if you temporarily get lost in the details of a particular piece of the mosaic. It also lets you radically reorganize documents with a few keystrokes or mouse clicks.

To the man with an ear for verbal delicacies...there is in writing the constant joy of sudden discovery, of happy accident.

—H. L. Mencken

When outlining in a word processor, you assign levels of importance to the various sections of your document (typically from 1 to 9). For example, for a book, the chapter titles could be designated level 1, the main subheadings level 2, and the body text beneath the subheadings level 3. Once you've established such a hierarchy, you could study chapter titles by displaying only level 1 text, or subheads by displaying only level 2 text, or both titles and subheads by displaying both levels 1 and 2, and so on. Also, while displaying, say, level 1 text, you could reposition an entire chapter by simply moving its chapter title to a different location in the outline; all the lower-level text associated with the chapter would automatically move with it. This ability to expand and contract sections of a document, and quickly reposition any section, can provide you with very useful perspectives on your work and great flexibility in managing it.

In most high-end word processors, you have the option of ignoring outline level assignments. In Ami Pro and Word for Windows, for example, you can do so by simply selecting Layout mode or Draft mode instead of Outline mode in the View menu. Any text you repositioned while in Outline mode will stay repositioned, but otherwise your document will look and behave as though it were never assigned any level hierarchies. And, of course, you can always just as easily switch back to Outline mode.

Outlining really is a very nice feature. Don't let childhood memories keep you away from it.

Desktop Publishing

In 1985, the software category of desktop publishing didn't even *exist*. Nowadays, however, it's a big business—big enough, in fact, to attract the attention of the word processing companies, which have proceeded to chip away at its customer base.

For example, all major word processors now support multiple columns, snaking columns (in which text automatically flows from one column to another), font control, and mixing text with graphics.

Ami Pro and Word for Windows even provide built-in drawing and charting programs; the ability to import a variety of graphics formats, and resize, crop, rotate, and flip graphics; resizable frames that can hold text and graphics; an editing screen that shows you almost precisely what your printed document will look like; and viewing options that let you adjust the magnification of your screen anywhere from 10 percent to 400 percent.

I do most of my work sitting down; that's where I shine.

—Robert Benchley

    Ami Pro is the superior package for desktop publishing work, thanks to its powerful drawing program, its exceptionally accurate display, and such unique options as gray-scale adjustment of imported graphics and automatic kerning to improve the spacing between letters.

Ami Pro's greatest desktop publishing strength, however, is its flexible control over frames. For example, you can make a frame transparent or opaque; adjust lines and shadows around a frame; anchor a frame to a particular line or paragraph, or to a particular spot on the page; repeat a frame on every page, or every alternating page; and partially or entirely layer frames on top of one another. You can also quickly move, resize, and delete frames. Since you can place any sort of text or graphic into a frame, it's very easy to reorganize various elements on a page.

Still, no word processor matches the full powers of a desktop publishing package. One basic feature that's lacking is the ability to jump text from one frame to another, which is especially useful for newsletter and magazine work (for example, to run an article across several nonconsecutive pages). There are also a number of sophisticated features unique to desktop publishing programs, such as fine typographic control and color separations. However, word processors can handle many layout tasks, from the design of a fancy business report to the production of an entire book. Whether you need a desktop publishing program to supplement your word processor ultimately depends on the particular type of work you're doing. For more information, see Chapter 22, *Laying Out Your Work*.

Document Notation

If you're in a workgroup environment where other people review your documents, programs such as WordPerfect, Word for Windows, and Ami Pro can ease the process by allowing your colleagues to insert comments directly into your files. Typically, these notes are invisible on-screen unless you request to see them, and aren't printed unless you set them to print. As a result, your co-workers can easily comment on various sections of your document without affecting any of its text. In addition, they can comment on each other's comments, in an attempt to build a consensus.

In WordPerfect for DOS, notes are handled as hidden text, while in WordPerfect for Windows, they're displayed on-screen in shaded boxes. Otherwise, however, they aren't treated very differently from standard text.

Word for Windows and Ami Pro go several steps further. First, they allow you to "lock" your document so that notes can be added, but the document's text can't be changed by anyone but you. Second, they automatically insert the initials of a word processor's owner (which are normally set during installation, but can be revised at any time) into every note the person creates, thus ensuring that the author of each note is identified. Third, they automatically number each note, and automatically renumber whenever a note is added or removed.

On top of that, Ami Pro prompts each person to specify a color to be automatically applied to all notes the person creates; this makes it easy to later identify the author of any note at a glance. Ami Pro also marks the creation date and time of each note, making it easy to see which notes are most recent.

Even with all these features, though, there are still gaps in word processor notation support. For example, while Ami's and Word's file locking prevents the document from being altered, it doesn't protect the notes themselves, and so fails to ensure an accurate audit trail. At the same time, the file locking allows only one person at a time to comment on the document, which can be a problem in some workgroup environments. Further, a word processor won't automatically notify appropriate workgroup members on the network whenever a document is available for review. If you require such extras (or, alternatively, if not everyone in your workgroup cares to use the same word processor), check out the standalone program CA-ForComment from Computer Associates, which works with WordPerfect, Microsoft Word, and ASCII file formats, and supports both Novell and (via a special version) Digital VAX/VMS PATHWORKS networks. Contact information appears at the end of this chapter.

Revision Tracking

Like document notation, revision tracking is especially useful when you're working with other people. However, its usefulness extends beyond a workgroup environment; people who need to manage document changes range from lawyers rewriting contracts to engineers honing technical specifications to editors fixing manuscripts. Word processors supporting this feature allow for revisions to be redlined as they occur; or for a comparison to be run between your original document and the edited one, producing a third document that points out all changes that were made.

For example, both the DOS and Windows versions of WordPerfect allow you to manually redline text you want to add and strike through text you want to delete. Ami Pro and Word for Windows can also mark changed text automatically as you edit. And all these programs provide a "compare" command that analyzes a specified original file and revised file, and then automatically generates a third document that marks where text has been deleted or added.

For casual use, these word processors are adequate; but they aren't precise enough for professional work. For example, if you've deleted a comma in a sentence, Ami Pro will mark as changed not only the comma, but also the word before it and the word after it; WordPerfect 5.2 for Windows will mark as changed the entire *sentence*; and Word for Windows is so inexact it will mark as changed the entire *paragraph*.

The word processors also lack bells and whistles, such as identifying text that's been both changed and moved, the ability to create different types of composite documents, generating comparison summaries and revision lists, and providing special handling for program source code files. If you need such high-level features, or if your word processor simply doesn't handle document revision, you can turn to the standalone program Docu-Comp II from Advanced Software, which supports the ASCII format, and a variety of Microsoft Word and WordPerfect file formats. DocuComp can even compare documents in two *different* formats and then generate the composite document in one of them, or in a third format—a timesaver if you're working with people who aren't using the same programs. It can also retain formatting information such as boldface, underlining, and font changes in your composite document (though you'll get the best results when generating the composite document in the same file format as your revised document). More information on DocuComp (and its main competitor, Comparite) appears in Chapter 15, *Tools for Lawyers*.

While there clearly are serious legal and technical uses for revision tracking, I've found the feature is especially handy for starting fights ("You rewrote *that*? I spent *hours* on that sentence!"), since it highlights even trivial changes you'd probably never notice if the software didn't point them out to you so effectively. God bless modern technology.

If you were a member of Jesse James' band and people asked you what you were, you wouldn't say "Well, I'm a desperado." You'd say something like "I work in banks" or "I've done some railroad work." It took me a long time just to say "I'm a writer." It's really embarrassing.

—Roy Blount, Jr.

The Top Ten

Just as a point of reference, here are the results of a recent *PC Computing* reader survey on the 10 features people want most in a word processor:

1. Spell-checking
2. Print preview
3. Multi-column formatting
4. Ability to import and integrate graphics
5. WYSIWYG (What You See Is What You Get)
6. Macros
7. Thesaurus
8. Table support
9. Style sheets
10. Table of Contents generation

The list represents a nice mix of editing and layout features. Most of them have already been covered in either this chapter or the previous one, but a few deserve comment.

For example, *print preview* allows you to see precisely what your printed page will look like (though you typically can't perform any editing while that view is displayed). On the other hand, *WYSIWYG* refers to getting a more-or-less accurate representation on your *editing* screen of what your printed page will look like. Ami Pro represents the best solution on both fronts, as its editing screen can display a representation of your printed page as accurate as any other program's print preview.

As for multi-column formatting, both Ami Pro and WordPerfect for Windows are particularly adept at it, since they let you easily adjust the column size with your mouse, and (unlike Word for Windows) let you set up columns of different widths on the same page. However, such programs as WordPerfect for DOS, XyWrite/Nota Bene, and Textra also do a fine job of creating multiple columns.

As mentioned in Chapter 1, Ami Pro, Word for Windows, and both the DOS and Windows versions of WordPerfect are fine at importing graphics, though Ami Pro provides the most graphics options. (Nota Bene, by the way, is especially poor at handling graphics.) As also mentioned, Ami Pro and both the DOS and Windows versions of Word offer exceptionally strong style sheet support.

Concerning tables, Ami Pro, Word for Windows, and the DOS and Windows versions of WordPerfect all shine, providing such options as the ability to perform addition and subtraction, and include simple math formulas. And virtually all high-end word processors offer some type of Table of Contents generation.

Lastly, as mentioned in Chapter 1, macros are collections of keystroke sequences—typically, sequences you use frequently. Macros are great for automating repetitive tasks, which both saves time and ensures consistency. Most word processors do a good job of providing basic macro support, letting you define, say, Ctrl+S as a keystroke that saves your document or Alt+P as a keystroke that prints it. However, for macro programming features (such as the ability to create your own menus and dialog boxes), nothing touches Ami Pro or Word for Windows. This can be significant because, even if *you* never plan to use sophisticated macro options, their existence allows *other* people to create add-on products you may one day use (for example, the scripting macro packages covered in Chapter 12).

For forty-odd years in this noble profession I've
harbored a guilt and my conscience is smitten.
So here is my slightly embarrassed confession—
I don't like to write, but I love to have written.

—Michael Kanin

Really, though, no one can say just how important any particular word processing feature should be to *you*. Ultimately, as with most everything else, it depends on your needs and the particular type of work you're doing.

What Your Word Processor Can't Do

Okay, we've covered some of the features word processors include. Now let's talk about what they *don't* provide.

For one thing, they aren't much use in helping you get started; that is, they don't offer any prompting or idea "hooks" to kick-start your writing process. For such aids, you need idea generators and software coaches, which are covered in Chapters 3 and 4.

Most word processors also lack writing reference tools, such as electronic dictionaries and style guides, and general-purpose reference tools, such as electronic encyclopedias and almanacs. These products are discussed in Chapter 5, *Electronic Dictionaries and Thesauruses*; Chapter 8, *Disk-Based References*; Chapter 9, *CD-ROM References*; and Chapter 10, *Online References*.

Word processors also fall short when it comes to certain high-end editing tools, such as full-featured grammar and style checkers, and search utilities for managing large amounts of text. Such packages are detailed in Chapter 6, *Grammar and Style Checkers*, and Chapter 7, *Other Editing Tools*.

Word processors are designed for a broad audience, so it's not practical for them to fully address the needs of people in specific fields. Such niche products are covered in Chapters 11 through 19, which discuss tools for journalists and book writers, scriptwriters, poets, businesspeople, lawyers, physicians, scientists and engineers, multilingual writers, and academics.

To work at maximum efficiency, you'll want to use PC enhancement utilities in addition to your writing-related programs. Such utilities are talked about in Chapter 20, *Essential General-Purpose Tools*.

While word processors typically offer file format conversion, layout, and printing features, they don't have the power of packages dedicated to such tasks. These supplementary programs are gone over in Chapter 21, *Converting File Formats*; Chapter 22, *Laying Out Your Work*; and Chapter 23, *Printing Your Work*.

Lastly, word processing packages generally don't offer you ways to save money on other writing-related programs. That deficiency is addressed in Appendix C, which features over $2,000 worth of software discount coupons.

Product Information

Note: Version numbers and prices may have changed by the time you read this.

Computer Associates
One Computer Associates Plaza
Islandia, NY 11788
(800) 225-5224; (516) 342-5224
Fax: (516) 342-4873

CA-ForComment 2.5: List Price, $895 for a 10-user license; generally not discounted

Advanced Software, Inc.
1095 East Duane Avenue
Suite 103
Sunnyvale, CA 94086
(800) 346-5392; (408) 733-0745
Fax: (408) 733-2335

DocuComp II 1.34: Single-User List Price, $199.95; Network (Novell and 3-Com) List Price, $695 for a 5-user license; Street Price N/A

For word processor product information, see the end of Chapter 1.

PART II

CREATING THE FIRST DRAFT

Writing is easy; all you do is sit staring at a blank sheet of paper until the drops of blood form on your forehead.
—Gene Fowler

CHAPTER
3

IDEA GENERATORS

Nothing in this world is so powerful as an idea whose time has come.
        —Victor Hugo

One of the great pains to human nature is the pain of a new idea.
        —Walter Bagehot

Everything has been thought of before, but the difficulty is to think of it again.
        —Goethe

The Bible tells us that "In the beginning, God created the heaven and the earth." I'd suggest something occurred before that, however...because first, He had to have the Idea. (And while you may have some quibbles with the execution, you've got to admit it was one *fantastic* idea.)

Every time you have an idea, you perform your own small act of creation. That can be absolutely thrilling; but it can also be awfully intimidating. It's no wonder, then, that so many of us freeze up when starting a new project.

In most cases, all the data we need is already in our heads; the difficulty is in teasing the information out. This is probably what Gene Fowler was thinking of when he made his classic statement, "Writing is easy; all you do is sit staring at a blank sheet of paper until the drops of blood form on your forehead."

Of course, there *are* some rare individuals who are constantly overflowing with ideas. They're the ones who are never at a loss for what to write about, and whose only frustration is that their typing fingers can't keep up with their fertile imaginations.

I put these folks in the same category as perfectly proportioned people who eat whatever they want and as much as they want and never gain any weight. That is, I find them depressing to be around. My advice is to avoid them like the plague.

As for the *rest* of us: It's very common, and very human, to have problems coming up with an idea...especially the right idea. Happily, computers can help.

For starters, PCs make it easy to enter, delete, and rearrange your text, which helps eliminate worries over writing something dumb or taking a wrong turn. That's important, because when you're beginning the creative process, you need to work in as nonjudgmental an environment as possible, to ensure that you don't block out fruitful new patterns of thought. You can always go back later and remove defective material with a few keystrokes ...and without disturbing any of the brilliant prose that surrounds it. (In contrast, with paper pages you have to live with ugly crossouts—which are constant reminders of your mistakes—or endure the tedium of retyping your entire document.)

Along similar lines, you can type a lot faster on a computer keyboard than on a typewriter or notepad; and one technique for brainstorming is to write as swiftly as you can, without letup. The theory is that by typing almost more quickly than you can follow, you make it easier for ideas to float up from your subconscious. Also, of course, the frenetic pace helps you get as much material out of your brain and into the PC as possible.

In fact, some experts recommend you go so far as to turn off your computer screen while churning out initial ideas. This ensures that while you're constructing the spine of your project, you aren't distracted by the urge to correct a typo or revise a clumsy sentence. When you finally become creatively exhausted, you can switch the monitor back on and let the "editor" part of you organize the raw material you've generated.

Then again, you may prefer a more relaxed approach. If the main obstacle you're facing is the terror of the blank page—or, in this case, the blank screen—try beginning every project by inserting a copy of some piece of writing you've done previously into your empty document. While it's not exactly rational, you may well find that writing in the presence of old, familiar words—words that provide confirmation that you *can* create successfully—is much easier than having to etch your thoughts onto an empty slate. Start overwriting your old text with stream-of-consciousness ideas; after a short while, you'll probably become immersed in your new document. When you're ready for a break, you can highlight and delete what's left of your previous prose.

The connecting theme in all of these techniques is to push past your mental barriers, bypassing your fears, insecurities, and internal censors. In many cases, you'll find that doing so is all you really need to come up with great ideas.

Nonetheless, there are solid reasons for turning to software dedicated to promoting ideas. It's very easy to become mired in your initial thoughts, and not push on to other perspectives that lead to more fruitful concepts. Computer programs will remain objective, nudging you to explore all facets of a situation. They will also remain patient and available, even while you're getting tired and frustrated. And they will never laugh at your ideas, or ask for a share of the profits that result from your sessions. (Indeed, electronic brainstorming partners have some clear advantages over human ones.)

This *is* a subjective area, so you may find that while some people derive great benefit from a particular program, the product just doesn't "click" for you. That being said, this chapter covers the seven idea generators generally considered most useful: IdeaFisher, The Idea Generator Plus, Idegen++, MindLink Problem Solver, Babble!, Just Joking, and The Humor Processor. None of these packages will hand you ideas at the press of a button. However, they can all help you to see combinations you didn't see before, and extract thoughts that you didn't know you had.

Before we get rolling, however:

A Cautionary Note

A few decades ago, some jokers at MIT put together a public-domain program called Eliza that was supposed to turn your PC into a therapist. It worked something like this:

COMPUTER: WHAT GOAL ARE YOU SEEKING?

YOU: I want to be rich and famous.

COMPUTER: WHY DO WANT TO BE RICH AND FAMOUS?

YOU: I like money, and I'm love-starved.

COMPUTER: TELL ME ABOUT LOVE-STARVED AND WHY YOU WANT IT.

YOU: I don't want it, I want to find love.

COMPUTER: WHOM ARE YOU TRYING TO REACH WITH YOUR LOVE?

YOU: I don't know right now, but I'll know her when I meet her. Of course, for meeting people, it helps to be famous.

COMPUTER: IS IT NORMAL FOR YOU TO BE FAMOUS?

YOU: Well, not for more than 15 minutes. You're really ignorant, aren't you?

COMPUTER: DEFINE IGNORANT AND WHY IT IS IMPORTANT TO YOU.

YOU: Oy.

On and on it went, continually picking out words to keep the conversation going. Eliza was a kick, and it was great at parties. Unfortunately, though, it also inspired some companies to produce similar products marketed as genuine personality analyzers, mind readers, and idea generators.

The point is, don't be taken in; whenever you see an ad for an obscure, low-priced idea generator, examine the claims skeptically, and try not to buy without a 30-day money-back guarantee.

On the other hand, all the products covered in this chapter, if used properly, often *can* kick-start a project or get stalled work flowing again. As I've said, they aren't suited to all tastes; but read on to see if they might be of help to you.

IdeaFisher

IdeaFisher is the big fish in this relatively small pond. Over a dozen years in the making, its development cost $3.5 million and involved the contributions of over 250 people. It's been variously described as a thesaurus for ideas, an idea supermarket, an associative lexicon, and an idiot savant.

Strangely enough, the seed for this product was planted when its creator, Marshall Fisher, took a comedy course in 1964 taught by a former head writer for Jack Benny. Fisher noticed that his classmates regularly came up with better gags than he did. After some thought, he decided this was because they were better at dredging relevant pieces of information out of their heads to kick off their ideas. Fisher went on to become a World War II B-25 pilot, a singer on "The Arthur Godfrey Show," a high school teacher, a staffer at *The Denver Post*, a travel manager for American Express in Hong Kong, and—most notably—co-founder of Century 21 Real Estate, which made him a multimillionaire. After selling his interest in Century 21 and retiring to Hawaii, he decided to finally pursue his dream of inventing a tool that facilitates creative thinking.

I always write a good first line, but I have trouble in writing the others.
—Moliere

IdeaFisher is actually two types of programs combined into one. Its first component is the QBank, which contains 5,970 common-sense questions designed to help you define your goals, hone your thoughts, and open your eyes to new possibilities. The questions are organized into three groups: Orient/Clarify identifies the contours of your project, Modify helps you look at your ideas from different directions and establish new concepts, and Evaluate assesses what you've come up with.

There's nothing to writing. All you do is sit down at a typewriter and open a vein.

—Red Smith

These three main categories are further organized into sub-categories. Specifically, under Orient/Clarify, you can choose questions relating to the development of a story or script, an advertisement or promotional campaign, a new product, a product name, a marketing strategy, or the solution to a particular problem. Under the Modify topic, you can select from among nearly two dozen sets of questions covering such areas as Perspective/Point of View, Purpose/Function, Opposites/Reversals, Combine Mix/Synthesize, Timing/Speed, and Emotions/Attitudes/Behavior. And under the Evaluate category, you can choose among the subjects Mission/Purpose/Process, Feasibility/Practicality/Implementation, Costs/Benefits Risk, Originality/Interest/Appeal, Simplicity/Efficiency/Effectiveness, and Human/Social/Environmental Concerns.

In some cases, the process of answering questions will be enough to give you all the ideas you need. If it isn't, though, you can have the program cull the key words and phrases contained in your answers and save them in a text editor called the Question Notepad. These terms can then be used as launching points for the second—and most important—component of IdeaFisher, which is the IdeaBank.

The theory behind IdeaBank is that our minds are great at storing information, but rather poor at retrieving it. Since creativity mostly consists of a fresh synthesis of old ideas, any tool that helps us remember what we already know can be a great asset. IdeaBank therefore provides over 60,000 words and phrases, with more than 700,000 associative links drawn between them.

For example, if you looked up the word *red* in a thesaurus, you'd find perhaps a dozen terms, such as *crimson, scarlet,* and *vermilion.* Looking up *red* in the IdeaBank, however, yields eight *categories*—such as People/Animals, Abstractions/Intangibles, and Activities/Events/Processes—encompassing 672 associated terms! For example, under People/Animals are such idea sparkers as *Lucille Ball, Scarlett O'Hara, The Pink Panther, Santa Claus, American Indian, lobster, robin, Little Red Riding Hood,* and *The Boston Red Sox.* Under Abstractions/Intangibles are such gems as *passion, rage, sexuality, Communism, red tape, deficit,* and *Valentine's Day.* And Activities/Events/Processes yields such subtle associations as *fever, measles, hot flash, bullfight, campfire, lava flow, Doppler effect,* and *sunrise.*

You can mark any terms that interest you using function key F10 (or mark *all* the terms by pressing Shift+F10), and copy them to a text editor called the Idea Notepad by pressing F9. You can then jot down ideas elicited by particular words in the Notepad; print the Notepad's contents; and/or choose to export its contents to a file you can later load into your word processor. If warranted, you can even jump back to the QBank to explore your newly discovered ideas more deeply—and then go back to the IdeaBank again.

To demonstrate how it all works, I decided to try to come up with the concept for a new book. All I knew up front was that I wanted it to be popular, and that I wanted to be able to write it quickly.

Since I didn't have even the glimmer of an idea yet, there wasn't much point in trying to clarify anything via the QBank. Therefore, I started off by selecting the IdeaBank and its Major Categories list, which is the top row of its hierarchy of topics. After a moment, 28 categories were displayed, including Animals, Business/Occupations, Emotions/Personality, Entertainment/The Arts, Military/War, Mind/Intellect, Families/Personal Relationships, and Time.

Soft and cuddly creatures are always popular, so I selected the Animals category. The response was a list of 22 topics, including Birds/Fowl, Dogs/Cats/Family Pets, and Insects/Spiders/Worms; plus more subtle associations, such as Smelling/Nose/Odors, Reproduction/Pregnancy/Birth, and Wild/Fierce/Uncivilized/Tame/Domesticated.

The "cats" topic clicked for me, as it reminded me of the myriad of best-selling cat books I've seen over the years. I was sure there was room in the market for another one, if I could just find an approach that hadn't been done yet; so I selected Dogs/Cats/Family Pets.

I was rewarded with 15 headings on the subject—Anatomy of Dogs and Cats, Domestic Cats, Famous Dogs and Cats, Pet Supplies and Equipment, and so on—encompassing 1,466 items. Rather arbitrarily, I decided to start with Anatomy of Dogs and Cats, and was provided with such warm 'n fuzzies as *bushy tail, cat's tummy, cold nose, curly tail, paws, rough tongue, scruff of the neck, smooth coat,* and *whiskers.* At first, these didn't do anything for me; but then I thought it might be interesting to contrast them with something ("reversal" being a standard brainstorming technique). So I tried to think of something that's the opposite of a soft and snuggly pet ...and yet is also found in the home...and is preferably something I'm already familiar with...and then I was suddenly hit with what IdeaBank is really designed for, what the creativity experts refer to as the "aha!" experience. In a flash, the answer leapt to my mind: computers!

Take a few sheets of paper and for three days in succession write down, without falsification or hypocrisy, everything that comes into your head. Write what you think...and when the three days are over, you will be amazed at what novel and startling thoughts have welled up in you.

—Ludwig Boerne

Well, of course! Almost simultaneously, two images also kicked in: a cartoon cat sleeping contentedly atop a PC monitor; and a cartoon cat with the look of a journalist on deadline pawing away furiously at a PC keyboard.

So, I thought, what's the title of this silly thing? Cats and computers? Computers and cats? No...computers *for* cats! Yeah, that's it. An pseudo-instructional guide titled *Computers for Cats*, executed with funny cartoons. (Hey, the title is even alliterative!)

With that major step accomplished (and in under 10 minutes, to boot), I decided to poke around and see if I could come up with more images for the book. The most energetic-sounding topic listed was Activities/Events/Processes, so I selected it, and quickly spun off the following ideas from these terms:

- *Animal worship*: Cats bowing down to a computer that has the form of an Egyptian cat-god.

- *Bird pecking at its reflection*: Cat pawing at its reflection in a computer monitor.

- *Cat-and-mouse behavior*: Cat batting around a PC, which is desperately trying to get away but is being held by a paw on its power cord.

- *Cat's nine lives*: A series of nine panels showing how a cat can get seriously injured through PC misuse (for example, electrocution, with the cat's fur standing on end).

- *Cross-breeding*: Um, on second thought, maybe not.

- *Life in a goldfish bowl*: Cat trying to get at a computer swimming around in a goldfish bowl.

- *Pet scratching furniture*: Cat using a PC as a scratching post.

- *Raining cats and dogs*: Raining cats and computers.

And so on, and so on.

Obviously, these were just preliminary notions, and I could do a lot better. Still, I appreciated being able to create foundation material so quickly; it gave the project a certain momentum, and encouraged me to believe there was some merit to it.

Rather than continue exploring the nearly 1,500 associations under the Dogs/Cats/Family Pets topic, I decided to narrow the field by using a nifty IdeaFisher feature named Compare. This command lets you specify two separate topics, and then displays only those associations that are common to both. In this case, I entered *cat*, and then *computer*. The result was 30 terms, including *home, laboratory,* and *school* (covering places where you could find both of our subjects); *learn, multiply, retrieve,* and *talk* (covering their abilities); *noise, security, size,* and *speed* (covering their physical attributes); and *dangerous, fast, intelligent,* and *uncontrollable* (covering their intangible attributes).

This list provoked yet more ideas. For example, *security* made me picture a guard-cat patrolling a computer facility; and then, reversing the image, a nerdy-looking hacker cat trying to break into a computer network. As another example, *learn* made me picture a *Jeopardy!*-type quiz show featuring three serious-minded cats competing against three bulky computer terminals.

You will have to write and put away or burn a lot of material before you are comfortable in this medium. You might as well start now and get the necessary work done. For I believe that eventually quantity will make for quality.

—Ray Bradbury

I also had the option of selecting any of the displayed terms, in case I wanted to explore a particular avenue of thought more deeply. For example, when I selected *security,* the program brought up 13 categories concerning the word, encompassing 1,612 terms. This ability to endlessly pursue association after association is one of the great charms of the IdeaBank, because it jibes with the way our minds work, and so promotes flow of thought.

I could've gone on brainstorming my *Computers for Cats* concept in the IdeaBank, but I didn't want to allow myself to get mired in my initial perspectives. Therefore, I turned to the QBank to subject my tentative notion to some thoughtful questioning.

I began by selecting the Orient/Clarify category and Generating Ideas for a Story or Script section. This grilled me with such fundamental queries as "What are you trying to accomplish?", "Who is the primary audience?", and "How sure are you that your premise has enough substance, or is compelling enough, to sustain audience interest?" It then moved on to character questions, such as "Do you truly understand them?", "Are all the characters believable?", and "Have you allowed the characters to form the plot and work out their own destinies, or have you forced them to fit a contrived plot?" It wrapped up by asking me to consider "What positive things might a discerning audience or critic say about your story?" and "What *negative* things?", suggesting that I consider such factors as whether it's convincing, whether the characters are three-dimensional, if conflict is unavoidable because of the nature of the characters, if everything that happens is relevant to the development of the story, and if the story is compelling and entertaining throughout. These questions weren't as directly relevant to the sort of book I was planning as they would be for, say, a novel. Still, they got me thinking about certain issues that I hadn't previously considered, such as whether I should create identifiable cat and computer characters, as opposed to using generic images; if I should emphasize the cats or the computers, or divide the book's focus evenly; and what style of drawing I should look for when choosing a cartoonist.

I next turned to the Modify category of the QBank and the Perspective/Point of View section, which challenged me to perform mental exercises. For example, I was prompted to identify my basic assumptions and then reverse them; exaggerate and reduce various aspects of my book to see how the whole would be affected; write a review of my idea as if I were a book critic; explain how a young child might view my project and handle aspects of it differently; and describe how a *lazy* person might handle the project. These helped me to think more creatively and critically about other approaches, such as doing the concept as a 16-month calendar instead of a book; or as a children's book; or as a simple graphics-based software package targeting quick sales during the Christmas season. It also made me consider making the concept even cutesier by going with a title like *Computers for Kittens*; or abandoning the feline motif entirely for something racier like *PCs for Punks*.

At that point, I was tired of answering questions, so I had the program cull the key words and phrases contained in my answers (that is, the text stripped of filler words such as *the* and *and*). With those terms in hand, I selected the IdeaBank again, to explore my concept further and generate more material. But at this point, you get the idea.

IdeaFisher can't claim to actually hand out concepts and solutions. However, it does provide a solid platform for brainstorming by tickling your memory cells and stretching your perspective. Its users include professional writers, such as novelists, comedians, and screenwriters (indeed, it's recently become a hot item in L.A.); people who are involved in research and development, such as educators, scientists, and marketers; and those who give presentations and speeches, such as Fortune 500 executives. Indeed, companies using IdeaFisher range from the Disney Corporation to NASA (which is using it to plan a mission to Mars!).

One of the reasons the program can support such a wide range of interests is that the IdeaBank supplies so many different types of associations. Further, you can optionally customize the IdeaBank, adding your own terms and associative links, to make it ideally suited to your particular area of expertise. Besides, it's actually *fun* to use, which is always desirable in a creative tool, no matter what field you're in.

The ideas I stand for are not mine. I borrowed them from Socrates. I swiped them from Chesterfield. I stole them from Jesus. And I put them in a book. If you don't like their rules, whose would you use?

—Dale Carnegie

Immature artists imitate. Mature artists steal.

—Lionel Trilling

Adam was the only man who, when he said a good thing, knew that nobody had said it before him.

—Mark Twain

Originality is the art of concealing your sources.

—Anonymous

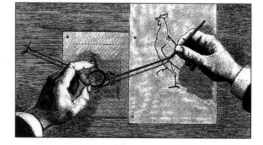

With all that being said, IdeaFisher also has a couple of drawbacks. First, though it's not difficult to use, it takes a while to learn because its design is somewhat unintuitive. Second, the program requires a hefty 7MB of hard disk space (which actually encompasses 25MB of highly compressed data).

Until recently, there was also a third drawback—a steep list price of $595. Happily, however, IdeaFisher Systems recently dropped its list price to only $199. And even better, the company has agreed to sell the package for a mere $99 to readers of this book! To take advantage of this terrific offer, simply use the IdeaFisher coupon near the back.

By the way, another inexpensive IdeaBank-type program worth considering is Inside Information from Microlytics. This product doesn't offer nearly as many words or associative links as IdeaFisher. However, it takes up less than 4MB of disk space, and has a street price of just $35. Further, it can be run memory-resident, which means you can call it up anytime from your word processor at the touch of a keystroke. For a detailed description of Inside Information, see Chapter 5, *Electronic Dictionaries and Thesauruses*.

If it's the QBank portion of IdeaFisher that most intrigues you, though —that is, if you're looking for a process-based system rather than a content-based one—you should explore The Idea Generator Plus, Idegen++, and MindLink Problem Solver. These products are covered in the following sections.

The Idea Generator Plus

Based on the book *The Art of Creative Thinking* by Gerard Nierenberg (Simon & Schuster, $7.95), The Idea Generator Plus supplies a tightly structured series of questions aimed at idea honing and problem solving. While IdeaFisher is best at free-form brainstorming, The Idea Generator Plus is most useful when you have a specific goal and need help generating ideas on how to achieve it. Also, The Idea Generator Plus is more geared toward solutions involving other people, and so can be especially effective when used as the foundation for group brainstorming sessions. Its questions are organized into three categories: Problem Statement, Idea Generation, and Evaluation.

In the Problem Statement section, you're asked to do such things as think of situations similar to yours and discuss how you'd approach them, list metaphors for your situation ("it's like climbing a mountain" or "it's like constructing a house of cards"), rate your goals from zero to nine, and specify which people you'd need to make your project happen.

In the Idea Generation section, you're encouraged to imagine other perspectives. For example, you're prompted to "suppose you were to hold a board meeting to discuss possible approaches to your situation. Who would you invite? Imagine going around the table and getting ideas from each person." Another scenario involves soliciting opinions from "voices in your head" belonging to the optimist, pessimist, realist, dreamer, and parent sides of your nature. Yet another exercise cleverly suggests that you reverse each of your goals, think of ways to reach the reversed goals, and then use your reversed ideas as springboards for achieving your actual goals (or, at minimum, as reminders of pitfalls to avoid).

Lastly, the Evaluation section makes you rate the various ideas you've generated during the session based on their relevance to your goals; and determine your ideas' costs, benefits, and effects on other people.

When you're finished answering all of the questions, you can have the program print the results, or save them to a text file you can later load into your word processor. In addition, you can save the data in file formats used by popular outliner and personal information manager packages, including SideKick Plus, GrandView, IBM Current, and Lotus Agenda. This allows you to pursue the ideas you've generated in familiar, open-ended environments.

The Idea Generator Plus has a list price of $97.50.

If you can afford to buy only one idea generator, I strongly recommend you go for IdeaFisher. However, if you'd like to have your creativity nudged in more than one way, or if you're ever involved in group problem-solving sessions, The Idea Generator Plus (with its 60-day money-back guarantee) is worth investigating.

Idegen++

While The Idea Generator Plus stresses a structured, businesslike approach, Idegen++ from Finntrade employs more playful, childlike techniques.

Idegen++ begins by cheering "quantity yields quality!" to encourage you to spend an hour or two generating a couple of dozen ideas. It also reassures you that, initially, "the main goal is to get your thoughts out of their normal rational tracks—not so much to find practical ideas."

The program takes on a California tone with such suggestions as "Begin this phase by relaxing. Breathe deeply and enjoy the sensation of calmness. This method is called 'Forced Relaxation.'" It then starts throwing random terms at you—*atom, ocean steamer, meadow, yeast, a good book, adult child, contagious disease*—and asks you to draw connections between each term and your goal. While some might find it silly, the spontaneity of this approach has a certain charm, and may suit you if you have an artistic personality.

After you're done generating your initial ideas, you're asked to evaluate each one by considering how relevant it is to your goals, whether it has valuable secondary benefits, and whether it can be made more practical. You're then given the opportunity to revise your ideas based on these criteria, while the program attempts to help by tossing more "springboard" terms your way.

Finally, you're prompted to rate each of your concepts using plus signs and asterisks. The program then sorts the ideas based on your ratings, and lets you print them to paper and/or save them to a text file you can later load into your word processor.

Idegen++ is clearly not for everybody. However, if you're intrigued by this product's approach, it won't cost you an arm and a leg to check it out. While the package has a list price of $295, you can buy it using the Finntrade coupon near the back of this book for only $99 (a $196 savings).

MindLink Problem Solver

MindLink Problem Solver is based on a series of field-tested techniques developed by Synectics Inc., a management consulting firm that has aided over a quarter of the companies in the Fortune 500. The program combines the structured approach of The Idea Generator Plus with the playfulness of Idegen++, and does so with surprising success.

MindLink further has the distinction of being the first Microsoft Windows-based program covered in this chapter. In fact, it uses the Windows platform to create an ambitious visual structure based on linked electronic "index cards" à la the Apple Macintosh HyperCard system. (It's written in PLUSRT from Spinnaker Software, which is a HyperCard clone for Windows.) As a result, it provides a very attractive, open-ended environment. The tradeoff is that its performance is somewhat sluggish, and it's initially more difficult to figure out how to use than its competition.

There's not much you can do about the sluggishness, aside from running the software on a 486. However, you can learn the program by patiently studying its manual, which does a superb job of conveying MindLink's creative philosophy. For example, here's what it has to say about following up on observations:

> The great thinkers like Pasteur, Archimedes, and Einstein had a special understanding of their thinking process. This was marked by an interested tolerance for "intuitive" lines of thought that did not, in the end, lead anywhere....They had learned that by pursuing anything that came along, one of a hundred or one of a thousand would pay off. But the payoffs were so valuable that the seemingly wasteful pursuits were well worth it....

> We only hear of the successful lines of thought and it is easy to draw the conclusion that great thinkers only pursue the ones that pay off. Common sense and observation of thousands of invention sessions have demonstrated to me that the successful thinkers are successful, not because they have an intuitive feel or intuition about which line of thought to follow, but because they try them all.

And here's a taste of the manual's discussion on the importance of wishing:

> Remember when you were five years old. What did you wish for? A bike? To fly? A skizillion dollars? A brother (or no brother)? Remember what it was like to wish? It was OK. It was free. Often it was not bound to reality. What we're looking for here is merely to reclaim that kind of wishing, one of our earliest and strongest creative abilities.

In fact, the program is structured around three types of activities: listing your wishes, listing ideas about your wishes (or about other ideas), and coming up with solutions for making your wishes and ideas come true. It allows you to do this in a myriad of ways. For example, you can tackle a particular goal on a Problem Card, and then generate relevant thoughts in a free-form manner using "wish worksheets" and "idea worksheets" that are automatically linked to the Problem Card. Or you can let the program guide you through problem solving in a carefully structured, step-by-step fashion. Or you can simply plunge directly into an idea generating session.

While you're brainstorming, you can always click on an "idea trigger" icon that provides a randomly generated perspective for you to interact with. For example, one trigger directs you to concentrate on "*Your intense self.* Forget about your problem while you generate thoughts and feelings vis-a-vis this part of your personality. Take your time and list enough descriptions to recall what you are thinking about." Another trigger gently suggests, "Reflect on these two questions for a few moments: What would the best possible outcome look like? And what *else* would come from the best possible outcome?" Other triggers ask you to play with one or more objects that are bundled with the package; in my copy, these included a turquoise plastic egg, a marble, a magnifying glass, a bell, a cork, a pipe cleaner twisted into a spiral, and a little plastic tractor. These randomized triggers give the program a spontaneous and organic feeling, since they ensure no two sessions will be exactly alike.

MindLink can even help when you don't have a specific problem to tackle but would simply like to stretch your mind. It does so via a section called the Gym, which provides randomly generated assignments to tickle your memory, stimulate your mind's eye, squash your self-censor, and enhance your ability to make connections. The directives can range from the concrete ("list several different ways to use a paper clip; and list several different situations where you cannot possibly use a paper clip for anything") to the poetic ("describe the view inside of a grain of sand"). When you're finished with the mental gymnastics, you may feel better prepared to use the problem solving features of the program; or you may want to simply turn to your word processor in the hopes that you'll write more creatively than you would have without performing the exercises.

MindLink Problem Solver has a list price of $295, which isn't unreasonable considering its technical slickness and complexity. However, through special arrangement with MindLink, Inc., you can purchase the package for only $99 (a $196 discount!) by using its coupon near the back of this book. If you're comfortable running Microsoft Windows, you'll likely find this program to be a marvelous idea stimulator, either by itself or in conjunction with IdeaFisher.

Babble!

Before I talk about Babble! (and yes, the "!" is indeed part of the name), journalistic ethics impel me to mention that one of its programmers, Tracey Siesser, is a dear friend of mine. With all due objectivity, though: Babble! is great!

I'm not alone in thinking so. Such luminaries as science fiction novelist Orson Scott Card and fantasy novelist Neil Gaimon have also heaped praise on it, and regularly use it to get "unstuck" on stories and come up with wild ideas.

Babble! is almost nothing like the other idea generators I've covered, however. It's actually more like a sound mixer...except that instead of sound, it mixes *text*.

Specifically, it takes a file that contains sample text (say, a story you're working on), analyzes it for style and content, and then spits out sentences consisting of grossly rearranged text that somehow retains the flavor of the original prose. While the new sentences seldom make perfect sense or hold up well grammatically, they're sufficiently comprehensible to help you see your work in fresh ways and spark new concepts.

Further, Babble! can handle more than one file at a time; it can manage as many as *four* simultaneously. As a result, you can mix different text styles together, in any ratio you desire. For example, you can set it to 50 percent your text and 50 percent William Shakespeare. Or you can set it to 40 percent Shakespeare, 40 percent Bible, and 20 percent Harold Robbins. Or to 20 percent Robbins, 20 percent Beatles, 20 percent Chinese Menu, and 40 percent Beaver Cleaver.

In fact, Babble! comes packaged with 48 files containing text from such sources as Shakespeare, the Bible, "Dick and Jane," Mother Goose, Little Red Riding Hood, *TV Guide*, movie blurbs, standard insults, horror fiction cliches, opening narrations from classic science fiction TV shows, excerpts from Orson Scott Card stories, Poe's "The Raven," Confucius sayings, Chinese menu selections, French phrases, and the Declaration of Independence—to name but a few. (Of course, you can always create more files on your own.)

For example, a mixture of the Bible and "Dick and Jane" produced sentences like "In my bones, I will put the house with me, and iron. See, I have gotten a pet." And a Shakespeare and "Leave it to Beaver" mix generated the soliloquy "She's pretty and sails upon her eyes of them. Aye me she smells good, oh, that birds would be something, and Juliet is what holds the slings and all the guys beat me and kill the rest of outrageous fortune. You watch me, but sick and she's pretty and I were a funny-lookin' goon. O, how she smells good."

If all that's not enough, Babble! also features 28 special effects (assigned to the 10 function keys alone and in combination with Alt and Ctrl). These effects include such niceties as Lisp (replaces *s* with *th*), Stutter (d-d-d-oes that to words), Censor (inserts lots of -*EXPLETIVE DELETED*- into the text), Elmer Fudd (great with Shakespeare: "Womeo, oh Womeo!"), and, for computer press fans, Dvorak (boldfaces words randomly). The package even includes a "Nifty Keyboard Template" to remind you of the effects available.

As already indicated, Babble! can be used to combat writer's block, or as an idea generator "finding connections which are not obvious to the naked mind" (to quote the manual). However, it can also be used just for kicks. As the manual states, "Babble! is a toy for people who love words....It's fun to play with on your own, and it also makes a great party program. It's terrific at disrupting work in an office—one person runs it and starts giggling, and then everyone gathers 'round."

Actually, the manual itself is a real charmer, with statements like "We tried [Babble!] on legal boilerplate, but the stuff that came out sounded just like the stuff that went in!" It also has lots of fun with blank pages, using lines such as "This left page is intentionally blank," "This page left intentionally blank except for this explanation," "This blank page is intentionally on the left," "This page was left in a maze of twisty little passages," and "See previous blank page."

Because its publisher, Korenthal Associates, wants every writer in America to own a copy of Babble!, it sells it for the ridiculously low price of $35. For readers of this book, however, KA is going one better and providing it for only *$25*. Don't pass this deal up! To take advantage of it, simply use the Korenthal Associates coupon near the back of this book.

As Babble! itself puts it, the program is "It, which you to create music from the stuff that went in this. So what it still babbles! In all that is generated and you to those who love words on." I couldn't have said it better myself.

Humor is the shortest distance between two people.
　　　　　　　　　　　—Victor Borge

You can pretend to be serious; you can't pretend to be witty.
　　　　　　　　　　　—Sacha Guitry

Comedy is the last refuge of the nonconformist mind.
　　　　　　　　　　　—Gilbert Seldes

Everybody likes a kidder, but nobody lends him money.
　　　　　　　　　　　—Arthur Miller

He who laughs, lasts.

　　　　　　　—Dr. Robert Anthony

Dying is easy. Comedy is difficult.
　　　　　—Edmund Gwenn, on his deathbed

Just Joking and The Humor Processor

On the theory that you should "always leave 'em laughing," I'm tying up this chapter by discussing joke processors.

Contrary to popular belief, this type of software isn't primarily for stand-up comedians. In general, a professional comic worth her salt will make better use of her time by simply scanning the daily newspapers, and by keenly observing life around her.

So who's the primary market for humor software? Interestingly, it's businesspeople and other professionals who are called upon to make speeches or presentations. Such folks, who aren't experts at being funny, often find a database of jokes searchable by topic a lifesaver when they're desperately groping for a lighthearted opening line.

There's also a secondary audience for comedic software, and that's anyone who's interested in brainstorming—which is why I'm covering these products here. Nothing breaks through preconceived notions and alters perspectives as effectively as a well-constructed joke. If you're stuck on a problem, and you have a good sense of humor, reading through gags on a related subject and trying to draw connections can be an effective way of achieving the epiphany you're seeking.

Just Joking, from The Writing Tools Group, provides more than 2,800 jokes and humorous quotations, organized into 250 topics. The witticisms are culled from two recent books, *The Comedy Quote Dictionary* by Ronald

Smith and *Friendly Advice* by John Winokur, and the overall quality is high. For example, on the subject of cats, it offered 12 bits, including the following:

> We have two cats. They're my wife's cats, Mischa and Alex. You can tell a woman names a cat like this. Women always have sensitive names: Muffy, Fluffy, Buffy. Guys name cats things like Tuna Breath, Fur Face, Meow Head.
>
> They're nice cats. They've been neutered and they've been declawed. So they're like pillows that eat.
>
> — Larry Reeb
>
> I found out why cats drink out of the toilet. My mother told me it's because it's cold in there. And I'm like: How did my mother know that?
>
> — Wendy Liebman
>
> The clever cat eats cheese and breathes down rat holes with baited breath.
>
> — W. C. Fields
>
> I gave my cat a bath the other day ... they love it. He sat there, he enjoyed it, it was fun for me. The fur would stick to my tongue, but other than that ...
>
> — Steve Martin
>
> Cats are intended to teach us that not everything in nature has a purpose.
>
> — Garrison Keillor

You can find material in Just Joking by topic, by author, by phrase, or by cross-reference. The program also lets you add your own jokes to existing topics, create new topics, and define additional cross-references. And it allows you to easily export jokes to a text file or print them to paper.

Just Joking has a list price of $29, and is available in both DOS and Windows versions. The Windows version is especially nice for its small touches. For instance, its icon looks like a bright yellow banana peel that's just waiting for someone to trip over it; and the program makes your PC speaker laugh uproariously when you select the Help/About Just Joking option. And if you're still not sold, know that a funny nose and glasses doodad—complete with bushy eyebrows and mustache—is included in both versions of the package. Recommended.

Providing a similar service is The Humor Processor from Responsive Software. This package isn't as technically slick as Just Joking, and supplies only 500 jokes in 122 topics. Further, the jokes are generally of a much cruder quality than those in Just Joking. For example:

Two men were preparing to go hiking in Yosemite National Park. One asked the other why he was putting on a pair of running shoes instead of hiking boots. "In case we meet a bear," he replied. "That's silly, you can't outrun a bear." "I don't have to outrun the bear, I only have to out-run you."

A couple had trained their parrot to say "Who is it?" One day, when no one was home, the plumber came to fix their leaky faucet. When he knocked, the parrot said "Who is it?" and he replied "The plumber." This went on for hours: "Who is it?" "The PLUMBER!" "Who is it?" "The PLUMBER!" When the couple finally comes home, the plumber has had a stroke and died, and is lying in a heap in front of the door. "I wonder who it was," says the husband, and the bird replies "The PLUMBER!"

A teenager writing away to a pet store was having trouble with the plural of "mongoose." After trying "Please send me two mongooses," and "Please send two mongeese," his final letter read: "Dear Sirs: Please send me one mongoose. And while you're at it, why don't you send me an-other one?"

"I've heard that sleeping outdoors is the best cure for insomnia." "Sure, so is sleeping indoors."

GROAN.

The thing is, for the purposes of brainstorming, these musty attacks on our sensibilities are probably more useful than the relatively sophisticated wit to be found in Just Joking. Like its competition, The Humor Processor provides searching, export, and printing features, and lets you add your own material to the database. In addition, The Humor Processor gives you one thing Just Joking does not: a gag generator.

Specifically, if you select its Brainstorming option, The Humor Proces-sor splits your screen into three sections: a small Setup box across the top, and huge Left and Right boxes below it. In the Setup box, you enter a model of the type of joke you want to create. The program's manual fur-nishes a number of examples, including Exaggeration ("I'm so ugly that every evening my kids flip a coin to see who has to kiss me goodnight"), Reversal ("I have a job at the local radio station; I get in my car at rush hour and report on helicopter traffic"), Misdirection ("I sold my house this week; I thought I got a good price for it, but the landlord was mad as hell"), Cliché Rewrite ("Gamblers are just people waiting for their chips to come in"), Combination ("I went to eat at a Chinese-German restaurant, and an hour later I was hungry for power"), and so on.

In the Left and Right boxes, you load in any of 17 data files filled with terms associated with a particular subject, such as automobiles, computers, politics, smallness, or stupidity; or containing hundreds of names of famous people, movie titles, song titles, and so on. You can then scroll through each of the two side-by-side lists—either manually or automatically—while keeping an eye on your Setup formula, in the hopes of hitting upon an appropriate connective spark. While this simple but clever setup can indeed be used for creating jokes, it's also useful for brainstorming on virtually any topic.

The Humor Processor has a list price of $49.95. You can also buy an add-on database, which dishes out 600 more jokes, for $24.

Whether you decide to purchase a humor program or not, try to keep in mind that some aspect of the creative process should always be fun. Take on the attitude of novelist Gene Wolfe, who has a sign on his desk that says "I am going to tell you something cool." Your positive attitude is certain to come through in your writing.

At the same time, don't confuse fun with frivolity. As Elbert Hubbard noted (with only slight exaggeration), "An idea that is not dangerous is unworthy of being called an idea at all." And as Victor Hugo astutely observed, "Nothing in this world is so powerful as an idea whose time has come."

I think I did pretty well, considering I started out with nothing but a bunch of blank paper.
                                                                    —Steve Martin

Product Information

Note: Version numbers and prices may have changed by the time you read this.

Experience in Software, Inc.
2000 Hearst Avenue
Suite 202
Berkeley, CA 94709-2176
(800) 678-7008; (510) 644-0694
Fax: (510) 644-3823

The Idea Generator Plus 3.11: List Price, $97.50; Street Price N/A

Finntrade, Inc.
2000 Powell Street
Suite 1200
Emeryville, CA 94608
(510) 547-2281
Fax: (510) 653-4784

Idegen++ 2.3: List Price, $295; via coupon near the back of this book, $99

IdeaFisher Systems
2222 Martin Street
Suite 110
Irvine, CA 92715
(800) 289-4332; (714) 474-8111
Fax: (714) 757-2896

IdeaFisher 4.0: List Price, $199; via coupon near the back of this book, $99

Korenthal Associates, Inc.
511 Avenue of the Americas, #400
New York, NY 10011
(800) 527-7647; (212) 242-1790
Fax: (212) 242-2599

Babble! 2.0: List Price, $35; via coupon near the back of this book, $25

MindLink, Inc.
Box 247
King's Highway
North Pomfret, VT 05053
(800) 253-1844; (802) 457-2025
Fax: N/A

MindLink Problem Solver 2.2 (for Windows): List Price, $299; via coupon near the back of this book, $99

Responsive Software
1901 Tunnel Road
Berkeley, CA 94705
(415) 843-1034
Fax: N/A

The Humor Processor 2.02: List Price, $49; generally not discounted

Humor Processor Add-On Database (600 more jokes): List Price, $24; generally not discounted

Writing Tools Group
One Harbor Drive
Suite 111
Sausalito, CA 94965
(800) 523-3520; (415) 382-8000
Fax: (415) 883-1629

Just Joking 1.0 (for DOS): List Price, $29; Street Price N/A

Just Joking 1.0 (for Windows): List Price, $29; Street Price N/A

CHAPTER

4

SOFTWARE
COLLABORATORS

Somebody gets into trouble, gets out of it again.
People love that story. They never get tired of it.

—Kurt Vonnegut

Fiction writing is lonely work. The advertised promise of an electronic writing partner, or a disk-based story coach, that will break through your mental barriers therefore has great appeal. (After all, running a program is a lot healthier than downing several stiff drinks.)

I wish I could tell you that for 50 bucks you need never feel alone at your writing desk again. Unfortunately, the products in this category aren't nearly smart enough yet to take the place of a human partner. And most of them cost considerably more than $50.

However, if you can move past the silly hype in *all* of these programs' ads and lower your expectations, you'll find the majority of these packages provide significant support and guidance, and are genuinely useful tools. This chapter explores the most popular "collaborator" products: Plots Unlimited from Ashleywilde, Collaborator II from Collaborator Systems, WritePro from WritePro Corp., and FirstAid for Writers from WritePro Corp.

Plots Unlimited

Plots Unlimited is one of the first programs I got in for this book. I spoke at length to its co-creator, Tom Sawyer, and found him to be an intelligent and charming man. He's also somebody who's eminently qualified to create such a product, since he's sold numerous teleplays, and is currently the producer of the CBS hit *Murder, She Wrote* (a mystery series which lives or dies on its plot points).

In addition, the notion behind the program is a fine one. Since, as the saying goes, there are no new ideas, it's theoretically possible to enter every plot under the sun into a large database, and set up links between all plots that are conceptually related to each other. Such a database would allow you to string plots together in thousands of diverse combinations, generating a practically unlimited number of rich storylines.

That is, in effect, what the Plots Unlimited designers tried to do. The goal is a laudable one. Unfortunately, there are problems with their execution.

For starters, Ashleywilde has chosen to impose two marketing problems on its product. First, it's copy protected; it requires that you place a dongle on your parallel port. (If you aren't sure why this is an unpleasant burden to deal with, see the Introduction's section on copy protection.) Second, it's very expensive, with a list price of $399 and street price of about $299.

These negatives might be overlooked if the package made it easy to generate stories. However, I found the software frustrating.

My unease began when I first ran Plots Unlimited and was presented with the obtuse message "Cannot locate the desired version of FoxPro" (FoxPro being the database software used to create Plots Unlimited 2.0). The 122-page manual lacks an index, and the table of contents is missing such standard sections as "Error Messages" and "Troubleshooting." By going through the booklet paragraph by paragraph, I was able to find the answer on page 12 under a section titled "If You Need to Reinstall"—a less than helpful heading since there's no way to know you need to reinstall until *after* you read the section. Just as irritating, the manual neglects to explain exactly why the default installation options don't work, or what the error message means. Not a good beginning.

Every novel should have a beginning, a muddle, and an end.

—Peter De Vries

The man who writes about himself and his own time is the only man who writes about all people and about all time.

—George Bernard Shaw

Once I got the program up and running, I was rewarded by a friendly opening screen that said "Welcome" at the top and bottom, and "Ready to Start" in the middle. Unfortunately, it left out any instruction on what to do next. While this is a small point—some puttering around revealed I could simply press any key to proceed—it's another indication of less than perfect attention to detail.

The next screen offered three menus on its top line: Info, File, and Characters. I tried selecting the first menu by pressing Alt+I, but nothing happened. I next tried pressing a few other keys typically used to activate menus, such as Esc and /, but none of them did the trick, either. Deciding I needed more information, I pressed F1, which is what virtually every modern PC program designates as the Help key. Not Plots Unlimited, though; in this product, F1 has no effect.

After some more experimentation, I discovered Alt actually *does* activate menus, but only after you press it by *itself* and then *release* it—a method that's both nonstandard and unintuitive. In a word, sloppy.

Opening the menus revealed an organizational structure that also left something to be desired. For example, the Info menu's first option is "About PLOTS Unlimited," which provides only a copyright notice. You have to move down to the second option, "Help with PLOTS," to (finally) access the program's Help feature. And when you do, you won't get help on what you're currently doing (that is, context-sensitive help); all that's available is a list of 27 topics you can select among for more information.

Moving onward, I followed the screen prompts to open a plot file, and was then asked to select one of seven plot types: Character Combination; Story Type; Characters and Story Type; Story Type and Sub-Type; Character, Story Type, and Sub-Type; MasterPlot; and Conflict. The display offered no description of what these selections meant. However, a help screen I brought up explained the options are filters that allow you to hone in on the types of plots you're most interested in. For example, Character Combination lets you choose plots centering on particular types of characters (say, a female protagonist and a male criminal); Story Type lets you view only plots that involve a specified broad theme (say, Romance); and MasterPlot lets you construct a plot definition by stringing together three selections from lists of protagonists, actions, and resolutions.

Returning to the plot filter menu, I opted for choice five, "Character, Story Type, and Sub-Type." This led to a screen filled with 165 character combinations like the following:

- Jack (male protagonist)

- Jack and subordinate/employee

- Jack, friend, and utility character

- Jack, criminal, and Jack's son

- Carol (female protagonist) and mysterious aunt

- Carol, female stranger, and inanimate/mysterious object

- Jack, Carol, his grandfather, and her father

Preferring to keep things simple, I chose the first selection, Jack (male protagonist). I was then given the opportunity to change "Jack" to a name more appropriate to whatever story I was considering; but since I had nothing in mind yet, I accepted the default name.

Next, I was asked to select one of the three Story Types the program divides *all* fiction plots into: Romance, Married Life, and Activities. (Hey, I'm just reporting here.) I selected what seemed to me the most expansive option, Activities. I was then asked to choose one of the following 15 "Story Sub-Types:" Chance, Crime/Immorality, Deception, Deliverance, Helpfulness, Idealism, Misfortune, Mistaken Judgement, Mystery, Necessity, Obligation, Personal Limitations, Pretense, Revelation, and Vengeance.

I decided to select Personal Limitations. However, my finger slipped and highlighted Obligation, and I pressed Enter before noticing. No problem, I thought; as in most programs, pressing Esc will return me to the previous screen. Unfortunately, Esc did no such thing; instead, it performed the same action as the Enter key, pushing me

The only sensible ends of literature are, first, the pleasurable toil of writing; second, the gratification of one's family and friends; and, lastly, the solid cash.

—Nathaniel Hawthorne

forward rather than backward. The only way to rectify my error was to select the File menu's Restart PLOTS option, which canceled the entire operation and threw me back to the first program screen. As a result, I had to grit my teeth and retrace all my steps from scratch. Worse than sloppy.

Finally, though, I got to the actual plots, and was pleased to discover meaty material. Some samples:

- Jack is a successful businessman with an overwhelming desire to quit the commercial world and become a romantic adventurer; only the fear of others' disapproval stops Jack.

- Writer Jack finds that he is losing touch with his public, becoming unable to write salable material.

- Jack, with average abilities, unrealistically views himself as being superior; Jack tries ambitious ventures, but loses confidence before finishing them.

- Mail room clerk Jack is held in low esteem, (then) solves a problem that has baffled his superiors and wins an executive position.

- Jack wants to engage in an honest venture but lacks the money to finance it, (so) temporarily turns to crime.

- Jack is obsessed with fear that he is being dogged by danger; convinced that he's being pursued, Jack seeks peace of mind.

- From early childhood, Jack has been programmed to believe that he lacks courage; Jack's belief that he lacks courage becomes a self-fulfilling prophecy.

These are all solid plot suggestions involving personal limitations. Further, the program supplied about 45 others that were equally good.

Of course, if this was *all* the program did, it couldn't justify its $399 price-tag. After all, you can get collections of plots grouped by theme from inexpensive books, such as *The Thirty-Six Dramatic Situations* by Georges Polti ($7.88 from mail-order vendor The Write Stuff), *How to Write Plots That Sell* ($11.40 from The Write Stuff), and—if you can find it in a used bookstore—the 1929 paperback *Plotto* by William Wallace Cook (which was actually the springboard for Plots Unlimited).

If you want to get rich from writing, write the sort of thing that's read by persons who move their lips when they're reading to themselves.

—Don Marquis

When in doubt, have two guys come through the door with guns.

—Raymond Chandler

The major promise of the program, then, is that it will let you build an entire storyline by linking the initial plot you choose with plotlines that lay the foundation for it (Leadins) and logically result from it (Leadouts).

To test this, I selected as my starting-point plot "From early childhood, Jack has been programmed to believe that he lacks courage; Jack's belief...becomes a self-fulfilling prophecy." I was then asked if I wanted to first expand this plot by Leadout (which is the conventional approach) or by Leadin (a "working backwards" method popular among mystery writers). I chose Leadout, and was presented with these follow-up ideas (which I had to view one by one through a narrow, unresizable window):

- Jack makes a heroic attempt to rescue a child, Lee, but both die.

- Soldier Jack disappears from his unit...and dies while performing a heroic act; but he is reported to have deserted under fire.

- Jack has a strange experience among a group which has beenbrainwashed... and finds the key to the brainwashing in a notebook belonging to Eric, one of the perpetrators. Using information obtained from the note book, Jack rescues the victims.

- Jack tries to correct a character flaw in his friend, Pete, by relating a story that subtly suggests a method of self-help.

- Jack is a cowardly braggart. He is manipulated into a dangerous test and must either eat his words or prove himself.

- Carol stops loving her husband, Jack, when she realizes he's a coward.

None of these are bad plots. However, I was hoping for more than a mere six endings. This set of closers felt very incomplete, and arbitrary.

Still hopeful, I next requested Leadins. That generated the following:

- Jack, on the run from a relentless process-server, pretends that his showgirl wife, Carol, is his sister. Jack...finds himself in jeopardy when Carol's new admirer turns out to be a notorious mob figure.

- Both Jack and Carol are too shy to admit their love for one another.

- Carol loves Jack; but, before she will commit to marry him, she insists that he must perform heroic deeds.

And that was it; only three plots. It's hard to create the feeling of inevitability a great story demands when you're presented with such a small base of ideas to choose from.

I write when I'm inspired, and I see to it that I'm inspired at nine o'clock every morning.

—Peter De Vries

Further, when I tried to generate extended plotlines from one of the Leadins or Leadouts, I quickly hit the *same* plots again and again, as if I was in some sort of infinite loop. Subsequent tests I ran produced similar results.

I don't know if the root of the difficulty is too few plots in the database, or too few program links drawn between the plots. Whatever the cause, though, it made the program too frustrating for me to use.

By the way, the program *does* offer an alternative: at any time, you can bypass the suggested Leadouts and Leadins, and just comb through randomly furnished plots. However, that substitutes the problem of having too few choices with having too many unstructured ones.

Reviewer Bob Levitus apparently came to a similar conclusion in the June 1993 *MacUser*. Discussing the Macintosh version, Levitus observed "Every plotting method we chose led to a ridiculously long list of conflicts...or to a disappointingly small set. And expanding the initial conflict forward or backward inevitably led us to a dead end all too quickly, with only two or three equally unworkable conflicts to choose from—often conflicts that really weren't applicable to the type of story we had in mind. If you play with the program long enough, you're sure to find one or two conflicts that sound good to you. But that's not the point. You can probably find one or two conflicts that sound good to you in the morning paper."

I'd soften that observation by pointing out that it takes only one strong idea to begin a screenplay, teleplay, or novel; and if you end up making tens of thousands of dollars from the sale of your work, a program like Plots Unlimited will have paid for itself many times over. Also, plot generation is a subjective enterprise, so just because the program's limitations kept it from clicking for me or Mr. Levitus doesn't necessarily mean it won't help spark useful storylines for you.

Therefore, if you're a professional writer with both the interest in using such a program and more than enough cash to spare (for example, if you're a working movie or TV scripter), I'd say buying Plots Unlimited is a worthwhile gamble—especially since it comes with a 30-day money-back guarantee. If you're a struggling beginner, though, your money will probably be better spent on other resources, such as writing workshops, books...and, yes, the morning paper.

Lastly, I want to repeat that Plots Unlimited is a terrific idea, and the goal it's shooting for is an ambitious one. Like a first draft manuscript, it needs a lot more rewriting and polishing; but it's a program to keep an eye on.

Collaborator II

Collaborator II is a rock-solid program that steps you through the process of writing a story by asking you 72 carefully chosen questions, and providing a large screen area for you to type in your answers.

The software's emphasis is on producing screenplays—for instance, it provides sample answers to each question based on *It's a Wonderful Life*, and even includes a videotape of the movie as part of the package—but it can used effectively for any kind of fiction writing project.

The program begins by asking such basics as "What is the working title

Ultimately, literature is nothing but carpentry. With both you are working with reality, a material just as hard as wood.

—Gabriel Garcia Marquez

of the story?", "Who is the intended audience?", "Why will this audience respond to your story?", "What is the theme of the story?", "Where does the story take place, and why is this imperative?", "What is the main conflict?", "What is at stake?", and so on.

It then nudges you into increasingly nitty-gritty thinking about your tale, with such queries as "What is the inciting action or event which begins your story?" "Is your protagonist required to resolve the conflict within a certain time?", "(For each of your plot points), does this event introduce a character, move the story forward, or propel your protagonist into action?", "How have your protagonist's and antagonist's special talents come into play?", "How has your protagonist grown?", "How did your antagonist change?", and "Has your protagonist 'gone the limit' to overcome the antagonist?"

The questions don't actually use vague terms such as "your story", though. Collaborator works hard to be interactive, and so plugs in the actual name of your story, protagonist, and antagonist as soon as you supply the necessary information. For example, in the *It's a Wonderful Life* sample, a typical question reads "How have George Bailey's and Herbert Potter's special talents come into play?"

Another way the program interacts is via a small-scale artificial intelligence routine. You can optionally call on this mini-program at any point to generate follow-up questions that pick up on words from your current answer.

Further, you can tackle the 72 prepared questions in any order you choose. To do so, you simply pop up a Goto Question box, highlight the phrase representing the question you want, and press Enter; or double-click on the phrase with your mouse. You can readily tell which questions you've already answered because a checkmark appears to the left of them.

The process of going through the questions is a genuinely valuable one. Based on the principles expounded in the classic book *The Art of Dramatic Writing* by Lajos Egri ($9.64 from The Write Stuff), they force you to think about crucial elements of your story in an objective manner, and also give you ample opportunities for experiencing insights about your material.

Of course, you might accomplish the same thing going through questions in a book—in fact, Collaborator's creators have written a paperback based on the program titled *The Screenwriter's Companion* ($14.95 from Silman-James, an imprint of Samuel French). However, irrational as it might be, using the program makes you feel less alone, and so makes it more likely that you'll stick through the process.

Besides, Collaborator sports other nifty features. One is an extensive five-screen form you can fill out for each of your characters, prompting you for such information as eye color, distinguishing marks or scars, addictions, special talents, idiosyncrasies, sexual preferences, phobias, and sample of character's dialogue. Another nice touch is a box containing Lajos Egri's List of 100% Characteristics, which furnishes traits ranging from Anti-Change, Arrogant, and Audacious to Whining, Wishy-Washy, and Worrisome that you can apply to characters you're dreaming up.

An additional memory-jogging aid is a built-in thesaurus which is designed to aid story and character development—for example, it provides antonyms you can use to boost conflict. On top of that, a no-frills word processor, 150,000-word spelling checker, and simple calculator are part of the package.

There are also two general positives worth noting. First, the overall program is smartly designed. While Collaborator is a DOS product, it uses Windows-like menus to organize its commands, employs resizable windows to display its data (and lets you keep several windows open at the same time), and is easy to operate with either the keyboard or a mouse.

(Writing a novel) is like driving a car at night. You never see farther than your headlights, but you can make the whole trip that way.

—E.L. Doctorow

Second, the manual is excellent. It carefully explains the reasoning behind each of Collaborator's questions, and in the process offers loads of wise advice and interesting movie examples. For instance, to begin explaining the question "Who is the intended audience?", the manual states:

> While all writers write for an audience, the professional writer must also write for himself. To quote Cyril Connelly: "Better to write for yourself and have no public than write for the public and have no self." Yet the screenwriter must keep in mind the words of Dr. Samuel Johnson: "The drama's laws, the drama's patrons give. For we that live to please, must please to live."

> Terry Bacon wrote: "How you write to people depends upon who you think they are." And E. B. White said: "No one can write decently who is distrustful of the reader's intelligence, or whose attitude is patronizing." Respect your audience and they will respect you. Know your audience as well as you know your story and your characters.

If Collaborator was $99, I'd unhesitatingly recommend it to everybody. Unfortunately, it has a list price of $329, and a street price of about $269. Also, I'm sorry to report that it's copy protected (via software and hidden directories).

On the plus side, though, the package comes with an unusually liberal 90-day money-back guarantee. Therefore, if you think you'd benefit from Collaborator II, and you can afford its high price, you might as well check it out. You have nothing to lose but your faulty story structures.

My mother, Southern to the bone, once told me "All Southern literature can be summed up in these words: 'On the night the hogs ate Willie, Mama died when she heard what Daddy did to Sister.'" She raised me up to be a Southern writer, but it wasn't easy.

—Pat Conroy

WritePro

Plots Unlimited and Collaborator II are professional tools aimed at helping you create salable fiction. In contrast, WritePro is a tutorial program that drums in fundamental rules about the craft of writing. Also, while the first two programs are targeted at working scriptwriters, WritePro is designed primarily for aspiring short story writers and novelists.

WritePro consists of eight lessons, sold in units of two. Each lesson covers about 20 distinct rules of writing.

For example, Lesson One has you perform exercises demonstrating such truisms as "Somebody has to want something badly," "That somebody should be your lead character," "What your lead character wants should be important," and "Writing is rewriting." And Lesson Two teaches that "Readers are more interested in an active hero or heroine than a passive one," "We need something visual on every page," "If a character is torn between two conflicting wants, it increases suspense if the matter is not resolved immediately," and "As a story continues, the obstacles should be greater, not smaller." This is uniformly solid advice, so if any of it is new to you—or if you once knew these rules but have since forgotten them—you may find WritePro worthwhile.

You won't experience much trouble using the program; in fact, it's virtually idiot-proof. The downside, of course, is that its instructions sometimes treat you like an idiot. (But if you had a thin skin, you wouldn't be a fiction writer in the first place, right?)

Have faith...arising out of the mad notion that your society needs to know what only you can tell it.

—John Updike

Also, the software doesn't pay close attention to what you're doing. For example, if you're supposed to type a scene in a text box but try to just skip to the next screen, the program will complain that you've left the box blank. However, if you enter even a single letter into the box, the program will quiet down and let you proceed. It would make more sense to provide a "look-only" mode for those who like to skim first, and a stricter "teaching" mode that carefully notes the quantity and content of the prose you're creating.

In a nutshell, if you're an established fiction writer, you probably won't have the patience to go through WritePro's lessons. If you're starting out, however, you can learn a lot from this program, which is based on the hard-won knowledge of bestselling novelist and topnotch fiction editor Sol Stein.

Also, unlike the first two products covered in this chapter, WritePro isn't copy protected. And it's not expensive, either; the list price of the first four lessons is only $99.95. Better yet, using the coupon near the back of this book, you can buy them at a "what the heck" price of $49.95. On top of that, the package comes with a 30-day money-back guarantee, so your risk is zero. If you think you'd benefit from a drilled-based writing class on disk, this is the product to buy.

FirstAid for Writers

FirstAid for Writers, which is also from WritePro Corp., is a sort of Write-Pro for journalists and professional fiction authors.

Rather than a series of sequential lessons that you go through once and then set aside, FAW consists of numerous short exercises you can jump to directly, and that you'll (theoretically) return to whenever the need arises. Also, its instructions are written at a higher level than WritePro's, since they're directed at working writers.

FAW consists of five modules. Gearing Up tries to help you break through writing blocks. QuickFix aims to improve your fiction's beginnings, descriptions, characterizations, plotting, pacing, and basic storytelling. Intervention guides you in tackling persistent challenges such as suspense, point of view, flashbacks, eliminating cliches, enhancing resonance, increasing literary values, writing erotica, and finding your own voice. Nonfiction targets how to compellingly begin a journalism piece, make the people you write about come alive in print, use conflict and suspense as tools, use dialogue properly, and tap your originality. And Refresher reminds you of the order in which various elements should appear in your work when you're ready to do a rewrite.

In addition, the package comes with a unique Professional Back-Up Service that allows you to mail or fax specific writing problems to WritePro Corp. for up to one year after your purchase. The company promises that a professional editor will study your letter, and then get back to you by mail, fax, or phone.

FAW is a hodgepodge, with some parts of it more clearly targeted at pros than others. Also, it has an unattractive low-tech look that I'd argue is inappropriate for a program purporting to be a serious tool. Perhaps its biggest problem, though, is that there may not be a great many veteran writers who actually *want* disk-based instruction on their craft.

Therefore, I suspect whether you like this program will depend largely on your experience level and your personal taste. If you're interested in giving it a spin, it has a 30-day money-back guarantee, it's not copy protected, and you can buy it using a coupon near the back of this book for a reasonable $149.

A book should serve as the axe for the frozen sea within us.

—Franz Kafka

Thomas Wolfe said of the writing life, "And the essential paradox of it is that if a man is to know the triumphant labor of creation, he must for long periods resign himself to loneliness, and suffer loneliness to rob him of the health, the confidence, the belief and joy which are essential to creative work." I don't know whether any of the software discussed in this chapter will enhance your health and joy; but if used properly, they should help you produce better work. (And as for the rest of it: See Chapter 10, *Online References*, and Chapter 11, *Tools for Newspaper, Magazine, and Book Writers*, for some suggestions on how to chat with your peers around the country using a modem.)

Product Information

Note: Version numbers and prices may have changed by the time you read this.

Ashleywilde, Inc.
23715 West Malibu Road
Suite 132
Malibu, CA 90265
(800) 833-7568; (310) 456-1277
Fax: (310) 456-8586

Plots Unlimited 2.0: List Price, $399; Street Price, about $299; copy protected via a dongle that attaches to the parallel printer port

Collaborator Systems, Inc.
P.O. Box 57557
Sherman Oaks, CA 91403
(800) 241-2655; (818) 980-2943
Fax: (818) 788-4192

Collaborator 2.2: List Price, $329; Street Price, about $269; copy protected via software

Silman-James Press
c/o Samuel French Theatre and Film Bookshop
7623 Sunset Boulevard
Hollywood, CA 90046
(800) 822-8669; (213) 876-0570
Fax: (213) 876-6822

The Screenwriter's Companion by Cary Brown, Francis X. Feighan, and Louis Garfinkle (softcover book): $14.95

The WritePro Corporation
43 Linden Circle
Scarborough, NY 10510
(800) 755-1124; (914) 762-1255
Fax: (914) 762-5871

FirstAid for Writers 1.0: List Price, $299; via coupon near the back of this book, $149

WritePro 1/2/3/4 (first four of eight lessons): List Price, $99.95; via coupon near the back of this book, $49.95

WritePro 5/6/7/8 (last four of eight lessons): List Price, $99.95; Street Price N/A

The Write Stuff
21115 Devonshire Street, #182
Chatsworth, CA 91311
(800) 989-8833; (213) 622-9913
Fax: (213) 622-9918

The Art of Dramatic Writing by Lajos Egri (softcover book): List Price, $10.95; The Write Stuff Price, $9.64

The Thirty-Six Dramatic Situations by Georges Polti (softcover book): List Price, $8.95; The Write Stuff Price, $7.88

How to Write Plots That Sell by F. A. Rockwell (softcover book): List Price, $12.95; The Write Stuff Price, $11.40

Many other writing-related books are also available at discount prices; call to get this mail-order vendor's jampacked free catalog.

PART III

HONING YOUR WORK

Our power is patience. We have discovered that writing allows even a stupid person to seem halfway intelligent, if only that person will write the same thought over and over again, improving it just a little bit each time. It is a lot like inflating a blimp with a bicycle pump. Anybody can do it. All it takes is time.

—Kurt Vonnegut

CHAPTER

5

ELECTRONIC DICTIONARIES AND THESAURUSES

Give me the right word and the right accent and I will move the world.

—Joseph Conrad

The odds are that you're already convinced of the value of electronic spelling checkers. (What else can go through your document in seconds and pick out all the typos?)

When it comes to electronic dictionaries and thesauruses, though, you may be skeptical. After all, if you need the definition of a word or a list of its synonyms, you can simply reach for a book to get the information. Why, you may reasonably ask, should you spend more money, and give up megabytes of disk space, for programs that may not even tell you as much as standard paper references will?

On the thesaurus side, there are two basic answers: speed and convenience.

For example, picture yourself desperately revising a document that has to be out the door by 5 P.M. Then consider the likelihood of your periodically taking out whole minutes to pick up *Roget's International*, look up its cross-references for the synonyms you're seeking, flip through its pages to locate each reference, and then finally enter the word you want.

In contrast (as noted in Chapter 2), a software thesaurus asks only that you place your cursor on the pertinent word and press an invoking keystroke (say, Alt+T). When you do so, it instantly pops up a list of synonyms on your screen. After you select the word you want, the software immediately returns you to your document, replaces your original word with the one you chose, and retreats again to the background so you can resume editing. For most people, this quickness and efficiency isn't just a welcome convenience; it makes the difference between using a thesaurus and not using one at all.

With electronic dictionaries, a similar case can be made...though not as solidly. That is, it's decidedly easier to move to a word and press a keystroke (say, Alt+D) to bring up a definition than it is to grope around for your paperback dictionary and look the word up. The savings in time and effort in this instance aren't enormous, however, and by themselves may not justify the cost of the software for you.

The real strengths of electronic dictionaries are actually more subtle. If properly exploited, they'll let you work with words in ways that are impossible for a paper reference to match.

To get a better sense of what I'm talking about, let's explore the best disk-based dictionary on the market: the Random House Webster's Electronic Dictionary & Thesaurus, College Edition.

The RHWEDT

WordPerfect Corporation's Random House Webster's Electronic Dictionary & Thesaurus, College Edition (which, for the sake of our collective sanity, I'll refer to from here on in as RHWEDT) has a street price of about $55, takes up about 9MB of your hard disk, and (for its DOS version) needs about 8K of memory when running resident in the background. In return for these requirements, though, it gives you quite a bit.

For one thing, RHWEDT provides 180,000 entries, more than any other disk-based dictionary on the market. (If you pore over software ads, you may notice the Writing Tools Group's American Heritage Dictionary, 2nd College Edition program claims 303,000 words. However, that number was arrived at using such methods as counting small variations of a word as separate entries. Based on traditional counting methods, The American Heritage Dictionary has about 160,000 entries, or 20,000 fewer than RHWEDT.)

Each RHWEDT entry provides the accepted spellings and syllabications of a word, followed by the word's pronunciations, its various definitions, and the period of its first recorded usage. For example, the entry for *computer* provides the pronunciation "kuhm pyU tuhr," notes the word is a noun, offers such definitions as "a programmable electronic device designed for performing prescribed operations on data at high speeds" and "one that computes," and traces the word back to the 1640s.

RHWEDT also includes an excellent thesaurus that you can use to either supplement or replace your word processor's thesaurus. The RHWEDT version contains a solid 275,000 entries; provides an illustrative sentence for each category of synonyms; and usually supplies antonyms, as well.

The program also keeps track of your lookup requests, maintaining a running list of the last 16 words you checked through either the dictionary or thesaurus. This is handy if you need to go back and recheck a word, or run a word through both the thesaurus and the dictionary.

Therefore, as the electronic equivalent of its hardcover version, RH-WEDT is affordable, complete, and convenient to use. However, where it really transcends its paper edition—and hits the strengths I alluded to earlier—is in its search capabilities.

Words are...the most powerful drug used by mankind.

—Rudyard Kipling

Let's say, for example, you need some Iraq-related terms to add color to a piece you're writing about the Middle East, but you can't think of anything past the name of the country. With a paper dictionary, you could look up Iraq and cross your fingers, but the chances are you wouldn't find much that was usable. With RHWEDT, however, you can select the Search Definitions command, type *Iraq*, and press Enter. You'd then be rewarded with the following words containing Iraq in their definitions: Baghdad, Basra, Ctesiphon, dinar, Erbil, Euphrates, fils, Gulf States, Gulf War, Hussein, id, Iraq (naturally), Iraqi, Kalakh, Kerbela, Kirkuk, Kish, Kufa, Kurdistan, Lagash, Mandaean, Mesopotamia, Middle East, Mosul, Najaf, Near East, Nineveh, Nippur, Seleucia, Shatt-al-Arab, Sippar, Syrian Desert, Telloh, Tigris, Ur, Uruk, and Zagros Mountains.

One of the things you might notice about this list is its considerable sweep. The number of words uncovered is partly the result of RHWEDT's enormous word-base. However, it's also due to software dictionaries typically being more current than their paper versions, since they're so much easier for their publishers to revise; that's why among the entries that turned up are Gulf War and Hussein.

If you decided you needed even more terms, you could apply the Search Definitions command to any of the listed words to generate additional lists. However, let's take the opposite tack and assume you want to *narrow* the search. You can do this using the Search Definitions command's AND/OR/NOT options, which allow you to search for two or more words that appear in the same definition.

For example, let's say you just want words for Iraqi currency. To get them, you select Search Definitions again, but this time type *Iraq AND monetary* (which tells the program to find entries with both "Iraq" and "monetary" in their definitions), and press Enter. This produces two words: *dinar* and *fils*.

Selecting *dinar* and pressing Enter yields a definition that says, in part, "The basic monetary unit of Algeria; of Bahrain; of Iraq, Jordan, and Kuwait; of Libya; of Tunisia; and of Yugoslavia." Bingo.

Further, plugging *fils* into the dictionary reveals that it's "a monetary unit of Bahrain, Iraq, Jordan, and Kuwait, equal to 1/1000 of a dinar." The definition goes on to explain that *fils* is also a French term meaning *son*, "often used after a name with the meaning of Jr., as in Duma fils." Live and learn.

What these examples illustrate is that RHWEDT, via its Search Definitions command, gives you the ability to turn the program into a "reverse dictionary"; in effect, it lets you look up the definition to locate the word. If you simply think about the number of times you've had a word on the tip of your tongue but couldn't quite remember it, you'll immediately appreciate the usefulness of this powerful feature.

That's not the only way RHWEDT lets you plumb its data, though. Another is pattern matching, which is accessed through the program's Search Wildcard command. This feature lets you represent any single letter using a question mark (?), and any combination of letters using an asterisk (*). For example, if you tell RHWEDT to search for *c?t*, it supplies the terms *cat, cot,* and *cut.* (the program ignores punctuation marks when determining matches), *CAT, cit., cot, CRT, CST, C.S.T., cut, cvt,* and *cwt.* On the other hand, if you have RHWEDT search for *c*t*, it generates 824 terms, including *cabalist, chief master sergeant, cnidoblast* (a type of cell found in jellyfish), *conflict of interest, corps de ballet, cryptozoologist* (someone who investigates mythic creatures like the yeti and Loch Ness monster), *Cuisinart, cyst,* and *czarist.*

Colors fade, temples crumble, empires fall, but wise words endure.

—Edward Thorndike

The uses for this Wildcard feature are unlimited. For example, say you're trying to remember the term for a chemical used in Vietnam containing the word *orange*. A paper dictionary will give you all the terms beginning with orange, such as *orangeade, orange milkwood, orange pekoe, orangewood,* and *orangey*; but the dictionary's static alphabetic organization won't be able to provide terms that contain orange in their middle or end. In contrast, by supplying RHWEDT with the search pattern **orange**, you're delivered a complete list containing such terms as *East Orange, mandarin orange, methyl orange, navel orange, temple orange*...and the phrase you were looking for, *Agent Orange*.

As another example, assume you were asked to create a product name that, for patriotic reasons, begins with a *u* and ends with an *s*; and that contains precisely seven letters. To get started, you might enter the search pattern *u?????s*, which turns up such idea-provoking words as *Ulysses* (heroic), *Ulfilas* (a missionary who translated the Bible into Gothic, for that touch of nobility), *uranous* (a substance containing uranium, to connote explosive possibilities), and *undress* (hey, stop looking, we've got a winner). This approach is, of course, also useful for tackling crossword puzzles.

As a last example, say you were writing a poem and needed a rhyme for *twilight*. Simply entering the pattern **ight* would give you 34 possibilities, including *airtight, dogfight, eyesight, inflight,* and *twi-night* ("of or denoting a baseball doubleheader begun late in the afternoon and continued into the evening," a term dating back to the 1940s). Actually, you're better off using WordPerfect Rhymer for poetry, because it's a more precise instrument (see Chapter 13, *Tools for Poets*); but RHWEDT will do in a pinch.

And if all that's not enough, RHWEDT even has a gimmick: an anagram generator. I don't know of a single practical use for this feature outside of prepping for a game of Scrabble; but if you want to be able to generate four other words out of *plate* (*petal, pleat, tepal,* and *leapt*), RHWEDT makes sure that you can.

The Random House Webster's Electronic Dictionary & Thesaurus, College Edition is available for both DOS and Windows. It's a terrific buy at a street price of about $55.

Other General-Purpose Dictionaries

While WordPerfect Corporation's RHWEDT is the best disk-based dictionary, you may find another program better suits your particular needs; or you may simply want another program to supplement RHWEDT. This section briefly describes the competition.

As I mentioned previously, the Writing Tools Group publishes The American Heritage Dictionary, 2nd College Edition, or AHD for short. This is a fine program that offers all the features RHWEDT does, including definition searching, pattern matching, and even anagram generation. RHWEDT handles a few things better, though; for example, it lets you scroll both forward and backward in a long list of words, while AHD only lets you scroll forward. Most important, RHWEDT has more entries and better definitions; for example, when I ran *Iraq* through AHD, neither *dinar* or *fils* turned up. On the other hand, AHD inevitably contains some information that RHWEDT lacks, so if you spend a lot of time looking up words, you might consider buying AHD as a supplemental reference source. AHD is available in both DOS and Windows versions, and has a street price of about $59.

Another product based on *The American Heritage Dictionary* is Word-Science Corporation's Instant Definitions. Perhaps the best thing about this program is its size; while it contains 116,000 entries, it occupies only 2.5MB on your hard disk, which makes it great for laptop use. (In contrast, the DOS version of RHWEDT requires about 8.5MB, and AHD needs 9.5MB.) Instant Definitions is small because it leaves out pronunciation and word origin information, and uses shorter definitions. It's very fast (as you might guess from its name), can run resident in as little as 4K of memory, and offers advanced features such as definition searching. Its street price is about $49.

The Concise Oxford Dictionary, Electronic Edition from Oxford University Press also sounds like a winner. Unfortunately, despite its distinguished title, the program has a number of limitations, including a relatively small word-base (though it requires 4.5MB of hard disk space), the inability to search through definitions, and the lack of a thesaurus. Also, its list price of $99 is seldom discounted, so it's nearly twice as expensive as its competition. If you're really interested in owning a world-class Oxford University Press dictionary...and you have deep pockets...I suggest turning instead to the OED CD-ROM, which is covered in the next section.

If all you want is a thesaurus, the best standalone DOS program is Microlytics' Word Finder, which contains over 220,000 synonyms (but no antonyms), requires a mere 615K of disk space, and has a street price of about $30. (Before purchasing Word Finder, though, check to make sure you don't already own it; it's built into several word processors, including XyWrite and Nota Bene.) If you use Windows, an even better buy is Word Finder Plus, which provides over twice as many synonyms as the DOS version (as well as 50,000 concise definitions and a vocabulary quiz), and only costs about $30.

On the other hand, if you want as many reference tools as possible stuffed into one product, consider The Writer's Toolkit from Systems Compatibility Corporation. This program includes a 115,000-word version of *The American Heritage Dictionary*; and a version of Houghton Mifflin's *Roget's II* thesaurus (which I found typically came up with about two-thirds the synonyms Word Finder did—though the words it *did* suggest were of good quality). The Writer's Toolkit also incorporates versions of Houghton Mifflin's CorrecText program (see Chapter 6, *Grammar and Style Checkers*); *The Concise Columbia Dictionary of Quotations*, containing 6,000 quotations searchable by author or topic; Houghton Mifflin's *Dictionary of Common Knowledge*, providing thousands of facts searchable by topic, person, place, or date; Houghton Mifflin's *The Written Word III* reference book on grammar and style; and a utility that translates abbreviations (such as NY, CIA, and ASPCA) into their full word equivalents, and vice versa.

It is just when ideas are lacking that a phrase is most welcome.
> —Johann Wolfgang von Goethe

A good catchword can obscure analysis for fifty years.
> —Wendell L. Wilkie

On the negative side, the dictionary and thesaurus of The Writer's Toolkit aren't as good as RHWEDT's; and the grammar checker isn't as full-featured and effective as WordPerfect Corporation's Grammatik (again, see

Chapter 6). However, The Writer's Toolkit has a street price of about $35, which is a fraction of what you'd pay if you bought comparable editing and reference tools separately. If you think the program's components will meet your needs—or if you're looking for a gift for a young student—this package offers very good value for the money.

Lastly, taking an entirely different approach to thesauruses and dictionaries is Microlytics' Inside Information. Based on the recent *Word Menu* reference book published by Random House, this program organizes all human knowledge into seven categories: Nature, Science & Technology, Domestic Life, Institutions, Arts & Entertainment, Language, and The Human Condition. It then divides these categories into sub-categories, and sub-sub-categories, until it gets you down to one of its 700 thesaurus-like word lists. At that point, you can select particular words and access brief definitions of them.

To demonstrate, I selected the initial window's last category, The Human Condition, and pressed Enter. In response, the program opened another window containing four sub-categories: Character, Cognition, The Dark Side, and Faith. I chose The Dark Side, and got a window holding seven more categories: Crime; Intrigue, Deception & Strategy; Drugs & Drug Abuse; Insanity & Mental States; Magic & The Occult; Violence; and Death. Rather than pussyfoot around, I went directly for Death. This resulted in a window with seven additional headings: Dead or Dying; Unnatural Deaths; Murder & Suicide; Dead Bodies; Burial & Funerals; Beyond the Grave; and Language of Death. After choosing Dead or Dying, I finally arrived at a word list; specifically, 50 terms along the lines of *bite the dust, cash in one's chips, done for, dust and ashes, gone to Davy Jones, iced, kick the bucket, meet one's Maker, six feet under,* and *wither and die.*

Not fully sated, I pressed Esc to back up one window, and then selected Language of Death. I was rewarded with such colorful phrases as *ante mortem* (which, I learned at a keypress, means "preceding death"), *black humor, body bag, coup de grace* ("deathblow"), *dead duck, dying breath, Enoch Arden* ("person presumed dead who turns up alive"), *fey* ("fated to die"), *Thanatos* ("primal, instinctual desire for death"), and 40 other terms.

Inside Information also offers lighter fare, of course; for example, if you select the topic thread Arts & Entertainment/Pop Culture/Cinema/Genres & Types of Pictures, you get 61 names for movie categories, including *A picture* (as opposed to a "B" picture), *blaxploitation, cinema verite, oater, screwball comedy, spaghetti western, tearjerker,* and *whodunit.*

To some extent, you can generate similar types of lists using the definition-searching feature of a program such as RHWEDT. However, the wording used in dictionary definitions isn't always consistent, so sometimes pertinent terms are skipped over in searches. Also, dictionaries often leave out slang and jargon terms, which may be precisely what you're looking for. In contrast, the Inside Information word lists were carefully developed over six years by novelist Stephen Glazier, his research assistants, and a horde of consultants, using a wide range of reference materials. The only product that provides comparable word lists is IdeaFisher (see Chapter 3, *Idea Generators*), which can be purchased using a coupon near the back of this book for $99; while Inside Information's street price is about $35.

Like IdeaFisher, Inside Information can be used to generate ideas about particular topics (though it's not designed to promote flow of thought the way IdeaFisher is). In addition, like dictionary definition searches and thesauruses, Inside Information can jog your memory about certain words and phrases, and lead you to new ones you weren't aware of. It can even help you quickly familiarize yourself with a particular field, by supplying you with the common terminology for the field and letting you look up phrases you aren't sure about. This function is especially useful if you're a journalist or fiction writer, since it provides you with both a pool of colorful terms you can include in your writing, and a foundation for further research.

Of course, if you're a language nut like me, you don't need any practical motivation for buying Inside Information. The fact that this program offers a neat new way of relating to words is reason enough.

The Oxford English Dictionary CD-ROM

Products such as WordPerfect Corporation's RHWEDT and Microlytics' Inside Information are terrific electronic dictionaries, and they'll fully serve the needs of most people. However, if you crave the ultimate in dictionaries—and, for that matter, one of the great reference works of our time—you should turn to the Oxford English Dictionary (Second Edition) on CD-ROM. (For information on what's required to use CD-ROMs, see Chapter 9, *CD-ROM References*.)

This product supplies, on a single shiny disc you can hold in your hand, the entire contents of the mammoth 20-volume, 137-pound paper version of the Oxford English Dictionary—or, as it's affectionately referred to worldwide, the *OED*. The result of over a century's labor by a small army of lexicographers and researchers, the OED contains 290,500 main entries encompassing the definitions of 616,500 words. (For example, the main entry *television* encompasses such sub-entries as *cable television, television evangelist,* and *television network*.) Like other dictionaries, the OED gives you a word's pronunciations, syllabications, and definitions. What sets the

OED apart is that it also provides extensive information on a word's etymology—that is, its origins and changing meanings over time. This etymology is documented with copious quotations from a wide range of print sources.

For example, the OED contains over 30 single-spaced pages on the word *love*. The actual definitions take up less than a page; the rest of the space is devoted to etymological details, and more than 600 *quotations* about love. The latter range from an 825 A.D. Latin Vespers prayer, to some sound animal-handling advice from 1653 ("Tie the frog's leg above the upper joint to the armed wire, and in so doing use him as though you loved him"), to a 1922 excerpt from James Joyce's *Ulysses* ("Lord love a duck, he said, look at what I'm standing drinks to!"), to a 1946 lament ("He loves me. He don't. He'll have me. He won't. He would if he could, but he can't."), to a modern excuse from 1975 ("But Sher love, it was only a read-through. You don't expect me to act?"). The quotations are organized by shades of meaning, and within each category by chronology; so strolling through them provides you with both a full understanding of the various ways a word can be used, and insight into how a particular meaning of the word has changed over time. The OED contains an awesome 2.4 million quotations, and a grand total of 60 million words. There's simply nothing else like it.

I never write metropolis *for seven cents because I can get the same price for* city. *I never write* policeman *because I can get the same money for* cop.
—Mark Twain

As you'd expect, the electronic version of the OED lets you exploit this tremendous data resource in ways that would be impossible with the printed version. For starters, of course, you can summon any entry by just typing it in; if you misspell it, the software will automatically offer suggestions on which word you really mean. You can also conduct wildcard searches for entries, using the standard question mark for single letters and asterisk for groups of letters.

Further, you can search for words within definitions, within quotations, within etymologies, or throughout the entire text. You can also narrow searches to find only, say, the verb forms of words, or quotations from a particular author, by checking off various pop-up options. You can even take advantage of a built-in data query language that lets you construct highly sophisticated search requests. Indeed, giving you the power to make pinpoint searches is taken so seriously in this product that program code occupies more space on the CD-ROM than the dictionary data.

When I *use a word...it means just what I choose it to mean—neither more nor less.*

—Humpty Dumpty
(via Lewis Carroll)

With all that being said, I'll hit you with the two bits of bad news.

First, the OED works exclusively under Windows, so if your system is DOS-only, you'll have to make some significant changes to run this software. On the positive side, however, the OED's Windows design makes it fairly easy to use. It also allows you to highlight all the text for an entry, copy it to the Clipboard, and then paste it into your favorite word processor for further study.

The second bit of bad news is the OED's cost: it's $895, with no lower price in sight. (I tried to talk the publisher into doing a discount coupon, but no go; the OED is, not unreasonably, being treated as a premium product.) Therefore, this isn't a purchase to make casually. If you have serious need for this heavy-duty research tool, however, be comforted by the fact that even at $895, the CD-ROM costs $1,855 less than its printed counterpart—and, at the same time, takes up a lot less space, and allows you to make much greater use of its data.

Frankly, I find it mind-boggling that we can buy and use a tool like the OED CD-ROM at all. It's an amazing age we live in.

Computer Dictionaries

In addition to general-purpose dictionaries that cover a little bit of everything, you may be interested in dictionaries that hone in on a particular subject area.

One obvious topic for a computer-based dictionary to tackle is, um, computers. Two products that do this are The Computer Language Company's Electronic Computer Glossary and Que Software's Computer User's Dictionary (both of which are available in separate DOS and Windows editions).

These two dictionaries actually have more similarities than differences. For example, they both have an informal style, sprinkling tips, anecdotes, and brief histories of terms into their definitions. They both let you "reverse" the dictionary by searching for words in the definitions (though only the Que dictionary lets you narrow the search using the AND/OR/NOT operators). And they both include among their entries a generous number of product names, such as WordPerfect, PC Tools, and QuarkXPress.

The Que dictionary has a slightly more attractive look; and it may be less intimidating to novices because it restricts itself to PC terms (the Glossary includes minicomputer and mainframe terms).

Overall, though, I prefer the Glossary. For one thing, it contains 5,000 entries versus the 2,000 in the Que package. For another, it's updated four times a year, so you can feel confident that the terminology is current. In addition, the Glossary provides such extras as explanatory charts and diagrams; a list of over 100 common DOS filename extensions; and (under the definition for *BBS*) the numbers of more than 200 popular electronic bulletin board systems. It even includes frequently misspelled words (such as "gooey" for GUI and "zywrite" for XyWrite), so if you enter them you can be directed to their correctly spelled counterparts.

Perhaps most important, the Glossary is easier to use. This is due to small touches, such as its clearing the entry window after each definition so you can readily type in a new word (the Que product leaves your previous word in the entry window, forcing you to manually delete it); its intuitive use of the PgDn key for viewing definitions (Que's usage is quirky); and its automatically issuing a command to your printer to push a page out after a definition has been printed (the Que program forces you to press your printer's Form Feed button to get the page out).

The list price of The Electronic Computer Glossary is a low $29.95, and Que's Computer User's Dictionary is $39.95. Browsing through either program can teach you a great deal about PCs and PC products.

Inductel Specialized Dictionaries

There's actually a third computer dictionary available; but it's not really directed at a mass audience, and is sold as part of a set.

Specifically, a company named Inductel, which is dedicated to serving niche markets, has broken down the popular *McGraw-Hill Dictionary of Scientific and Technical Terms* into six electronic dictionaries covering Biology, Chemical Terms, Computers, Electrical and Chemical Engineering, Mechanical and Design Engineering, and Physics. Together, these products contain over 120,000 definitions and take up about 9MB of your hard drive (though, if you're short on disk space, you can opt to install only the dictionaries you most need). The entire package costs $149, and is aimed primarily at techies. For more information on it and related products, see Chapter 17, *Tools for Scientists and Engineers*.

Lexicographer: a writer of dictionaries, a harmless drudge.

—Samuel Johnson

When the last sheet of Dr. Johnson's lexicography was put into his hands, his printer heaved a sigh and said, "Thank God I have done with him at last!"

—Laurence J. Peter

If you're a physician, you may want Brody's Medical Dictionary. This Inductel product contains over 40,000 definitions, and costs $59.95.

Brody's, by the way, shouldn't be confused with Dorland's Electronic Medical Speller or Stedman's/25 Plus for WordPerfect; the latter are purely word lists that help smooth spell-checking in WordPerfect. More information on all these packages appears in Chapter 16, *Tools for Physicians*.

And if you want an inexpensive, broad-based multilingual dictionary, Inductel offers The Concise Dictionary of 26 Languages, an electronic version of the book by Lyle Stuart. This $49 product handles languages ranging from Czech to Yiddish, and requires only 1.5MB of disk space; but, on the down side, it covers only the 1,000 most commonly used words in each language. For more information about it, and other multilingual dictionaries, such as the excellent Lexica from the Writing Tools Group, see Chapter 18, *Tools for Multilingual Writers*.

Finally, to round out its product line, Inductel sells the general-purpose Funk & Wagnalls Standard Desk Dictionary, which contains over 100,000 words, takes about 5.5MB of disk space, and costs $79.95.

The nice thing about buying into the Inductel product line is that all of its dictionaries are managed by a single program called KAS (Knowledge Acquisition System). When loaded memory resident, KAS takes up as little as 12K, and displays the definition of the word your cursor is on at a keystroke.

You should be warned that KAS's screen display is unattractive, and its method for setting options is unintuitive. However, once you get used to it, you'll find that it searches through the dictionary of your choice at lightning speed. Even better, if you set it to do so, it will automatically search through *all* the Inductel dictionaries you've installed whenever you look up a word, and then show you all the definitions found—with each definition preceded by the name of the dictionary it came from. In addition, KAS lets you add your own definitions, and even revise existing ones. Therefore, if you work with a wide range of specialized terminology, Inductel's KAS system may prove ideal. The entire Inductel product line, which is called the Micro Library, can be purchased for a very reasonable $229.95.

Product Information

Note: Version numbers and prices may have changed by the time you read this.

The Computer Language Company, Inc.
5521 State Park Road
Point Pleasant, PA 18950
(215) 297-5999
Fax: (215) 297-8424

Electronic Computer Glossary 6.37 (for DOS): List Price, $29.95; generally not discounted

Electronic Computer Glossary 6.37 (for Windows): List Price, $29.95; generally not discounted

IdeaFisher Systems
2222 Martin Street
Suite 110
Irvine, CA 92715
(800) 289-4332; (714) 474-8111
Fax: (714) 757-2896

IdeaFisher 4.0: List Price, $199; via coupon near the back of this book, $99

Inductel, Inc.
5339 Prospect Road
Suite 321
San Jose, CA 95129-5028
(408) 866-8016
Fax: (408) 243-1762

Brody's Medical Dictionary: List Price, $59.95; generally not discounted

The Concise Dictionary of 26 Languages: List Price, $49.95; generally not discounted

Funk & Wagnalls Standard Desk Dictionary: List Price, $79.95; generally not discounted

The McGraw-Hill Dictionaries (Biology, Chemical Terms, Computers, Electrical and Chemical Engineering, Mechanical and Design Engineering, and Physics): List Price, $149.95; generally not discounted

Medical Library (Brody's Medical Dictionary, McGraw-Hill Dictionary of Biology, McGraw-Hill Dictionary of Chemical Terms, and McGraw-Hill Dictionary of Physics): List Price, $99.95; generally not discounted

Micro Library (all the Inductel dictionaries): List Price, $229.95; generally not discounted

Microlytics, Inc.
2 Tobey Village Office Park
Pittsford, NY 14534
(800) 828-6293; (716) 248-9150
Fax: (716) 248-3868

Inside Information 1.0: List Price, $49.95; Street Price, about $35 (direct from Microlytics during discount periods)

Word Finder 4.0: List Price, $39.95; Street Price, about $30 (direct from Microlytics during discount periods)

Word Finder Plus 1.0 for Windows: List Price, $39.95; Street Price, about $30 (direct from Microlytics during discount periods)

Oxford University Press
200 Madison Avenue
New York, NY 10016
(800) 334-4249, ext. 7370; (212) 679-7300, ext. 7370
Fax: (212) 725-2972

The Oxford English Dictionary (Second Edition) on CD-ROM (for Windows): List Price, $895; generally not discounted

The Concise Oxford Dictionary, Electronic Edition: List Price, $99; generally not discounted

Que Software
11711 North College Avenue
Carmel, IN 46032-5634
(800) 992-0244; (317) 573-2500
Fax: (317) 593-2655

Que's Computer User's Dictionary 1.0 for DOS: List Price, $39.95; Street Price N/A

Que's Computer User's Dictionary 1.0 for Windows: List Price, $39.95; Street Price N/A

Systems Compatibility Corporation
401 North Wabash
Suite 600
Chicago, IL 60611
(800) 333-1395; (312) 329-0700
Fax: (312) 670-0820

The Writer's Toolkit 2.0 for DOS: List Price, $59.95; Street Price, about $35

The Writer's Toolkit 2.0 for Windows: List Price, $59.95; Street Price, about $35

WordPerfect Corporation
1555 N. Technology Way
Orem, UT 84057
(800) 321-4566; (801) 225-5000
Fax: (801) 228-5377

Random House Webster's Electronic Dictionary & Thesaurus, College Edition 1.0 for DOS: List Price, $99; Street Price, about $55

Random House Webster's Electronic Dictionary & Thesaurus, College Edition 1.0 for Windows: List Price, $99; Street Price, about $55

WordScience Corporation
1415 Oakland Blvd.
Suite 220
Walnut Creek, CA 94516
(800) 869-9673; (510) 939-1190
Fax: N/A

Instant Definitions 3.0: List Price, $69; Street Price, about $49

Writing Tools Group
One Harbor Drive
Suite 111
Sausalito, CA 94965
(800) 523-3520; (415) 382-8000
Fax: (415) 883-1629

The American Heritage Dictionary, 2nd College Edition 1.1 for DOS: List Price, $99; Street Price, about $59

The American Heritage Dictionary, 2nd College Edition 1.1 for Windows: List Price, $99; Street Price, about $59

CHAPTER
6

GRAMMAR AND STYLE CHECKERS

Word has somehow got around that the split infinitive is always wrong. That is a piece with the outworn notion that it is always wrong to strike a lady.

                   —James Thurber

Like other things forced upon us at a tender age, the word "grammar" carries some negative connotations with it.

For me, they go back to grade school (a.k.a. "grammar school"), where I spent laborious hours poring over an obtuse red book filled with rules about gerunds and participles and dangling modifiers. I had trouble connecting the hard-sounding words and rigid statements about English to the organic ways in which language weaves and bobs; and so I quickly developed a "bad attitude" about grammar. As a result, to this day I can't deconstruct a sentence, or even say with any certainty which word is the subject, which is the object, and which is the reject (or whatever).

At the same time, I know that correct syntax and punctuation are extremely important. Like fine clothing or a sharp letterhead, they convey to an audience a certain level of competence and effort. Similarly, when we allow grammatical errors to creep in, they call into question both overall accuracy and sincerity of effort. (For example, if I'd begun this chapter by stating "Grammar checkers is good things. Very unique. Hopefully, you like them.", it would've demolished my credibility with any reader outside of The Incredible Hulk.)

Even worse, such errors threaten clarity. There's a world of difference between "I love you." and "I, love you?!" Indeed, fortunes have turned on the placement of a single comma in a contract. (The problem has even become a plot device in fiction. For example, if you're a fan of the TV series *The Prisoner*, recall that the show would have ended immediately if Patrick McGoohan's character realized the answer to his question "Who is Number One?" was not the non sequitur "You are Number *Six*."—in response to which he roared "I am not a number, I am a free man!"—but rather "*You* are, Number Six.") It's difficult enough to be understood without placing such impediments in our way.

How do we reconcile a resistance to language rules with our need for them? A course is suggested by the Arthur Zeiger in his book *Encyclopedia of English*:

There is only one "law" of grammar: if any construction is used often enough and widely enough, it is right and proper.

There are no invariable "rules of grammar." However, there are descriptive generalizations concerning grammar. They are valuable, when they conform to reality, in the same way that a periodic chart of chemical elements is valuable; both abridge the total learning process.

But remember: if a generalization and a usage do not agree, the generalization is not necessarily wrong, and the usage certainly is not. It is merely that the generalization is not comprehensive enough to cover the usage.

In other words, if you have a good ear for language, trust it; but when in doubt, don't hesitate to seek guidance from existing rules. (Or, as Ken Kesey once wisely advised, "Take what you can use and let the rest go by.")

This same attitude should be held toward grammar checkers. It's likely that you won't agree with much of what these programs tell you about your documents (*especially* if you write well). However, if you patiently work with them, and fine-tune them to accommodate your particular writing style, they'll help you catch errors that no other type of program can.

This chapter first discusses the pros and cons of grammar checkers. It then demonstrates grammar and style checking features by exploring the best product in this category, Grammatik 5. The chapter also covers the two other leading grammar checkers, Correct Grammar and RightWriter; and a dedicated style-checking program named Corporate Voice, which helps you to mimic a particular writing style (be it that of H. David Thoreau, Danielle Steele, or the Department of Defense).

Do You Really Need a Grammar Checker?

As noted in Chapter 2, spelling checkers are great for finding typos in individual words. However, they pay no attention whatsoever to context. A spelling checker will therefore never be able to recognize that you meant *it's* (short for *it is*) rather than *its* (the possessive form of *it*); or except ("I'll do everything except clean windows") instead of accept ("I accept your offer"). It also won't notice if you use "are" (plural) when your sentence about a crate of oranges demands "is" (singular, for the one crate). It won't be aware of your misplaced commas, or your failure to match a left parenthesis with a right one. And it certainly won't be able to warn you about overlong sentences, or your use of the same word to start three sentences in a row, or the perils of passive voice.

For all of these sins of usage, punctuation, and style, you must turn instead to a grammar checker. This category of software will valiantly try to figure out what you meant—or should have meant—to say in each sentence. It will point out all the problems it can find, offer explanations for why they *are* problems, and provide suggestions for correcting the errors.

As you might imagine, grammar checkers are highly sophisticated products. However, because of the difficulty of their goal—that is, to correctly interpret the sense and structure of English sentences—they're far from 100 percent effective. A recent *PC Magazine* test of the most popular program, Grammatik 5, scored it as identifying only 53 percent of the errors in test documents. The next most popular program, Correct Grammar, fared even worse, identifying only 35 percent of the errors.

"Whom are you?" said he, for he had been to night school.
—George Ade

Just as bad, grammar checkers often flag problems that aren't problems at all. Until recently, this made the checking process so slow and annoying that many people refused to use the software. The programs now partially address this issue by letting you select a category of writing (say, fiction versus business) and level of strictness (say, informal versus formal) that conforms to your personal style, thus lessening the chance of unwelcome suggestions. You can further customize a program by turning specific grammatical rules off or on, and even by writing your own rules. When using the software straight out of the box, however, you'll still likely be hit with a lot of false error reports.

So should you bother with a grammar checker? If you're in tight control of your craft, and your documents don't have to be absolutely perfect grammatically (for example, if you're a professional writer whose text will be checked over by an editor before it sees print), then probably not; the benefits likely won't justify the time and hassle of using the program.

If what you write goes directly to your audience, however (for example, if you're creating business letters for important clients, or a newsletter without the help of a skilled proofreader), you may find a grammar checker worthwhile even if it only occasionally ferrets out a serious error. In addition, you may benefit from being forced to look at each of your documents one last time, especially since the grammar checker provides a fresh perspective you could never get from simply rereading your prose.

This morning I took out a comma and this afternoon I put it back again.

—Oscar Wilde

And if you tend to commit the kinds of mistakes this software excels at uncovering—for example, words misspelled in context, problems with tense, and stylistic lapses—then you absolutely should try a grammar checker and see if it helps. Even if the program finds only half your errors, you'll be a lot better off than when *none* of them were being caught. You'll also naturally become more adept at your craft as you note the kinds of suggestions that keep cropping up and adjust your writing accordingly. After all, a grammar checker will tell you things about your writing that no one around you may notice...or, perhaps, has the courage to bring to your attention.

Before you buy a standalone grammar checker, though, first see if a program you own already provides a version of one. Such popular word processors as Ami Pro and Word for Windows, and the reference package The Writer's Toolkit, contain versions of Houghton Mifflin's CorrecText grammar checker, which is the same software engine used in Correct Grammar. (The main difference is that Correct Grammar tacks on important customization options.) In addition, WordPerfect includes a near-complete version of Grammatik 5; the only significant component missing is a programming utility for creating your own grammar and style rules.

If you have one of these add-ins, you should run it to determine whether a grammar checker supports your style of writing. In some cases (most notably, the WordPerfect/Grammatik 5 combination), you may not only find the answer is yes, but that your add-in provides all the help you need. For more information about word processors with grammar components, see Chapter 2, *What Your Word Processor Can and Can't Do*; and for more information on The Writer's Toolkit, see Chapter 5, *Electronic Dictionaries and Thesauruses*.

Grammatik 5

WordPerfect Corporation's Grammatik is by far the most popular grammar checker on the market, with over 1.5 million copies sold. Through its various incarnations, it hasn't always been the best; but version 5, which was rewritten almost from scratch, *is* significantly better than anything else available.

Starting with the basics, Grammatik 5 is available in both DOS and Windows editions, each of which has a street price of about $55. The DOS version takes up only 1.4MB of hard disk space, and the Windows version around 2MB, so both are suitable for laptop use.

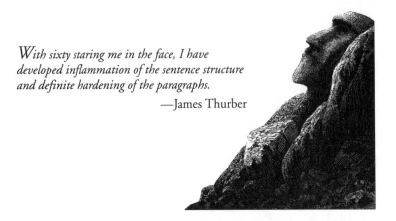

With sixty staring me in the face, I have developed inflammation of the sentence structure and definite hardening of the paragraphs.

—James Thurber

The DOS version works with the file formats of virtually all popular DOS word processors, as well as integrated programs with word processing components. These include Bank Street Writer, DisplayWrite, Enable, IBM Writing Assistant, Interleaf, LetterPerfect, Microsoft Word, Microsoft Works, MultiMate, OfficeWriter, PC-Write, PFS:First Choice, PFS:Write, Professional Write, Q&A Write, Signature, Sprint, Volkswriter, WordPerfect, WordStar, and XyWrite. It also supports Windows Write and RTF, which are file formats that retain most document formatting information (such as underlining, boldfacing, and font changes), and can be written and read by most Windows word processors. Lastly, it supports ASCII, the generic format that *all* PC word processors can handle but that strips a document of its formatting information. Therefore, if your word processor isn't supported in any other way, you can save a copy of your document in ASCII, run that file through Grammatik, and then manually apply the suggestions that were generated to your original file.

In addition, if you're using a recent version of LetterPerfect, Microsoft Word, PFS:First Choice, Professional Write, WordPerfect, WordStar, or XyWrite, you can invoke Grammatik from within your program with a keystroke. Unlike many other DOS utilities, Grammatik doesn't manage this by operating memory resident. Instead, it asks you to run your word processor using the special command GMKWP, which first loads an 18K Grammatik program and *then* your word processor. When you've completed your document and want to check it, you simply press Alt+G. Grammatik saves your document, closes your word processor, and runs itself; and when you're finished checking grammar and exit Grammatik, it automatically starts your word processor up again and reloads your document. While this procedure isn't as elegant as using a TSR, it has the advantage of taking up memory only when you explicitly ask it to; when you exit your word processor, Grammatik also exits, freeing the 18K it occupied.

The only man, woman, or child who ever wrote a simple declarative sentence with seven grammatical errors is dead.

—e. e. cummings
on the passing of
Warren G. Harding

If you want optimum convenience in switching between programs, though, turn to Grammatik for Windows. This version works with all the file formats covered by the DOS version, plus the formats of the Windows applications Ami Pro, Microsoft Word, PFS:WindowsWorks, Professional Write Plus, and WordPerfect. In addition, Grammatik works with any text that has been copied to the Windows Clipboard. This means you can easily use it with desktop publishing programs such as Ventura Publisher and QuarkXPress, electronic mail packages such as ProComm Plus, and even spreadsheet and database products such as Microsoft Excel and FoxPro.

You can run Grammatik in its own window, which you can switch to with a mouse click or a few presses of Alt+Tab. Alternatively, if you install Grammatik as a menu option or icon within Ami Pro, Microsoft Word, or WordPerfect, you can invoke it from your word processor without having to leave your document. In fact, if you want to be able to access Grammatik quickly from *anywhere* in Windows, you can install it to appear as an option on every Windows program's Control menu! On the other hand, if you don't have an appropriate application open, you can check a file by simply dragging its name from the File Manager to a minimized Grammatik icon. The Windows version therefore provides you with tremendous flexibility.

Now that we've covered what Grammatik needs to run and how you can access it on your system, let's talk about what the program actually does.

When you give Grammatik a document, it first breaks it apart sentence by sentence. It then breaks down each sentence into clauses, phrases, and individual words, and analyzes each piece using 96 grammatical attributes. (For example, the word *crate* might be assigned such attributes as *noun*, *countable*, and *singular*).

Grammatik then tries to figure out whether the pieces work together properly. To do so, it tests them against thousands of built-in rules on such topics as pronoun number agreement, tense shift, proper use of possessives, end of sentence punctuation, spelling errors, clichés, and run-on sentences. These rules are divided into 58 *rule classes*, which are organized into three general categories: Grammar, Mechanical, and Style.

The Grammar category is devoted to parts of speech and sentence construction. It consists of the following 24 rule classes: Adjective, Adverb, Article, Clause, Comma Splice or Fused Sentence, Comparative/Superlative, Conjunction, Double Negative, Homonym, Incomplete Sentence, Incorrect Verb Form, Infinitive, Noun Phrase, Object of Verb, Possessive Form, Preposition, Pronoun Case, Pronoun Number Agreement, Relative Pronoun, Run-On Sentence, Sequence of Tenses, Subject-Verb Agreement, Subordination, and Tense Shift.

The Mechanical category tries to catch various kinds of typos. It contains the following 12 rule classes: Capitalization, Doubled Word or Punctuation, Ellipsis, End of Sentence Punctuation, Number Style, Punctuation, Question Mark, Quotation Marks, Similar Words, Spelling, Split Words, and Unbalanced Parentheses/Brackets/Quotes.

And the Style category concerns itself with subjective style and word choices. It encompasses the following 22 rule classes: Abbreviation, Archaic, Cliché, Colloquial, Commonly Confused, End of Sentence Preposition, Foreign, Formalisms, Gender Specific, Jargon, Long Sentence, Overstated, Paragraph Problem, Passive Voice, Pejorative, Questionable Usage, Redundant, Sentence Variety, Split Infinitive, Trademark, Vague Adverb, and Wordy.

Actually, the program doesn't apply all of these rules to every document. If it did, many items you consider perfectly fine for your writing style would end up being flagged as errors, which would waste your time and cause you needless irritation.

You can be a little ungrammatical if you come from the right part of the country.

—Robert Frost

To get around this problem, Grammatik doesn't check your document until you select one of 10 writing styles—the choices being General, Business Letter, Memo, Report, Technical, Documentation, Proposal, Journalism, Advertising, and Fiction. These styles are distinguished, quite simply, by which rules they disallow. For example, Business Letter retains a rule that forbids incomplete sentences, while Fiction turns that rule off. In addition, the styles adjust the thresholds for certain rules; for example, Memo sets the Long Sentence rule to permit no more than 25 words per sentence, while Technical pushes that allowance up to 40.

After selecting the style closest to the type of writing you're doing, you are allowed to choose one of three levels of formality for it: Formal, Standard, or Informal. These levels go a step further in turning certain rules on or off, and so provide additional flexibility within a certain style. In effect, then, you really have 30 styles to choose from (though the differences between formality levels are relatively minor).

But Grammatik's options don't stop there—if you find that none of its existing styles quite fits your writing, you can create your own customized style. To do so, you select one of the existing styles for use as a template, turn off all of the grammar rules that are inappropriate for your type of writing, and turn on all the rules that you believe will be genuinely useful in catching errors. Your style is then saved under a name of your choosing, and is permanently listed with the other styles. You can create up to three custom styles in this way; and, of course, you can revise your styles at any time.

Further, using a powerful programming utility called the Rule Designer, you can create your *own* grammar and style rules. These can be added to existing rule classes, or can form the basis of up to three rule classes of your own making.

The Rule Designer has a number of uses. For example, if you're managing a workgroup that produces business documents, you can make Grammatik accept one version of trade terms, while flagging all other versions as being inconsistent with your company's style. Or you can set the program to flag industry jargon and suggest universally understood phrases as substitutes.

At first blush, the numerous customization options Grammatik provides may seen like overkill. Well...they're not. That's because, despite its relative sophistication as a computer program, Grammatik can be pretty stupid. Indeed, as one software reviewer observed, "If you're ever worried that your computer is smarter than you are, try spending some time evaluating grammar checkers."

To demonstrate, I did a test run of Grammatik on a fairly popular section of text: the first dozen verses of the Book of Genesis. For my style, I accepted the program's default General style and Standard formality options. I also used the program's batch mode, which goes through a document in seconds, inserts each suggestion directly before the section of text being critiqued, and then saves the whole marked-up document to disk. (The alternative is interactive mode, which lets you go through the suggestions one by one, and call up additional information about each suggestion.)

On the first sentence, "In the beginning God created the heaven and the earth," Grammatik offered an astonishing one-word recommendation: "Simplify." (Fair warning: Nothing that follows tops this one. Sorry.)

Regarding the next few passages, "And the earth was without form, and void; and darkness was upon the face of the deep. And the Spirit of God moved upon the face of the waters," Grammatik noted that "You have used *and* to begin the last three sentences. Consider more variety with your sentence openers." Well, in this case the repetition creates a poetic effect, but the observation is at least a tolerable one.

I have never been able to understand why it is that just because I am unintelligible nobody understands me.

—Milton Mayer

Concerning the sentence, "And God said, Let there be light: and there was light," Grammatik griped "You need an *object* before the colon to complete the thought." That's just wrong. In fact, this verse represents one of the clearest expressions of a thought in our language.

Regarding "And God saw the light, that it was good: and God divided the light from the darkness," Grammatik stated "When introducing a nonessential relative clause, *which* is preferable to *that*. If the clause is essential, then remove the commas. If this clause is an appositive, then *that* is fine." The clause isn't essential, but it *is* an appositive, so we'll score that as a correct (albeit unhelpful) call.

The fragment "And God said, Let the waters under the heaven be gathered together unto one place..." garnered two complaints. First, "be gathered" was criticized as being "passive voice, consider revising using active voice." That may be a valid warning in general, but it really doesn't apply here.

Second, "gathered together" was protested because "*together* is implied in the definition of *gather* and could be omitted." This one's a reasonable point, especially since it doesn't mandate eliminating the second word, but instead leaves the esthetic choice to the writer.

Concerning "And God called the dry land Earth; and the gathering together of the waters called He seas: and God saw that it was good," Grammatik grumbled that "the subject pronoun *he* should not be used in

the object position." Well, *I* like it, but I'll admit it's not standard usage.
(At the same time, it's interesting that the program inconsistently didn't
object to "gathering together," which is just as redundant as "gathered together.")

The final verse, "And the earth brought forth grass, and herb yielding
seed after his kind, and the tree yielding fruit, whose seed was in itself, after
his kind: and God saw that it was good," brought forth two comments.
First, Grammatik warned that "this sentence may have two independent
clauses without a conjunction in between." No, it doesn't (though it *is* a
long and winding passage).

Second, on the phrase "in itself," Grammatik groused that "in most
cases this expression can simply be omitted." If it was spouted by a cliché-
ridden corporate executive, I'd agree; but this instance happens to be one of
the few times when the phrase is absolutely correct.

All in all, then, Grammatik came up with a lot of wrongheaded advice.
If you constantly had to put up with this many unhelpful suggestions,
you'd probably give up on the program.

It would be preferable if Grammatik were smart enough to do better.
Until that happens, however, the next best solution is to turn off various
Grammatik rules to accommodate a document's style. For our current text,
this can be done by simply selecting the Fiction style at the Informal level.
So I did precisely that, and then ran the test again.

The results? Much cleaner. Only four complaints survived the change:
the one about beginning too many sentences with "And" (which isn't un-
reasonable); the demand that an object is needed before the colon to complete the thought (which is still wrong); the observation that "gather" often
works as well as "gather together" (which is a fair one); and the objection
that "called He seas" is incorrect (which it really isn't, though it's nonstandard). This shows that Grammatik's options aren't merely gimmicks; they
really can make a significant difference in how useful the program is to you.

On top of its grammar, punctuation, and style checking, Grammatik
provides several extras of varying benefit.

One is a 100,000-word dictionary that can check your document's
spelling. Both the manual and the program's marketing materials make a
big deal about this new feature; and indeed, it's the best spelling checker
available in a grammar checker. However, in the DOS version the spelling
suggestions don't appear automatically; you always have to press a function
key to display them, making checking slow and arduous. Worse, in both
the DOS and Windows versions, the suggestions that appear aren't as good

as those provided by more established spelling checkers, such as Word-Perfect's or the Microlytics speller in XyWrite. In most cases, you'll therefore be better off spell-checking your document in your word processor before sending it off to Grammatik.

A more intriguing feature is Grammatik's set of statistics screens. These provide you with information on noteworthy patterns in your writing, and on how readable your document is.

If you would like to write better than everybody else, you have to want to write better than everybody else. You must take an obsessive pride in the smallest details of your craft.

—William Zinsser

For example, if you select the Single-Document Profile option, you're presented with an alphabetical list of every word in your document and the number of times each word appears. This quickly shows you whether you're overusing or underusing particular words. (In case you're curious, in our Genesis text the most-used words are *the*, with 42 appearances; *and*, with 35; *God*, with 14; and *was*, with 10. Of the 71 remaining distinct words, none of them appear more than eight times.)

A related option, Historical Profile, presents you with the same type of alphabetical word list and word count. However, instead of restricting itself to your current document, it covers all the documents you've checked with Grammatik. This lets you inspect your patterns of word usage over an extended period of time.

To learn even more about your current document, you can select the Show Statistics option. This displays the number of paragraphs in the document, the average number of sentences per paragraph, the total number of sentences, the average number of words per sentence, the number of sentences ending with a question mark or exclamation point, the number of words, and the average number of letters and syllables per word.

Show Statistics also goes a step further by using these numbers to indicate the clarity of your document. It does so by plugging them into three standard readability tests: the Flesch Reading Ease Index, the Flesh-Kincaid Index, and Gunning's Fog Index.

The Flesch Reading Ease Index was developed in the 1940s by educator Rudolph Flesch, and consists of two simple formulas: 1.015 × (average number of words per sentence) + .846 × (number of syllables per 100 words); and 206.835 − (result from the first formula). The Flesch test was originally used by magazine publishers as a quick way of making sure their articles were geared to their intended audiences. For example, on a scale of 1 to 100, a score of 75 corresponded to the level of *Reader's Digest*, while a score of 35 meant that you would be understood only by *Scientific American* readers. Use of the Flesch test has since expanded to a wide range of fields; for example, some states won't approve an insurance policy that scores less than 40. As another point of comparison, our Genesis text scored an impressive 89, indicating that the vast majority of people will be able to read it effortlessly.

Fashions fade, style is eternal.
—Yves St. Laurent

If you are getting the worst of it in an argument with a literary man, always attack his style. That'll touch him if nothing else will.

—J. A. Spender

Find a subject you care about and which you in your heart feel others should care about. It is the genuine caring, and not your games with language, which will be the most compelling and seductive element in your style.

—Kurt Vonnegut

The Flesch-Kincaid Index is a modification of the Flesch test, and was developed in the 1970s by J. Peter Kincaid. It consists of just one formula, which determines the grade school level: .39 × (average number of words per sentence) + 11.8 × (number of syllables per word) – 15.59. The Flesch-Kincaid test was originally developed for the Navy to ensure its technical documentation would be clear to sailors. However, the test's use has since expanded to many government agencies, including the Department of Defense, the Social Security Administration, and the IRS. Our Genesis text scored a 4 on this one, meaning Flesch-Kincaid approves it for anyone who's made it to 4th grade.

The Gunning's Fog Index was first published in Robert Gunning's 1952 book, *The Art of Clear Writing*. It uses two formulas, which also determine grade school level: (average number of words per sentence) + (number of words of 3 or more syllables); and .4 × (result from the first formula). Gunning is used mostly by the publishing industry, and is based on the skeptical assumption that one's reading level is about two grades behind one's actual schooling. It therefore gave our Genesis text a 6, for 6th grade, versus the 4 score from Flesch-Kincaid.

Finally, if you prefer getting your data in visual form, Grammatik provides a Comparison Chart option which graphs the readability of your document against three other documents. The latter can be anything you want; some typical choices are previous documents you've created, or company standards that you're expected to adhere to. You can also simply accept for comparison the three default documents: the Gettysburg Address, the Hemingway short story "The Snows of Kilimanjaro," and a life insurance policy.

Overall, between its thousands of usage rules, its (relatively) careful checking, its effective style and customization options, and its statistical information, Grammatik is an impressive package that gives you a lot of value for its $55 street price.

Correct Grammar

Another solid grammar checker is The Writing Tools Group's Correct Grammar. It comes in both DOS and Windows versions (each of which takes up around 1.3MB of hard disk space), and has a list price of $49.95.

Correct Grammar doesn't sport nearly as attractive a screen design as Grammatik, and it's not as easy to use. In addition, it doesn't support as many word processors as Grammatik (though it covers all of the popular ones); and the DOS version can be set up to run only from within Word-Perfect and WordStar. Also, its suggestions tend to be more brusque than Grammatik's.

Take what you can use and let the rest go by.

—Ken Kesey

In most other ways, though, Correct Grammar's features are competitive with Grammatik's. It also does a few things better; for example, it lets you see a lot more of your document on-screen than Grammatik does when you're performing interactive checking.

Correct Grammar offers a total of 10 styles (with no formality levels): Academic, Advertising, Basics, Business, Custom, Fiction, Informal, Legal, Reviewer, and Technical. To demonstrate the program's checking, I ran the "Genesis test" on it using the Fiction style. The results were as follows:

The first verse ("In the beginning...") escaped unscathed. However, the next sentence—"And the earth was without form, and void; and darkness was upon the face of the deep"—got fingered because "the semicolon seems inappropriate in this context." The comment strikes me as rather picky for a Fiction style, but it's not flat-out wrong.

All the sentences about "light" made it through okay. However, the program didn't care for the two instances of *which* in "And God made the firmament, and divided the waters which were under the firmament from the waters which were above the firmament." Specifically, it suggested we "consider using *that* as the restrictive relative pronoun," which is perfectly sound advice.

Regarding "And God said, Let the waters under the heaven be gathered together unto one place," Correct Grammar had two comments. First, it suggested we "use a form of *be* that agrees with the subject." This is the program's first real error; the use of "be" is fine. On the plus side, like Grammatik, the program correctly noted that *gathered together* is a "redundant expression" and we should "consider deleting *together*."

On the closing two verses, Correct Grammar began by complaining "sentence exceeds recommended length." Since the sentences respectively contain 34 and 33 words, I'd call this suggestion overly restrictive for fiction writing.

However, it's on the phrase "Let the earth bring forth grass..." that the program became most agitated. First, it stated that "the word *earth* does not agree with *bring*," which is simply not true. Next, it suggested we "consider *brings* instead of *bring*." If we obliged, we'd turn a grammatically correct clause into an incorrect one ("let the earth *brings* forth grass").

Lastly, about the word "forth" (in *bring forth*), Correct Grammar cautioned "This word sounds like *fourth*. Check the spelling you intend." This is the kind of advice that drives me up the wall. For one thing, there's nothing in the sentence to even remotely indicate the word is being misused. For another, it makes me feel scolded for daring to use a word that sounds like another word. Such warnings can be useful if you often have problems with homonyms; but when they appear in a purportedly open-ended style such as Fiction, they're just stultifying. (Also, during other tests I ran, Correct Grammar ironically failed to find fault with the genuinely incorrect sentences "I like words, two." and "I like words, to.")

Overall, though, Correct Grammar didn't do badly. It's also interesting to note how little overlap there is between this program's suggestions and those of Grammatik's—yet another indication that grammar checking is still far from being an exact science.

Most reviewers, including me, consider Grammatik to be the more flexible and helpful program. However, no two people have precisely the same writing problems. If you find that Grammatik's suggestions aren't suited to your style, Correct Grammar offers a very capable alternative.

RightWriter

The third contender in the grammar checker market is Que Software's RightWriter. Like its competitors, it comes in both DOS and Windows versions (each of which takes up around 1.5MB of hard disk space), and provides solid word processor support. It has a street price of about $29.

The quality of RightWriter's grammar checking isn't quite in the same league as Grammatik's or Correct Grammar's. However, it outdoes both programs with its wealth of customization options.

For starters, it provides the standard 10 prepared styles: General, Newsletter, Proposal, Scholarly, Fiction, Technical Manual, (Nontechnical) Manual, Technical Articles/Books, Spelling Only, and All Rules On. It then goes a big step beyond its competition by allowing you to create an *unlimited* number of custom styles.

On top of that, it lets you adjust any style you're using via a "grammar equalizer," which works a bit like a sound mixer. Specifically, it displays six vertical scroll bars labeled Punctuation, Usage, Grammar, Style, Capitalization, and Structure. Each bar contains a control box that is initially in the middle, indicating that a medium number of rules are turned on. If you're especially weak in, say, Usage, you can move the control box all the way to the top, switching all the usage rules on. At the same time, if your document has a lot of strangely spelled names (a particular hazard in the computer industry, which is filled with products containing capital letters in the middle—for example, WordPerfect, QuarkXPress, and, uh, Right-Writer), you can move the Capitalization control bar toward the bottom, switching most of the rules in that area off.

Still not satisfied, RightWriter also lets you fine-tune your style by specifying whether your document is addressed to the general public, a high school-level audience, or a college-level audience. In most cases you'll want to stick to the default General level, but the other options can prove handy when you're targeting select groups of readers.

Ultimately, I think most people will find all of these options more confusing than helpful, and will prefer Grammatik's cleaner approach. But if you need to work with many different styles, and you like having a quick, visual way to adjust them, you might want to give RightWriter a look.

I ran the Genesis test against this program, too, once again employing the Fiction style. Here are the results:

The first verse ("In the beginning...") passed without comment. Regarding the second, though—"And the earth was without form, and void; and darkness was upon the face of the deep"—RightWriter politely queried "Is this sentence too complex to read easily?" Some might be tempted to respond, "I dunno; what do *you* think, dummy?" Others, however, will prefer this tentative tone to Correct Grammar's drill-sergeant wording. At any rate, the verse is clear as crystal, so the program wins no points here.

On the phrase "And God saw the light, that it was good...", RightWriter asked "Is this comma needed?" and recommended "replace with *light that*."

Unfortunately, "And God saw the light that it was good" doesn't cut it. Strike two.

Regarding the fragment "And God said: Let there be a firmament," the program wanted to know "Is *firmament* misspelled?" Um, no, it's not...and so much for RightWriter's spelling dictionary. Strike three. (Also, of course, the question comes up four more times, for the four additional places where *firmament* appears; but we won't knock the software for being consistent.)

After asking its timorous "Is this sentence too complex...?" a couple more times (no, and no), RightWriter got down to some solid observations. Like Correct Grammar, it noted "divided the waters which" could be better phrased as "divided the waters that." Also, like both Grammatik and Correct Grammar, it gently suggested to "consider replacing *gathered together* with *gathered* if no loss of essential information occurs." Further, it bettered both programs by additionally suggesting that "gathering together" be replaced with "gathering."

Just when things were looking up, though, RightWriter committed an error in the very same clause. Specifically, regarding "and the gathering together of the waters called He seas: and God saw that it was good," the program asked "Is a comma missing? Replace with: He, seas." That's not even close to being right.

Finally, on each of the last two verses, RightWriter inquired hesitantly "Is this sentence too long?" As I noted in the Correct Grammar section, the sentences are, respectively, 34 and 33 words in length, which I consider well within bounds for fiction writing.

In summary, RightWriter made an awful lot of mistakes, including some really dumb ones. On the positive side, however, it caught all the significant items that its competitors flagged as errors, and even uncovered one that Grammatik and Correct Grammar missed. Overall, I consider Grammatik a significantly better program; but if you like the idea of tinkering with a Grammar Equalizer, or prefer a checker that politely queries instead of ordering you around, RightWriter is worth a look.

Corporate Voice

The three grammar checkers covered in this chapter can all provide some statistics on your document's readability. However, if it's vital that you effectively target a particular audience, you should also consider buying Scandinavian PC Systems' Corporate Voice.

For starters, this unique program lets you modify the Flesch, Flesch-Kincaid, and Gunning's Fog tests to ignore trade words with which your audience is familiar. As a result, it's capable of giving positive readability scores to, say, training manuals that contain long technical words but are otherwise written at a 5th-grade level.

For further analysis, Corporate Voice divides your document's words into four categories: the 450 words that make up 60 percent of most documents; the larger group of 2,450 words that make up 80 percent of most documents (which the program refers to as *mortar*); the aforementioned terms you designate as trade words; and words that are less frequently used. This provides additional criteria for evaluating your work; for example, Corporate Voice's designers say every book they've analyzed from a bestselling author consists of at least 78 percent "mortar" words.

Where the program really shines, though, is as a "style replicator." That is, if you feed it the text of a writer you admire, it will show you in what ways your documents do and don't match that writer's style, using such criteria as the percentage of sentences in each sample that are, in the program's terms, *simple, normal, complicated, wordy,* and *pompous.* In all, the program uses 25 statistical measures and 17 types of graphs to guide you in duplicating the style.

This function is especially useful for a corporation that wants all its documents to carry the same distinctive voice (hence the program's name). For example, with the software used as a measuring tool, a company can require its writers to always match the style of some respected in-house text by 90 percent or better before their documents are even submitted for approval.

On the other hand, if a business doesn't have a history of good writing, it can use Corporate Voice to copy the style of a competitor known for the quality of its prose. The program can also aid a firm entering new markets by helping it to copy the styles of other companies already selling in those markets.

Similarly, if you're a professional writer targeting a new magazine, you can use Corporate Voice to match your style against writers already published there. You can even use it to try and write a bestseller in the style of Raymond Chandler, or Ian Fleming, or Margaret Mitchell...come to think of it, those have all already been done, but you get the idea.

The worst thing about Corporate Voice is its price, which is $249.95, and is seldom discounted. However, by special arrangement with Scandinavian PC Systems, you can get the program for only $125 through the coupon near the back of this book. This is a terrific deal, and if the program sounds at all useful to you, I recommend you go for it. The chances are you'll make your money back on the first business sale or writing contract it helps you to win.

Product Information

Note: Version numbers and prices may have changed by the time you read this.

Que Software
11711 North College Avenue
Carmel, IN 46032-5634
(800) 992-0244; (317) 573-2500
Fax: (317) 593-2655

RightWriter 6.0 for DOS: List Price, $49.95; Street Price, about $29

RightWriter 6.0 for Windows: List Price, $49.95; Street Price, about $29

Scandinavian PC Systems
P.O. Box 3156
Baton Rouge, LA 70821-3156
(800) 487-7727; (504) 338-9580
Fax: (504) 338-9670

Corporate Voice 1.0: List Price, $249.95; generally not discounted; Via coupon near the back of this book, $125

Corporate Voice ProStyles Volume 1 (over 50 writing styles, ranging from Andy Warhol and *Arabian Nights* to Walt Whitman and *Woman's Day*, that can be plugged into Corporate Voice): List Price, $19.95; generally not discounted

WordPerfect Corporation
1555 N. Technology Way
Orem, UT 84057
(800) 321-4566; (801) 225-5000
Fax: (801) 228-5377

Grammatik 5 for DOS: List Price, $99; Street Price, about $55

Grammatik 5 for Windows: List Price, $99; Street Price, about $55

Writing Tools Group
One Harbor Drive
Suite 111
Sausalito, CA 94965
(800) 523-3520; (415) 382-8000
Fax: (415) 883-1629

Correct Grammar 4.0 for DOS: List Price, $44.95; Street Price N/A

Correct Grammar 2.0 for Windows: List Price, $44.95; Street Price N/A

CHAPTER

7

OTHER EDITING TOOLS

No passion in the world is equal to the passion to alter someone else's draft.

—H. G. Wells

The strongest force in the world, people who put words on paper soon learn, is neither love nor sex, but the desire to change another person's copy.

—John Kador

Every book should have a "miscellaneous" section. You're now reading the one in this book.

And it's quite appropriate, actually, because this chapter discusses products that help you deal with a miscellany of data. That is, in one way or another, they all comb through the vast jumbles of text on your hard disk and help you to extract precisely the information you need. The programs covered are Info Select, the FileFind utility in the PC Tools and Norton Utilities product lines, ZyINDEX, and Windows Personal Librarian. With one or more of these tools, you'll be able to pluck order from the chaos.

Info Select

Info Select from Micro Logic is a quirky, wonderful program that lets you enter an infinite number of electronic Post-It notes. If you use it faithfully, you'll be spared searching for scraps of paper that contain critical information, or straining your memory for facts about the important client you have on the phone, or forgetting a loved one's birthday.

The program lets you bring up a window with a keystroke, enter as little or as much text as you want, and then save the window's contents with another keystroke. After that, whenever you need the information, you can bring the window back to your screen by simply calling up a search box and entering a word or phrase that's contained in the window. The only practical limit to the number of windows you can create is the size of your hard disk.

While the basic idea is simple, the execution is slick. Info Select runs as a 7K memory-resident program under DOS that you can invoke with a keystroke, or as a Windows program you can switch to with a mouse click, so you can always access it in seconds. It automatically fits as many text windows as it can on-screen. To see more windows, you can simply press the Down Arrow and Up Arrow keys, which makes your current windows disappear and other windows pop up to take their place. This design is highly intuitive, and also makes for a fun and dynamic display.

The heart of Info Select is its lightning-fast Search command, which lets you retrieve data by entering a word or phrase contained in the window you're seeking. If the search turns up too many matches, you can eliminate irrelevant windows using several special options, or *operators*, named AND, RETURN, DATE, and SIZE. Specifically:

- AND requires that a window contain both of the terms you specify. For example, *cotton AND candy* matches only windows containing both *cotton* and *candy*.

- RETURN excludes windows containing your second term. For example, *cotton RETURN candy* ignores windows containing the phrase *cotton candy* from its list of windows containing *cotton*.

- DATE restricts searching to the time range you specify. For example, *cotton 05/01/93 05/14/93* finds cotton references in windows saved during the first two weeks of May 1993.

- SIZE restricts searching to the amount of text you specify. For example, *cotton < 500* matches cotton references only in windows with fewer than 500 characters.

Alternatively, you can opt to *expand* a search by using the OR operator; for example, *cotton OR candy* turns up windows that contain *cotton*, or *candy*, or both words. And you can even search for words that are conceptually related to your phrase using the NEURAL operator; for example, the grouping *circus children treat fluffy sticky* brings up windows that contain the most number of matches for those five words, and are therefore likely to contain information connected to cotton candy.

Info Select also furnishes some useful miscellaneous features. For example, if you bill by the hour, you can insert a timer into a window with a few keystrokes, allowing Info Select to keep track of the time you're on the phone with a client. And you can create reminder windows—say, about an important business meeting, or a hot date—that pop up on your screen at appropriate times to jog your memory. The Windows version of Info Select even provides links to the Calculator and Calender programs bundled with Windows to further aid you in getting through billing and scheduling chores.

The many uses for Info Select include electronic Rolodex functions (store each business card in a separate window!), to-do lists, memo and letter writing (the program provides ready-made forms for such common documents as business letters and purchase orders), and reference lists (the package includes sample windows containing area codes, metric conversions, PC graphic symbols, and so on). You can also use the program's windows as loosely structured databases, because Info Select can sort information, alphabetically or numerically, based on any column of data you specify. Indeed, it can even generate form letters and envelope addresses via a Mail Merge option.

Blot out, correct, insert, refine, enlarge, diminish, interline.

—Jonathan Swift

Because it's designed to be so open-ended, Info Select can readily serve diverse professional needs. For example, if you're a salesperson, you'll find it's great for jotting down leads and other random bits of information during phone calls; and for instantly bringing up handy facts on a client such as the size of her last order, or the names of his children. If you're a lawyer, you can use it on a laptop to store briefs, legal precedents, case notes, and other pertinent trial data you'll want to access instantly. And if you're a novelist or screenwriter, you'll appreciate being able to devote a window to each scene and then shuffle the windows around until you find the order that works best.

Info Select also offers a number of general purpose technical features. For example, it allows you to view the first line of each window, providing an overview of what's available; copy or move data among windows; duplicate a window, or quickly split its contents into multiple windows; import text from and export text to ASCII files used in conjunction with your word processor; and organize your windows into groups, called *stacks*, in case you prefer to keep one type of data separate from another.

Info Select isn't for every taste. If you want a structured foundation for your information, you'll be happier with a PIM (Personal Information Manager) such as Lotus Organizer, or a database program such as Borland's Paradox. However, if you like the idea of typing anything that comes to mind and saving it in a window, and having windows appear and vanish at a dizzying pace, give Info Select a try. It's available for both DOS and Windows (the Windows version being significantly prettier and easier to use), and has a list price of $149. However, you can buy the package using the Micro Logic coupon near the back of this book for $79.95.

FileFind

Info Select is fine at locating data in its own windows, but it's useless when you need to find information created by other programs. To perform a basic search through *all* your files, you may therefore want to turn to a simple utility such as the FileFind program in Central Point's PC Tools, or the identically named and functionally similar FileFind component of Symantec's Norton Utilities product line.

FileFind performs a couple of basic tasks. First, if you remember at least the beginning portion of your file's name but don't recall which of your hundreds of directories it resides in, FileFind can scour your entire hard disk to uncover the file's location—and typically in under a minute. For example, if you're seeking a file involving taxes, the search pattern TAX*.* (with the asterisks representing any combination of characters) will turn up files like TAX93, TAXES.WKS, TAXINFO, and TAXCHEAT, along with their directory locations. After the operation, FileFind allows you to view the contents of each matched file until you hit upon the one you're seeking.

Alternatively, FileFind can conduct a search based on the *contents* of your files. To use this feature, you simply enter a word or phrase that's likely to be in the file you want...and *not* likely to be in many other files. This type of search can take a lot longer, because it requires sifting through millions of characters, as opposed to just checking through a few thousand filenames. (Of course, if you know the directory your file is in, you can speed things up enormously by restricting the search to that directory.) Again, when the search is completed, you can view the contents of each file within FileFind, which will show you the spot in the file where the match occurred.

FileFind provides an effective way to conduct simple searches. It's also virtually free, since it's bundled in with PC Tools, The Norton Utilities,

The Norton Desktop for DOS, and The Norton Desktop for Windows—and you should own *at least* one of these packages, if only for their critical data protection and recovery utilities. For more information about these products, see Chapter 20, *Essential General-Purpose Tools*.

ZyINDEX

If you need to conduct more complex searches on your data, a good choice is ZyLAB's ZyINDEX.

Unlike the FileFind utility, this program first needs to "index" the contents of your hard disk—that is, to identify what's there and then create a system of pointers to your files for each word or phrase. The completed index can occupy about a third to half as much space as your actual data, and the indexing can take several hours (in fact, it's best to set the operation to run at night while you're away from your PC). Once the process is completed, though, ZyINDEX can search through the contents of your word processing and dBASE-compatible database files in a flash, and then inform you of which ones hold the information you need.

I have performed the necessary butchery. Here is the bleeding corpse.

—Henry James, after honoring an editorial request to cut three lines from a 5,000-word article

ZyINDEX offers a number of sophisticated search options. As in Info Select, its operators include AND, OR, NOT (called RETURN in Info Select), QUORUM (called NEURAL in Info Select), and DATE. In addition, ZyINDEX supplies a WITHIN operator, which finds a phrase within n words of another phrase (with n being any number from 1 to 16,382). For example, *operators W/15 neural* matches the second sentence in this paragraph, because "operators" and "NEURAL" are within 15 words of each other; but *operators W/5 neural* doesn't match the sentence because of the search request's narrower focus.

To exercise even more control, you can use a RANGE operator, which finds a phrase within a text area specified by the two numbers *n,n* (*n* again being any number from 1 to 16,382). The first number defines how many words to search in front of the initial phrase, and the second defines how many words to search past it. For instance, both *control /-5,15/ exercise* and *control /-5,15/ phrase* match the first sentence in this paragraph, while *control /-15,5/ phrase* does not.

If that's not enough, you can also use a TO operator, which locates a phrase that falls between two other phrases—for example, it can find every occurrence of *William Blake* that appears after *William Shakespeare* but before *William Faulkner* in the same file.

You can combine these ZyINDEX operators and your terms in any order, constructing complex search requests. And using parentheses, you can precisely control how your command is executed.

If you aren't sure of the spelling of your term, or you want to match several words that are similar to it, another handy option is using the question mark (?) to represent any single character, and the asterisk (*) to represent any group of characters. (These wildcards can significantly slow the search process, though, since they work against the software's indexing scheme.)

Everyone needs an editor.

—Tim Foote

Some editors are failed writers, but so are most writers.

—T. S. Eliot

You can even apply a built-in electronic thesaurus to words in your search command, to ensure that you don't miss an important file because you neglected to include an appropriate synonym. And you can create a virtually unlimited number of *concepts*, which are groups of terms (say, *dark, athletic, brooding, rich, obsessed, caped*) that you've assigned to shorthand words (say, *Batman*) and that you can use in all your subsequent searches.

If you only occasionally search through your files for data, ZyINDEX is overkill. However, if you regularly need to pluck information from the thousands of files on your hard disk—or the hundreds of thousands of files on a network server—you'll find ZyINDEX's speed and precision a godsend. ZyINDEX is available for both DOS and Windows at a list price of $395. However, using the ZyLAB coupon near the back of this book, you can purchase the package for $199, or nearly 50 percent off.

Windows Personal Librarian

Windows Personal Librarian from Personal Library Software does everything ZyINDEX does...but more so.

Like ZyINDEX, Windows Personal Librarian creates an index based on the text files you specify, which can occupy about 50 percent as much space as the data itself. However, in addition to text, WPL can index graphics, sound, animation, and hypertext (programmed links between text sections).

It can also deal comfortably with enormous amounts of data—specifically, up to 4 gigabytes (that is, 4,000MB) containing up to 16 million files. Of course, if you have that many files, you'll probably want to organize them into separate groups for indexing purposes; but that's no problem, either, because the program can search through multiple indexes simultaneously.

WPL provides virtually all the search options that ZyINDEX does, including the AND, OR, and NOT operators, word proximity operators, and parentheses for specifying the execution order of a complex combination of operators. In fact, about the only ZyINDEX feature it doesn't include is a built-in thesaurus (but it provides a Thesaurus button, and the option of installing your own synonym finder software).

In addition, WPL allows you to type your requests as standard sentences —for example, "Who were the leaders of the surrealist movement in France?" If you type in a misspelled word, it will conduct a "fuzzy" search that brings up a list of similar words you can select from. And if you want to peruse an alphabetical list of all the words in your textbase, or see how many times a particular word appears, the program can readily accommodate you.

Even nicer, the software operates with dizzying speed. For example, complex multi-word searches on a 3MB textbase typically execute in less than a second, while similar searches on a 500MB textbase execute in three to six seconds.

What makes WPL most exciting, however, is its ability to intuit connections between terms and rank their relative importance on the fly.

For starters, if you enter a word in the Search box and select an Expand command, WPL will supply all the terms in your textbase that are likely to be related to your word (and, optionally, all the files the terms appear in). It accomplishes this impressive feat using a sophisticated computer algorithm that notes all the documents your word appears in, the number of times other words appear near your word in those documents, and the relative rarity of those other words in your textbase.

Would you convey my compliments to the purist who reads your proofs and tell him or her that I write in a sort of broken-down patois which is something like the way a Swiss waiter talks, and that when I split an infinitive, God dammit, I split it so it will stay split?
—Raymond Chandler

In conversation you can use timing, a look, inflection, pauses. But on the page all you have is commas, dashes, the amount of syllables in a word. When I write I read everything out loud to get the right rhythm.
—Fran Lebowitz

A man who writes well writes not as others write, but as he himself writes; it is often in speaking badly that he speaks well.
—Baron De Montesquieu

To demonstrate this amazing feature, I loaded the sample textbase packaged with the product, which is a collection of over 1,000 newspaper articles from 1991; typed *BCCI* in the Search box; and selected Expand. In about a second, the program searched through the 3MB of data and displayed a list of 127 words it decided, based on their frequent proximity to *BCCI* and their uniqueness in the textbase, were in some way related to the term. The list included some clunkers, such as *announced, expected, important,* and *accused.* However, it also furnished a surprising number of useful terms, including *scandal, laundering, auditors, creditors, liquidators, London, Luxembourg, Waterhouse, Altman, Katzenbach, indictments,* and *justice.* It's important to understand that this list did not result from any previous work in which the terms were linked together—it was generated spontaneously from the data in the textbase. As a result, each time we added BCCI articles to the textbase, we'd get a different—and probably superior—list of words.

The Expand feature is an enormously powerful tool; for example, when you're working with a large enough textbase, it can actually be used to construct reference products such as thesauruses. However, its main function is to lead you to relevant terms to include in your Search command.

Further, WPL makes the process especially easy. To add any displayed term to your Search box, you simply need to click on the word (which both turns it red and runs a line through it) and click on the Include button. The program appends a space, and then the term, to whatever is already in the Search box. When you execute the search, each space is considered to be an OR operator. As a result, each added term expands the search to include more documents.

Vigorous writing is concise. A sentence should contain no unnecessary words, a paragraph no unnecessary sentences, for the same reason that a drawing should have no unnecessary lines and a machine no unnecessary parts. This requires not that the writer make all his sentences short, or that he avoid all detail and treat his subjects only in outline, but that every word tell.

—William Strunk, Jr.

Of course, if you're a text-retrieval pro, you may balk at this point, because a good search technique often involves *narrowing* your focus, not expanding it to the point where you have too many documents to deal with. However, this approach has a serious downside—namely, when you eliminate too many search words, you risk passing over the document you most need. Perhaps WPL's *best* feature, then, is that it solves this thorny problem: It lets you use as expansive a search as you want, and then *ranks* the documents it retrieves in order of importance! The program is able to do this using algorithms similar to the ones involved in the Expand command; namely, it notes all the words in your search command, and then assigns priority to those documents that contain the greatest number of search words in closest proximity to one another and with the greatest degree of rarity in the textbase.

WPL numbers each matched document in ascending order (that is, 1, 2, 3,..., with 1 being the most important). If you want a clearer idea of the priorities WPL assigned, though, you can click on an icon to display a color chart that graphs the ranking assigned to all the matched documents! This ranking system, which can be astonishingly effective, puts WPL miles above other text retrieval programs.

WPL even lets you glimpse the process it goes through via a Search Detail box that lists the number of matches it found for each search word. These include not only the exact word, but derivations based on the word's root; for example, if you tell the program to search for *indictment*, it automatically looks for *indict* and *indictments*, as well. Of course, you have the option of switching this feature off and seeking exact matches only; but in most cases, you'll find this "root" feature to be a great aid to your research.

All this power doesn't come without a price...specifically, a list price of $995, which is seldom discounted. While this places WPL outside the budget of most individuals, it's quite reasonable for companies that regularly deal with large chunks of information, such as law firms and corporate libraries. WPL counts among its customers the Department of Justice, the Department of Agriculture, the Army, the Air Force, Unisys, Apple computer (which uses it for answering technical support calls), a number of CD-ROM publishers (WPL is perfect for browsing through the several hundred megabytes of data CD-ROMs can hold), *The Economist*, *The Financial Times*, *The Congressional Quarterly*, and—naturally—the Library of Congress.

Personal Librarian is also available for DOS, but that version isn't as easy to use, and it lacks some important features such as "fuzzy" searches and graphics support. Therefore, if you have Windows on your system, buy the Windows version. In addition, if you're in a multi-platform corporate environment, you may want to explore the Personal Librarian editions for the Macintosh, UNIX, and VMS, all of which are compatible with one another.

Of course, as your data files continue to expand and multiply, you may find even the most powerful software can't prevent areas of your hard disk from becoming whirlpools of anarchy. If you ever feel overwhelmed by it all, however, be comforted by the words of Carl Jung: "In all chaos there is a cosmos, in all disorder a secret order."

Product Information

Note: Version numbers and prices may have changed by the time you read this.

Borland International
1800 Green Hills Road
P.O. Box 660001
Scotts Valley, CA 95066-0001
(800) 331-0877; (408) 438-8400
Fax: (408) 439-9262

Paradox 4.5 for DOS: List Price, $795; Street Price, $529

Paradox 1.0 for Windows: List Price, $795; Street Price, $139.95 direct from Borland during sales periods, otherwise $529

Central Point Software
15220 N.W. Greenbrier Parkway
Suite 200
Beaverton, OR 97006
(800) 445-4208; (503) 690-8090
Fax: (503) 690-8083

PC Tools 8.0 for DOS: List Price, $179; Street Price, about $109

Lotus Development Corporation
55 Cambridge Parkway
Cambridge, MA 02142
(800) 343-5414; (617) 577-8500
Fax: (617) 253-9150

Lotus Organizer 1.0 (for Windows): List Price, $149; Street Price, about $99

Micro Logic
P.O. Box 70
Dept. 510
Hackensack, NJ 07602
(800) 342-5930; (201) 342-6518
Fax: (201) 342-0370

Info Select 2.0 for DOS: List Price, $149; via coupon near the back of this book, $79.95

Info Select 1.0 for Windows: List Price, $149; via coupon near the back of this book, $79.95

Personal Library Software
2400 Research Blvd., #350
Rockville, MD 20850
(301) 990-1155
Fax: (301) 963-9738

Windows Personal Librarian 3.0: List Price, $995; generally not discounted

Personal Librarian 2.3: List Price, $995; generally not discounted

Symantec Corporation
10201 Torre Avenue
Cupertino, CA 95014-2132
(800) 441-7234; (408) 252-3570
Fax: (800) 554-4403

The Norton Utilities 7.0: List Price, $179; Street Price, about $115

The Norton Desktop 1.0 for DOS: List Price, $179; Street Price, about $115

The Norton Desktop 2.2 for Windows: List Price, $179; Street Price, about $115

ZyLAB
100 Lexington Drive
Buffalo Grove, IL 60089
(800) 544-6339; (708) 459-8000
Fax: (708) 459-8054

ZyINDEX 4.0 for DOS: List Price, $395; via coupon near the back of this book, $199

ZyINDEX 5.1 for Windows: List Price, $395; via coupon near the back of this book, $199

PART IV

GETTING INFORMATION

A world of facts lies outside and beyond the world of words.
—Thomas H. Huxley

Information is where you find it.
—Librarian's motto

CHAPTER
8

DISK-BASED REFERENCES

A beautiful theory, killed by a nasty, ugly, little fact.

—Thomas H. Huxley

There's more to writing than style and craft; you also (sigh) need content. This ranges from the foundation knowledge you require to get started, to niggling little facts that simply flesh out your work but nonetheless have to be accurate.

The importance of accuracy is clear-cut in a company report, a magazine article, or any other prose that seeks to convey information. But even if you're writing a fiction piece, you should make sure that the street in L.A. where your hero hangs out really exists, that you have the correct caliber for his gun, that his favorite Raymond Chandler quote was really said by Chandler, and so on. Every time you get a detail wrong, you risk losing the trust of a reader who knows better.

For in-depth information on a subject, there's still nothing that beats conducting interviews and reading a few good books. However, for checking the occasional fact, you may find disk-based references more convenient.

Ordinarily, you look something up by leaving your PC, scrounging around for the appropriate book, scanning an index, and flipping through pages. This takes time, and can break the flow of your work. In contrast, an electronic reference is always available on your hard disk; can be called up with a keystroke (if you're running it memory resident) or in a separate window (if you're running Windows); and displays the data you need in seconds. In most cases, the program even lets you copy the information you find back into your document, sparing you the trouble of typing it in.

On the other hand, electronic references are a lot more expensive than their print equivalents. Also, they take up space on your hard disk whether you're using them or not and, if they're run memory resident, occupy a slice of your PC's limited memory. You therefore have to balance these financial and hardware costs against the time and effort an electronic reference can save you.

One determining factor is whether the program lets you work with information in ways that a book doesn't. For example, with an electronic encyclopedia you can not only look up topic headings, but search through the full text of the explanatory articles, enabling you to locate *all* the places where the subject you're interested in is mentioned. Along the same lines, with an electronic atlas you can get information on an area of a map by just clicking on that area with your mouse. Such added functionality is sometimes the best reason to use a disk-based reference.

Another consideration is, quite simply, how often you think you'll need it. If you expect to access an electronic reference several times a week, buy it; it'll pay for itself by speeding the flow of your work. Otherwise, you might want to just move your bookshelf closer to your PC.

A third question is *where* you'll be using the program. For example, if you're usually on the road with your laptop, disk-based references may rescue you from having to carry around a number of large, heavy books.

Sit down before fact as a little child, be prepared to give up every preconceived notion, follow humbly wherever and whatever abysses nature leads, or you will learn nothing.

—Thomas H. Huxley

You should also keep in mind that there are other types of electronic references available. For example, if your main interest is plumbing the depths of a large and complex reference work, your best bet is to get a version of that work on CD-ROM (see Chapter 9, *CD-ROM References*); while if you need an occasional esoteric fact, or require extremely timely information, you should turn to an online service (see Chapter 10, *Online References*). The main thing to remember is that research isn't an either/or proposition; you should grab information from any source that provides it efficiently and affordably.

This chapter covers two categories of disk-based software: general reference works (except for dictionaries, which are discussed in Chapter 5, *Electronic Dictionaries and Thesauruses*); and writing-related reference works. What follows isn't comprehensive, but it hits the highlights and tries to give you a taste of what's available.

All solid facts were originally mist.

——Henry S. Haskins

Nothing is so fallacious as facts, except figures.

——Sydney Smith

Get your facts first, and then you can distort them as much as you please.

——Mark Twain

General Reference Works

A search for fundamental references has to start with Microlytics' The Random House Encyclopedia, Electronic Edition, which is available in both DOS and Windows versions. This program commandeers about 9MB of your hard disk, but in return offers 20,000 entries ranging from abacus ("a mathematical tool made up of beads strung on wire in units of 10; the Chinese abacus dates from the 12th century") to zygote ("cell formed by fusion of male and female gametes").

The encyclopedia initially displays 11 topics: Geography; History; Philosophy, Religion and Mythology; Social Science; The Arts; Science; Sports and Leisure; Law; Government; and Timechart, which lets you explore world events organized chronologically. If you select one of these categories, you're presented with sub-categories; for example, choosing The Arts yields Literature; Visual Arts; Music and Instruments; Sculpture, Textiles, Ceramics, and Jewelry; Art History; Photography; Performing Arts; Architecture; and Publishing and Journalism. Selecting one of these headings leads to the encyclopedia's entries; for example, choosing Publishing and Journalism opens a window holding 83 related topics, including Alexandrian Library, (Ted) Edward James Koppel, Library of Congress Classification System, Pulitzer Prizes, and John Peter Zenger. Choosing one of these topics displays a brief pertinent article in a text window, which you can read, copy to a text file, and/or print.

Stepping through the category hierarchy isn't the only way to find a topic; you can alternatively type a word, phrase, or year to jump directly to the topic you want. You can even conduct a search through the articles themselves, which enables you to locate every mention of a subject in the entire encyclopedia.

Facts, when combined with ideas, constitute the greatest force in the world.

—Carl W. Acherman

You can buy The Random House Encyclopedia for DOS as a solo product, but it's actually one of a trio of reference works from Microlytics running under a program called INFODESK. The other two products are Inside Information (which is covered in Chapter 5, *Electronic Dictionaries and Thesauruses*); and The Elements of Style, Electronic Edition (which is covered in the next section). When INFODESK is run memory resident, it takes up a mere 6K; and when you invoke it with a keystroke, it allows you to use *any* of the three Microlytics reference works you have installed on your hard disk. This elegant system therefore gives you instant access to a great deal of information with a minimum of memory overhead. The DOS and Windows versions of The Random House Encyclopedia each have a street price of about $55.

An even more integrated solution is provided by The Writer's Toolkit from Systems Compatibility Corp. This jam-packed package includes *The Concise Columbia Dictionary of Quotations*, containing 6,000 quotations searchable by author or topic; Houghton Mifflin's *Dictionary of Common Knowledge*, providing thousands of facts searchable by topic, person, place, or date; Houghton Mifflin's *The Written Word III* reference book on grammar and style; and a utility that translates abbreviations (such as NY, CIA, and ASPCA) into their full word equivalents, and vice versa. As noted in Chapter 5, this program also includes versions of *The American Heritage Dictionary*, *Roget's II* thesaurus, and Houghton Mifflin's CorrecText grammar checking program; but at its low street price of about $35, it can be worth picking up The Writer's Toolkit for its reference tools alone. The program is available in both DOS and Windows versions.

A reading machine,
always wound up and going,
he mastered whatever
was not worth the knowing.

—James Russell Lowell

One thing The Writer's Toolkit *doesn't* have is maps. For those, the first programs to consider are The Software Toolworks World Atlas and The Software Toolworks U.S. Atlas. Both of these packages start you off with an overview (of the world and the United States, respectively), and let you progressively hone in on the area you want by mouse-clicking on increasingly detailed maps.

We don't know a millionth of one percent about anything.
—Thomas Alva Edison

For example, if you open the World Atlas and click on Europe, you're quickly switched to a 256-color map of Europe with the names of its countries. If you then click on, say, France, the European map is replaced by one of France. The most important cities are highlighted in red; if you click on one, you can obtain a wealth of data about it, including total area, climate, population, birth and death rates, education, number of newspapers, number of dentists, number of farm animals (subdivided by chickens, goats, pigs, and so on), crime statistics, travel information, tourist attractions—there are 12 single-spaced pages of information on Paris alone. With a few more clicks, you can display the current time in that city; with another couple of clicks, you can learn the distance between the city and another major city; and with another click, even play a few bars of the country's national anthem! You can also revise map data, add notes to maps, and place electronic "pins" into areas of importance to you. And you can print out any map, or save it as a graphic to be imported later into your word processor or desktop publishing program.

The U.S. Atlas works similarly, except that it gives you data on states, cities, and major counties. The atlases are available for both DOS and Windows, and range in street price from about $29 to $48. The only significant knock against these smartly produced programs is that while they tell you a great deal about famous cities, they don't provide data on a lot of others you might be interested in. Even so, they contain so much statistical information that they take up from 4MB (for the U.S. Atlas for DOS package) to 8MB (for the World Atlas for Windows package). If you'd rather keep your disk space open for other programs, you can buy this software on CD-ROM; for more information, see Chapter 9, *CD-ROM References*.

The most merciful thing in the world... is the inability of the human mind to correlate all its contents.

—H. P. Lovecraft

Then again, if you're seeking something more utilitarian, consider the DOS or Windows version of the Automap Road Atlas. This program performs one simple function: after you tell it where you are and what city or town in the U.S. you want to drive to, it uses its database on over 350,000 miles of highways and roads to tell you how to get there! Specifically, it generates a list of routes with excellent detailed directions, estimates of the time required and distance traveled for each leg of the trip, and the overall time and distance of the trip. Automap can provide you with the fastest route, the shortest route, or (if you want to meander a bit) alternate routes. It can also overlay the locations of national parks and landmarks on its maps, in case you're interested in sightseeing. (You can even purchase an add-on database that covers ski resorts!) If you're often on the move, Automap is a great program to keep on your laptop. In addition, if you're a fiction writer, this software will help you provide your readers with realistic travel information on places you've never visited. Automap requires 4MB of disk space and has a street price of about $55. An add-on database that covers European cities is also available, for about $29.

Yet another useful travel program is the Zagat-Axxis CityGuide from Axxis Software. This product won't help you get to a city, but it'll give you a lot of good advice on how to enjoy yourself once you get there. It provides detailed information on a city's landmarks, restaurants, and hotels (even to the point of noting whether a hotel's rooms have fireplaces). It also functions as a sort of walker's Automap, by bringing up maps of addresses you supply and giving you detailed directions for the most efficient route within the city for getting to them. Zagat-Axxis CityGuide is actually a *series* of packages, with each one dedicated to a particular major city such as New York, Los Angeles, Chicago, or Washington, D.C. Like Automap, CityGuide is great for travelers, and for authors who set their stories in cities they aren't familiar with. The program runs only under Windows, and carries a list price of $99 for each city edition.

After conquering the highways and streets, you can choose to turn inward via a Software Marketing Corp. guide to human anatomy. Aptly named Bodyworks, the program is crammed with text and graphics explaining how your various parts operate. This reference is useful both for fiction and nonfiction writing—and, as a bonus, can help keep you healthy. The same publisher also sells Chemistry Works, which provides clear explanations and 3-D color illustrations of atomic structures, elemental properties, and all the other stuff that intimidated you in school; and Orbits, which provides impressive 3-D color animated sequences demonstrating how planets orbit the sun, moon-planet gravitational effects, and other facets of our solar system. Each package has a street price of about $50.

If your interest lies not with flickering stars but rather with a flickering screen, you may instead opt for Roger Ebert's Deluxe Computerized Movie Home Companion. This package is a disk-based version of famed film critic Ebert's book guide to over 1,000 popular films. Its main value is its ability to quickly generate lists of films based on searches you conduct on the movie descriptions. If you have a CD-ROM drive, however, a vastly superior reference work is Microsoft's Cinemania, which is based on Leonard Maltin's *Movie and Video Guide 1993*. For more information on Cinemania, as well as on a CD-ROM version of the Ebert program, see Chapter 9.

Finally, if literature is your love, can you pass up all of Shakespeare's plays on disk? The most carefully edited PC version is probably William Shakespeare: The Complete Works, Electronic Edition from Oxford University Press. In addition to its accuracy, and its plain ASCII text format, this edition is a good choice because it's in a line-numbered form that makes it readily searchable by Micro-OCP, a text analysis program also published by Oxford University Press (see Chapter 19, *Tools for Students and Academics*). The Shakespeare package is $150, and requires 7MB of hard disk space; the Micro-OCP program is $295.

If you're not planning to perform scholarly studies on Shakespeare, though, a much more cost-effective alternative is to buy World Library's Library of the Future CD-ROM, which gives you Shakespeare, the Bible, and hundreds of other classic works packed together on a single disc for only $299. For more information on the incredible Library of the Future, see Chapter 9.

Writing-Related Reference Works

A number of disk-based reference packages center on providing advice to writers about grammar, punctuation, and style. Unlike the grammar checkers covered in Chapter 6, which read through your prose and point out errors, these reference packages simply allow you to look up directives on the proper way to construct a sentence, business letter, report, or what have you. The most popular ones are based on best-selling books, can be run memory resident under DOS for quick access, and allow you to conduct searches for phrases throughout the entire text.

The classiest such program is Microlytics' Elements of Style, Electronic Edition. As the name indicates, this is a PC version of the classic, concise guide to writing by William Strunk and E. B. White. As mentioned previously, it's also part of the INFODESK series and, at a street price of about $25, makes a nice supplement to The Random House Encyclopedia and Inside Information products. If you're a fan of *The Elements of Style*, and think you'd refer to its electronic version frequently—or simply believe you'd feel comforted by its ever-ready presence in your computer's memory —no more need be said.

If you prefer lots of data in a writing reference, though, consider Parsons Technology's Resident Expert for Effective Writing. This program contains five government (that is, public domain) handbooks on clear, effective communication. At first this may seem like an oxymoron, but the advice provided is generally good; in fact, some of the wording indicates that the handbook writers studied *The Elements of Style* very closely before creating their own works. What makes Resident Expert stand out, though, is that it additionally offers information on geography (area codes and time zones for major cities; state, territory, and province capitals; etc.), history (the Declaration of Independence, the Constitution, U.S. Presidents, etc.), language (sample business letters, the Greek alphabet, quotations, etc.), math (formulas for discrete compounding, logarithm identities, etc.), science (physical constants, table of the elements, unit conversion, etc.), and computers (ASCII tables, PC video modes, etc.). On top of that, it kicks in a list of 20,000 often-used words, correctly spelled and syllabified. This smorgasbord of data can be loaded memory resident, and will take up only 1K of main memory *if* you have expanded memory; otherwise, though, it requires a whopping 65K. Resident Expert's list price is $29.

Going to the other extreme, Grammar Quick from THC Press offers a short, simple guide to basic grammatical rules. Written unpretentiously and loaded with examples, this product takes up about 6K when running resident, and has a "what the heck" price of $35. (By the way, if you subscribe to *Writer's Digest* magazine, this is the program it has been advertising.)

A logical supplement to Grammar Quick is the Writing Tools Group's Correct Writing, which tells you almost nothing about grammar, but provides a cornucopia of punctuation and style advice. Specifically, it covers abbreviation, capitalization, punctuation, and spelling (via an extensive list of the most commonly misspelled words); creating stylistically correct tables of contents, footnotes, bibliographies, and indexes; and miscellaneous topics such as italics, numerals, math, and symbols. The DOS version takes up only 215K of your hard disk, making it handy for laptop use, while the Windows version requires about 900K. Correct Writing's list price is $29.

Another product in the Correct line is Correct Letters, which supplies you with more than 250 standard business letters created by the respected American Management Association. The letters are divided into categories such as marketing and PR; customer service; credit and collection; personnel; confirmation; replies; permissions; and personal/social. Every letter is in a plain text format you can load into your word processor and quickly customize for your business, thus saving hours spent reinventing the wheel. In addition, the package includes a guide to effective letter writing. Both its DOS and Windows versions have a list price of $29.

A third Correct package is Correct Quotes, which supplies over 5,000 quotes organized into 600 topics. You can locate a quote either by category or by a word search. For example, under the topic Humor, I found such gems as "Everything is funny as long as it is happening to somebody else (Will Rogers)," and "The satirist shoots to kill, while the humorist brings his prey back alive and eventually releases him again for another chance (Peter De Vries)." Being a *Citizen Kane* fan, I next decided to do a word search on "Welles," and turned up "Now we sit through Shakespeare in order to recognize the quotations (Orson Welles)." Such pithy lines can be used to add zest to almost any kind of writing, from fiction to articles to business speeches. (Indeed, under some strange circumstance, they might even be used to liven up a computer book.) The DOS version of Correct Quotes requires about 500K of hard disk space, and the Windows version a little over 1MB; each package carries a list price of $29. By the way, if you want even more quotes, keep in mind that one of the components of The Writer's Toolkit (covered in the previous section) is *The Concise Columbia Dictionary of Quotations*, with 6,000 quotations searchable by author or topic.

It may be true, as Thomas Edison stated, that "We don't know one millionth of one percent about anything." Still, with the help of reference works like the ones covered in this chapter, maybe we'll squeak by.

Product Information

Note: Version numbers and prices may have changed by the time you read this.

Automap, Inc.
1309 114 Avenue SE
Suite 110
Bellevue, WA 98004-6999
(800) 440-6277; (206) 455-3552
Fax: (206) 455-3667

Automap Road Atlas 3.0 for DOS: List Price, $99.95; Street Price, about $55

Automap Road Atlas 3.0 for Windows: List Price, $99.95; Street Price, about $55

Automap Destination Europe (add-on to Automap that provides data on European cities): List Price, $49.95; Street Price, about $29

Automap Destination Ski (add-on to Automap that provides data on ski resorts): List Price, $29.95; Street Price N/A

Axxis Software
644 Haverford Road
Haverford, PA 19041
(800) 394-3549; (215) 896-0576
Fax: (215) 896-0584

Zagat-Axxis CityGuide 1.0 for Windows (separate edition for each city): List Price, $99 per city edition, $249 for three city editions; Street Price N/A

Infobusiness, Inc.
887 South Orem
Orem, Utah 84058-5009
(800) 657-5300; (801) 221-1100
Fax: (801) 225-0817

Roger Ebert's Deluxe Computerized Movie Home Companion 1.0: List Price, $59.95; Street Price N/A

Microlytics, Inc.
2 Tobey Village Office Park
Pittsford, NY 14534
(800) 828-6293; (716) 248-9150
Fax: (716) 248-3868

The Elements of Style, Electronic Edition 1.0: List Price, $29.95; Street Price, about $25 (direct from Microlytics during discount periods)

The Random House Encyclopedia, Electronic Edition 1.0 for DOS: List Price, $69.95; Street Price, about $55 (direct from Microlytics during discount periods)

The Random House Encyclopedia, Electronic Edition 1.0 for Windows: List Price, $69.95; Street Price, about $55 (direct from Microlytics during discount periods.)

Oxford University Press
200 Madison Avenue
New York, NY 10016
(800) 334-4249, ext. 7370; (212) 679-7300, ext. 7370
Fax: (212) 725-2972

William Shakespeare: The Complete Works, Electronic Edition 1.0: List Price, $150; generally not discounted

Micro-OCP 1.0: List Price, $295; generally not discounted

Parsons Technology, Inc.
1 Parsons Drive
Hiawatha, Iowa 52233
(800) 223-6925; (319) 395-9626
Fax: (319) 393-1002

Resident Expert for Effective Writing 2.3: List Price, $59; Street Price, about $29

Software Marketing Corporation
9830 S. 51st Street
Building A-131
Phoenix, AZ 85044
(800) 545-6626; (602) 893-2400
Fax: (602) 893-2042

Bodyworks 3.0 for DOS and Windows: List Price, $69.95; Street Price, about $50

Chemistry Works 2.0 for DOS and Windows: List Price, $69.95; Street Price, about $50

Orbits 2.0: List Price, $59.95; Street Price, about $50

The Software Toolworks, Inc.
60 Leveroni Court
Novato, CA 94949
(800) 234-3088; (415) 883-3000
Fax: (415) 415-883-0293

The Software Toolworks World Atlas 4.0 for DOS: List Price, $59.95; Street Price, about $40.

The Software Toolworks World Atlas 4.0 for Windows: List Price, $79.95; Street Price, about $48

The Software Toolworks U.S. Atlas 4.0 for DOS: List Price, $49.95; Street Price, about $29

The Software Toolworks U.S. Atlas 4.0 for Windows: List Price, $59.95; Street Price, about $35

Systems Compatibility Corporation
401 North Wabash
Suite 600
Chicago, IL 60611
(800) 333-1395; (312) 329-0700
Fax: (312) 670-0820

The Writer's Toolkit 2.0 for DOS: List Price, $59.95; Street Price, about $35

The Writer's Toolkit 2.0 for Windows: List Price, $59.95; Street Price, about $35

THC Press
P.O. Box 536
Camarillo, CA 93011
(805) 485-5575
Fax: N/A

Grammar Quick 1.0: List Price, $35; generally not discounted

Writing Tools Group
One Harbor Drive
Suite 111
Sausalito, CA 94965
(800) 523-3520; (415) 382-8000
Fax: (415) 883-1629

Correct Letters 1.0 for DOS: List Price, $29; Street Price N/A

Correct Letters 1.0 for Windows: List Price, $29; Street Price N/A

Correct Quotes 1.0 for DOS: List Price, $29; Street Price N/A

Correct Quotes 1.0 for Windows: List Price, $29; Street Price N/A

Correct Writing 1.0 for DOS: List Price, $29; Street Price N/A

Correct Writing 1.0 for Windows: List Price, $29; Street Price N/A

CHAPTER

9

CD-ROM REFERENCES

Knowledge is of two kinds. We know a subject ourselves, or we know where we can find information upon it.

           —Samuel Johnson

Storing vast amounts of data on a shiny, hand-sized disc used to be the stuff of science fiction novels. Thanks to the pioneering work of the Philips Company and Sony Corporation in the late 1970s and early 1980s, however, that wild notion is now reality. A single 4.72-inch Compact Disc Read-Only Memory, or *CD-ROM*, can hold up to 630MB of information. That's the equivalent of 275,000 pages of text, or 1,800 double-density floppy disks, or thousands of images, or 74 minutes of music.

The last example is especially appropriate, because a CD-ROM looks and functions very much like a music CD. In both cases, data is broken down into complex patterns of zeros and ones, which are represented by the presence or absence of pits on the disc's surface. When you play the disc, a low-power laser beam focuses on its surface to pick up its microscopically coded information, which is then translated into digital data that your stereo or PC system can understand. CDs and CD-ROMs are actually so similar that most CD-ROM drives, when used with the appropriate software, are able to play your music CDs.

Where the two media part company is in the type of data they store, and their degree of accuracy. CDs deliver audio exclusively, and so don't require stringent error checking, because your ear is unlikely to detect minuscule glitches. CD-ROMs, on the other hand, can contain computer programs, text, graphics, animation, and video in addition to audio. Indeed, this mixed-media aspect of a CD-ROM is one of its great charms, and is used to great effect by some of the products covered in this chapter (such as Microsoft's Encarta encyclopedia and Multimedia Beethoven packages). However, because even tiny misreading of a disc's surface can ruin an image or crash a program, CD-ROMs need more rigorous error-handling standards, and so their drives employ a more sophisticated technology. As a result of their special manufacturing requirements, and the fact that they don't yet enjoy economies of scale (to date, the number sold to consumers is a relatively small 1.5 million), CD-ROM drives are more expensive than CD players.

For example, two of the best drives are NEC Technologies' Multispin 74, which attaches outside your PC and sells for about $550; and NEC's Multispin 84, which installs inside your PC like a floppy drive, and sells for about $450. (And these prices don't even include the "SCSI interface" kit you'll typically require to connect either device to your system; that costs about $95.) The nicest quality of these models is their relatively quick speed: their access time for locating a file is 280 milliseconds, and their data transfer rate for relaying information to your PC is 300 kilobytes per second. There are far less costly drives available but, unless you're really squeezed for cash, you should avoid them because their slow access speeds make them frustrating to use.

Knowledge is the amassed thought and experience of innumerable ideas.

—Ralph Waldo Emerson

Despite the initial expense, CD-ROM has too many advantages to ignore. The most obvious is the medium's ability to save enormous amounts of storage space—for example, a single disc easily holds a 21-volume encyclopedia, or 1,000 classic works of literature, or 1,000,000 detailed maps of U.S. streets. CD-ROMs also typically provide search software that let you locate data in seconds, as opposed to the hours or days you might otherwise have to spend combing through bookshelves and flipping pages. Further, the search software will do a more thorough job, since it can find references to your topic buried within any section of text on the disc. And once you've found your information, it's usually easy to print it, or save it to a file you can later load into your word processor—a vast improvement over having to type it in yourself. CD-ROMs can even mimic TV and film by mixing words, pictures, and sound to give you a multi-sensory understanding of a subject. On top of all that, some popular CD-ROMs are actually *cheaper* than their print equivalents, because their publishers pass on the huge savings they're realizing from being spared high paper and shipping costs.

There are more than 4,000 CD-ROMs commercially available, so it would take volumes to fully cover the field. Therefore, this chapter touches on only the cream of the crop, with an emphasis on reference works of interest to writers. The areas it covers are literature; movies; music and art; atlases, travel guides, and almanacs; encyclopedias; general reference; book and magazine guides; and CD-ROM guides.

Knowledge is the only instrument of production that is not subject to diminishing returns.

—J. M. Clark

Literature

I'd always intended to assemble a home library of classic books that I could refer to and study whenever the mood struck me. I never got around to it, though. I was put off by the effort involved in locating the many different volumes, the $1,000 or more they'd cost, and—most of all—the amount of space they'd require.

It was therefore with enormous pleasure that I received my review copy of the Library of the Future, Second Edition from World Library. This phenomenal product gathers the most popular books of the ages and stuffs them all onto one platter.

Included on the disc are all the plays of Shakespeare; the King James Bible, the Koran, two books of Buddha, three books of Confucius, and the Egyptian Book of the Dead; 25 books by Plato and 29 books by Aristotle; *The Iliad* and *The Odyssey* by Homer, *Oedipus the King* and *Electra* by Sophocles, and *The Aeneid* by Virgil; *War and Peace* and *Anna Karenina* by Leo Tolstoy, *The Brothers Karamazov* by Fyodor Dostoevsky, *A Tale Of Two Cities* by Charles Dickens, and *Moby Dick* by Herman Melville; *Tom Sawyer, Huck Finn,* and a large collection of speeches by Mark Twain; 127 tales by Hans Christian Andersen, 30 Aesop's Fables, 60 Sherlock Holmes stories by Arthur Conan Doyle, and *The Wizard of Oz* by L. Frank Baum; and numerous other works by such immortal writers as Geoffrey Chaucer, Miguel De Cervantes, Thomas Hobbes, Nicolo Machiavelli, Jonathan Swift, John Milton, Mary Shelley, Edgar Allan Poe, Lewis Carroll, Emily Bronte, Charlotte Bronte, Jane Austen, Ralph Waldo Emerson, Stephen Crane, Rudyard Kipling, Oscar Wilde, Henrik Ibsen, H. G. Wells, Jules Verne, Charles Darwin, Karl Marx, Henry David Thoreau, Walt Whitman, and William Butler Yeats.

In all, it provides 971 classic works of literature, philosophy, drama, poetry, science, and religion, drawn from 111 of the finest authors in human history.

There are two caveats worth noting. First, because the text format is ASCII, there's no italic or boldface information, which can be a significant loss with certain novels. Second, the folks at World Library didn't check every line for accuracy as carefully as they might have. My quick skim found only minor mistakes, though; for example, the beginning of *The Adventures of Tom Sawyer* has Aunt Polly shouting as follows:

"Tom!"
No answer.
"TOM!"
No answer.

The CD-ROM, however, has it as

"TOM!"
No answer.
"Tom!"
No answer.

which nonsensically implies that Aunt Polly's voice starts out loud and then, as she becomes impatient, gets *softer*. The point is that if you need pinpoint accuracy, you shouldn't rely *exclusively* on this disc. The vast majority of it is fine, though.

Library of the Future, Second Edition has a list price of $299. You may find that cost justified simply for the convenience of being able to browse these classic works at your leisure without having to dedicate multiple bookshelves to them.

But the disc also offers other advantages over paper books. These include an attractive color text viewer that lets you easily adjust the width of the pages you're reading; a split screen option for viewing two works simultaneously; an auto-scrolling option that spares you from having to keep pressing the PgDn key; a bookmark option for marking a spot you'll want to return to later; a simple text editor for jotting down notes; capsule information on each author you can pop up at a keystroke; easy-to-use search commands that rapidly locate all the works on the CD-ROM containing the words or phrases you specify; and 180 accompanying illustrations that you can access in seconds.

Further, the disc lets you select a section of the book you're reading (or select the entire book), and then direct it to be printed, or to be saved as an ASCII text file on your hard disk. In the latter case, you can then bring the text into your word processor for further study and/or inclusion in your documents. This feature is especially handy for academics writing about the classics, and for authors seeking inspiration from them.

And in addition to its DOS programs, the product includes Windows software on the same disc! The Windows version furnishes an especially attractive display, and enhances certain features; for example, it lets you view up to eight documents at a time, and allows you to display the text in the font of your choice.

Considering everything it offers, this disc is a bargain. But if you still don't find it an irresistible buy, check out Library of the Future, Third Edition, which is due out by the time you read this, and is scheduled to feature over *1,700* titles...plus about 20 minutes of full motion video! These are precisely the kind of products I fantasized about owning when I first learned about CD-ROMS.

One other package worth mentioning here is the Bureau of Electronic Publishing's bestselling Monarch Notes on CD-ROM, which contains the text of every Monarch Notes booklet ever published (including many now out of print). If you don't have the time to read a classic, or if you need your memory jogged, you'll find this $69.95 disc to be a great timesaver. More information about it appears in Chapter 19, *Tools for Students and Academics.*

Movies

Any discussion of basic film research must begin with Leonard Maltin, who is a national treasure. While most know him only as the guy with the nervous smile and encyclopedic knowledge of film on "Entertainment Tonight," Maltin's biggest achievements have been his wonderful books. These include *Of Mice and Magic*, an indispensable guide to the history of cartoons; *The Disney Films*, a treasure chest of facts and photos concerning the studio that helped shape American culture; and *The Art of the Cinematographer*, which sheds light on some of the most underappreciated players in the movie business.

His ultimate work, however, is his *Movie and TV Video Guide*, which is a spectacular combination of scholarship and accessible writing. It covers more than 19,000 films, with each entry including such basic (but scrupulously researched) information as title, release date, country of origin, playing time, director, and actors. What makes the book really shine, however, are its carefully thought out rating assignments (from four stars to BOMB, in half-star increments), and its witty and incisive capsule reviews. For example, here's what it offers on Edward Wood's infamous *Plan 9 from Outer Space*:

> Hailed as the worst movie ever made; certainly one of the funniest. Pompous aliens believe they can conquer Earth by resurrecting corpses from a San Fernando Valley cemetery. [Star Bela] Lugosi died after two days' shooting in 1956; his remaining scenes were played by a taller, younger man holding a cape over his face! So mesmerizingly awful it actually improves (so to speak) with each viewing. And remember: it's all based on sworn testimony!

Jumping to the other side of the spectrum, here's what the book has to say about *Casablanca*:

> Everything is right in this WW2 classic of war-torn Casablanca with elusive nightclub owner Rick (Bogart) finding old flame (Bergman) and her husband, underground leader Henreid, among skeletons in his closet. Rains is marvelous as dapper police chief, and nobody sings "As Time Goes By" like Dooley Wilson. Three Oscars include Picture, Director, and Screenplay (Julius & Philip Epstein and Howard Koch). Our candidate for the best Hollywood movie of all time.

This is smart, enthusiastic writing from someone who really knows what he's talking about. The book is also full of interesting tidbits: for example, the *E. T.* review informs us that Debra Winger (!) contributed to the alien's voice; and the *Citizen Kane* entry reminds us that Orson Welles was only 25 when he made the picture, and that the reporter with the pipe is a young Alan Ladd. The consistent excellence and vitality of these reviews spanning over 1,400 pages is mind-boggling. Maltin's *Movie and Video Guide* is one of the great reference works of our time.

In fact, the only thing wrong with the book is you can't search through it easily. For example, there's no easy way to find all films that contain "ice skating" in their titles or descriptions; or all movies that feature cowboy hero Roy Rogers; or even all movies that receive four stars. That's why Microsoft performed a great service recently by giving us Cinemania, a

Liberty cannot be preserved without a general knowledge among the people.... The preservation of the means of knowledge among the lowest ranks is of more importance to the public than all the property of all the rich men in the country.

—John Adams

Windows CD-ROM that contains all the text in Maltin's *Movie and Video Guide*, and search commands that let you generate lists of movies on any subject in seconds. (Specifically, the commands let you search based on genre, director, actor, quality rating, Academy Award, MPAA rating, or any phrase in the movie titles and/or reviews.)

However, Microsoft didn't stop there. The disc also contains thousands of entries from *The Motion Picture Guide* and *The Encyclopedia of Film*, which are standard references published by the respected entertainment information service Baseline. And it has more than 1,000 stills from classic films, numerous excerpts of classic movie dialog, and an extensive glossary of film terms. It even gives you a simple text editor for taking notes on your discoveries...or for printing out a list of movies to take with you to the video store. And, happily, all this wonderful stuff can be purchased for a street price of only $49. If you have any interest in movies, Cinemania is a must-have reference work. (And if you don't, it's a *great* birthday present for someone who does.)

In case Cinemania doesn't sate your appetite for film references, you might also check out Roger Ebert's Home Movie Companion, a CD-ROM version of Ebert's popular book. Covering only about 1,000 films, this disc from Quanta Press doesn't approach the comprehensiveness of Cinemania; and it's not as technically slick, either. However, the Ebert reviews are longer than Maltin's, and offer an informed alternative perspective. Also, the disc contains scores of interesting interviews and essays that Ebert's written over his distinguished career as a film critic. At a street price of about $49, it makes a nice supplement to the Cinemania CD-ROM.

Music and Art

As mentioned previously, one of the neat things about a CD-ROM is its capacity for storing text, music, and art together. Perhaps the best example of a disc that creatively mixes all three of these elements is Microsoft's Multimedia Beethoven: The Ninth Symphony, which requires Windows, an audio card (such as the $155 Sound Blaster Pro Basic from Creative Labs), and speakers or headphones.

At its basest level, you can use this product like a standard music CD to play the Ninth Symphony—in this case, a 1964 recording by the Vienna Philharmonic conducted by Hans Schmidt-Isserstedt, running about an hour. However, you can also choose to display a running commentary by Beethoven expert Robert Winter that's synchronized to the music! Further, the program makes it easy to pause, skip, and replay portions of the symphony. For example, if you're puzzled by a musical term in Winter's remarks, you can click on it to bring things to a halt and pop up a definition from the package's extensive glossary.

The disc also provides four other fascinating sections. The Pocket Guide lists the major movements of the symphony, and allows you to listen to any of them with a mouse click. Beethoven's World offers an excellent 124-screen description of the man and his times, complete with photos from the period. The Art of Listening features Winter's down-to-earth explanations of musical concepts, beautifully illustrated by pieces from the symphony, and running 103 screens. Lastly, The Ninth Game lets you (and up to three others) play a fun multiple-choice trivia-style game concerning music in general and Beethoven in particular; among this one's charms is a digitized voice with a silly German accent that cheers you on. Multimedia Beethoven is one of the cleverest and classiest CD-ROMs ever published, particularly because it's so accessible to those without musical expertise. If you have an audio board, don't hesitate to snap up this package at its low street price of $50.

Another noteworthy Microsoft product is Musical Instruments, which also requires Windows and an audio board. This one lets you explore more than 200 musical instruments from around the world through 500 terrific photographs, 1,500 sound samples, and a variety of articles based on the acclaimed Eyewitness Guide book series. It's a great package if you're at all interested in the subject, or if you're looking for an educational plaything for your kid—especially at its inexpensive street price of $50.

A third package requiring Windows and an audio board comes from Dr. T's Music Software (a company I'm guessing was founded by a fan of the surreal Dr. Seuss film *The 5,000 Fingers of Dr. T*... see the Cinemania disc for details). Called Composer Quest, it guides you through musical his-

It is said that desire for knowledge lost us the Eden of the past; but whether that is true or not, it will certainly give us the Eden of the future.
—Robert G. Ingersoll

tory, and lets you read news items and view art masterpieces from the same period as the music you're listening to. It also features a game that has been described as a highbrow version of "Name That Tune." This is a fine educational gift for a child who's beginning to show an interest in music. It has a list price of $99.

If you're more interested in painting, and especially if you're a student or reviewer, you should check out Coate's Art Review—Impressionism from Quanta Press, which features over 600 masterpieces from Degas, Gauguin, Manet, Monet, Renoir, Van Gogh, and many other giants. At the heart of the disc is an impressionist art database covering the paintings and drawings, background information, museums and collections, demographics, schools, and other pertinent facts. After conducting a search on the database, you can bring up appropriate paintings on your screen with a keystroke. The VGA and Super VGA pictures don't hold a candle to the beauty of the originals, of course, but they work quite well as references; and the disc's street price of $49 isn't a lot more expensive than a comparable book full of art plates.

CD-ROMs are also a great source of clip art, which you can use to liven up anything from a newsletter to a glossy magazine ad. Publique Art from Quanta Press will supply you with over 2,500 cartoon-like public domain images at a list price of $99.95. And if it's more businesslike graphics you need, the premium drawing program CorelDraw includes an awesome 18,000 high-quality images and symbols on CD-ROM as part of its $395 street price package. In addition, CorelDraw is an invaluable tool for revising clip art, and creating your own artwork (as detailed in Chapter 22, *Laying Out Your Work*).

Atlases, Travel Guides, and Almanacs

If you like maps, the first products to look at are The Software Toolworks World Atlas and The Software Toolworks U.S. Atlas. As explained in Chapter 8, *Disk-Based References*, each package starts you off with an overview (of the world or the United States, respectively), and then lets you progressively hone in on the area you want by mouse-clicking on increasingly detailed maps. The advantage of the CD-ROM versions is, quite simply, that they spare you from dedicating up to 8MB of hard disk space per program. The atlases are available in both DOS and Windows versions, and range in price from $59.95 to $69.95.

Another winner is DeLorme's Street Atlas USA, an amazing product that maps virtually every street in the country! It accomplishes this feat by packing over one *million* detailed maps on the disc. This product is great for when you're making travel plans, or are writing fiction about an area you've never been to, or simply feel nostalgic and yearn to see the street names of your old neighborhood. DeLorme also just came out with Global Explorer, which reportedly offers lots more information than The Software Toolworks World Atlas. Both DeLorme products require Windows, and have a street price of about $99 each.

If you crave to experience the actual look and feel of a city, and you have Windows and an audio board, go for Great Cities of the World from Inter-Optica Publishing. This set of discs delivers sights and sounds that evoke the spirit of, on Volume I: Bombay, Cairo, London, Los Angeles, Moscow, New York, Paris, Rio de Janeiro, Sydney, and Tokyo; and on Volume II: Berlin, Buenos Aires, Chicago, Jerusalem, Johannesburg, Rome, San Francisco, Seoul, Singapore, and Toronto. These fun products display a slide show of landmarks in each city, while a narrator provides commentary and local music plays in the background. They also offer nitty-gritty information on hotels, restaurants, and other vital tourist facts. Great Cities of the World is a enjoyable way to prep for travel, or take a vicarious exotic vacation. Each disc has a list price of $49.95.

If you need more in-depth information, though, turn to the CIA World Fact Book from Quanta Press, which offers a slew of statistics and text gathered by the CIA on 249 countries and international territories. Sometimes called the world almanac of the Federal Government, this product covers such subjects as business, communications, disputes, drug traffic, economy, environment, geography, government, and military capabilities. The disc offers a search facility (which is unintuitive, but quite functional), and has a low street price of about $35. Further, if you want the same territory covered from a very different perspective, pick up Quanta Press' KGB World Factbook, which also costs about $35.

If you want yet more, Countries of the World from the Bureau of Electronic Publishing will give you the full text of 106 U.S. Army Country Handbooks (with each running between 200 and 500 pages), plus a hodgepodge of additional data gathered from 151 U.S. embassies, the Department of the Navy, the CIA World Factbook, and other sources. At the steep price of $395, though, you'll want it only if you have a serious business need for its extra information.

Lastly, if you'd like to know what's happening on this side of the Atlantic, buy the USA State Factbook from Quanta Press, which covers economics, geography, politics, population, traditions, and other subjects concerning the 50 states and U.S. territories. Like the two international Factbooks, it can be purchased for about $35.

Encyclopedias

The word "encyclopedia" used to represent a collection of relatively stodgy books filled with grey text, and an occasional picture, that spent most of its time making shelves groan under its weight. The 20 to 30 volumes in the set were a pain to comb through for information, and the information was a nuisance to copy by hand once you found it. On top of all that, encyclopedias cost a small fortune. If it wasn't for parental guilt and libraries, there probably wouldn't have been a market for the things at all.

Thanks to discs, those days are gone forever. A CD-ROM encyclopedia takes up almost no space. It's also quite affordable—a street price of $249 is typical. It lets you easily search through all its articles in seconds to uncover the information you're seeking. And once you have, it allows you to print the information, or copy it to your word processor.

And, perhaps best of all, encyclopedia publishers are taking advantage of the fact that CD-ROMs are interactive by creating products that are actually *fun*. Using vibrant pictures, sound bites, animation, and even video clips, they make dry facts about our world come alive. (In other words, these are *not* your father's encyclopedias.)

Knowledge is power, if you know it about the right person.
                    —Ethel Watts Mumford

The package that epitomizes the multimedia approach—and, in fact, is one of the most brilliantly designed CD-ROMs ever made—is Microsoft's new Encarta for Windows. This product is enormously accessible, and so is perfect for kids and computerphobes. However, it also provides the in-depth information needed for serious research. It's simply wonderful.

When you start up Encarta, you're greeted with a beautifully sculpted title screen. Even better, though, is that near its center is a picture randomly selected from the 7,000 high-quality photographs and drawings stored on the disc—say, a frowning gorilla, or yellow flowers, or a speckled bird, or the vibrant colors of a nation's flag. After a few moments, the picture is replaced by another, and another, creating a continuous art slide show that's a delight to watch.

When you're ready to get down to business, you can select several routes for obtaining information. The most straightforward is Encyclopedia Contents, which displays an alphabetical list of topics you can jump around in by typing the initial letters of the subject you're after.

If you'd prefer a more leisurely path, Category Browser presents you with topic categories. The topmost ones in the hierarchy are Art, Language and Literature; Geography; History; Life Science; Physical Performing Arts; Religion and Philosophy; Science and Technology; Social Science; and Sports, Games, Hobbies, and Pets. Selecting one of these leads to subcategories, and selecting one of them displays the names of relevant articles.

A third route for exploration is Open Encyclopedia, which in effect opens the encyclopedia's "pages" to the last entry you looked at. The first time you select this command, it displays the very first topic, which is the letter *a*. Like all Encarta's articles, this is accompanied by a gorgeous picture; specifically, a highly stylized "A" with rich colors, flowing curves, and assorted animals perched around it. Further, if you click on an icon by the picture, you're rewarded with a summary caption. In this case, the caption reads "The letter A gets its shape from an ancient Egyptian hieroglyph of an eagle. The Phoenicians later named it aleph, meaning ox, the head of which they thought the letter resembled. The Greeks then called the letter alpha, and the Romans gave the letter the name we recognize: A." This is the kind of clear, concise writing found throughout the encyclopedia and its more than 21,000 articles.

If you look up a topic that has some relation to sound, you can also click on icons to hear appropriate sound bites. For example, the article on African languages supplies about a dozen phrases in Swahili; the entry on Robert Frost features the writer reading his classic poem "Fire and Ice;" and the section on the flute will present you with music played with that instrument. In all, the disc contains more than 6,500 sound selections, encompassing over seven hours worth of words, music, and noises from nature.

In case all that's not enough, Encarta bundles in a number of superb additional programs. These include a fine 83,000-word dictionary and 40,000-word thesaurus; a Software Toolworks-type atlas with over 800 color maps that display appropriate encyclopedia entries when you request textual information; a superb visual timeline spanning from 15 million

B.C. to the present that runs 20 feet horizontally, and furnishes you with textual information about any displayed item at a mouse click; a collection of more than 100 marvelous animations, including such treasures as a butterfly emerging from its cocoon; and a game called Mind Maze that tickles your memory and teaches you interesting facts.

Encarta is much more than a paper encyclopedia translated into electronic form. In fact, over 93 percent of its content was created exclusively for the CD-ROM; for example, all its photographs were selected in part on how attractive they'd look on a PC screen. Encarta is a landmark product, and an example to all other CD-ROM publishers of how to exploit the medium. It has an affordable street price of $249, and is one of the best reasons for buying a CD-ROM drive.

Of course, there *are* other worthwhile CD-ROM encyclopedias. The best of these is Compton's Interactive Encyclopedia, which holds 32,000 well-written articles encompassing nine million words. In addition, it offers most of the same pictorial and sound features as Encarta—though not with the same degree of technical brilliance. It has a street price of about $249 and, if you conduct a lot of research, is worth considering as a supplementary information source.

Lastly, if you have fond memories of the 21-volume Academic American Encyclopedia, check out its electronic counterpart, The New Grolier Multimedia Encyclopedia, which contains 33,000 articles. This product is less technically adept than either Encarta or Compton's, and its articles aren't as consistently well written. Still, it provides some information the other two don't, and is especially good about citing sources for further research. Its street price is also $249.

General Reference

One of the first important works to come out in CD-ROM, and still one of the best, is Microsoft Bookshelf. Its appeal is quite simple—it holds the text of several of the most popular reference books of our time. Specifically, it contains *Bartlett's Familiar Quotations*, *The Concise Columbia Dictionary of Quotations*, *The Concise Columbia Encyclopedia*, *The World Almanac and Book of Facts*, *The Hammond Atlas*, *The American Heritage Dictionary*, and *Roget's II Thesaurus*.

These books are the products of decades of meticulous scholarship, and together form a strong foundation for anyone's research library. Purchasing their paper versions would cost several hundred dollars, but Microsoft Bookshelf has a street price of only $129. Further, the CD-ROM allows you to conduct searches for information through individual books, or through all of them simultaneously, in mere seconds, sparing you hours of tedious page-flipping. It also makes it easy to print an entry or copy it to your word processor.

In fact, the Windows version of Bookshelf has special links to Microsoft Word for Windows, so if you own that word processor, you'll be able to copy any displayed entry with a single mouse click—a great convenience. And if you don't have Word, Microsoft will happily rectify the situation with an alternative CD-ROM, Word for Windows & Bookshelf, that supplies the reference works and word processor on the same disc for a street price of about $379.

Another smorgasbord CD-ROM worth considering is the Toolworks Reference Library from The Software Toolworks. This gives you *The New York Public Library Desk Reference, The Dictionary of 20th Century History, Webster's New World Dictionary of Quotable Definitions, Webster's New World Dictionary: Third College Edition, Webster's New World Thesaurus, Webster's New World Guide to Concise Writing, The National Directory of Addresses and Telephone Numbers*, and *J.K. Lasser's Legal and Corporation Forms for the Smaller Business*.

While not as distinguished as the Microsoft Bookshelf lineup, this disc's collection of reference works makes a nice supplement to Bookshelf. Also, if you run a business, the telephone directory (which contains more than 210,000 entries) and the J.K. Lasser book (which furnishes 300 ready-to-use business forms) will prove especially helpful. The Toolworks CD-ROM's list price is $79.95.

Of course, there are also noteworthy reference discs devoted to one particular area. For example, if your main interest is dictionaries, nothing comes close to the Oxford English Dictionary on CD-ROM. This extraordinary Windows product provides definitions for 616,500 terms, and 2.4 million quotations to illustrate various shades of meanings, for a total of 60 million words. Even at its price of $895, this disc is a bargain. More information about it appears in Chapter 5, *Electronic Dictionaries and Thesauruses*.

And if you're seeking a multilingual dictionary, a solid one-stop shopping choice is Languages of the World from the NTC Publishing Group. This disc holds 18 complete monolingual and bilingual dictionaries covering 12 languages—including Chinese, Japanese, Swedish, and Norwegian —and totaling seven million words. Its list price is $249.95, and more information about it appears in Chapter 18, *Tools for Multilingual Writers*.

If you're a history buff, you'll enjoy U.S. History on CD-ROM from the Bureau of Electronic Publishing, which offers the full text of 107 public domain books on U.S. history. Included are such government documents as the Nixon Watergate tape transcripts and Congress' three-volume Iran-Contra affair report, plus over 1,000 historical photos, maps, and tables. There are more typos in the keyed-in text than one might reasonably expect, especially considering the disc's $395 list price; but it's still a valuable resource.

For more recent history, you should go to the Windows-based Facts On File News Digest, which delivers more than 10,000 pages (12 million words) of national and international news from 1980 through 1992. The data is in the form of abstracts written by Facts On File staffers, and is based on articles from major newspapers and other media sources. The disc's $695 cost precludes buying it for casual use, but it's a reasonable purchase for information-driven businesses.

What can I know? What ought I to do? What may I hope?
—Immanuel Kant

The more we know, the more we want to know; when we know enough, we know how much we don't know.
—Carol Orlock

Apart from the known and the unknown, what else is there?
—Harold Pinter

All I ever needed to know I learned in kindergarten.
—Robert Fulghum

Finally, if your field is science, you'll probably want the McGraw-Hill Science and Technical Reference Set from McGraw-Hill Publishing, which integrates two standard works: *The McGraw-Hill Concise Encyclopedia* and *The McGraw-Hill Dictionary of Scientific Terms*. The CD-ROM offers 7,300 articles and 115,500 definitions, ranging from astronomy to zoology, and has a street price of about $265.

Book and Magazine Guides

Another valuable role for CD-ROM is as a guide to traditional print media. A disc's storage capabilities, combined with search software, make it a perfect platform for delivering data on the millions of books and magazine articles available.

The classic references on books, of course, are Bowker's *Books in Print* and *Children's Books in Print*. For $1,095, you can buy a CD-ROM version called Books in Print Plus that incorporates both of these works, offering data on over one million books. These are ordered into 18 categories, including author, title, publisher, ISBN number, LCCN number, subject, audience, publication year, and price. The disc also furnishes the names, addresses, and phone numbers of virtually all U.S. book publishers. If you can stretch your budget a bit further, though, $1,595 will get you Books in Print with Books Reviews Plus, which contains everything in Books in Print Plus, and in addition has the full text of more than 150,000 reviews from *Publishers Weekly, Kirkus, Library Journal, School Library Journal, Choice, Booklist, SciTech Book News, Reference & Research Book News, BIOSIS*, and *University Press Book News*. Both CD-ROMs are sold as annual subscriptions that get you 12 discs, updated monthly.

For general interest magazines, you can turn to the Magazine Article Summaries CD-ROM series from EBSCO Publishing. The base package, which costs $399, provides hundreds of thousands of article abstracts for 383 popular publications, such as *Newsweek, Time, The Economist, Foreign Policy, Library Journal, Rolling Stone, Psychology Today, New England Journal of Medicine, Omni*, and even *The New York Times*; and also features about 5,000 Magill Book Reviews. For $1,399, you can get a disc that additionally contains the full text of 60 of the magazines (including all the publications just mentioned, except for *The New York Times*); and $1,999 will buy you a disc that features 90 full-text magazines. The abstracts cover magazine articles from 1984 to the present, and the full-text articles typically range from 1990 to the present.

Lastly, if you're heavily involved with computers, and you can spare its $695 annual subscription fee, don't hesitate to buy Computer Select from Computer Library (a division of Ziff Communications). This superb CD-ROM spans the past year of computer literature, providing abstracts for 170 computer publications covering 80,000 articles. Even better, it supplies full-text articles for 75 major magazines such as *PC Magazine, PC Week, InfoWorld, PC Computing, PC Sources*, and *MacUser*; and the text of respected newsletters such as Esther Dyson's *Release 1.0* and Stewart Alsop's *P.C. Letter*. (A newsletter like *Release 1.0* is provided under a three-month time delay, however, since a subscription to it alone normally costs $395.) Computer Select is therefore a great product to turn to when you're considering a software or hardware purchase.

In addition, Computer Select gives you contact information and brief profiles on 13,000 computer companies; price, version number, compatibility, and contact data on 72,000 hardware and software products; and definitions for 12,000 computer and telecommunications terms drawn from the Electronic Computer Glossary (see Chapter 5, *Electronic Diction-*

aries and Thesauruses) and the book *Telecom Dictionary* by Harry Newton. Helping you to make sense of all this information is Lotus' excellent Blue-fish search technology, which is easy to learn and a joy to use. Also, your $695 supplies you with 12 discs, updated monthly, so that you're ensured of always having current information—a critical point in the fast-moving computer business.

In a nutshell, Computer Select is a *great* product. I heartily recommend it, not only as a reviewer, but as a grateful user; it's the CD-ROM I used most frequently when putting this book together.

CD-ROM Guides

As we've seen in this chapter, CD-ROMs have been used as reference guides to films, music, books, and magazines. It's therefore only natural that there are also CD-ROMs acting as guides to...other CD-ROMs.

In fact, there are two: CD-ROMs in Print 1994 from Meckler Publishing, and The CD-ROM Directory 1994 from Pemberton Press. Both cover virtually every disc currently available, and both typically base their sketchy product descriptions on information from the publishers, so there's not an enormous difference between the products.

There *are* nuances worth mentioning, though. In general, Meckler covers a slightly higher number of CD-ROMs than Pemberton, while Pemberton provides a bit more information on each entry. Also, the software on the Meckler disc that lets you work with the data is *much* easier to learn and use than Pemberton's. At the same time, however, you can perform sophisticated searches with the Pemberton software that are beyond Meckler's capabilities.

As for price, Meckler charges $95 for one disc; or $165 for two biannual discs (you're given one at your time of purchase, and mailed the updated version within six months); or $165 for one disc and an annual book version. And Pemberton Press charges $225 for two biannual discs, or $330 for the two discs and an annual book version.

Therefore, if you don't require esoteric search commands or detailed product descriptions, you'll probably want to choose Meckler. For example, whenever I needed CD-ROM information for this book, I always reached for Meckler first, and used Pemberton only occasionally as a supplement. However, you won't go wrong with either of them.

One other CD-ROM reference worth mentioning is the *Gale Directory of Databases, Volume 2*. This is actually more comprehensive than the Meckler and Pemberton products, and comes out twice a year; but it's available in book form only. It's a terrific buy if you're also interested in online databases, since that's the subject covered in great detail in its companion *Volume I* (as explained in Chapter 10, *Online References*). An annual subscription to the two-volume, biannual book set is $300, while a subscription to *Volume 2* alone is $130.

Product Information

Note: Version numbers and prices may have changed by the time you read this.

Bowker Electronic Publishing
(A division of Reed Reference Publishing)
121 Chanlon Road
New Providence, NJ 07974
(800) 323-3288; (908) 665-2866
Fax: (908) 665-3528

Books in Print Plus: List Price, $1,095 for 12 monthly discs; generally not discounted

Books in Print with Books Reviews Plus: List Price, $1,595 for 12 monthly discs; generally not discounted

Bureau of Electronic Publishing
141 New Road
Parsippany, NJ 07054
(800) 828-4766; (201) 808-2700
Fax: (201) 808-2676

Countries of the World: List Price, $395; Street Price N/A

Monarch Notes CD-ROM: List Price, $69.95; Street Price N/A

U.S. History on CD-ROM: List Price, $395; Street Price N/A

Compton's NewMedia
2320 Camino Vida Roble
Carlsbad, CA 92009
(800) 862-2206; (619) 929-2500
Fax: (619) 929-2600

Compton's Interactive Encyclopedia for Windows: List Price, $395; Street Price, about $249

Computer Library
Ziff Communications
One Park Avenue
New York, NY 10016
(800) 827-7889; (212) 503-4400
Fax: (212) 503-3695

Computer Select: List Price, $995 for 12 monthly discs; generally not discounted

Corel Systems Corporation
1600 Carling Avenue
Ottawa, Ontario, Canada K1Z 8R7
(800) 836-3729; (613) 728-8200
Fax: (613) 761-9176

CorelDRAW 4.0 (for Windows): List Price, $595; Street Price, about $395

Creative Labs
1901 McCarthy Blvd.
Milpitas, CA 95305
(800) 998-5227; (408) 428-6600
Fax: (408) 428-6633

Sound Blaster: List Price, $149; Street Price, about $99

Sound Blaster Pro Basic: List Price, $229; Street Price, about $155

Sound Blaster Pro (includes MIDI kit): List Price, $299; Street Price, about $189

DeLorme Mapping Company
Lower Main Street
P.O. Box 298
Freeport, Maine 04032
(800) 452-5931; (207) 865-1234
Fax: (207) 865-9291

Street Atlas USA (for Windows): List Price, $169; Street Price, about $99

Global Explorer (for Windows): List Price, $169; Street Price, about $99

EBSCO Publishing
P.O. Box 2250
83 Pine Street
Loading Dock I
Peabody, MA 01960
(800) 653-2726; (508) 535-8500
Fax: (508) 530-8661

Magazine Article Summaries CD-ROM (base product): List Price, $399; generally not discounted

Magazine Article Summaries CD-ROM (with full text for 60 magazines): List Price, $1,399; generally not discounted

Magazine Article Summaries CD-ROM (with full text for 90 magazines): List Price, $1,999; generally not discounted

Facts On File, Inc.
460 Park Avenue South
New York, NY 10016
(800) 443-8323; (212) 683-2244
Fax: (212) 213-4578

Facts On File News Digest (1980-1992): List Price, $695; generally not discounted

Gale Research
835 Penobscot Building
Detroit, MI 48226
(800) 877-4253; (313) 961-2242
Fax: (313) 961-6083

Gale Directory of Databases, Volume 1: Online Databases and Gale Directory of Databases, Volume 2: CD-ROM, Diskette, Magnetic Tape, Handheld, and Batch Access Database Products: List Price, $300 for the two-volume biannual book set, $130 for *Volume 2* alone; generally not discounted

Grolier Electronic Publishing, Inc.
Sherman Turnpike
Danbury, CT 06816
(800) 356-5590; (203) 797-3530
Fax: (203) 797-3835

The New Grolier Multimedia Encyclopedia: List Price, $395; Street Price, about $249

InterOptica Publishing, Ltd.
300 Montgomery Street
Second Floor
San Francisco, CA 94104
(415) 788-8788
Fax: (415) 788-8886

Great Cities of the World, Volume I: List Price, $49.95; Street Price N/A

Great Cities of the World, Volume II: List Price, $49.95; Street Price N/A

McGraw-Hill Publishing Company
Professional and Reference Division
11 West 19th Street
New York, NY 10011
(800) 262-4729; (212) 512-2000
Fax: (212) 337-4092

McGraw-Hill Science and Technical Reference Set: List Price, $495; Street Price, about $265

Meckler Publishing
11 Ferry Lane West
Westport, CT 06880
(800) 632-5537; (203) 226-6967
Fax: (203) 454-5840

CD-ROMs in Print 1994: List Price, $95 for one disc, $165 for two biannual discs, $165 for one disc and annual book version; generally not discounted

Microsoft Corporation
One Microsoft Way
Redmond, WA 98052
(800) 426-9400; (206) 882-8080
Fax: No generic sales or information fax number

Cinemania (for Windows): List Price, $79.95; Street Price, about $49

Bookshelf (for DOS): List Price, $195; Street Price, about $129

Bookshelf (for Windows): List Price, $195; Street Price, about $129

Multimedia Beethoven (for Windows): List Price, $79.95; Street Price, about $50

Musical Instruments (for Windows): List Price, $79.95; Street Price, about $50

Encarta (for Windows): List Price, $395; Street Price, about $249

Word for Windows & Bookshelf, Multimedia Edition: List Price, $595; Street Price, about $379

NEC Technologies, Inc.
1255 Michael Drive
Wood Dale, IL 60191
(800) 632-4636; (708) 860-9500
Fax: (800) 366-0476

MultiSpin 38 (portable): List Price N/A for this line; Estimated Selling Price (provided by NEC), $350

MultiSpin 74 (external): List Price N/A for this line; Estimated Selling Price (provided by NEC), $550

MultiSpin 84 (internal): List Price N/A for this line; Estimated Selling Price (provided by NEC), $450

Parallel to SCSI Interface: List Price N/A for this line; Estimated Selling Price (provided by NEC), $95

NTC Publishing Group
4255 West Touhy Avenue
Lincolnwood, IL 60646
(800) 323-4900; (708) 679-5500
Fax: (708) 679 2494

Languages of the World: List Price, $249.95; Street Price N/A

Pemberton Press, Inc.
462 Danbury Road
Wilton, CT 06897
(800) 248-8466; (203) 761-1466
Fax: (203) 761-1444

The CD-ROM Directory 1994: List price: $225 for two biannual discs, $170 for annual book version, $330 for discs/book combination; generally not discounted

Quanta Press, Inc.
1313 Fifth Street SE
Suite 208C
Minneapolis, MN 55414
(612) 379-3956
Fax: (612) 623-4570

Roger Ebert's Movie Home Companion: List Price, $79.95; Street Price, about $49

Coate's Art Review—Impressionism: List Price, $79.95; Street Price, about $49

Publique Art: List Price, $99.95; Street Price N/A

CIA World Factbook: List Price, $49.95; Street Price, about $35

USA State Factbook: List Price, $49.95; Street Price, about $35

The Software Toolworks, Inc.
60 Leveroni Court
Novato, CA 94949
(800) 234-3088; (415) 883-3000
Fax: (415) 415-883-0293

The Software Toolworks World Atlas 4.0 for DOS or Windows, CD-ROM version: List Price, $69.95; Street Price N/A

The Software Toolworks U.S. Atlas 4.0 for DOS or Windows, CD-ROM version: List Price, $59.95; Street Price N/A

Toolworks Reference Library: List Price, $79.95; Street Price N/A

World Library, Inc.
12914 Haster Street
Garden Grove, CA 92640
(800) 443-0238; (714) 748-7197
Fax: (714) 748-7198

Library of the Future, Second Edition (for DOS and Windows): List Price, $299; Street Price N/A

Two mail-order vendors that carry most of the products covered in this chapter are:

Bureau of Electronic Publishing
141 New Road
Parsippany, NJ 07054
(800) 828-4766; (201) 808-2700
Fax: (201) 808-2676

S & S Enterprises
CD-ROM Software and Publishing
P.O. Box 552
Lemont, IL 60439
(800) 766-3472; (708) 257-7616
Fax: (708) 257-9678

The Bureau of Electronic Publishing often charges close to list price, so it's not ideal for bargain shopping. However, you should contact BEP if only to get its information-packed catalog, which is a terrific guide to popular discs from a variety of publishers (including BEP itself).

S & S, on the other hand, offers significant discounts on CD-ROMs, as well as special offers you're unlikely to find elsewhere. For example, when the Toolworks Reference Library was retailing for $129.95, S&S was selling the disc, sans packaging, for only $29. This vendor is therefore a great place to check into for comparison shopping.

CHAPTER
10

ONLINE REFERENCES

I find that a great part of the information I have was acquired by looking up something and finding something else on the way.

—Franklin P. Adams

If you're using your phone line only for talking, you're missing out on a dynamic universe of information. Millions of PC users now routinely dial into enormous data carriers, called *online services*, which provide databases covering virtually every interest, from literature and poetry, to business and law, to sports and games. Just as important, these services allow callers to communicate with each other in a relaxed environment where all are encouraged to share their knowledge and wisdom.

It doesn't take much to hook into this exciting world. All you need is a modem, a telecommunications program, and a few appropriate phone numbers.

A *modem* is a device that converts data from your PC into audio tones that can be transmitted over phone lines, and converts similar tones from other computers into data your PC can understand. These processes are called *modulation* and *demodulation*, and it's from the first few letters of these two terms that we get the word "modem."

When shopping for a modem, the main characteristics you should look for are Hayes compatibility, high speed, and fax capability. In addition, you need to decide whether you prefer the unit to be internal or external.

Hayes compatibility simply means the modem uses a collection of industry standard command codes. These codes are built into virtually all modern modems.

A modem's speed is rated in bits-per-second, or *bps*. At minimum, you should buy a 2,400 bps modem, which will cost around $50. If you can afford it, however, I recommend buying a 14,400 bps modem, which operates six times faster, and costs about $180. Operating at a higher speed allows you to spend less time reading in, or *downloading*, data, which not only gives you more time to do other things, but cuts down on your phone bill charges.

Many modems now include the ability to send and receive fax transmissions. This allows you to send a document you've created in your word processor directly to someone else's fax machine without ever having to touch a sheet of paper. Since this fax capability adds very little to the cost of the modem, you should seek it even if you don't foresee an immediate need for it.

Finally, you have to choose between an external and internal modem. An external unit connects to your PC's serial port via a modem cable, while an internal unit is set on a board you install in a slot in your PC. In general, if you're short on slots, select the external option. Otherwise, an internal modem is less expensive, takes up no space on your desk, and is sure to run at high speeds without problems (an external 14,400 bps modem can be too fast for your serial port and require the addition of a special UART chip).

Once you've decided on the options you want, you'll find excellent inexpensive modems are available from a number of companies, including U.S. Robotics, Practical Peripherals, and Zoom. For example, one of the finest modems on the market is U.S. Robotics' internal Sportster 14,400/PC Fax, which has a low street price of $179.

You do not need to leave your room. Remain sitting at your table.... The world will freely offer itself to you.

—Franz Kafka

As for telecommunications programs, one of the best DOS packages is Telix SE, which is distributed as shareware—that is, software that you're allowed to use for free during a trial period (say, 30 days). If you then decide that you don't care for the program, you can simply delete it from your hard disk. On the other hand, if you want to keep using it, you're honor-bound to mail the publisher a check for the cost of the product. Once you do so, you become an official registered user, and are entitled to such extras as technical support and notification of new releases. As noted in Chapter 1, shareware is based entirely on the honor system; the nice thing is, it works.

If you don't know someone who can simply give you a copy of Telix SE, you can buy it from a shareware vendor for $2 to $6; or you can download it from an online service using some *other* telecommunications program. You can also buy it directly from the publisher, deltaComm Development, for $39 (or $51 if you want a printed manual included), and become a registered user immediately.

Try to know everything of something; and something of everything.

—Henry Peter

You can't have everything. Where would you put it?

—Steven Wright

Of course, if you own Microsoft Windows, you have a capable telecommunications program named Terminal included in the package. If you want snazzy features, though (such as the ability to view a GIF graphics file as you're downloading it, so you can be sure you're not devoting time to a file you don't need), the best bang for the buck is provided by Datastorm Technologies' excellent Procomm Plus for Windows, which costs about $99.

Once you're set up with your hardware and software, you can begin dialing into other computer systems. You may want to start by calling a local electronic bulletin board service, or BBS, which is typically operated by an enthusiastic hobbyist as a free service, and offers such basics as a message board for trading information and gossip, a program section that contains hundreds of shareware programs you can download, and (buried somewhere) a file with the phone numbers of other BBSs in your area. Another good source for BBS phone numbers is the Ziff-Davis monthly magazine *Computer Shopper*, which is available at many newstands and computer stores. You can also dial into a large national BBS, such as EXEC-PC at (414) 489-4210 or Channel 1 at (617) 354-8873, and then download several of its BBS lists.

To get the most out of your telecommunications system, though, you'll want to join a few online services. Therefore, the rest of this chapter briefly describes the biggest and best services available: CompuServe, GEnie, Delphi, America Online, Prodigy, BIX, MCI Mail, BRS, DIALOG, NEXIS, NewsNet, Dow Jones News/Retrieval, and Internet.

The answer to almost any question you might have can be found on one of these services. On top of that, many of them are lots of fun, and offer a great way to make friends with fellow modem users across the country.

CompuServe

When it comes to general purpose services, CompuServe is both the biggest and the best. It offers a staggering 1,500 reference databases, and 350 discussion forums, on such topics as astrology, astronomy, biorhythms, business, cars, CB radio, comic books, disabilities, flying, food, foreign languages, gardening, human sexuality, intelligence, journalism, law, medicine, movies, new age themes, photography, psychology, religion, roleplaying games, science fiction, show business, stamp collecting, stocks, weather, and wine (to name but a few).

In addition, if you do business with other computer users, you may find CompuServe's electronic mail service indispensable, since it allows you to trade private information quickly and conveniently. Virtually all services provide e-mail, but CompuServe is the system most businesspeople have access to, either directly or through its gateway to MCI Mail (which is covered later in this chapter).

Perhaps CompuServe's greatest strength, however, is its support forums devoted to various software and hardware packages. Run by the products' vendors, these sections give you the opportunity to post technical questions at any time and receive in-depth answers within 24 hours. Often, though, your answer will appear within a few hours from a fellow member, since many computer "power users" hang out on CompuServe and are quick to generously share their hard-earned knowledge.

CompuServe's standard membership costs $8.95 a month and $8 an hour, and includes free access to about 35 services (such as stock quotes, movie reviews, and an electronic encyclopedia). An alternative plan charges $2.50 a month and $12.80 an hour, which can be preferable for infrequent users.

The main downside of CompuServe is that you can easily get hit with large monthly bills if you don't take keep an eye on the clock while using it. To reduce your online time and reduce costs, try OzCIS from Ozarks West Software, which automates many CompuServe functions, and is only $30 (or $40 with a printed manual). Also, if you use Windows, don't hesitate to obtain CompuServe's own WinCIM program, which greatly simplifies getting around the labyrinth of options available. WinCIM costs $25, but comes packaged with a $25 CompuServe usage credit, so it's virtually free.

In a nutshell, if you must restrict yourself to just one service, it probably should be CompuServe.

GEnie

GEnie has a similar structure to CompuServe, but is smaller and cozier. It's also much less expensive. During off-peak hours (6 P.M. to 8 A.M. your local time, and weekends), it charges $8.95 per month for your first four hours of use, and $3 for each additional hour. During the business day, however, it charges $12.50 an hour.

Perhaps the best area on GEnie is its famous Science Fiction/Fantasy/Horror RoundTable (SFRT), which has become an indispensable tool, and beloved hangout, for hundreds of genre fiction authors. Actually, you can learn a great deal about writing from the SFRT no matter what type of fiction you're interested in. Indeed, the SFRT's biggest drawback is that it can become addictive and cut into your professional writing time. (I speak from experience here.)

Another nice aspect of GEnie is the way it organizes public messages. Most services (including CompuServe) create message "chains" by having you respond to the last person who left a comment on a subject. GEnie, in contrast, allows you to create a topic category in which anyone can then leave messages directed at the topic, rather than at a particular person. This creates a more communal atmosphere, helps ensure that messages stay centered on the subject, and generally produces a more readable format for messages.

Yet another unique feature of GEnie is that its stock quotes use decimal points, while all other services give you fractions. This is useful if you're in the habit of importing your stock data into a spreadsheet for quick calculations.

GEnie is also the best text-based system for kids, due to its low cost, and the availability of such features as an online encyclopedia and "homework help" sections.

On the downside, GEnie doesn't carry nearly as many online databases as CompuServe; and aside from a few exceptions such as the SFRT, it doesn't attract as many sharp people who can answer your questions. Still, it's an excellent resource and, if you use it during off-peak hours, a real bargain.

The mind is the man, and knowledge mind; a man is but what he knoweth.

—Francis Bacon

Knowledge and human power are synonymous.

—Francis Bacon

Delphi

Delphi is the tiniest online system covered here, with only 20,000 members (versus GEnie's 500,000 members and CompuServe's one million). It also provides one of the narrowest range of services, concentrating on online games and entertainment information.

On the other hand, it's cheap. Delphi charges a flat rate of $10 for four hours of use a month, and $4 an hour for additional use. Alternatively, you can sign up for $20 a month covering 20 hours of use, and $1.80 an hour for additional use. If you dial in using SprintNet or Tymet (which you'll probably have to do if you live outside of Massachusetts, where Delphi is based), a $9 an hour fee is tacked on for use during business hours.

If you're looking for a homey community to hang out or play games with, Delphi is a good choice. It's also a economical resource for small businesses, since it provides stock quotes, the Dow Jones Averages, Donohue's Money Fund Report, the UPI Business News, the Financial Commodity News, PR Newswire press releases, and a few other fundamentals either entirely under its flat fee plan or for just a little extra.

Perhaps Delphi's best feature, however, is its unique gateway to Internet, a worldwide computer system with millions of subscribers. Internet can be difficult to join if you aren't connected with a government, university, or corporate R&D department. Most of the services covered in this chapter provide electronic mail connections to Internet, but Delphi also offers full access to the millions of messages and files on the system. More information about Internet appears later in this chapter.

America Online

This system provides the same basic features as CompuServe, GEnie, and Delphi. The difference is that it lets you access them through Microsoft Windows-style screens, complete with overlapping windows, menu commands, and buttons for you to click with your mouse.

America Online is relatively new, but its unique look and affordable pricing (a flat rate of $9.95 a month for five hours of use, and $3.50 an hour for additional use) have garnered it rapid growth. It's a service to keep an eye on.

Prodigy

Let me state my bias up front—I don't like Prodigy. It's the only major graphics-based system aside from America Online. However, it's much slower and uglier than America Online, and (unlike every other service in this chapter) doesn't allow you to capture the text that appears on your screen to a disk file. It has also developed a reputation for unpleasant censorship policies, and (based on personal experience) appears to regard its customers a bit contemptuously. And it's the only service that plasters paid advertisements—that's right, *advertisements*—at the bottom of its screens.

That being said, Prodigy is quite cheap; a flat fee of $14.95 a month covers virtually all services. It also offers a number of reference works and interactive programs of special interest to children. Therefore, if you have kids, it's worth subscribing to. Otherwise, you may prefer tapping into the inexpensive resources on GEnie, Delphi, or America Online.

Never try to tell everything you know. It may take too short a time.
—Norman Ford

It's what you learn after you know it all that counts.
—AJohn Wooden

MCI Mail

All the services discussed so far offer electronic mail as a feature. It may therefore seem strange that MCI Mail provides electronic mail as virtually its *only* feature. However, MCI Mail's commands for composing, editing, sending, and receiving messages are easier to use than those of other systems. And with over 800,000 subscribers, and a tie-in to CompuServe's and Internet's electronic mail systems, it has a long reach.

Further, MCI Mail never charges you for the time you spend on the system receiving and composing messages. Like the Post Office, it asks for money only when you *send* mail. Specifically, it charges 50 cents for the first 500 characters; 10 cents for second 500; then 10 cents per 1,000 characters up to 10,000 characters; and then 5 cents per 1,000 characters. Most messages are typically under 1,000 characters, and so cost a mere 60 cents for instantaneous delivery.

Alternatively, you can opt for a Preferred Pricing plan that lets you send up to 40 messages a month for a flat fee of only $10. Each message can be up to 5,000 characters; any text past that is simply counted as a new message.

While e-mail is its main business, MCI Mail can also dispatch your text as a fax, as a telex message, as a First Class letter, or as a letter to be delivered overnight. It also offers private read-only bulletin boards for, say, consultants who want to keep their clients updated. And it provides a gateway to the Dow Jones News/Retrieval service, a valuable news and business resource covered later in this chapter.

If you don't send messages, MCI Mail's sole cost is an annual membership fee of $35. Therefore, there's little risk to joining it; and you never know when you'll bump into a business prospect who can reach you electronically only through MCI Mail.

BIX

As mentioned previously, CompuServe is the place where you'll find knowledgeable computer owners discussing the finer points of using their hardware and software. However, BIX (short for Byte Information Exchange) is the place where you'll find the engineers who actually designed the hardware and software. In other words, it's a haven for techies. Not surprisingly, popular topic areas include programming in Windows, programming in DOS, using Borland C++, science fiction, and modem-to-modem game-playing.

BIX is somewhat pricey, charging $13 a month just for membership, and $3 an hour during off-peak hours (6 P.M. to 7 A.M. your local time, and weekends) or $9 an hour during business hours (7 A.M. to 6 P.M. your local time). An alternative off-peak hours plan lets you pay $33 a month for the first 20 hours of use, and then an hourly rate of $1.80 an hour.

If you're interested in technical matters, this system is worth investigating. Otherwise, though, stick to the mainstream services.

BRS

BRS encompasses two services centered around research databases: BRS/After Dark, which is available only from 6 P.M. your local time to 4 A.M. Eastern time; and BRS Search Service, which is always available, but more expensive.

BRS/After Dark provides the full text of over 85 major reference works, including Books in Print Online, Book Review Digest, Magazine ASAP, Magazine Index, National Newspaper Index, Newsearch, UMI Article Clearinghouse, Biography Index, Bibliographic Index, Business Periodicals Index, Harvard Business Review Online, DISCLOSURE Database, Federal Register Abstracts, Legal Resource Index, Art Index, ERIC, Academic Index, Peterson's College Database, Linguistics and Language Behavior Abstracts, Sociological Abstracts, Religion Index, Health Periodicals Database, MEDLINE, AIDS Database, CANCERLIT, PsycINFO, and TOXLINE.

To give you a sense of how much information this covers, Magazine ASAP supplies the complete text or abstracts for 380,000 articles from 100 general-interest periodicals; Books in Print Online contains citations to 1.9 million books from 22,000 publishers; the National Newspaper Index furnishes 2.8 million citations to articles, editorials, and letters from *The New York Times*, *The Washington Post*, *The Wall Street Journal*, *The Los Angeles Times*, and *The Christian Science Monitor*; and MEDLINE holds nearly seven million abstracts and citations on biomedical literature. And that's just *four* of the references offered on this service.

BRS/After Dark is quite affordable, charging an $80 one-time fee, plus $12 a month, plus extra fees depending on the databases you access (ranging from $10 to $50 an hour) and number of searches you conduct.

If you need to conduct searches during business hours, you can turn to BRS Search Service, which carries all the databases BRS/After Dark does, *and* about 50 others. It charges an annual fee of $80, plus $45 to $75 an hour depending on the databases you access, plus additional charges for the text you retrieve. In general, BRS Search Service is a lot pricier than its sister service; but if you can afford it, it's a fine resource.

DIALOG

Like BRS, DIALOG concentrates on major reference works. However, it provides many more of them than BRS; and also offers the full text of publications such as *The Washington Post* and *The Los Angeles Times*. In all, DIALOG carries over 420 databases, encompassing billions of articles and citations.

DIALOG's software isn't very well-designed, so it can be difficult to figure out how to navigate the system (the service is typically used by skilled librarians). If you patiently study its fine manuals, however, and keep a command reference card by your PC, you'll get by. DIALOG charges a $295 signup fee, which includes classroom or videotape training, and $100 worth of connect time. In addition, it charges an annual $75 subscription fee, and from $1 to $300 an hour depending on the databases you access.

Alternatively, you can choose a superb sister service called Knowledge Index, which is available from 6:00 P.M. to 5:00 A.M. your local time and weekends. Knowledge Index carries only about 100 of DIALOG's reference works, but it still covers over 50,000 publications. These include hundreds of general-interest books and periodicals, and thousands of specialized journals for businesspeople, lawyers, physicians, scientists and engineers, academics, and artists. Knowledge Index is easier to use than the full DIALOG system, and is significantly less expensive—a flat $24 an hour.

Further, you don't need to join DIALOG to access Knowledge Index. In fact, Knowledge Index is available *exclusively* through CompuServe! To access it, simply type GO KI at the CompuServe system prompt.

NEXIS

If your main interest is news articles, the best source is NEXIS, which carries the full text of over 650 publications. These include *The New York Times, The Washington Post, The Wall Street Journal, The Los Angeles Times, USA Today, Newsweek, Time, U.S. News & World Report, The Economist,* and many other general interest newspapers and magazines, often dating back to the 1970s. Some of the periodicals, such as *The New York Times,* are available exclusively through NEXIS.

NEXIS also supplies more specialized journals, such as *Consumer Reports, Adweek, Advertising Age, Industry Week, Legal Times, Congressional Record, Movie Reviews Data Base,* and *Sports Illustrated.* In addition, it pro-

Anyone who has begun to think places some portion of the world in jeopardy.
                                    —John Dewey

vides stories from news outlets such as the AP, Reuters, and the Japan Economic Newswire; and transcripts of television programs such as *ABC News* and *The MacNeil-Lehrer News Hour.*

NEXIS is one of the most expensive services, charging $43 an hour, plus hefty additional fees per search, plus a monthly subscription fee of $50. If you expect to use the service frequently, you may prefer a flat-fee option; call Mead Data Central for details.

NewsNet

While BRS, DIALOG, and NEXIS concentrate on major references and publications, NewsNet is devoted to specialized newsletters. It carries nearly 550 of them, and the topics they cover range from global warming to ice cream.

More specifically, the newsletters provided on the service include *Aerospace Daily, Affluent Markets Alert, Biotech Business, Bond Buyer, Coal Outlook, Corporate Job Outlook, Defense Week, Editors Only, Education Weekly, Energy Daily, FCC Daily Digest, The FDIC Watch, Food & Drink Daily, Food Chemical News, Foundation Giving Watch, FX Week, Global Environment Change Report, Helicopter News, High Tech Ceramics News, Ice Cream Reporter, International Country Risk Guide, International Merger Law, Japan High Tech Review, Liability Week, Military Robotics Sourcebook, Mobile Satellite Reports, Nuclear Waste News, PhotoMarket, Political Risk Newsletter, Real Estate Buyers Directory, Space Daily, Wall Street S.O.S., Wine Business Insider,* and *World Bank Watch.*

Many of these newsletters charge hundreds of dollars for an annual subscription to their paper editions. NewsNet gives you the opportunity to look over a newsletter without making a large payment up front. It also

Once there was an elephant

Who tried to use the telephant—

No! No! I mean an elephone

Who tried to use the telephone.

—Laura Howe Richards, "Eletelephony"

Have I reached the party to whom I am speaking?

—Ernestine (Lily Tomlin)

The telephone is a device for connecting you with strangers.

—Anonymous

supplies you with timely information a lot faster than the U.S. Postal service can. And it allows you to store the data in a text file you can later load into your word processor for further study.

Of course, you pay for these privileges. NewsNet charges a $79.95 signup fee, plus $15 a month, plus $90 an hour, plus $60 to $300 an hour for reading full-text articles. Therefore, it's not a service to be used casually. But if you have a serious business need for one or more of the newsletters it stocks, you'll appreciate the conveniences NewsNet offers.

Dow Jones News/Retrieval

If you're involved in business and finance, nothing beats Dow Jones News/Retrieval. This service carries the full text of all the articles in *The Wall Street Journal*, *The Washington Post*, *Business Week*, *Barron's*, *Forbes*, and many other publications, often going back for years. It also provides several constantly updated newswires; tracking reports on stocks that suddenly deviate from their normal trading patterns; voluminous analytical information on tens of thousands of companies; and much more.

During business hours, DJN/R charges a high $117 an hour, plus $1.14 for every 1,000 characters accessed. If you can wait until after 6 P.M., however, the rate plunges to $9 an hour plus 30 cents for every 1,000 characters accessed. There's even a flat fee plan of $29.95 a month if you restrict your calls to between 8 P.M. and 6 A.M. and access only the more popular features. For more information about this excellent service, see Chapter 14, *Tools for Businesspeople*.

Internet

The largest online system in the world, Internet isn't a centralized service, but rather a sprawling conglomeration of more than 500,000 computers spread out across over 100 countries. These linked-up computers typically reside in government offices, universities, and corporate R&D departments, because the system (which, in the U.S., is funded by the Federal government) has traditionally been dedicated to scientists, educators, and researchers. However, Internet is becoming increasingly commercialized, and may soon be an important tool for business.

Internet's most popular feature is its electronic mail system, which allows you to reach millions of people around the world cheaply and instantaneously. Further, many online services offer a two-way gateway to Internet's e-mail, which means you can trade messages with modem users on a wide variety of services through Internet.

In addition, Internet provides dynamic discussion areas covering just about every subject you can imagine; thousands of data and program files you can download for free; and gateways into other online reference systems, such as DIALOG and NEXIS.

Internet has some hassles associated with it, though. First, it's not easy to learn or use. Two items that can help in this regard are the 96-page booklet *Zen and the Art of the Internet* by Brandon P. Kehoelearning, which can be ordered through the system by sending a message to "ftp.cs.widener.edu;" and an educational comic book from the California Education and Research Federation, which can also be ordered through Internet. In addition, software may soon become available that greatly simplifies navigating the system.

Another hassle is that it's difficult to join Internet if you don't belong to a university or corporation. It *is* possible, though; to learn more, contact InterNIC, a nonprofit information clearinghouse that will send you a free packet identifying the companies or institutions providing Internet access in your area.

Alternatively, you can join Delphi, the inexpensive online service mentioned previously, which provides a gateway to *all* the features on Internet

The information we need is not available. The information we want is not what we need. The information we have is not what we want.

—John Peer

We don't care. We don't have to. We're the phone company.

—Ernestine (Lily Tomlin)

Many are called, but few are called back.

—Sister Mary Tricky

(as opposed to just e-mail). Delphi is currently the only popular service to offer such a gateway, but it's likely other services will soon follow suit.

Because of its history of being difficult to join and use, many people think of Internet as an arcane system for techies. However, that's rapidly changing, and the system is undergoing explosive growth. In fact, Vice President Al Gore has stated Internet should form the foundation of a "national data highway" that reaches into high-tech homes and businesses, and eventually deliver not only programs and text, but digitized video and sound. Whether that day comes or not, the system is advanced enough to make it well worth exploring right now.

Reference Books

This chapter has only touched on what's available online. For more information, I recommend you pick up some books devoted to telecommunications services.

The best and most comprehensive reference is the *Gale Directory of Databases, Volume 1: Online Databases* from Gale Research. This 1,300-page tome furnishes detailed information on every significant database available via modem, as well as complete lists of the databases offered on each service. It comes out twice a year, along with a companion volume covering CD-ROMs titled *Gale Directory of Databases, Volume 2: CD-ROM, Diskette, Magnetic Tape, Handheld, and Batch Access Database Products*. The price for the two-volume, biannual book set is $300, while a subscription to *Volume I* alone is $210.

If you'd prefer a more informal approach, *Dvorak's Guide to PC Telecommunications, Second Edition* by John Dvorak and Nick Anis gives you nitty-gritty advice on a wide range of topics, including how to install your modem and telecommunications software, which online services are most useful, and even how to run your own BBS. This 1,100-page book also supplies a disk containing useful shareware (including the Telix SE program recommended earlier in this chapter), and has hundreds of dollars worth of discount coupons. It's published by Osborne/McGraw-Hill, and costs $39.95.

Finally, you may find it helpful to read books devoted to particular online services you're interested in. These dedicated references vary wildly in quality, but a reliable rule of thumb is that you won't go wrong with anything written by Alfred Glossbrenner or Stephen Manes.

Now go out and buy that modem.

Product Information

Note: Version numbers and prices may have changed by the time you read this.

America Online, Inc.
8619 Westwood Center Drive
Vienna, VA 22182
(800) 827-6364; (703) 448-8700
Fax: (703) 883-1509

Charges flat rate of $9.95 a month for five hours of use, and $3.50 an hour for additional use

BIX (Byte Information Exchange)
General Videotex Corporation
One Phoenix Mill Lane
Petersborough, NH 03458
(800) 227-2983; (603) 924-7681
Fax: (603) 924-2530

Charges $13 a month for membership, plus $3 an hour during off-peak hours (6 P.M. to 7 A.M. your local time, and weekends) or $9 an hour during business hours (7 A.M. to 6 P.M. your local time). Alternative off-peak hour plan charges (on top of the $13 a month) $20 a month for the first 20 hours of use, and then an hourly rate of $1.80 an hour; the business hour rate remains $9 an hour.

BRS Online Products
InfoPro Technologies
8000 Westpark Drive
McLean, VA 22102
(800) 955-0906; (703) 442-0900
Fax: (703) 893-0490

BRS/After Dark online service: $80 one-time fee, plus minimum charge of $12 a month, plus additional charges depending on the databases you access (ranging from $10 to $50 an hour) and number of searches you conduct. This service is available only from 6 P.M. your time to 4 A.M. Eastern time, and most of the weekend; and doesn't allow access to all the databases BRS Search Service does.

BRS (online) Search Service: Typically, $45 to $75 an hour (depending on the databases you access), plus additional charges for the text you retrieve, plus an $80 annual subscription fee; call for more information

CompuServe Information Service
5000 Arlington Center
Columbus, OH 43220
(800) 848-8199; (614) 457-0802
Fax: (614) 457-8149

Standard membership costs $8.95 a month and $8 an hour, and includes free access to about 35 basic services. Alternative "pay as you go" plan costs $2.50 a month and $12.80 an hour.

WinCIM 1.0: List Price, $25 (which is refunded via a $25 usage credit); generally not discounted

Datastorm Technologies
P.O. Box 1471
3212 Lemone Blvd.
Columbia, MO 65205
(314) 443-3282
Fax: (314) 875-0595

Procomm Plus 2.01 for DOS: List Price, $129; Street Price, about $69

Procomm Plus 1.02 for Windows: List Price, $179; Street Price, about $99

Delphi
General Videotex Corporation
1030 Massachusetts Avenue
Cambridge, MA 02138-5302
(800) 695-4005; (617) 491-3393
Fax: N/A

Flat rate of $10 an hour a month for four hours of use, and $4 an hour for additional use. Also offers alternative plan of $20 a month for 20 hours of use, and $1.80 an hour for additional use. If you dial in using SprintNet or Tymet (which is typical for anyone living outside of Massachusetts), there's a $9 surcharge for use during business hours.

deltaComm Development
P.O. Box 1185
Cary, NC 27512-1185
(800) 859-8000; (919) 460-4556
Fax: (919) 460-4531

Telix SE 3.21: List Price, $51 ($39 without printed manual); generally not discounted

DIALOG Information Services, Inc.
3460 Hillview Avenue
Palo Alto, CA 94304
(800) 334-2564; (415) 858-3785
Fax: (415) 858-7069

Charges $295 for signup fee (which includes classroom or videotape training, and $100 worth of connect time), $75 for annual subscription fee, and from $1 to $300 an hour depending on the database you're accessing.

Alternatively, during off-peak hours (6 P.M. to 5 A.M., and weekends) you can use Knowledge Index for $24 an hour through CompuServe.

Dow Jones News/Retrieval
Dow Jones & Company, Inc.
P.O. Box 300
Princeton, NJ 08543-0300
(800) 522-3567; (609) 520-4000
Fax: (609) 520-4775

During off-peak hours (6 P.M. to 6 A.M., and weekends), $9 an hour plus 30 cents for every 1,000 characters accessed; during business hours (6 A.M. to 6 P.M.), $117 an hour plus $1.14 for every 1,000 characters accessed. Additionally requires fees of $29.95 for signup and $18 for annual subscription. Flat fee plan of $29.95 a month (for use between 8 P.M. and 6 A.M. and on weekends) also available; call for details.

Gale Research
835 Penobscot Building
Detroit, MI 48226
(800) 877-4253; (313) 961-2242
Fax: (313) 961-6083

Gale Directory of Databases, Volume 1: Online Databases and Gale Directory of Databases, Volume 2: CD-ROM, Diskette, Magnetic Tape, Handheld, and Batch Access Database Products: List Price, $300 for the two-volume biannual book set, $210 for *Volume I* alone; generally not discounted

GEnie Information Services
401 North Washington Street
Rockville, MD 20850
(800) 638-9636; (301) 251-6475
Fax: (301) 251-6421

During off-peak hours (6 P.M. to 8 A.M., and weekends), $8.95 a month for your first four hours, and $3 for each additional hour; during business hours, $12.50 an hour

InterNIC
P.O. Box 85608
San Diego, CA 92186-9784
(800) 444-4345; (619) 455-4600
Fax: (619) 455-4640

Ask this nonprofit information clearinghouse for the free packet that
identifies the companies or institutions providing Internet access in your area

MCI Mail
1133 19th Street NW
Washington D.C. 20036
(800) 444-6245; (202) 833-8484
Fax: (202) 416-5858

Charges $35 annual membership fee, plus the following for every message you send: 50
cents for the first 500 characters, 10 cents for next 500, then 10 cents per 1,000
characters up to 10,000 characters, and then 5 cents per 1,000 characters. There's *no*
charge for time spent on the system and for receiving messages.

A Preferred Pricing plan is also available, which lets you send up to 40 messages a
month for a flat fee of $10 a month. Each message can be up to 5,000 characters; text
over 5,000 characters is counted as a new message.

NEXIS
Mead Data Central
9393 Springboro Pike
P.O. Box 933
Dayton, OH 45342
(800) 227-4908; (513) 859-1608
Fax: (513) 865-1666

Charges $43 an hour, plus additional fees per search, plus monthly subscription fee of
$50. A flat-fee option is available for frequent users; call for more information.

NewsNet, Inc.
945 Haverford Road
Bryn Mawr, PA 19010
(800) 345-1301; (215) 527-8030
Fax: (516) 527-0338

Charges a $79.95 signup fee, plus $15 a month, plus $90 an hour, plus $60
to $300 an hour for reading full-text articles

Osborne/McGraw-Hill
2600 Tenth Street
Berkeley, CA 94710
(800) 227-0900; (510) 549-2805
Fax: (510) 549-6603

Dvorak's Guide to PC Telecommunications, Second Edition: List Price, $39.95; generally not discounted

Ozarks West Software
Steve Sneed
14150 Gleneagle Drive
Colorado Springs, CO 80921
CompuServe mailbox 70007,3574
Fax: (719) 260-7151

OzCIS 2.0: List Price, $40 ($30 without printed documentation); generally not discounted

Practical Peripherals, Inc.
(Subsidiary of Hayes Microcomputer Products, Inc.)
375 Conejo Ridge Avenue
Thousand Oaks, CA 91361
(800) 442-4774; (805) 497-4774
Fax: (805) 374-7200

Sells a variety of quality modems at low prices; call for details

Prodigy Services Company
445 Hamilton Avenue
White Plains, NY 10601
(800) 776-3449
Fax: N/A

Flat fee of $14.95 a month covers virtually all services. Exceptions are about a dozen special sections, most of which involve interactive games; and electronic mail, which costs 25 cents per message after you've used your allotment of 30 messages per month. Available seven days a week, 21 hours a day (the service closes for maintenance between 4 A.M. and 7 A.M. Eastern time daily).

U.S. Robotics, Inc.
8100 North McCormick Blvd.
Skokie, IL 60076-2920
(800) 342-5877; (708) 982-5010
Fax: (708) 982-5235

Sells a variety of quality modems at low prices, such as the internal U.S. Robotics Sportster 14,400/PC Fax (Street Price, about $180); call for details

Zoom Telephonics, Inc.
207 South Street
Boston, MA 02111
(800) 631-3116; (617) 423-1072
Fax: (617) 423-9231

Sells a variety of quality modems at low prices; call for details

PART V

HANDLING SPECIALIZED
WRITING TASKS

Contrary to general belief, writing isn't something that only "writers" do; writing is a basic skill for getting through life.... Writing isn't a special language that belongs to English teachers and a few other sensitive souls who have a "gift for words." Writing is thinking on paper. Anyone who thinks clearly should be able to write clearly—about any subject at all.

—William Zinsser

There are no dull subjects; there are only dull writers.

—H. L. Mencken

CHAPTER

11

TOOLS FOR NEWSPAPER, MAGAZINE, AND BOOK WRITERS

What! Another of those damned, fat, square, thick books! Always scribble, scribble, scribble, eh, Mr. Gibbon?

    —The Duke of Gloucester, on being presented a copy of Volume III of *The Decline and Fall of the Roman Empire*

This chapter is a little different, because the tools for newspaper, magazine, and book writers are actually sprinkled throughout this entire book. As a result, I'm not going to discuss new products here. Instead, I'll be pointing out the software covered in other chapters that are of particular interest to professional writers, and explain why they merit your attention.

Further, I'll be getting somewhat personal, because I began my career working as a journalist (for the now-defunct National News Council), then moved into magazine freelancing (albeit for unusual publications, such as *Mad* and *Spy*), and finally got into writing the sort of thing you're holding in your hands. Since this chapter hits close to home, I'll be letting you know what *I* use, and share some less than objective opinions.

Let's get to it.

Word Processors

XyWrite.

XyWrite, XyWrite, XyWrite.

While I tried to keep it under control in Chapter 1, *Choosing a Word Processor*, I'm really a *fanatic* about XyWrite for DOS. I spend more than 70 percent of my PC time in the program (even taking into account my game-playing time).

If you're working for a newspaper or magazine using the Atex system, no more need be said, because XyWrite is a PC version of Atex. Otherwise, the main reasons for my fervor are speed, flexibility, simplicity, and power. But mostly speed.

When you're rushing to meet a deadline, you don't want anything to distract you from pumping words into your machine. XyWrite (unlike Windows word processors) never has any trouble keeping up with my typing. It's also blindingly fast at executing searches, finding the phrase I need almost as soon as I press Enter. Its excellent built-in spelling checker and thesaurus are equally quick. And on my 386 PC, it stores a chapter like this one to disk in under a second, so I don't even hesitate to save my document every few minutes. As a result, though my machine crashes as frequently as anyone else's, I never lose much of my work.

When I want to read a good book, I write one.
    —Benjamin Disraeli

XyWrite expedites things even more by allowing you to ignore menus and do everything using either two-letter commands, or single keystrokes you've programmed into its uniquely pliable software keyboard system. For example, I've assigned single keystrokes to perform such functions as saving my current document, printing my document, switching me to one of several frequently used directories, listing my files in an alphabetically ordered text window (which is editable, and so great for batch file creation), and deleting the file at my cursor position. (In fact, I perform a number of file operations from XyWrite instead of the DOS prompt, because it's faster that way.) Programs such as WordPerfect also let you assign shortcut keystrokes for operations, but they don't approach XyWrite's flexibility.

Yet another nice aspect of the product is that it's ideal for laptop use. While it's as powerful as WordPerfect, its essential files require less than 3MB of disk space. Also, XyWrite's software "engine" loads itself entirely in memory, so the program seldom needs to access your hard disk. This not only makes XyWrite operate even faster, but helps extend the life of your laptop's battery, which is important if you're a journalist on the run. XyWrite even saves its files in a form of ASCII, which means its documents can easily be exchanged with others or sent across phone lines as electronic mail.

As I noted in Chapter 1, some find XyWrite hard to learn; and it virtually *requires* you to impose your own design decisions on it. Also, it enjoys nowhere near the training support that exists for WordPerfect or Microsoft Word. However, if you don't need much hand-holding, and you aren't entirely satisfied with your current word processor, check out XyWrite. It may turn out to be the program you've been looking for all along.

Writing is like prostitution. First you do it for love, then for a few friends, and finally for money.
—Moliere

The two most beautiful words in the English language are "Check enclosed."
—Dorothy Parker

Marry money.
—Max Schulman,
providing advice to aspiring writers

Composing and Editing Tools

It's a standard joke that the question most often asked pro writers is "Where do you get your ideas?" Answer #1: "From a small suburb in Cincinnati. I subscribe for $3,500, and every week the service sends me two ideas. I'd be a bum without it." Answer #2 (from columnist William F. Buckley): "The world irritates me three times a week."

Actually, some writers are just naturally bursting with ideas; so many that if they *weren't* writers, they'd probably explode. But there are also those unfortunate few—like me, for instance—who can use any help they can get. If you're in this latter group, some mind ticklers worth exploring are IdeaFisher and Inside Information, both of which offer large collections of related words; and Babble!, which reads in your text, optionally combines it with the text of other writers of your choosing, and slings out strange new sentences. IdeaFisher and Babble! are covered in Chapter 3, *Idea Generators*; and Inside Information is covered in Chapter 5, *Electronic Dictionaries and Thesauruses*.

There are three rules for writing the novel.
Unfortunately, no one knows what they are.

—W. Somerset Maugham

Once you've started writing, you'll want software that can swiftly provide you with synonyms and definitions for your words. The program that's best at both tasks is the excellent, inexpensive Random House Webster's Electronic Dictionary & Thesaurus, College Edition. Even if you think you're getting by fine with a paperback dictionary, give RHWEDT a try. My guess is that you'll quickly get hooked on it.

Everything goes by the board: honor, pride, decency…to get the book written. If a writer has to rob his mother, he will not hesitate; the Ode on a Grecian Urn *is worth any number of old ladies.*

—William Faulkner

If you can risk getting sucked into hours of idle browsing, an even more impressive reference source is the Oxford English Dictionary (Second Edition) on CD-ROM. It's not quite as fast as RHWEDT, since it has up to 60 million words to search through; and at $895, it's not a casual purchase. However, if you love words, and you have lots of time on your hands, nothing else touches this product. Both the RHWEDT and the OED are covered in Chapter 5, *Electronic Dictionaries and Thesauruses.*

Another program for word lovers is WordPerfect Rhymer, which will read the word at your cursor position and generate first syllable rhymes, last syllable rhymes, first and last *sound* rhymes (which encompass a broader range than syllable rhymes), double and triple rhymes, and so on. While this superb tool is of most interest to poets, it's useful to any writer who cares about such things as rhythm, assonance, and alliteration. A complete description of it appears in Chapter 13, *Tools for Poets.*

If your craft is under control, you probably do *not* have to bother getting a grammar checker. Despite continuing improvement, these programs are still stupid enough to be more irritating than helpful to most professional writers. However, if you're a patient soul, the best of the breed is Grammatik 5, which provides both suggestions and interesting statistical data about your work.

For even more statistical info, you should check out the unique Corporate Voice. Despite its name, this program can help you target new magazines, or break into diverse book markets, or ghost for established authors. That's because, using 25 statistical measures and 17 types of graphs, it can guide you in duplicating the style of any writing sample you feed into it. If you consider the success Alexandra (*Scarlett*) Ripley garnered from cloning Margaret Mitchell's style, you'll begin to see the possibilities. More information on both Grammatik 5 and Corporate Voice is in Chapter 6, *Grammar and Style Checkers*.

Reference Tools

There are a number of disk-based references, but for me the sentimental favorite is Microlytics' The Elements of Style, Electronic Edition, based on the classic book by William Strunk and E. B. White. Even when I don't agree with the authors, I always admire how well they state their opinions. For example, on the topic of writing naturally:

> The use of language begins with imitation. The infant imitates the sounds made by its parents; the child imitates first the spoken language, then the stuff of books. The imitative life continues long after the writer is on his own in the language, for it is almost impossible to avoid imitating what one admires. Never imitate consciously, but do not worry about being an imitator; take pains instead to admire what is good.

The first thing to look out for after your first big success are drugs and screenplays.
                    —Richard Price

This is a work brimming with style, insight, and attitude. If you're still shaky on some aspects of writing, you'll appreciate its great tips and clear examples on rules of usage, principles of form, and commonly misused words and expressions. And if you're an old pro, you'll want this product for its inspirational value alone. More information on it—and on other electronic writing guides—can be found in Chapter 8, *Disk-Based References*.

On Journalism

Journalism is literature in a hurry.

—Matthew Arnold

I can write better than anybody who can write faster, and I can write faster than anybody who can write better.

—A. J. Liebling

The art of newspaper paragraphing is to stroke a platitude until it purrs like an epigram.

—Don Marquis

The difference between journalism and literature is that journalism is unreadable and literature is not read.

—Oscar Wilde

Every journalist has a novel in him, which is an excellent place for it.

—Russell Lynes

It is only fair to state, with regard to modern journalists, that they always apologize to one in private for what they have written against one in public.

—Oscar Wilde

Modern journalism, by giving us the opinions of the uneducated, keeps us in touch with the ignorance of the community.

—Oscar Wilde

Enquiring minds want to know.

— *The National Enquirer*

Journalism consists in buying white paper at 2 cents a pound and selling it at 10 cents a pound.

—Charles A. Dana

Never argue with people who buy ink by the gallon.

—Tommy Lasorda

For comprehensive information on a subject, you'll want to turn to CD-ROMs and online databases, which let you rapidly search through the text of dozens of major newspapers and magazines, plumb data from such fundamental reference works as *Books In Print* and *Literary Marketplace*, and access a mind-boggling array of other sources. There's too much of interest to note here, but you can get the details in Chapter 9, *CD-ROM References*, and Chapter 10, *Online References*.

Aside from formal research, though, you really ought to join an online service to hang out with your peers. My favorite writers' haunt is GEnie's SFRT (Science Fiction Roundtable), where you can find some of the sharpest minds in genre literature, including such luminaries as Neil Gaiman, Damon Knight, Judy Tarr, Peter David, Janna Silverstein, Adam-Troy Castro, and Lois Tilton (to name but a few). Editors from book publishers such as Bantam, Tor, and Ace, and from magazines such as *Fantasy & Science Fiction*, also take time out to schmooze there.

If SF/fantasy/horror isn't your thing, both GEnie and CompuServe offer sections devoted to other branches of writing, such as general nonfiction, technical books, romance novels, movies and television, and comic books. The quality of a section depends primarily on who happens to be frequenting it during a given period; for example, at the time of this writing, Roger Ebert is a regular visitor to CompuServe's ShowBiz forum, making that section rather special. Poke around, and see what you can see. While chatting in these forums can be awfully time-consuming, there are few more effective ways of obtaining writing tips, picking up valuable business news, or making some new friends.

Other Tools

Most writers simply write, and allow the production aspects of their work to be taken care of by others. However, an increasing number of us are exploring the joys and terrors of self-publishing. That's due in no small measure to advances in desktop publishing software, which allow even neophytes to create aesthetically pleasing pages.

For simple projects, such as a newsletter or a short book, you'll find Microsoft Publisher for Windows inexpensive, easy to learn, and very effective. For more complicated jobs, such as creating a magazine, products like QuarkXPress for Windows are your best choice. More information about both low-end and high-end DTP packages appears in Chapter 22, *Laying Out Your Work*. Also, if you need to deal with a variety of electronic graphics, you should read about Hijaak for Windows in Chapter 21, *Converting File Formats*.

William Faulkner 1949 Nobel Prize Acceptance Speech

I feel that this award was not made to me as a man, but to my work—a life's work in the agony and sweat of the human spirit, not for glory and least of all for profit, but to create out of the materials of the human spirit something which did not exist before. So this award is only mine in trust. It will not be difficult to find a dedication for the money part of it commensurate with the purpose and significance of its origin. But I would like to do the same with the acclaim too, by using this moment as a pinnacle from which I might be listened to by the young men and women already dedicated to the same anguish and travail, among whom is already that one who will someday stand here where I am standing.

Our tragedy today is a general and universal physical fear so long sustained by now that we can even bear it. There are no longer problems of the spirit. There is only the question: When will I be blown up? Because of this, the young man or woman writing today has forgotten the problems of the human heart in conflict with itself which alone can make good writing, because only that is worth writing about, worth the agony and the sweat. He must learn them again. He must teach himself that the basest of all things is to be afraid; and, teaching himself that, forget it forever, leaving no room in his workshop for anything but the old verities and truths of the heart, the old universal truths lacking which any story is ephemeral and doomed—love and honor and pity and pride and compassion and sacrifice. Until he does so, he labors under a curse. He writes not of love but of lust, of defeats in which nobody loses anything of value, of victories without hope, and, worst of all, without pity or compassion. His griefs grieve on no universal bones, leaving no scars. He writes not of the heart but of the glands.

Until he relearns these things, he will write as though he stood among and watched the end of man. I decline to accept the end of man. It is easy enough to say that man is immortal simply because he will endure; that when the last ding-dong of doom has clanged and faded from the last worthless rock hanging tideless in the last red and dying evening, that even then there will still be one more sound: that of his puny inexhaustible voice, still talking. I refuse to accept this. I believe that man will not merely endure: He will prevail. He is immortal, not because he alone among creatures has an inexhaustible voice, but because he has a soul, a spirit capable of compassion and sacrifice and endurance. The poet's, the writer's, duty is to write about these things. It is his privilege to help man endure by lifting his heart, by reminding him of the courage and honor and hope and pride and compassion and pity and sacrifice which have been the glory of the past. The poet's voice need not merely be the record of man; it can be one of the props, the pillars, to help him endure and prevail.

One problem with doing large projects and messing with graphics files is that they eat up a lot of hard disk space. If you start feeling squeezed, don't hesitate to install Stacker, a miraculous piece of software that typically doubles the room available on your drive. Information on Stacker, plus other useful PC utilities, is located in Chapter 20, *Essential General-Purpose Tools*.

Finally, if you ever decide to take a sabbatical from the noble realm of print and go for the megabucks, the best program for writing a screenplay is Scriptware. This is a very thoughtfully designed package that enormously reduces the hassles involved with script formatting, and is so superior to everything else on the market that it's practically revolutionary. For a detailed description of Scriptware, see Chapter 12, *Tools for Movie, Television, and Theatre Writers*.

Product Information

Note: Version numbers and prices may have changed by the time you read this.

Cinovation, Inc.
204 West 20th Street
Suite 37
New York, NY 10011
(800) 788-7090; (212) 924-4495
Fax: (212) 924-1005

Scriptware 1.2: List Price, $299; via The Write Stuff coupon near the back of this book, $259, with Linda Seger's *Making a Good Script Great* and Rick Reichman's *Formatting Your Screenplay* thrown in. Supports screenplay, sitcom, and stage play formats; copy protected via software.

CompuServe Information Service
5000 Arlington Center
Columbus, OH 43220
(800) 848-8199; (614) 457-0802
Fax: (614) 457-8149

Standard membership costs $8.95 a month and $8 an hour, and includes free access to about 35 basic services. Alternative "pay as you go" plan costs $2.50 a month and $12.80 an hour.

IdeaFisher Systems
2222 Martin Street
Suite 110
Irvine, CA 92715
(800) 289-4332; (714) 474-8111
Fax: (714) 757-2896

IdeaFisher 4.0: List Price, $199; via coupon near the back of this book, $99

GEnie Information Services
401 North Washington Street
Rockville, MD 20850
(800) 638-9636; (301) 251-6475
Fax: (301) 251-6421

During off-peak hours (6 P.M. to 8 A.M., and weekends), $8.95 a month for your first four hours, and $3 for each additional hour; during business hours, $12.50 an hour

Inset Systems
71 Commerce Drive
Brookfield, CT 06804-3405
(800) 374-6738; (203) 740-2400
Fax: (203) 775-5634

HiJaak 2.0 for Windows: List Price, $169; Street Price, about $85

Korenthal Associates, Inc.
511 Avenue of the Americas, #400
New York, NY 10011
(800) 527-7647; (212) 242-1790
Fax: (212) 242-2599

Babble! 2.0: List Price, $35; via coupon near the back of this book, $25

Microlytics, Inc.
2 Tobey Village Office Park
Pittsford, NY 14534
(800) 828-6293; (716) 248-9150
Fax: (716) 248-3868

Inside Information 1.0: List Price, $49.95; Street Price, about $35 (direct from Microlytics during discount periods)

The Elements of Style, Electronic Edition 1.0: List Price, $29.95; Street Price, about $25 (direct from Microlytics during discount periods)

Microsoft Corporation
One Microsoft Way
Redmond, WA 98052
(800) 426-9400; (206) 882-8080
Fax: No generic sales or information fax number

Microsoft Publisher 2.0 for Windows: List Price, $139; Street Price, about $89

Oxford University Press
200 Madison Avenue
New York, NY 10016
(800) 334-4249, ext. 7370; (212) 679-7300, ext. 7370
Fax: (212) 725-2972

The Oxford English Dictionary (Second Edition) on CD-ROM (for Windows): List Price, $895; generally not discounted

Quark, Inc.
1800 Grant Street
Denver, CO 80203
(800) 788-7835; (303) 894-8888
Fax: (303) 343-2086

QuarkXPress 3.2 for Windows: List Price, $895; Street Price, about $549

Scandinavian PC Systems
P.O. Box 3156
Baton Rouge, LA 70821-3156
(800) 487-7727; (504) 338-9580
Fax: (504) 338-9670

Corporate Voice 1.0: List Price, $249.95; generally not discounted; via coupon near the back of this book, $125

Corporate Voice ProStyles Volume 1 (over 50 writing styles, ranging from Andy Warhol and "Arabian Knights" to Walt Whitman and *Woman's Day*, that can be plugged into Corporate Voice): List Price, $19.95; generally not discounted

Stac Electronics
5993 Avenida Encinas
Carlsbad, CA 92008
(800) 522-7822; (619) 431-7474
Fax: (619) 431-9616

Stacker 3.0: List Price, $149; Street Price, about $85

Stacker AT/16 2.0: List Price, $249; Street Price, about $185

The Technology Group
36 South Charles Street
Suite 2200
Baltimore, MD 21201
(410) 576-2040
Fax: (410) 576-1968

XyWrite 4.0 for DOS: List Price, $495; via coupon near the back of this book, $149

WordPerfect Corporation
1555 N. Technology Way
Orem, UT 84057
(800) 321-4566; (801) 225-5000
Fax: (801) 228-5377

Rhymer 1.0 (for DOS): List Price, $89; generally not discounted

Grammatik 5 for DOS: List Price, $99; Street Price, about $55

Grammatik 5 for Windows: List Price, $99; Street Price, about $55

Random House Webster's Electronic Dictionary & Thesaurus, College Edition 1.0 for DOS: List Price, $99; Street Price, about $55

Random House Webster's Electronic Dictionary & Thesaurus, College Edition 1.0 for Windows: List Price, $99; Street Price, about $55

CHAPTER

12

TOOLS FOR MOVIE, TELEVISION, AND THEATRE WRITERS

*If you can tune into the fantasy life of an 11-year-old
girl, you can make a fortune in this business.*

—George Lucas

*Whom God wishes to destroy, He first makes
successful in show business.*

—Francis Ford Coppola

You have to have a talent for having talent.

—Ruth Gordon

Scripting is one of the most exacting forms of writing. It forces you to keep in mind a slew of formatting conventions, and to set up the same formats (such as margin settings for character names, and dialogue, and action) over and over again. Because of its complexity and mechanical repetitiveness, the chore of scripting cries out for automation via a solid software package.

It's taken awhile, because the market for scripting programs is so much smaller than the one for general-purpose word processors. However, the need has finally been answered by a terrific new standalone program called Scriptware, as well as by a more modest product called SuperScript Pro that works in conjunction with WordPerfect. This chapter describes these two packages, as well as their competition: ScriptPerfection, The Warren Script Applications, Movie Master, and Scriptor. In addition, it briefly discusses pertinent software tools that are covered in depth in other chapters (such as Plots Unlimited, Collaborator II, and Cinemania); and supplementary resources such as online services, books, and the Guild.

Evaluating Scriptwriting Programs

A typical movie script looks something like this:

CHARACTER NAME (V.O.)

(continuing)

Dialogue dialogue dialogue dialogue
dialogue dialogue dialogue dialogue
dialogue dialogue, y'know?

CUT TO:

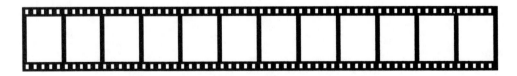

INT. SAMPLE LOCALE - DAY

Velma enters, stares intently at Character Name, and then slaps him in the face to stop his meaningless babbling.

This sample, short as it is, contains most of the basic elements used in real scripts. These elements are:

- Character Name: The name of the character currently speaking, set in all caps and on a margin near the center of the page.

- Dialogue: What a character says, appearing below the character name and a bit to the left of it.

- Transition: A directive such as FADE IN:, CUT TO:, DISSOLVE TO:, or FADE OUT: that indicates a new shot. The transition margin is near the right side of the page.

- Scene Heading: Typically, a line that starts with INT. or EXT., is set in all caps, and indicates the place and time of day the scene occurs. The scene heading margin is near the left side of the page. This element is also referred to as a *slugline*.

- Action: Descriptions of character behavior, scenery, and so on. The action margin is usually the same as the scene heading margin.

- Parenthetical: An aside to the scriptreader, such as "(V.O.)" to indicate a voiceover, or "(continuing)" to indicate a character's dialogue that was interrupted by an action description is now picking up where it left off. A parenthetical typically appears directly to the right of the character name (where it's also called an *extension*); or directly below the name, which is typical for actor directions, such as "(talking rapidly)".

There are other script elements (for example, act headings); and the formatting for stage plays uses a different margin scheme. Still, the six items above encompass over 90 percent of any script. A useful scriptwriting program will therefore make it as easy as possible to enter each of these elements.

You write a hit play the same way you write a flop.
—William Saroyan

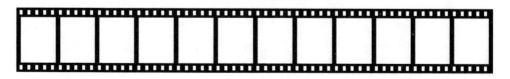

In addition, a good program should be able to lay out your script accurately and attractively. For example, it should be smart enough to create page breaks without separating elements that belong together (such as a character name and initial dialogue). It should also be able to quickly add elements, such as customized page numbers, or scene numbers, or "(CONTINUED)" lines at the bottom of every page.

Further, your software should support all the formats you're likely to need. Every program covered in this chapter lets you create screenplays; most also provide settings for TV sitcoms and stage plays. The supported formats for each package are listed at the end of this chapter.

Lastly, all things being equal, it's always preferable to buy software that's not copy protected, as explained in the section on copy protection in the Introduction. Unfortunately, the scripting market has a tradition of treating its customers with suspicion, so virtually all its products *are* copy protected. (In fact, the only unprotected scripting software covered in this chapter is The Warren Script Applications; and that's got *other* problems.) If you need the programs, you're stuck with this hassle; but be sure to complain long and often to the software publishers taking your money, until they join the rest of the civilized world and drop copy protection from their products.

A dramatic writer should never tell anything he can show.
—Nunnally Johnson

If you're going to tell people the truth, make them laugh, or they'll kill you.
—Billy Wilder

Don't use your conscious past. Use your creative imagination to create a past that belongs to your characters.
—Stella Adler

If all that's going on in your scenes is what's going on in your scenes, think about it for a long time.
—William Goldman

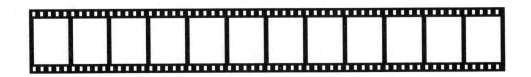

Scriptware

Cinovation's new Scriptware is the best tool available for scriptwriting, period. Nothing else matches its smarts, its intuitiveness, its flexibility, and its power.

Scriptware is a great example of "less is more." While it provides a full range of menu options and mouse support, its basic operation is centered around two keys—Tab and Enter. The program can boil things down to this extent because it's smart enough to guess what you want to do next, based on where you currently are in your script. More specifically, the program's designers, Steve Sashen and Stuart Greenberg, fully exploit the fact that the elements of a script have consistent relationships both to document margins and to each other.

For example, if you're on the left margin of a film script and type *int.* or *ext.*, Scriptware immediately understands you want to enter a scene heading, and so sets everything in your paragraph to uppercase. When you end the heading by pressing Enter, it returns you to normal upper- and lower-case typing so you can write action descriptions.

When you're done with action and are ready for dialogue, simply press Tab. Scriptware knows that the element appearing to the right of action is usually a character name, and so moves you to the character name margin. (If what you really wanted to do was insert a CUT TO:, though, pressing Tab one more time would push you over to the transition margin.)

You call this a script? Give me a couple of
$5,000-a-week writers and I'll write it myself.
          —Movie producer Joe Pasternak
Days off.
—Spencer Tracy, on what he looks for in a script

Disney, of course, has the best casting. If he doesn't
like an actor, he just tears him up.
          —Alfred Hitchcock
Television is a medium because anything well
done is rare.
          —Fred Allen

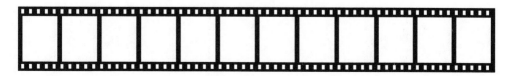

After placing you at the character name margin, Scriptware automatically pops up a "cast box" listing the names of the characters you've already used in your script. You can insert any listed name by simply typing its first letter (or first few letters, if more than one name has the same initial letter). Alternatively, you can select a listed name directly with your arrow keys or mouse. The cast box therefore spares you the tedium of typing the same names over and over.

On the other hand, if you want to enter a new name, just type it in. In addition to being inserted into your script (in all caps, even if you didn't bother typing in uppercase), the name is automatically added to the cast box so you can quickly select it the next time you need it.

Once your character name is in place, you have several options: you can enter a parenthetical direction to its right (which is also referred to as an *extension*); a parenthetical direction directly below it; or go straight into dialogue.

To enter an extension, you simply press Tab again. Scriptware knows you must want a parenthetical, and so inserts a set of parentheses for you to type in. In addition, it pops up an extension box containing the directions "v.o." (for voiceover) and "o.s." (for off-screen). As with character names, you can choose one of the box entries by typing its first letter, or selecting it with your arrow keys or mouse. Alternatively, you can type a new direction, which will automatically be added to the extension box for future selection.

Similarly, to enter a parenthetical below the character name, press Enter and Tab. This instantly places you on the appropriate margin, and inserts a set of parentheses in which you can type your direction (typically, some helpful hint to the actor, like "sighing impatiently" or "raging helplessly").

Imitation is the sincerest form of television.
—Fred Allen

I don't want to achieve immortality through my work. I want to achieve it by not dying.
—Woody Allen

When you're done with any parentheticals and are ready to enter dialogue—yep, you guessed it—just press Enter. This moves you immediately to the dialogue margin. All the talk you subsequently type stays within the dialogue margins established for the particular format you've selected—the possibilities being film, standard TV sitcom, alternate TV format, play, two-column A/V (for video projects), or a custom format of your own design.

Finally, when you've completed your dialogue, simply press Enter again. You're automatically moved back to the action margin...where you can begin a new cycle of typing.

The automated steps just described will by themselves save you *enormous* amounts of time and effort. However, Scriptware doesn't stop there.

Unlike most of its competitors, Scriptware always accurately shows you where each page ends, or *breaks* (via thin lines across the screen). This means that when you add or remove text in the middle of your script, the program automatically reformats all subsequent pages, allowing you to immediately see the new page breaks created by your changes. Similarly, if you widen your margins, or add a line to your header, or make any other kind of change, the program quickly displays the effects of your revisions on-screen.

Scriptware can also perform such clever functions as automatically spilling dialogue from the bottom of a page over to the next page, by repeating the character's name at the top of the next page and inserting a parenthetical "(cont'd)" beneath the name. (In addition, it lets you set such factors as whether to split dialogue only after two or more lines; whether to split the dialogue only at the ends of sentences; whether to add a "(more)" to the bottom of the page where the dialogue begins; and, for that matter, whether you want to allow dialogue splitting at all.)

Good evening, ladies and gentlemen—and welcome to darkest Hollywood. Night brings a stillness to the jungle. It is so quiet you can hear a name drop. The savage beasts have already begun gathering at the water holes to quench their thirst. Now one should be especially alert. The vicious table-hopper is on the prowl, and the spotted back-biter may lurk behind a potted palm.

—Alfred Hitchcock

As another example of Scriptware's smarts: If you have a character named Bob talking, then interrupt him with an action paragraph, and then start up his dialogue again, the program will notice what's going on and automatically insert a "(continuing)" under the second appearance of Bob's name. Further, if you later remove the first occurrence of Bob's dialogue, the program instantly removes the "(continuing)" from the second occurrence of Bob's dialogue! It's these sorts of automatic actions that make the program seem like an alert assistant, ever-ready to take care of humdrum details.

Along the same lines, it's extremely easy to change your script's formatting. For example, if you've just sold your screenplay and need to switch it from its submission format (which is relatively uncluttered, for ease of reading) to a shooting format (which is filled with such elements as scene numbers and "(CONTINUED)" lines at the bottom of each page), you can do so using only a few keystrokes or mouse clicks; in seconds, your entire script is reformatted, and the changes you've requested appear on-screen. You can similarly adjust the margins for one or more elements throughout your script; or even quickly convert your script into an entirely different format (say, from screenplay to sitcom).

It's a snap for Scriptware to make such changes, because it constantly keeps track of every element of your script. This is made evident by the status line at the bottom of the screen; as you move through your document, the line instantly identifies whether the text you're on is Action, Dialogue, Transition, or some other element. (This status line feature, by the way, is very handy whenever you need to verify that a section of text is formatted properly.)

In Hollywood, writers are considered only the first drafts of human beings.
—Frank Deford

In Hollywood, if you don't have happiness, you send out for it.
—Rex Reed

I don't want any yes-men around me. I want everybody to tell me the truth even if it costs them their jobs.
—Samuel Goldwyn

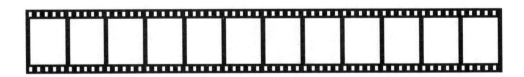

While Scriptware works hard to do things for you, it doesn't *force* anything on you; in fact, it's quite flexible. For example, if you don't want to look at the status line or menu bar, you can turn them off and make the entire screen available for editing text. You can also change other aspects of your display, such as the screen colors, or (if you have an EGA or VGA monitor) the number of lines displayed on your screen.

As for the keyboard: If you're more comfortable using traditional short-cut keystrokes than Scriptware's Tab-Enter procedure, you can press Alt+S or Shift+Enter to start a scene heading, Alt+C or Ctrl+Enter to insert a character name, and so on. And if you don't care for the (fairly intuitive) Scriptware editing keystrokes, you can set the program to accept the keystrokes of WordPerfect or Microsoft Word instead.

There are also nice small touches. For example, to insert a parenthetical, you can choose to press the left parenthesis instead of Tab; and you can exit a pop-up box by pressing the Left Arrow key instead of Enter. Scriptware also provides subtle conveniences; for example, you can use a GoTo command to jump not only to a particular page number, but to a particular *scene* number; and you can insert electronic "notes" in your script, which appear on-screen but won't be printed.

You can even adjust the program's rules for handling script elements. For example, you can set it to move you to a character name margin after you're finished writing dialogue, instead of to the default action margin (useful if you tend to write talk-heavy scenes).

"Hello," he lied.
—Don Carpenter, quoting a Hollywood agent

You can take all the sincerity in Hollywood, place it in the navel of a fruit fly, and still have room enough for three caraway seeds and a producer's heart.
—Fred Allen

Hollywood is a place where they place you under contract instead of under observation.
—Walter Winchell

Another important facet of Scriptware is that when you select Text mode, it operates as a standard word processor, which means that you don't need to buy an additional program for writing memos, letters, and proposals. Scriptware gives you such basic word processing features as a spelling checker, a thesaurus, headers and footers, macros, an outline mode, and the ability to work with multiple documents at the same time.

Scriptware isn't perfect—for example, it lacks an Undo command, and it uses a copy protection scheme that places hidden files on your hard disk—but because it's so far ahead of anything else on the market, its few shortcomings become irrelevant. Scriptware makes writing scripts a pleasure. If you earn your living in film, television, or theatre—or hope to do so shortly—this is the program to buy.

Scriptware's list price is $299. However, using the coupon from mail-order vendor The Write Stuff near the back of this book, you can get the program for $259...and have two superb books, Linda Seger's *Making a Good Script Great* and Rick Reichman's *Formatting Your Screenplay*, thrown in as a bonus.

Hollywood is like being nowhere and talking to nobody about nothing.

—Michelangelo Antonioni

In the picture business, intelligence and taste are to be found only among the office help.

—Joseph Hansen

In California, everyone goes to a therapist, is a therapist, or is a therapist going to a therapist.

—Truman Capote

It's a scientific fact that if you stay in California, you lose one point of your IQ every year.

—Truman Capote

There's nothing wrong with Southern California that a rise in the ocean level wouldn't cure.

—Ross MacDonald

Macro Scripting Packages

While Scriptware is great, it isn't necessarily the right choice for everyone.

For one thing, as just mentioned, it costs about $259. If you plan to write scripts only occasionally and casually, it may not make sense for you to shell out that much for a dedicated script processor.

More important, if you're one of the millions of longtime WordPerfect users, you may not care to switch to another program. Even though Scriptware will accept many WordPerfect keystrokes, it doesn't really look and feel like WordPerfect. In addition, Scriptware lacks the hundreds of special editing, formatting, and printing features (and fabled toll-free technical support) that have made WordPerfect famous.

Similarly, if you're a Microsoft Word user, you may settle for less powerful scripting capabilities to stay within a program you're already comfortable with.

In these cases, you should consider buying a program that plugs into your word processor and works in conjunction with it. Such packages are written in the programming, or *macro*, language of the word processor itself, and typically stay hidden within the program until you invoke them with special keystrokes (say, Ctrl+B to begin an act or scene heading, or Ctrl+C to insert a character name). They also typically cost about half as much as Scriptware does.

There are two macro packages available for WordPerfect—SuperScript Pro and ScriptPerfection—and one for Microsoft Word, The Warren Script Applications. To learn more about these products, read on.

We are drawn to our television sets each April the way we are drawn to the scene of an accident.

—Vincent Canby, on the Academy Awards

Strip away the phony tinsel of Hollywood and you find the real tinsel underneath.

—Oscar Levant

Why don't you come up and see me sometime?

—*She Done Him Wrong* (1933)

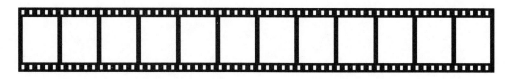

SuperScript Pro

SuperScript Pro, from Inherit the Earth Technologies, is a simple yet elegant package. It stays out of sight until you need it, and then operates in a fashion that feels perfectly natural for WordPerfect.

The program is centered around Ctrl+letter combinations, which you pretty much have to memorize. However, doing so isn't hard; you can get by just keeping in mind that Ctrl+B inserts the codes to start a script; Ctrl+C is for inserting a character name and, after you press Enter, dialogue; Ctrl+A is for writing an action description; and Ctrl+T is for inserting a transition (such as CUT TO: or DISSOLVE TO:) and, after you press Enter, optionally a scene heading. When you're done writing, pressing Ctrl+P puts the script into its final form, automatically inserting page numbering, and such optional extras as scene "(Continued)" lines, scene numbers, omitted scene references, and revision marks.

There are about 15 other Ctrl+letter combinations available, but most are more esoteric timesavers (for example, Ctrl+G repeats the last character name and inserts "(continuing)" below the name, for when a character's dialogue has been interrupted by an action description). Some scriptwriters comfortable with PCs will relish memorizing every keystroke shortcut provided, while others will probably go faster by just ignoring them. The nice thing is that both options are available, and the SuperScript Pro manual is very nonjudgmental about which approach you take; it even has a section targeted at people who don't want to learn a lot of keystrokes.

Speaking of the manual, it's excellent. It holds you by the hand from the start and shows you how to use SuperScript Pro step-by-step. It also sprinkles general advice about good scriptwriting practices along the way. There are even two fine essays on writing included, by USC professor James Boyle and by playwright/screenwriter David Scott Milton.

I was once so poor I didn't know where my next husband was coming from.
              —She Done Him Wrong (1933)

Toto, I have a feeling we're not in Kansas any more.
              —The Wizard of Oz (1939)

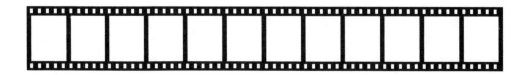

The program provides several customization screens, which are designed to look and work precisely like WordPerfect option screens. It also adds to the WordPerfect print screen an inconspicuous extra line that lets you output selected scenes from your script. Similarly, in case you get stuck, it reminds you via an extra line on the WordPerfect Help screen that scripting information is available by pressing Ctrl+H; when you access this help system, you find that it works exactly like WordPerfect's online help. This level of consistency and intelligent design is evident throughout the package.

However, SuperScript Pro provides nowhere near the level of automation that Scriptware does. For instance, it provides no special way to insert extensions; forces you to press Ctrl+A after you're done with dialogue, instead of returning you to the action margin automatically; and requires you to format your script with proper page breaks and page numbering as a separate, extra step.

The latter is particularly noteworthy, because it means you need to deal with two documents for each script: your editing draft, and the formatted version. It also means that every time you make a change in your draft, you have to generate a new formatted version before printing. Since formatting takes a while to execute, this can become pretty tedious.

There can also be disadvantages to the program's reliance on Ctrl keystrokes; for example, since the letters "S" and "A" are right next to each other on the keyboard, I sometimes found myself inserting sluglines (via Ctrl+S) when I meant to start action descriptions (via Ctrl+A). On the other hand, the Ctrl keystroke/typing/Ctrl keystroke/typing rhythm the program imposed generally worked very well, and at times was even fun.

Heathcliff, make the world stop right here. Make everything stop and stand still and never move again. Make the moors never change and you and I never change.
> —*Wuthering Heights* (1939)

Frankly, my dear, I don't give a damn.
> —*Gone With the Wind* (1939)

Basically, SuperScript Pro makes you do more work than Scriptware, and doesn't give you nearly as many options as Scriptware does. However, if you're already comfortable with the way WordPerfect operates, you'll be pleased with SuperScript Pro's seamless integration, which makes it look and feel like a natural extension of WordPerfect. Also, for casual use, its score of scriptwriting shortcuts are probably all you need. If you do most of your work in WordPerfect, anyway; or you like having access to the zillion-and-one features this comprehensive word processor offers; or you simply want to save some money, SuperScript Pro (at a cost of about $95) is a very reasonable alternative for script production.

ScriptPerfection

While SuperScript Pro tries to be as unobtrusive and natural an extension of WordPerfect as possible, ScriptPerfection treats WordPerfect more as a launching pad, and imposes its own method of doing things. Unfortunately, ScriptPerfection is a bit like a well-meaning relative who tries so hard to be helpful that he ends up getting in the way.

Instead of lurking in the background until you need it, ScriptPerfection requires that you start it up explicitly from the DOS prompt, along with WordPerfect, by typing SCRIPT and pressing Enter. When you do so, you're prompted to answer several questions about the script you're going to write. The program then uses your information to create a cover page and act heading, switches into an all uppercase mode, and prompts you to select Int., Ext., Fullshot, POV, or None to start your first scene heading. So far, so good.

Have you every noticed how grateful you are to see daylight again after coming out of a tunnel?....Always try to see life around you as if you'd just come out of a tunnel.

      —*Mr. Smith Goes to Washington* (1939)

I'm going to live through this, and when it's all over, I'll never be hungry again. No, nor any of my folks. If I have to lie, cheat, or kill. As God is my witness, I'll never be hungry again.

      —*Gone With the Wind* (1939)

After you make a selection, type your heading, and press Enter, the program prompts you to select Day, Night, Morning, Afternoon, Evening, Continuous, Later, or None. At first glance, this appears to be a helpful little timesaver. In practice, I found it distracting, because it broke the flow of my typing. I'd rather just type *Day* myself at the end of a scene heading than have to remember the program wants to do it for me.

(Along similar lines, instead of a single keystroke for starting a scene heading, the program provides *five*: Ctrl+I to start the heading with INT., Ctrl+E to start it with EXT., Ctrl+F to start it with FULL SHOT, Ctrl+P to start it with POV, and Ctrl+B to start it with no initial text. Some may applaud expending this much effort on entering a few initial letters, but I found it distracting and confusing.)

Upon completing my scene heading, I was ready to write an action description. Unfortunately, I found that I was still in uppercase mode—and despite repeated presses of the Caps Lock and Shift keys, I couldn't switch it off! After several minutes of frantic Ctrl+letter and Enter keystrokes, I broke back into normal typing mode; but I didn't enjoy the feeling of helplessness. (In retrospect, I probably did something "wrong" by the criteria of the program to have stayed in all caps mode; but the situation should have been easier to correct.)

Moving on, I found that, like SuperScript Pro, ScriptPerfection provides a number of keystroke shortcuts for entering script elements. However, its selection of keystrokes isn't nearly as intuitive and consistent. For example, to enter a transition you press Ctrl+T; but to enter action, you press Ctrl +Enter; and to enter a character name, you press Tab! Most bizarrely, for a parenthetical the required keystroke is Alt+9. Yep, that's right; Alt+9. Go figure.

You keep your feet on the ground and your head on those shoulders of yours and go out and, Sawyer, you're going out a youngster, but you've got to come back a star.
> —*42nd Street* (1933)

Mother of Mercy, is this the end of Rico?
> —*Little Caesar* (1930)

Also, as just indicated, too many keystrokes add clutter instead of helping. For instance, do you really need Ctrl+V and Ctrl+O shortcuts for inserting V.O. and O.S.? Or a Ctrl+X keystroke that does nothing but delete an occurrence of (O.S.), (V.O.), or (CONT'D)?

Because the keystroke assignments are confusing, I'd often press the wrong one. When I'd try to change the incorrect formatting using the Backspace key, however (a normal procedure in WordPerfect), I found it had no effect. I then used WordPerfect's Reveal Codes command, zeroed in on the unwanted formatting code, and pressed the Del key. That didn't work, either!

After repeated frustrating attempts, I combed the manual for an explanation. It turns out that ScriptPerfection paternally protects you from deleting codes it feels you shouldn't be messing with. (As the manual puts it —on page 22—"no longer will a slip of a finger turn your DIALOGUE into ACTION.") The manual also notes that such codes can be eliminated with a Ctrl+Del keystroke; but that information appears in a single sentence buried among 80 text-filled pages.

Then close your eyes and tap your heels together three times, and think to yourself, "There's no place like home."
　　　　　　　　　　—*The Wizard of Oz* (1939)

You know, Mildred, in the spring a young man's fancy lightly turns to what he's been thinking about all winter.
　　　　　　　　　　—*Mildred Pierce* (1945)

Of all the gin joints in all the towns in all the world, she walks into mine.
　　　　　　　　　　—*Casablanca* (1942)

What a dump.
　　　　　　　　　　—*Beyond the Forest* (1949)

She drove me to drink. That's the one thing I'm indebted to her for.
　　　　—*Never Give a Sucker an Even Break* (1941)

ScriptPerfection also provides a menu bar, which the manual mentions early on. Unfortunately, there's no explanation of how to *display* the bar until halfway into the manual (you press Esc). Once I had the menu bar up, I found it wouldn't let me scroll through its menu options using the Left Arrow key (as virtually all other modern programs do); every menu closed when I pressed Left Arrow, so I had to repeatedly move to a menu and press Enter to view its contents.

And the way the menus operate is also inconsistent; for example, selecting the Thesaurus menu doesn't display options, but instantly plunges you into WordPerfect's thesaurus. Further, there's no Help menu, which is the last menu of nearly all programs nowadays. Instead, the last menu is Exit; and its options are worded vaguely enough to allow you to lose your script if you're not careful.

ScriptPerfection really tries hard to help automate your work; and once you become accustomed to its design flaws and quirks, it's a genuinely useful tool. However, you'll probably find SuperScript Pro easier to learn and use.

As you grow older, you'll find that the only things you regret are the things you didn't do.
              —Mildred Pierce (1945)

I think it would be fun to run a newspaper.
              — Citizen Kane (1941)

My religion? My dear, I'm a millionaire.
              —Major Barbara (1941)

Badges? We ain't got no steenkin' badges. We don't need no badges. I don't have to show you any steenkin' badges!
        — The Treasure of the Sierra Madre (1948)

He just swallowed his pride. It'll take him a moment or two to digest it.
              — The Hasty Heart (1949)

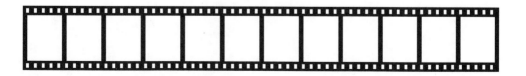

The Warren Script Applications

SuperScript Pro and ScriptPerfection work only with WordPerfect. In Hollywood, however, a whole lot of people use Microsoft Word. The Warren Script Applications, from Stefani Warren & Associates, are macro collections designed to turn MS Word for DOS or Windows into state-of-the-art script processors. Unfortunately, the versions I examined didn't perform as expected.

The installation for the Word for DOS macros consisted of two batch files: one if your hard drive is C, the other if it's D. As it happens, I wanted to install to my hard drive F. Worse, both batch files work only if you install from drive A; like many people, I need to install from my 3.5-inch drive B. The manual doesn't say a word about any of this; and, unlike every other software company discussed in this book, Stefani Warren & Associates doesn't provide telephone technical support. (The austere manual states that if you encounter a problem, "letters of inquiry may be sent by mail or FAX and will be answered promptly.") I opted to simply rewrite the batch file; but not everyone will have the technical know-how to do this.

When a man's partner's killed, he's supposed to do something about it. It doesn't make any difference what you thought of him; he was your partner, and you're supposed to do something about it.

          —The Maltese Falcon (1941)

People all say I've had a bad break, but today...today I consider myself the luckiest man on the face of the Earth.

          —The Pride of the Yankees (1942)

Every time you hear a bell ring, it means that some angel's just got his wings.

          —It's a Wonderful Life (1946)

Made it, Ma! Top of the world!!!

          —White Heat (1949)

My job is to teach these natives the meaning of democracy. And they're going to learn democracy if I have to shoot every one of them.

          —The Teahouse of the August Moon (1956)

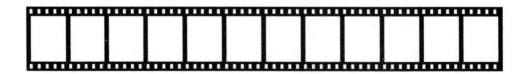

Once I got the package running, I found the menu system painfully slow on my 33MHz 386; on a less powerful machine, it would likely be intolerable. The menus also seemed incomplete, with "(Option not installed)"—sometimes in parentheses, sometimes not—appearing sporadically in various places.

As for entering script elements, you have to use either arduous Ctrl+Shift+letter combinations, such as Ctrl+Shift+C to enter a character name; or entirely unintuitive Ctrl+number combinations, such as Ctrl+4 to enter action. Worse, the results I got by pressing such keystrokes didn't always correspond to the manual's descriptions of what they're supposed to do. At that point, I gave up on the version for Word for DOS.

The Word for Windows version let me install from any floppy drive, but gave me no choice about the hard drive; it just placed itself, without asking, on the same drive as my copy of Word for Windows. (Fortunately, there was room for it.) I then tried to start up by double-clicking the Warren icon, but no go. After awhile, I figured out I needed to run a batch file that copies the WinWord program to the WARREN subdirectory. That started Word for Windows, so I turned to the manual for the next step. It told me I was now ready to make a selection from the Script Project Manager dialog box. Unfortunately—you guessed it—no such dialog box was anywhere in sight, nor was there any way I could see of bringing up the box. At any rate, according to the manual, the WinWord version also depends on irritating Ctrl+Shift+letter and Ctrl+number combinations. So goodbye, Warren Script Applications, goodbye.

I have always depended on the kindness of strangers.
> —*A Streetcar Named Desire* (1951)

You know, a dozen press agents working overtime can do terrible things to the human spirit.
> —*Sunset Boulevard* (1950)

Kirk was wrong when he said I didn't know where movie scripts left off and life begins. A script has to make sense, and life doesn't.
> —*The Barefoot Contessa* (1954)

It may be that by the time you read this, The Warren Script Applications will have improved immensely. It may also be that I just had bad luck with the two packages; after all, Nicholas Pileggi reportedly wrote the brilliant script for *Goodfellas* using TWSA. Given the lack of telephone tech support, however, you may want to try out the version you're interested in at your local dealer and/or be assured of a 30-day money-back guarantee policy before making a purchase. (Then again, there's always Scriptware...)

Movie Master

Movie Master has been around since 1987 and, until the release of Scriptware in November 1992, it was the only full-featured scriptwriting program on the market. Movie Master does a solid job of automating the writing process; but, at risk of sounding like a broken record, I have to report it doesn't perform as well as Scriptware. It also doesn't provide explicit support for as many varied film, TV, and stage formats as Scriptware does.

Getting started with Movie Master is quick and straightforward. To initiate a script, you activate the menu bar at the top of the screen by pressing Esc, press Enter twice to select the File menu's Open command, type a name such as MYSCRIPT, and press Enter again. Your script name appears in the status bar at the bottom of the screen, and you're switched to uppercase mode in the editing area so you can type something appropriate such as FADE IN:.

I've wrestled with reality for 35 years, and I'm happy, Doctor. I finally won out over it.
> —*Harvey* (1950)

Fasten your seatbelts. We're in for a bumpy night.
> —*All About Eve* (1950)

Gauguin: What I see when I look at your work is just you paint too fast.
Van Gogh: You look too fast.
> —*Lust for Life* (1956)

Nobody's perfect.
> —*Some Like it Hot* (1959)

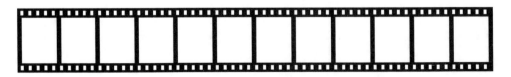

To begin your first scene heading, or slugline, you simply press F1. That key assignment isn't necessarily intuitive, but it *is* easy to remember, because the description 1SLUG is displayed near the bottom of the screen—along with 2ACTION, 3CHAR, 4PAREN, 5DIALOG, and definitions for the five other function keys. If you press Shift, Ctrl, or Alt, the display changes accordingly to show the actions of other function key combinations. (For example, if you press Ctrl, the bottom display shows that Ctrl+F1 inserts INT. into your script, Ctrl+F2 inserts EXT., Ctrl+F3 inserts - DAY, Ctrl+F4 inserts - NIGHT, Ctrl+F5 inserts CUT TO:, and so on.)

When you're done with your heading and press Enter, you're automatically moved to the character name margin...and here's where things get a bit dicey.

In addition to being moved to the margin, the program inserts the text NAME? into your script. If it happens that what you *really* want to do next is write some action descriptions, you can press F2 to get to the action margin; but that NAME? text stays put. You can delete it with several presses of the Backspace key, but that breaks the flow of your typing, and the point of scripting software is to be as helpful and unobtrusive as possible.

He'll regret it to his dying day—if he lives that long.
> *—The Quiet Man* (1952)

Years from now, when you talk about this—and you will—be kind.
> *—Tea and Sympathy* (1956)

Give me a girl of an impressionable age, and she is mine for life.
> *—The Prime of Miss Jean Brodie* (1969)

Mrs. Robinson, you're trying to seduce me, aren't you?
> *—The Graduate* (1967)

I'm a bagel on a plate of onions.
> *—Funny Girl* (1968)

Goshers! Chow! Is sure smelling good, Mr. Dealey-Buddy! Is tasting good too?
> *—Dondi* (1960)

Further, it can also be a problem if you actually *do* want to enter a character name. When you type the appropriate name, nothing happens; the NAME? text just sits there, unmoved. The reason is you first have to create a cast list using the Lists menu's Roles command. There's no message on the screen to even hint at this non-obvious requirement. It's also a real nuisance if all you want to do is create a spontaneous draft, letting your muse and keyboard take you where they will. (On the plus side, though, after you've created your cast list, you can enter a character name by just typing its first letter.)

Once you've got your character name in, you may want to add an extension—that is, a parenthetical direction to the right, such as (V.O.). However, the program won't let you type *anything* next to the character name, and there's no shortcut keystroke for inserting an extension. (If you notice that the function key display includes 4PAREN and so try pressing F4, you're moved to the line below the name. That lets you insert an acting-related parenthetical, but it doesn't help with the extension.)

Then why did God plague us with the power to think,
Mr. Brady? Why do you deny the one faculty of Man that
raises him above the other creatures of the Earth, the
power of his brain to reason?

> —*Inherit the Wind* (1960)

We rob banks.

> —*Bonnie and Clyde* (1967)

That's exactly why we want to produce this play, to show
the true Hitler; the Hitler you loved, the Hitler you
knew, the Hitler with a song in his heart.

> —*The Producers* (1968)

Now truth is not always a pleasant thing, but it is
necessary now to make a choice, to choose between two
admittedly regrettable, but nevertheless distinguishable,
postwar environments. One where you got 20 million
people killed, and the other where you got 150 million
people killed.

> —*Dr. Strangelove* (1964)

The answer turns out to be another menu command. Specifically, you have to press Esc to activate the menu bar, press L for the Elements menu, press A to select the Add option, press C to select Character Ext, and press Enter. You can then type, say, an opening parenthesis, the text "V.O.," and a closing parenthesis. Frankly, that's quite a workout for inserting a six-character instruction. In contrast, Scriptware asks only that you press Tab and V to achieve the same result. For that matter, any word processor—heck, any *typewriter*—requires only that you type a space and the text "(V.O.)".

On top of that, for some strange reason your extension doesn't appear near the character name, but way off to the right of it (though it's placed properly when printed). Worst of all, though, is the inconsistency; when one type of parenthetical can be executed with the press of a function key and is placed normally on-screen, while the other requires a stroll through Menu City and is set off to the side, it's an invitation for confusion.

When you're done with parentheticals, pressing Enter moves you directly into dialogue, which is a convenient bit of automation. When you're finished with dialogue and press Enter again, though, you're moved to another character name margin, with that NAME? text inserted (or an actual name, if you've filled out your cast list). If you really want to write action instead, pressing F2 will do the job; however, as before, it doesn't affect the character name text, which has to be manually deleted.

*I'll just sit here and be quiet, just in case they do
suspect me. They're probably watching me. Well, let
them. Let them see what kind of a person I am. I'm not
even going to swat that fly. I hope they* are *watching.
They'll see. They'll see and they'll know and they'll say,
"Why, she wouldn't even harm a fly."*
　　　　　　　　　　　　　　　　—Psycho (1960)

She's my sister!...

She's my daughter!...

She's my sister and *my daughter!*
　　　　　　　　　　　　　　　　—Chinatown (1974)

I like to watch.
　　　　　　　　　　　—Being There (1979)

There actually *is* a way to get around this problem: You can press the function key you want (say, F2 for action, or F6 for a transition, or F1 for a scene heading) *instead* of Enter, which bypasses invoking the character name function. This isn't a great solution, though, for two reasons. First, saying that sometimes it's fine to press Enter at the end of a paragraph, but other times you have to press a function key instead, creates yet another confusing inconsistency. Second, pressing Enter at the end of paragraphs is an ingrained habit for most PC users—a fact which most programs exploit, rather than work against.

Aside from these design flaws (and several others I'm skipping over), Movie Master has one critical technical shortcoming: it won't show you accurate formatting and page breaks as you write and edit your script. Instead, it requires that you explicitly format your document using a Paginate command. This means that every time you make a change in your script, you have to select Paginate to see where page breaks really occur and/or to print your script. This sort of major hassle is barely acceptable from a macro package, which can stretch the word processor it works with only so far; but it's simply inexcusable in a standalone product.

Bottom line: Scriptware is much more intuitive than Movie Master, offers many more options, and formats your script on-screen as you're editing it. At the same time, Scriptware has a list price of $299, while Movie Master's list price is $325. Movie Master is a nice program but, at least for now, it's just not competitive.

Hey, don't knock masturbation. It's sex with someone I love.

—Annie Hall (1977)

I know what you're thinkin': Did he fire six shots, or only five? Well, to tell you the truth, in all this excitement, I've kinda lost track myself. But being this is a .44 Magnum, the most powerful handgun in the world, and would blow your head clean *off, you've got to ask yourself* one *question: Do I feel lucky? Well, do ya, punk?*

—Dirty Harry (1971)

I won't be wronged. I won't be insulted. I won't be laid a hand on. I don't do these things to others and I require the same of them.

—The Shootist (1976)

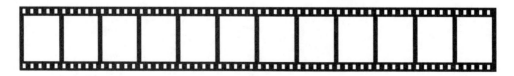

Scriptor

Screenplay System's Scriptor is a pioneer; it was the first program that addressed the problem of turning word-processed documents into scripts. Its approach was to take an already-written script created within a word processing package and "smooth out" the formatting to make the margins perfect, the pages break at the right places, optionally number scenes and insert "(CONTINUED)" lines, and so on. In other words, it didn't assist at all in the creation of your script, it just made your existing script look great.

Unfortunately, 10 years after the first release of the program, that's still about all Scriptor does. The program supplies macros for WordPerfect, Microsoft Word, and WordStar that provide some minimal help in script creation—basically, six keyboard shortcuts for setting margins for character names, dialogue, action, transitions, scene headings, and parentheticals. However, these don't approach the writing help provided by products such as SuperScript Pro or Scriptware; while *all* scriptwriting packages offer the basic output services of Scriptor.

A relationship, I think, is like a shark. You know—it has to constantly move forward or it dies. And I think what we have on our hands is a dead shark.
> —*Annie Hall* (1977)

I love the smell of napalm in the morning. It smells like...victory.
> —*Apocalypse Now* (1979)

You're out of order! You're out of order! This whole trial is out of order! They're out of order!
> —*...And Justice for All* (1979)

I want all of you to get out of your chairs. I want you to get up right now and go to the window, open it and stick your head out and yell, "I'm mad as hell, and I'm not going to take it anymore!"
> —*Network* (1976)

Scriptor is unique in one area, though: it contains a strong set of analysis and report tools. For example, a utility called Vocabulate can list all the words used in dialogue, broken down for each character; or list only words that are unique to each character, which is handy for checking to see whether you've really tailored each character's dialogue to his or her personality.

Scriptor can also generate cast lists, detailing the number of paragraphs of dialogue spoken by each character, plus the page and scene numbers each paragraph appears in.

And it can even produce outlines that list the number of each scene, the scene heading, the page the scene starts on, the scene's length in eighth-page increments (for example, "2 7/8" for a scene just under three pages long), and all the characters speaking in the scene. Such outlines can then be read into the popular Movie Magic Scheduling program (from Comprehensive Cinema Software, the publishers of Movie Master) for the purpose of creating breakdown sheets for each scene.

So, if you're already used to creating scripts in your own word processor without special help, and/or you have a genuine need for script analysis tools, Scriptor is worth a look. However, keep in mind that Scriptor won't help much with the physical process of creating your script, and won't help at all in letting you see your script in the proper format as you're writing it. Indeed, given its deficiencies, and its street price of about $255, Scriptor may be of most interest to script production folk who need to generate various breakdowns of scenes and character dialogue.

May the Force be with you.
　　　　　　　—Star Wars (1977)

Goooooooooooooooooooood morning, Vietnam!
　　　　　— Good Morning, Vietnam (1987)

We're on a mission from God.
　　　　　　— The Blues Brothers (1980)

I'll be back.
　　　　　　— The Terminator (1984)

Other Tools and Resources

There's a lot more to creating a script than the physical process of writing it.

For example, you can't begin your script until you have a solid idea for a story. If you're ever blocked, you can turn to Plots Unlimited, which can generate thousands of movie and TV oriented plot suggestions, and is covered in Chapter 4, *Software Collaborators*.

Once you've settled on an idea, you can flesh it out using Collaborator II, which asks you scores of questions that help you focus in on various aspects of your movie script. This product is also covered in Chapter 4.

If you have a CD-ROM drive and need to research films, you'll find the best way to do so is through Microsoft's great new Cinemania disc, which is based on Leonard Maltin's superb *Movie and Video Guide 1993* book and features over 19,000 capsule reviews, 745 extended reviews, 1,000 photographs, and a wide range of data-searching capabilities. If that's not enough, you can also get Roger Ebert's *Movie Home Companion* book in either a disk or CD-ROM format. These products are covered in Chapter 9, *CD-ROM References*.

Further, if you have a modem, you can get the answers to your script-related questions, or simply network and pick up juicy bits of information, by hanging out in the media sections on GEnie and CompuServe. If you're a member of the Writer's Guild of America, you should also check out the Guild's own electronic bulletin board, which provides a great way of getting to know your peers. And if you need industry information such as box office results, what projects are in development, or who worked on a particular film or TV show, BASELINE provides in-depth online databases to answer your questions. More information about online services appears in Chapter 10, *Online References*.

They're ba-a-ack.
> —*Poltergeist II* (1986)

Greed is good. Greed is right. Greed works.
> —*Wall Street* (1987)

Snakes! Why does it always have to be snakes?!
> —*Raiders of the Lost Ark* (1981)

Another important resource to exploit is writing-related *books*. Among the ones most useful to scriptwriters are:

- *Adventures in the Screen Trade* by William Goldman (Warner Books, 1983), $14.95

- *Selling Your Screenplay* by Cynthia Whitcomb (Crown, 1988), $11.95

- *The Art of Dramatic Writing* by Lajos Egri (Touchstone, 1960), $10.95

- *Making a Good Script Great* by Linda Seger (Samuel French, 1987), $11.95

- *The Art of Adaptation: Turning Fact and Fiction into Film* by Linda Seger (Owl, 1992), $14.95

- *Screenplay: The Foundations of Screenwriting* by Syd Field (Dell, 1982), $9.95

- *The Screenwriter's Workbook* by Syd Field (Dell, 1984), $9.95

- *The Craft of the Screenwriter: Interviews with Six Celebrated Screenwriters* by John Brady (Touchstone, 1981), $10.95

- *Formatting Your Screenplay* by Rick Reichman (Paragon House, 1992), $10.95

If you don't live near a bookstore that carries these titles, you can order them from mail-order vendor The Write Stuff, which offers both a wide range of software and over 250 books on writing, *all* of which are sold at aggressive discount prices.

Hello. My name is Inigo Montoya. You killed my father. Prepare to die.
> —*The Princess Bride* (1987)

Go ahead. Make my day.
> —*Sudden Impact* (1983)

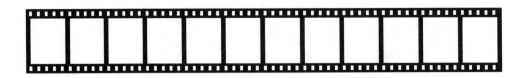

It's also a good idea to study the scripts of past and current masters. The best source for these is The Hollywood Book and Poster Company, which stocks over 2,000 unpublished scripts, and charges a low $15 per film script and $10 per television script. If it's plays you're after, though, New York's Drama Bookshop, and Applause Theatre and Cinema Books, have the most complete selections in the country.

Lastly, for nitty-gritty information about working in film or television (such as what to look out for in a contact), contact the Writer's Guild of America East or the Writer's Guild of America West. These two organizations are separate entities, but they cooperate with each other and share many resources. In general, you may find WGA West more helpful, because it has more members and thus a larger budget to work with. (For example, the Guild electronic bulletin board is owned and run by WGA West.) Anyone who's made a professional film or TV sale can—indeed, typically *must*—join one of these two guilds. Which one you join, however, is purely a matter of taste; there are lots of WGA West members in New York, and plenty of WGA East members in Los Angeles.

Contact information on the Guild, and on the mail-order vendors just mentioned (plus several others), appears at the end of this chapter.

Arthur: "I think I'll take a bath."
Butler: "I'll alert the media."
> —*Arthur* (1981)

You're not too bright. I like that in a man.
> —*Body Heat* (1981)

I won't be ignored.
> —*Fatal Attraction* (1987)

If you build it, he will come.
> —*Field of Dreams* (1989)

E.T. phone home.
> —*E.T. The Extra-Terrestrial* (1982)

Where does he get those wonderful toys?
> —*Batman* (1989)

Product Information

Note: Version numbers and prices may have changed by the time you read this.

Ashleywilde, Inc.
23715 West Malibu Road
Suite 132
Malibu, CA 90265
(800) 833-7568; (310) 456-1277
Fax: (310) 456-8586

Plots Unlimited 2.0: List Price, $399; Street Price, about $299. Copy protected via a dongle that attaches to the parallel printer port.

BASELINE
838 Broadway
New York, NY 10003
(800) 242-7546; (212) 254-8235
Fax: (212) 529-3330

Movie and television related online databases; call for prices and more information

Cinovation, Inc.
204 West 20th Street
Suite 37
New York, NY 10011
(800) 788-7090; (212) 924-4495
Fax: (212) 924-1005

Scriptware 2.0: List Price, $299; via The Write Stuff coupon near the back of this book, $259, with Linda Seger's *Making a Good Script Great* and Rick Reichman's *Formatting Your Screenplay* thrown in. Supports screenplay, sitcom, and stage play formats; copy protected via software.

Collaborator Systems, Inc.
P.O. Box 57557
Sherman Oaks, CA 91403
(800) 241-2655; (818) 980-2943
Fax: (818) 788-4192

Collaborator 2.2: List Price, $329; Street Price, about $269. Copy protected via software.

Comprehensive Cinema Software
148 Veteran's Drive
Northdale, NJ 07647
(800) 526-0242; (201) 767-7990
Fax: (201) 767-7377

Movie Master 4.0: List Price, $325; Street Price N/A. Supports screenplay and TV sitcom formats; copy protected via software.

CompuServe Information Service
5000 Arlington Center
Columbus, OH 43220
(800) 848-8199; (614) 457-0802
Fax: (614) 457-8149

Standard membership costs $8.95 a month and $8 an hour, and includes free access to about 35 basic services. Alternative "pay as you go" plan costs $2.50 a month and $12.80 an hour.

Inherit the Earth Technologies
1800 S. Robertson Blvd.
Suite 326
Los Angeles, CA 90035
(310) 559-3814
Fax: (310) 559-3814 (same as voice number; ITET's machine automatically senses whether you're a person or a fax)

SuperScript Pro 2.1: List Price, $119; Street Price, about $95. Supports screenplay, sitcom, and stage play formats; copy protected via software.

Infobusiness, Inc.
887 South Orem
Orem, Utah 84058-5009
(800) 657-5300; (801) 221-1100
Fax: (801) 225-0817

Roger Ebert's Deluxe Computerized Movie Home Companion 1.0 (disk-based): List Price, $59.95; Street Price N/A

GEnie Information Services
401 North Washington Street
Rockville, MD 20850
(800) 638-9636; (301) 251-6475
Fax: (301) 251-6421

During off-peak hours (6 P.M. to 8 A.M., and weekends), $8.95 a month for your first four hours, and $3 for each additional hour; during business hours, $12.50 an hour

Microsoft Corporation
One Microsoft Way
Redmond, WA 98052
(800) 426-9400; (206) 882-8080
Fax: No generic sales or information fax number

Cinemania: List Price, $79.95; Street Price, about $49

Quanta Press, Inc.
1313 Fifth Street SE
Suite 208C
Minneapolis, MN 55414
(612) 379-3956
Fax: (612) 623-4570

Roger Ebert's Movie Home Companion: List Price, $79.95; Street Price, about $49

Screenplay Systems
150 East Olive Avenue
Suite 203
Burbank, CA 91502-1849
(818) 843-6557
Fax: (818) 843-8364

Scriptor 4.0: List Price, $295; Street Price, about $255. Supports screenplay format; copy protected via software.

ScriptPerfection Enterprises
3061 Massasoit Avenue
San Diego, CA 92117-2522
(619) 270-7515
Fax: N/A

ScriptPerfection 3.0: List Price, $95; Street Price N/A. Supports screenplay and sitcom formats; copy protected via software.

Stefani Warren & Associates
The Warren Script Applications
3204 Dos Palos Drive
Los Angeles, CA 90068
No voice telephone sales or technical support number; but may be purchased through The Writer's Computer Store (see end of chapter)
Fax: (310) 874-6028

The Warren Script Applications 2.1 for Word for Windows: List Price, $175; generally not discounted. Supports screenplay, sitcom, stage play, and other formats.

The Warren Script Applications Screenplay Edition 6.05 for Word for DOS: List Price, $95; generally not discounted. Supports screenplay, TV, and stage play formats.

While you can order directly from software publishers, you'll save money by going through mail-order venders. Two companies that carry the computer products covered in this chapter are:

The Writer's Computer Store
11317 Santa Monica Boulevard
Los Angeles, CA 90025
(800) 272-8927; (310) 479-7774
Fax: (310) 477-5314

The Write Stuff
21115 Devonshire Street, #182
Chatsworth, CA 91311
(800) 989-8833; (213) 622-9913
Fax: (213) 622-9918

As mentioned previously, The Write Stuff also offers a wide range of writing-related books at discount prices. For a complete list, call the company to get its jampacked free catalog.

On the other hand, for unpublished movie and television scripts, the best source is:

The Hollywood Book and Poster Company
P.O. Box 539
Hollywood, CA 90078
(213) 465-8764
Fax: (213) 465-0413

And for plays, the best sources are:

The Drama Bookshop
723 Seventh Avenue
2nd Floor
New York, NY 10019
(800) 322-0595; (212) 944-0595
Fax: (212) 921-2013

Applause Theatre and Cinema Books
211 West 71st Street
New York, NY 10023
(212) 496-7511
Fax: (212) 721-2856

Samuel French Theatre and Film Bookshop
7623 Sunset Boulevard
Hollywood, CA 90046
(800) 822-8669; (213) 876-0570
Fax: (213) 876-6822

Finally, for information about working in film or television, contact:

Writer's Guild of America East
555 West 57th Street
New York, NY 10019
(212) 767-7800
Fax: (212) 582-1909

Writer's Guild of America West
8955 Beverly Boulevard
Los Angeles, CA 90048
(310) 550-1000
Fax: (310) 550-8185

CHAPTER
13

TOOLS FOR POETS

What is poetry?...It is much easier to say
what it is not. We all know what light is;
but it is not easy to tell what it is.

—Samuel Johnson

I'll play it first and tell you what it is later.

—Miles Davis

If I feel physically as if the top of my head
were taken off, I know that is poetry.

—Emily Dickinson

Frankly, there isn't much out there right now for poets, so this is going to be a short chapter.

There *were* several relevant packages a few years ago; but most faded away, presumably as software publishers discovered that poets aren't a market representing wealth and mass appeal. After all, as Don Marquis observed, "Publishing a volume of verse is like dropping a rose-petal down the Grand Canyon and waiting for the echo." (Then again, as Robert Graves pointed out, "There is no money in poetry; but then there is no poetry in money, either.")

At any rate, the single poetry package still extant is Rhymer, from Word-Perfect Corporation. Rumor has it one of the brilliant creators of Word-Perfect's spelling checker realized its phonetic recognition abilities (which allow the checker to read a misspelled word such as "sikolojee" and come up with the suggestion "psychology") could just as easily be applied to a rhyming dictionary, and so pushed for permission to write one. Word-Perfect Corp. reportedly wasn't too keen on the idea, but decided to give a "what the heck" green light. Thus was Rhymer born, in mid-1990...and that's also where it remains. No update was ever released, no Windows version is planned, and one can be hard-put to discover the program even exists. Like all its brethren, the thing apparently didn't fly.

Nonetheless, Rhymer is *wonderful*. For example, it's the only product I've ever encountered that can provide multiple rhymes for "orange." (More on this later.)

Using Rhymer is easy. When you run it, it automatically loads itself into memory, taking up about 33K, and then waits in the background until needed. Because it's memory resident, you can access it from *any* program —your word processor (which need not be WordPerfect), your desktop publishing program, a spreadsheet, a database, or even the DOS prompt. In general, though, you'll want to use it from your word processor as you're constructing your poem (or song, or ad copy).

A poem should not mean but be.
　　　　　—Archibald MacLeish

Poetry is the revelation of a feeling that the poet believes to be interior and personal (but) which the reader recognizes as his own.
　　　　　—Salvatore Quasimodo

When you get stuck in your writing, simply press the special keystroke that invokes Rhymer. (The default is Alt+Shift+F8, which is only intuitive if your keyboard has its function keys on the left; but you have the option of assigning virtually any other keystroke, such as Alt+R or Ctrl+R.) First, a message on the bottom of the screen instructs you to place your cursor on the word you want to rhyme. After you do so and press Enter, the section of text that contains your word is displayed in the top half of the screen, while these Rhymer options appear in the bottom half: Ending Rhyme, Last Syllable Rhyme, Double Rhyme, Triple Rhyme, Beginning Rhyme, First Syllable Rhyme, Phonetic Finder, and Options.

Ending Rhyme finds words that have the same last sound as your word —typically, a vowel sound followed by a consonant sound. When I chose this option for the word *beautiful*, Rhymer searched its 93,492-word dictionary and came up with 3,629 matches for the ending sound "ul." These included abysm*al*, barnac*le*, du*el*, minstr*el*, mong*ol*, nostr*il*, and petr*ol*.

Never show her your poetry until the third date.
—Allison Bell

I hope that one or two immortal lyrics will come out of all this tumbling around.
—Poet Louise Bogan on her romance with poet Theodore Roethke

Last Syllable Rhyme is more specific, finding only words that have the same last *syllable* sound as your word—typically, a consonant sound, a vowel, and another consonant sound. For example, when I chose this option for *beautiful*, Rhymer provided 174 matches for the last syllable sound "ful." These included apocry*phal*, cheer*ful*, forethought*ful*, of*fal*, ri*fle*, and zest*ful*.

Double Rhyme narrows things further, matching only words with the same vowel and consonant sounds in their next-to-last syllables, and same sound in their last syllables, as your word. When I selected this option for *beautiful*, Rhymer generated nine matches: beaut*iful* (Rhymer always includes the source word as a match), dut*iful*, fanc*iful*, merc*iful*, overfanc*iful*, pit*iful*, plent*iful*, undut*iful*, and unmerc*iful*.

Triple Rhyme is the narrowest search option, matching only words with the same vowel and consonant sounds in their third-to-last syllable, and same sounds in their last two syllables, as your word. When I chose it for *beautiful*, Rhymer achieved just three matches: bea*utiful*, d*utiful*, and und*utiful*.

Beginning Rhyme, as you might guess by now, locates words that have the same first sound as your word. When I selected it for *beautiful*, Rhymer yielded 28 words, including *beau*teous, *beau*tification, *bu*gle, *bu*gling, *bui*ck, *bu*tane, and *bu*tte.

And First Syllable Rhyme gives you words that have the same sounds preceding the first syllable break. In the case of *beautiful*, these are identical to the Beginning Rhyme words. However, when I fed Rhymer the word *scenery*, I turned up 235 words using the Beginning Rhyme option (including *cae*sar, *cc*, *ce*dar, *sea*food, *sea*l, *se*quel, *si*esta, and *si*kh); but only these 13 words with the First Syllable Rhyme option: *scene*, *scene*ries, *scene*ry, *scen*ic, *scen*ically, *seen*, *sen*ior, *sen*iority, *sen*iors, *sign*or, *sign*ora, *sign*oras, and *sign*ore.

Every poem is a momentary stay against the confusion of the world.

—Robert Frost

The poet's business is not to save the soul...but to make it worth saving.

—James E. Fletcher

If all these options aren't enough, you can turn to the Phonetic Finder, which is a sophisticated feature that lets you search using a combination of phonetic symbols ("E" for the "beet" sound, "e" for the "bet" sound, "aw" for the "caught" sound, and so on). What makes this especially powerful is the ability to mix in *wildcards*—that is, placeholders for various sounds. Specifically, you can use the asterisk (*) to represent one or more sounds; the question mark (?) to represent any single sound; C for any single consonant sound; V for any single vowel sound; and the hyphen (-) to indicate a syllable break. This gives you the freedom to, say, find words that rhyme only with a word's second syllable; or only with its middle syllables; or only that quadruple rhyme.

The aim of the artist is to arrest motion, which is life. A hundred years later, a stranger looks at it, and it moves again.

—William Faulkner

Finally, you can fine-tune Rhymer's output by using its WordPerfect-like Options screen. This lets you set the following ranges for matching words:

- Alphabetic, with the default being words starting with the letter A through words starting with the letter Z (that is, all words)

- Number of Syllables, with the default being 1 to 10 syllables

- Number of letters, with the default being words from 1 to 22 letters long

In addition, you can set Rhymer to send all matching words to a specified text file, which is especially convenient when hundreds of matches are found. The default is to display matching words on the screen, in bunches of 24.

And that's about all there is to say about Rhymer, so I guess...pardon me? Forgot something? Oh. Oh, yes.

So I type *orange*, press Alt+Shift+F8, press Enter, press D for Double Rhyme, and press Enter a few times to skip some options. With bated breath, I wait as the program searches through 93,492 words and turns up ...one match. Orange.

Well, okay, that's disappointing; but it was just a first stab at the problem. So I press Esc to return to the main menu, and this time select Ending Rhyme. Rather than immediately begin the search, Rhymer brings up the Phonetic Finder screen and informs me that two pronunciations are possible: or-unj and or-inj. A native New Yorker, I unhesitatingly select the former, and am rewarded with these nine words in response: challenge, expunge, lozenge, lunge, muskellunge, orange, plunge, scavenge, and sponge.

Okay, now we're getting somewhere! (I mean, *muskellunge*; wow.) Next, I select First Syllable Rhyme, and turn up *185* words ranging from *aura* to *orwellian*. These are too many to deal with, so I use the Options screen to narrow the search to words of one syllable. That gets us down to four: o'er, oar, or, and ore. And that's the last bit of data we need.

Rhymer couldn't provide a single word that rhymes with "orange." However, by having it generate single-syllable beginning and ending rhyme words, we can put together such mellifluous double-word rhymes as "o'er lunge," "or plunge," and "ore sponge." All right, maybe it's not Shakespeare; but it's still fodder for winning bar bets. More important, this same process can be applied effectively to any word. Rhymer can therefore be invaluable in providing both exact and subtle rhymes you never would have thought of on your own. It's a terrific product; and at $89, it's eminently affordable. Support poetry software and buy this program.

By the way, in addition to a rhyming dictionary, you should have available an excellent thesaurus, either via your word processor or from a separate program. For more information, see the "Thesauruses" section in Chapter 2, *What Your Word Processor Can and Can't Do*; and Chapter 5, *Electronic Dictionaries and Thesauruses*.

Also, you may find the word-toy Babble!, which reads in sentences and then spits them out in interesting new ways, to be especially helpful when applied to your poetry. Babble! is covered in Chapter 3, *Idea Generators*.

Product Information

Note: Version numbers and prices may have changed by the time you read this.

WordPerfect Corporation
1555 N. Technology Way
Orem, UT 84057
(800) 321-4566; (801) 225-5000
Fax: (801) 228-5377

Rhymer 1.0 (for DOS): List Price, $89; generally not discounted

Korenthal Associates, Inc.
511 Avenue of the Americas, #400
New York, NY 10011
(800) 527-7647; (212) 242-1790
Fax: (212) 242-2599

Babble! 2.0: List Price, $35; via coupon near the back of this book, $25

CHAPTER
14

TOOLS FOR
BUSINESSPEOPLE

Frenzy yourself into sickness and dizziness
Christmas is over and Business is Business.

— Franklin Pierce Adams

Gentlemen: You have undertaken to ruin me. I will not sue you, for law takes too long. I will ruin you. Sincerely, Cornelius Vanderbilt.

— Cornelius Vanderbilt, "Letter to associates"

The above epitomizes what great business writing is all about.

Business is driven by information. However, as the saying goes, time is money. Therefore, business communication must be clear, concise, and pointed.

Of course, these same rules apply to the highest standards of professional writing. As a result, most of the tools of the business writer are the same as those for the journalist trying to hook readers with a snappy lead, or the author seeking to quickly thrust a book audience into a different world.

These tools include a word processor built for speed and flexibility, such as WordPerfect or XyWrite (see Chapter 1, *Choosing a Word Processor*); a powerful idea generator, such as IdeaFisher (see Chapter 3, *Idea Generators*); an excellent word reference, such as the Random House Webster's Electronic Dictionary & Thesaurus, College Edition (see Chapter 5, *Electronic Dictionaries and Thesauruses*); and, if you're not entirely secure about your grammar and punctuation, or if you need to emulate a particular in-house style, Grammatik 5 or Corporate Voice (see Chapter 6, *Grammar and Style Checkers*).

Where you *do* part company from general-interest writers is in the type of information you require. Typically, you'll need such data as company profiles, stock and bond prices, and news items that affect the financial market. Therefore, this chapter covers business-related electronic references. Specifically, it discusses databases provided on CD-ROMs and on-line services.

CD-ROMs are convenient to use, and especially good at providing comprehensive information (for example, a telephone/address directory with millions of entries). The downside is that business discs are often very expensive. However, if your time is valuable and you expect to use a title frequently, you may decide it's well worth writing off as an expense on your company's balance sheet; or at least worth requesting as an item to be purchased by your public or corporate library.

Online services are also comprehensive, and excel at supplying fast-breaking news (for example, the latest gold prices). Further, they don't require the up-front financial commitment that a CD-ROM does. However, if you spend a lot of time online, you'll find the charges add up very quickly.

Both CD-ROMs and online services are enormously useful resources, and in today's competitive marketplace, you can't afford to ignore them. For general information on how to make use of these media, see Chapter 9, *CD-ROM References*, and Chapter 10, *Online References*.

Business-Related CD-ROMs

When you need information on a company, there are a variety of discs you can turn to.

If the company is on the New York Stock Exchange, American Stock Exchange, or Over-the-Counter, regional, or Canadian stock exchanges, COMPUSTAT PC Plus Standard & Poor's Stock Reports will provide a detailed report on it, including such data as its sales and revenues, its common share earnings, its next earnings report, its balance sheets for the past 10 years, significant events in its history, its current outlook, and statistical summaries and charts. Over 4,100 stock reports are included. An annual subscription is $6,000, and includes monthly updates.

Casting the net a bit wider, Compact Disclosure/SEC from Disclosure Inc. covers *all* U.S. public companies, which total about 11,000. For each, the CD-ROM offers financial data (culled from SEC filings and other public sources) such as balance sheet, income, cash flow, price/earning statistics, full text financials, and management discussions. Seven years of annual financial information and two years of quarterly data are included, as well as the Zacks earnings estimate. In addition, you're given such basic information as the company address and phone number, the SIC (Standard Industrial Classification) codes that indicate the types of business the company is involved in, a description of the markets the company is pursuing, shareholder data (number of shares outstanding, total number of shareholders, and so on), and the salaries of corporate officers. The disc costs $2,300, or $5,800 for 12 monthly updates.

Broadening the search further, if the company you're seeking has a net worth of $500,000 or more, Dun's Million Dollar Disc will provide its address and phone number, the names of its CEO and top executives, its number of employees, its annual sales, the year it was founded, its D-U-N-S number, its SIC code, its stock exchange and ticker symbol, and its import/export indicator. Over 216,000 public and private U.S. companies are covered. In addition, the disc furnishes biographical profiles on more than 660,000 senior executives. An annual corporate subscription, which includes quarterly updates, costs $5,295.

If you're interested in smaller firms, Duns (without the apostrophe, for bizarre marketing reasons) Reference Plus covers over four million U.S. businesses. Each entry includes the company name, address and phone number, headquarters location, parent company, D&B rating, D-U-N-S number, and SIC code. The price of the disc varies depending on the options you purchase; contact Dun & Bradstreet for details.

If writers were good businessmen, they'd have too much sense to be writers.

—Irvin S. Cobb

Whenever I'm asked what kind of writing is the most lucrative, I have to say ransom notes.

—Literary agent H. N. Swanson

Income tax returns are the most imaginative fiction being written today.

—Herman Wouk

Even wider coverage is provided by Business America On Disk, which supplies data on 10 million U.S. businesses, including address and phone number, SIC code, number of employees, annual sales, and contact name. The product comes with a hardware counter that limits you to 20,000 lookups, and has an annual lease fee of $7,500. If that's too pricey, you can opt for a scaled-down version named the Ten Million Business Database, which leaves out the employee, sales, and contact information, gives you no disk saving and printing options (aside from using your PC's Print Screen key), and has a hardware counter that limits you to 5,000 lookups, at a cost of $695. And if you can get by with just company names, partial addresses (no street numbers), and phone numbers, and a software counter that limits you to 5,000 lookups, choose The American Business Phonebook, which has a low street price of about $50. All three products are published by American Business Information.

Do other men for they would do you.
That's the true business precept.

—Charles Dickens

Don't steal; thou'lt never thus compete
Successfully in business. Cheat.

—Ambrose Bierce

For yet more comprehensive phone books, PhoneDisc from DAK Industries covers an awesome 72 million business and residential addresses and phone numbers (spread out over three discs) at the bargain price of $149.90. A competing product, ProPhone from ProCD, consists of six discs, organized by region, covering 70 million residential addresses and phone numbers; plus a disc containing seven million U.S. business addresses, phone numbers, and SIC numbers, searchable by over 2,000 business headings. ProPhone allows you to compile mailing lists from its data, which DAK does not; but it's a bit more expensive, with a street price of about $309. To supplement either product, you may also want the North American Facsimile Book from Quanta Press, which features 150,000 U.S. and Canadian fax numbers (along with business names and addresses), and has a street price of about $49.

For more in-depth (and expensive) business information, consider the OneSource series from OneSource Information Services, Inc. This line includes CD/Corporate, which offers financial and analytical data on 10,000 U.S. public companies and 6,000 private ones, more limited data on 100,000 other U.S. companies, details on 45,000 U.S. mergers and acquisitions, and full-text SEC filings for 5,000 U.S. corporations. In addition, the disc has profiles of 7,000 international public companies, financial data on 130,000 U.K. companies, and details on 25,000 U.K. and European mergers and acquisitions. Other similarly comprehensive products in the OneSource line are CD/Investment, CD/Banking, and CD/Insurance. Their prices can range from $10,000 to $70,000, depending on the information you want and how frequently you want it updated; call for details.

Of course, the popular press is also an invaluable resource. Business Index from Information Access gives you an amazing three million citations (and occasional abstracts) to over 800 business journals, 80 key regional magazines and newspapers, and business-related articles appearing in 3,000 additional periodicals. An annual subscription with monthly updates is $3,500. If you can make do with less comprehensive data, though, Business Periodicals Index from H. W. Wilson supplies more than 545,000 citations to over 345 business magazines, and costs $1,495 for an annual subscription with monthly updates.

Frank Munsey, the great publisher, is dead.... *(He) succeeded in transforming a once-noble profession into an eight per cent security. May he rest in trust.*

—Ambrose Bierce

Business without profit is not business any more than a pickle is a candy.

—Charles F. Abbott

Finally, if you often need to look up complete business articles, Business ASAP from Information Access offers the full text of over 350 business magazines, such as *Forbes, Fortune, The Economist,* and *Business Quarterly,* for an annual subscription price (including monthly updates) of $9,500. If you (or, more likely, your library) don't need quite that many articles, however, Information Access also sells Business ASAP Select, which includes 100 full-text magazine titles—including the four just mentioned—for a lower cost; call the company for details.

Business-Related Online Services

Virtually everything available on CD-ROM is also available online. In addition, online services are great at supplying timely information ranging from stock prices to election results.

The service that most directly targets businesspeople is Dow Jones News/Retrieval. This superb resource carries the full text of all articles in *The Wall Street Journal, The Washington Post, Business Week, Barron's, Forbes, Fortune, Financial World, The PR Newswire, The Business Wire,* and many other publications, often going back for years. For example, *The Wall Street Journal* database contains every issue from January 1984 to the present, and is updated daily.

DJN/R also provides an up-to-the-minute newswire that gives you stories within 90 seconds of their being filed by Dow Jones reporters around the country. This is a great place to turn to when seeking the latest developments in the stock market, or government, or some other area that affects your interests. A similar section is available for international news, stocked by items from 16 Dow Jones news bureaus around the world, and the European and Asian editions of *The Wall Street Journal*. And if that's not enough, a Business and Finance Report section offers a constantly updated collection of news stories related exclusively to commercial matters (such as the most active stock issues and the current Dow Jones Industrial Average).

Business is a good game—lots of competition and a minimum of rules. You keep score with money.

—Nolan Bushnell

Whoever said money can't buy happiness didn't know where to shop.

—Anonymous

If you require more analytical information, you can go to the Company, Industry Statistics & Forecasts section, which offers such treasures as Dun & Bradstreet's Reports on 75,000 Companies, Standard & Poor's Earnings and Income Estimates, Earnings Forecasts, Technical Analysis Reports, Analysts' Reports on Companies and Industries, Statistical Comparisons of Companies and Industries, SEC Filing Extracts, and Insider Trading Filings.

And, of course, like virtually every major online service, DJN/R gives you the latest stock prices. These are normally on a 15-minute time delay, as required by the various exchanges. However, if you've contracted with an exchange to allow it, DJN/R can just as easily give you *immediate* access to stock prices, something other services can't do. In addition, DJN/R monitors the price and volume of each stock, and quickly issues a report when it detects deviations from a stock's normal trading patterns. And it even offers a historical perspective by letting you locate the closing price of a stock on any day over the past year.

During business hours, DJN/R is quite pricey, charging $117 an hour plus $1.14 for every 1,000 characters accessed. If you can wait until after 6 P.M., however, the rate plunges to $9 an hour plus 30 cents for every 1,000 characters accessed. There's even a flat fee plan of $29.95 a month if you restrict your calls between 8 P.M. and 6 A.M., and access only the more popular features. If nothing else, the flat fee scheme offers a comfortable way of becoming acquainted with the system before you start spending megabucks on it during business hours.

Another extremely useful, and even more expensive, service is NEXIS, which carries the full text of over 650 publications. These include *The New York Times, The Los Angeles Times, The Economist, Newsweek, Time, U.S. News & World Report, ABA Banking Journal, American Banker, Adweek, Advertising Age*, and many other newspapers and magazines not available on DJN/R. (Indeed, some periodicals, such as *The New York Times*, are available *exclusively* through NEXIS.) Also online are stories from news outlets such as the AP, Reuters, and the Japan Economic Newswire; and transcripts of influential television programs such as *ABC News* and *The MacNeil-Lehrer News Hour*. NEXIS charges $43 an hour, plus hefty additional fees per search, plus a monthly subscription fee of $50. If you expect to use the service frequently, you may prefer a flat-fee option; call Mead Data Central for details.

Using Dow Jones News/Retrieval and NEXIS together will probably satisfy most of your business needs. However, other services also have special charms.

The business of America is business.
—Calvin Coolidge

For example, NewsNet is the best source for specialized newsletters, such as *Bond Buyer, Small Business Tax Review, MUNIWEEK,* and *Corporate Job Outlook.* GEnie is the only service that provides stock quotes using decimals instead of fractions, which makes it easy to import the numbers into a spreadsheet. Delphi is the least expensive service (charging as little as $20 a month for 20 hours of use and $1.80 an hour for additional use), yet provides stock quotes and the Dow Jones Industrial Average, and such valuable information sources as UPI Business News, Financial Commodity News, Donohue's Money Fund Report, and PR Newswire. And online giant CompuServe offers scores of business-related references among its awesome 1,500 databases.

For more information about these services, see Chapter 10, *Online References.* Also, if you do a lot of research work, consider purchasing the *Gale Directory of Databases* two-book set, which supplies comprehensive guides to online databases *and* CD-ROM databases, and costs $300.

Product Information

Note: Version numbers and prices may have changed by the time you read this.

American Business Information, Inc.
5711 South 86th Circle
P.O. Box 27347
Omaha, NE 68127
(402) 593-4500
Fax: (402) 331-1505

Business America On Disk: List Price, $7,500 for annual license; generally not discounted; requires dongle on printer port

Ten Million Business Database: List Price, $695 for annual license; generally not discounted; requires dongle on printer port

The American Business Phone Book: List Price, $298; Street Price, about $50; copy protected via software

CompuServe Information Service
5000 Arlington Center
Columbus, OH 43220
(800) 848-8199; (614) 457-0802
Fax: (614) 457-8149

Standard membership costs $8.95 a month and $8 an hour, and includes free access to about 35 basic services. Alternative "pay as you go" plan costs $2.50 a month and $12.80 an hour.

DAK Industries
8200 Remmet Avenue
Canoga Park, CA 91304
(800) 325-0800; (818) 888-8220
Fax: (818) 888-2837

PhoneDisc: List Price, $149.90; discounted if purchased with DAK's CD-ROM drive (which is very inexpensive, but too frustratingly slow for business use). Be sure to ask for DAK's free, fun catalog.

Delphi
General Videotex Corporation
1030 Massachusetts Avenue
Cambridge, MA 02138-5302
(800) 695-4005; (617) 491-3393
Fax: N/A

Charges flat rate of $10 an hour a month for four hours of use, and $4 an hour for additional use. Also offers alternative plan of $20 a month for 20 hours of use, and $1.80 an hour for additional use. If you dial in using SprintNet or Tymet (which is typical for anyone living outside of Massachusetts), there's a $9 surcharge for use during business hours.

Disclosure Inc.
5161 River Road
Bethesda, MD 20816
(800) 945-3647; (301) 951-1350
Fax: (301) 718-2343

Compact Disclosure/SEC: List Price, $2,300 for single disc, $5,800 for annual subscription (monthly updates); generally not discounted.

Dow Jones News/Retrieval
Dow Jones & Company, Inc.
P.O. Box 300
Princeton, NJ 08543-0300
(800) 522-3567; (609) 520-4000
Fax: (609) 520-4775

During off-peak hours (6 P.M. to 6 A.M, and weekends), $9 per hour plus 30 cents for every 1,000 characters accessed; during business hours (6 A.M. to 6 P.M.), $117 an hour plus $1.14 for every 1,000 characters accessed. Additionally requires fees of $29.95 for signup and $18 for annual subscription. Flat fee plan of $29.95 a month (for use between 8 P.M. and 6 A.M. and on weekends) also available; call for details.

Dun & Bradstreet Information Services
Three Sylvan Way
Parsippany, NJ 07054-3896
(800) 223-1026; (201) 605-6000
Fax: (201) 605-6921

Dun's Million Dollar Disc: List Price, $5,295 for annual corporate subscription (quarterly updates), $3,995 for annual library subscription; generally not discounted

Duns Reference Plus: Price varies by geographic region and data requested; call for details

H. W. Wilson Company
950 University Avenue
Bronx, NY 10452
(800) 367-6770; (718) 588-8400
Fax: (718) 590-1617

Business Periodicals Index: List Price, $1,495; generally not discounted

IdeaFisher Systems
2222 Martin Street
Suite 110
Irvine, CA 92715
(800) 289-4332; (714) 474-8111
Fax: (714) 757-2896

IdeaFisher 4.0: List Price, $199; via coupon near the back of this book, $99

Information Access Company
362 Lakeside Drive
Foster City, CA 94404
(800) 227-8431; (415) 378-5000
Fax: (415) 378-5369

Business Index: List Price, $3,500 for annual subscription (monthly updates); generally not discounted

Business ASAP (350 full-text magazine titles): List Price, $9,500 for annual subscription (monthly updates); generally not discounted

Business ASAP Select (100 full-text magazine titles): Call for price

Gale Research
835 Penobscot Building
Detroit, MI 48226
(800) 877-4253; (313) 961-2242
Fax: (313) 961-6083

Gale Directory of Databases, Volume 1: Online Databases and *Gale Directory of Databases, Volume 2: CD-ROM, Diskette, Magnetic Tape, Handheld, and Batch Access Database Products*: List Price, $300 for the two-volume, biannual book set; generally not discounted

GEnie Information Services
401 North Washington Street
Rockville, MD 20850
(800) 638-9636; (301) 251-6475
Fax: (301) 251-6421

During off-peak hours (6 P.M. to 8 A.M., and weekends), $8.95 a month for your first four hours, and $3 for each additional hour; during business hours, $12.50 an hour

NEXIS
Mead Data Central
9393 Springboro Pike
P.O. Box 933
Dayton, OH 45342
(800) 227-4908; (513) 859-1608
Fax: (513) 865-1666

Charges $43 per hour, plus additional fees per search, plus monthly subscription fee of $50. A flat-fee option is available for frequent users; call for more information.

NewsNet, Inc.
945 Haverford Road
Bryn Mawr, PA 19010
(800) 345-1301; (215) 527-8030
Fax: (516) 527-0338

Charges a $79.95 signup fee, plus $15 a month, plus $90 an hour, plus $60 to $300 an hour for reading full-text articles.

OneSource Information Services, Inc.
One Cambridge Center
Cambridge, MA 02142
(800) 554-5501; (617) 693-7400
Fax: (617) 693-7058

OneSource line: CD/Corporate, CD/Investment, CD/Banking, and CD/Insurance. Prices range from $10,000 to $70,000, depending on the information and update frequency desired; call for details.

ProCD, Inc.
8 Doaks Lane
Little Harbor
Marblehead, MA 01945
(617) 631-9200
Fax: (617) 631-0810

ProPhone: List Price, $449; Street Price, about $309

Quanta Press, Inc.
1313 Fifth Street SE
Suite 208C
Minneapolis, MN 55414
(612) 379-3956
Fax: (612) 623-4570

North American Facsimile Book: List Price, $299.95; Street Price, about $49

Scandinavian PC Systems
P.O. Box 3156
Baton Rouge, LA 70821-3156
(800) 487-7727; (504) 338-9580
Fax: (504) 338-9670

Corporate Voice 1.0: List Price, $249.95; generally not discounted; via coupon near the back of this book, $125

Corporate Voice ProStyles Volume 1 (over 50 writing styles, ranging from Andy Warhol and *Arabian Nights* to Walt Whitman and *Woman's Day*, that can be plugged into Corporate Voice): List Price, $19.95; generally not discounted

Standard & Poor's Compustat Services, Inc.
7400 South Alton Court
Englewood, CO 80112
(800) 525-8640; (303) 740-4548
Fax: (303) 740-4548

COMPUSTAT PC Plus Standard & Poor's Stock Reports: List Price, $6,000 for annual subscription, updated monthly; generally not discounted

The Technology Group
36 South Charles Street
Suite 2200
Baltimore, MD 21201
(410) 576-2040
Fax: (410) 576-1968

XyWrite 4.0 for DOS: List Price, $495; via coupon near the back of this book, $149

WordPerfect Corporation
1555 N. Technology Way
Orem, UT 84057
(800) 321-4566; (801) 225-5000
Fax: (801) 228-5377

WordPerfect 6.0 for DOS: List Price, $495; Street Price, about $269

Random House Webster's Electronic Dictionary & Thesaurus, College Edition 1.0 for DOS: List Price, $99; Street Price, about $55

Random House Webster's Electronic Dictionary & Thesaurus, College Edition 1.0 for Windows: List Price, $99; Street Price, about $55

Grammatik 5 for DOS: List Price, $99; Street Price, about $55

Grammatik 5 for Windows: List Price, $99; Street Price, about $55

CHAPTER
15

TOOLS FOR LAWYERS

A verbal contract isn't worth the paper it's written on.
—Samuel Goldwyn

The big print giveth and the small print taketh away.
—Fulton Sheen

A large portion of your work as a lawyer involves writing and research.

You have to write briefs, deposition questions, oral arguments, notes on clients, memos to colleagues, and an assortment of other documents.

And you have to conduct research on case law, available expert witnesses, news stories related to your cases, and a wide spectrum of other items.

There are many PC software tools available to aid you in this work. This chapter provides a brief overview of what's out there, and where you can go to obtain more information.

Writing, Editing, and Formatting Tools

To begin with, you need an excellent word processor. In law, that's a no-brainer, because there's one clear-cut standard: WordPerfect for DOS. This is partly thanks to the program's speed and comprehensiveness (as detailed in Chapter 1, *Choosing a Word Processor*); but it's also due to WordPerfect's long history of providing features lawyers need, such as redlining and line numbering; its superb toll-free technical support; and the many supplementary products created for it by third-party vendors.

A good example of the latter is Black's Legal Speller—Electronic Edition from West Publishing, which adds to WordPerfect's fine general-purpose speller over 20,000 legal words and phrases. The job of the Black's product is to keep WordPerfect from flagging your correctly spelled legal terms— and, just as important, to allow WordPerfect to provide appropriate suggestions when a legal term *is* misspelled. The program works with both the DOS and Windows versions of WordPerfect 5.0 and up, and costs $99.

Another useful package from West Publishing is Black's Law Dictionary —Electronic Edition. A complete version of the famous reference book, it furnishes definitions of over 30,000 legal terms and expressions, as well as discussions, examples of usage with citations, and internal cross-references. Unlike the print version, however, the software is always available on your hard disk; can be run memory-resident, popping up from any DOS application with a keystroke; and allows you to search through its definitions, acting as a "reverse dictionary." The program takes up about 15MB of disk space, and costs $169.

Once you've finished editing a document, you may wish to see how it now differs from the original. Alternatively, you may need to study how someone else has revised a document you've supplied—say, a negotiated contract. As noted in Chapter 2, *What Your Word Processor Can and Can't Do*, programs like WordPerfect contain a few revision tracking features, but they aren't precise enough for legal work. A better choice is DocuComp II from Advanced Software, which supports a variety of WordPerfect and Microsoft Word file formats, as well as the generic ASCII format. Docu-Comp II will analyze a specified original file and revised file, and then generate a third document that shows exactly where text has been deleted, added, or moved. In addition, it can generate comparison summaries and revision lists, which save you from searching for tiny changes in long documents. And while WordPerfect can note only that a sentence has been changed, DocuComp II will nail a change down to a revised word. The package costs $199.95.

When you go to court, you are putting your fate into the hands of 12 people who weren't smart enough to get out of jury duty.

—Norm Crosby

How to win a case in court: If the law is on your side, pound on the law; if the facts are on your side, pound on the facts; if neither is on your side, pound on the table.

—Anonymous

I learned law so well, the day I graduated I sued the college, won the case, and got my tuition back.

—Fred Allen

DocuComp II's main competitor is CompareRite from Jurisoft (a division of Mead Data Central). CompareRite can be extremely precise, pinpointing even comma changes (as opposed to DocuComp II, which will mark both the comma and the word next to it). However, it has trouble tracking text moved further than eight pages. Also, it's unable to transfer certain formatting information to your composite document, while DocuComp II excels as maintaining boldfacing, italics, font changes, and so on. Then again, CompareRite supports 10 word processing formats, so if you're using a program other than WordPerfect or Microsoft Word, CompareRite may spare you from always having to convert your document to ASCII before running a comparison. The program costs $160.

Jurisoft also offers three other noteworthy programs: CiteRite II, FullAuthority, and CheckCite.

CiteRite II locates each citation in your brief, compares it against the *Harvard Bluebook*, and then provides a report detailing each citation and the pertinent Bluebook rules; and it does it all extremely quickly. There's also a version available for the California style manual. CiteRite II costs $180.

Similarly, FullAuthority locates each citation in your brief, and in seconds creates a fully formatted Table of Authorities that you can print and attach to your document. Some word processors, such as WordPerfect, can also create a Table of Authorities, but only if you manually mark each citation, a procedure that's not only tedious but runs the risk of your missing citations in a long document. FullAuthority costs $160.

Lastly, CheckCite locates the citations in your brief, dials the LEXIS online service (which will be covered shortly), and makes sure the details of each citation are correct, and that the case wasn't later overturned. It can then create a printed report. Because it encourages you to spend time and money on LEXIS (which, like Jurisoft, is part of Mead Data Central), CheckCite is provided free to any LEXIS user.

For searches that extend beyond citations, you should turn to text retrieval programs. Such software helps you pluck precisely the information you need out of the thousands of files on your hard disk or office server. Two excellent general-purpose programs are ZyLAB's ZyINDEX, which you can buy using a coupon near the back of this book for only $199 (50 percent off list); and Windows Personal Librarian from Personal Library Software, a powerhouse package that costs $995. Both of these products are covered in Chapter 7, *Other Editing Tools*. Also, two solid programs created specifically for the legal market are SUMMATION II from Summation Legal Technologies ($1,092) and Discovery Pro for Windows from Stenographic Legal Services ($1,195), which are both especially good at deposition retrieval.

An appeal is when you ask one court to show its contempt for another court.
—Finley Peter Dunne

Another very helpful tool for dealing with depositions—and, for that matter, court transcripts, trial notes, and other documents you'll want to refer to on paper—is 4Print from Korenthal Associates. This program allows you to print two, three, or four pages of text on one side of a sheet of paper. It also makes it simple for you to print on both sides of your paper, giving you up to eight pages of text on a sheet. Further, you can set it to number every line (starting with 1 on each page), insert titles and borders, replace multiple blank lines with a single line, and perform a number of other handy formatting tricks. 4Print comes packaged with both DOS and

Windows versions, and can be purchased for only $39.95 using the Korenthal Associates coupon near the back of this book. More information about it appears in Chapter 23, *Printing Your Work*.

If your problem isn't so much managing documents as creating them, you can buy software that helps you to construct standard legal documents from scratch. Called *document assembly* programs, these packages ask you detailed questions and then pull together appropriate paragraphs of boilerplate text based on your answers. There are many document assembly programs available; West Publishing alone sells about 15 packages covering such areas as bankruptcy filings, jury instructions, and benefit plans, at prices ranging from $179 to $650.

I have always believed that to have true justice we must have equal harassment under the law.

—Paul Krassner

To save even more effort, you can buy standard legal forms on disk. For instance, West Publishing sells dozens of Federal, state-specific, and topical legal forms you can load into your word processor, at the price of $49 a package.

Finally, you're creating an undue burden on yourself if you don't take advantage of electronic mail. This marvelous service lets you send a letter you've just created in your word processor to its intended audience in minutes. The person(s) you sent it to can then read your letter immediately, or at some more desirable time. E-mail therefore combines the immediacy of a phone call with the convenience of a paper letter; and it's considerably less expensive than both long distance calls and overnight mail. A number of online services provide e-mail, including MCI Mail and CompuServe (which are discussed in Chapter 10, *Online References*), and ABA/net (which is covered shortly). In addition, some services (such as MCI Mail) let you maintain bulletin boards you can use to keep your clients updated on what's happening in your firm. Alternatively, you may want to set up internal e-mail and bulletin board systems. The products to accomplish this are beyond the scope of this book, but one source of more information is *Dvorak's Guide to PC Telecommunications, Second Edition* by John Dvorak and Nick Anis (Osborne/McGraw-Hill, $39.95).

Research Tools

There are two principal sources for legal research: the online service LEXIS from Mead Data Central, and the online service WESTLAW from West Publishing. You can access either of these services directly, or through gateways on a third service named ABA/net that's run jointly by AT&T and the American Bar Association.

LEXIS and WESTLAW actually have a lot more in common than differences. Both provide comprehensive coverage of federal and state court cases, U.S. code and state statutes, Federal regulations, administrative law decisions, legal topics (intellectual property, bankruptcy, health law, environmental law, and so on), full-text articles from legal publications (*ABA Journal, National Law Journal, California Lawyer*, and so on), and a wide assortment of other legal material. Both also offer relatively easy-to-use search commands, and provide excellent customer support. And both are invaluable tools for checking citations, studying fast-breaking cases, researching news stories, locating expert witnesses, and answering virtually any legal research question you can imagine.

There *are* a few notable differences between the services, though. One is that WESTLAW puts in more editorial work on statutes and court cases before placing them online. For example, WESTLAW's large staff of lawyer/editors verified over one million citations last year and made 80,000 corrections. These corrections ranged from fixing transposed citations, to noticing contradictory reasoning in a judge's decision and going to the judge to request official clarification.

In addition, for both Federal and state court decisions, WESTLAW provides synopses you can read quickly to help avoid wasting time with irrelevant cases; headnotes that identify the exact points of law addressed in each decision, which enhance your odds of locating pertinent cases when you're conducting a search; and a key-number system that classifies cases into minute sub-categories of law, which is another valuable tool for conducting searches.

On the other hand, LEXIS gives you a much wider range of pricing plans, including a very affordable plan for small firms using ABA/net (which will be covered shortly). Also, LEXIS offers more databases (about 4,700, versus about 4,000 on WESTLAW); and its nonlegal databases include all 650 full-text newspapers and magazines carried by its sister service NEXIS (see Chapter 10), such as *The New York Times*, *The Washington Post*, *The Wall Street Journal*, *Newsweek*, and *Time*. These online publications are tremendously useful resources when you need information about recent events or people in the news. WESTLAW's nonlegal databases are also very impressive—they include about 90 percent of the databases on DIALOG (again, see Chapter 10), which centers on major reference works such as Books in Print Online, Biography Index, DISCLOSURE Database, Federal Register Abstracts, ERIC, and MEDLINE. But these more scholarly reference tools aren't as helpful to many lawyers as the timely periodicals on NEXIS.

To some lawyers, all facts are created equal.

—Justice Felix Frankfurter

I'm not an ambulance chaser. I'm usually there before the ambulance.

—Melvin Belli

The word shyster *(doesn't) come from Shakespeare's Shylock, (but) from a Mr. Scheuster, an unscrupulous American criminal lawyer in the 1840s.*

—The NY Public Library Book of Answers

Therefore, while there's a great deal of overlap between the two services, it generally makes sense to belong to *both*, so that you're ensured of having available what may, quite suddenly and unexpectedly, become a critical source of information.

You can sign up for LEXIS and WESTLAW directly, or access them through ABA/net. Large firms that use the two services frequently can save money by joining directly, while solo practitioners and small firms will find joining ABA/net more economical and straightforward.

If you join LEXIS directly, you have three payment plans to choose from. Under the first one, you pay $125 a month, plus $46 an hour, plus additional charges per search. This is the best way to go if you're an inexperienced user, since it allows you to spend time on the system at a relatively low cost while you're figuring out how to get at the information you want.

Under the second LEXIS plan, you pay $125 a month, plus a hefty $406 an hour. However, these fees cover all your activities online; in other words, there are no additional charges for accessing databases. This is the most cost-effective plan for experienced LEXIS users, such as law librarians, who can go directly to the information they require, download the data, and quickly log off.

At the other extreme, the third LEXIS plan charges nothing for connect time, but asks for significantly more money per search. It's used mostly by government agencies.

(Actually, there's also a fourth plan, which is named Maximum Value Products, or MVP; but it's best to sign up for it through ABA/net, which will be discussed shortly.)

WESTLAW offers just two payment plans, both of which are based exclusively on the amount of time you're on the system.

Under the first plan, you pay $125 a month, plus $195 an hour for up to 50 hours of use. After that, the rate goes down as your use goes up: $185 an hour for hours 51 through 100, $175 an hour for hours 101 through 200, and $160 an hour for hours 201 and up. In most cases, you also have to pay a "connection" charge of $35 to $50 an hour. Further, you're charged for a minimum of three hours of use a month ($579), whether you actually utilize that time or not.

The second WESTLAW plan requires no monthly subscription fee, but costs $240 an hour, plus a connection charge of about $30 to $40 an hour. Also, it charges you for a minimum of 20 minutes of use a month ($80). This plan is therefore most appropriate if you're going to use WESTLAW infrequently.

Of course, it may be that the prices mentioned so far are significantly more than you're comfortable paying. If so, take heart. ABA/net, in conjunction with LEXIS, offers a very affordable alternative.

For starters, you can join ABA/net for a monthly charge of only $3 a month. This gives you access to the electronic mail system and a few other services.

More important, it allows you to join LEXIS under its Maximum Value Products, or MVP, plan, which charges an amazingly low flat fee of $95 a month! In other words, you can use the system as long as you want, and conduct as many searches as you want, for a single monthly charge of $95.

To live outside the law, you must be honest.

—Bob Dylan

As you might guess, there's a catch: MVP covers only the cases and statutes for your own state, and Federal circuit and district court cases. However, if you're a typical solo practitioner or member of a small firm, that's really all you need. (In fact, if you don't require even the Federal cases, you can skip access to them and pay just $85 a month.) If more than one attorney will be online, you can simply add $70 per head (or $60 minus Federal case access); for example, in a two-attorney firm, both lawyers can use LEXIS' MVP service for a total of just $165 a month.

Further, ABA/net allows you to access *all* LEXIS databases, even if you're on the MVP plan. You simply have to keep in mind that when you conduct searches on non-MVP databases, you're charged the regular LEXIS rate—which on ABA/net is $48 an hour, plus $6 to $91 per database search (or $3.75 per cite using Shepherd Citation/Autocite, or $5 per cite using LEXSEE and LEXSTAT).

In contrast, WESTLAW is no bargain on ABA/net. You have to explicitly join it at the cost of $45 a month, and pay $270 an hour. You're also charged for a minimum of 10 minutes of use a month ($27), whether or not you utilize that time. Further, the ABA/net gateway doesn't include access to WESTLAW's DIALOG databases. On the plus side, though, WESTLAW doesn't charge anything extra for the number or type of databases you access; and it's quite convenient to be able to access both WESTLAW and LEXIS from a single service.

The minute you read something you can't understand, you can almost be sure it was drawn up by a lawyer.

—Will Rogers

If online charges start getting too onerous, you can always turn to disk-based and CD-ROM references.

On the disk-based side, there are a variety of books you can purchase in electronic form that can be loaded memory resident and popped up at a keystroke. For example, West Publishing offers dozens of /FAST (Fast Access Searchable Text) disks containing state codes, federal codes, and codes on special topics such as bankruptcy and insurance, with prices ranging from $115 to $150 per package.

And scores of publishers offer CD-ROM titles, covering state and Federal law, tax codes, patents, military justice, constitutional law, and hundreds of other subjects. The up-front costs of a disc can be high; but if you and your colleagues expect to use one frequently, it can ultimately prove both cheaper and more convenient than getting the data online.

An excellent source of information on legal CD-ROMs—and on many other law-related PC products—is *Winning with Computers: Trial Practice in the 21st Century* from the American Bar Association. The book costs $99.95, but is well worth it for its numerous articles by practicing attorneys on the computer tools they've discovered to make their lives easier and their practices run more efficiently. I highly recommend it, and (to a lesser extent) *Winning with Computers, Part 2,* which costs $69.95. And I also recommend the ABA Technology Clearinghouse Information Packets, which cover over 20 topics (such as litigation support, document management, case management, and estate/pension planning), and cost $20 for one packet and $55 for three packets (or, for ABA members, $10 and $25). These books and packets will help lead you to other products and sources of information beyond the scope of this chapter.

Product Information

Note: Version numbers and prices may have changed by the time you read this.

ABA/net Department
American Bar Association
750 North Lake Shore Drive
Chicago, IL 60611
(800) 242-6005 ext. ABA (Dallas AT&T division)
Fax: (214) 308-4235 (Dallas AT&T division)

Charges $3 a month for subscription to basic services.

For LEXIS MVP plan, charges flat fee of $85 a month for access to the cases and statutes in your state, or $95 a month if you also want access to Federal circuit and district court cases. For each additional attorney on the plan, add $60 for state access only, or $70 for both state and Federal access.

For standard LEXIS access, charges $48 an hour, plus $6 to $91 per database search (or $3.75 per cite using Shepherd Citation/Autocite, or $5 per cite using LEXSEE and LEXSTAT).

For WESTLAW access (sans the DIALOG databases), charges $45 a month and $270 an hour; and charges for a minimum of 10 minutes of use a month ($27).

Advanced Software, Inc.
1095 East Duane Avenue
Suite 103
Sunnyvale, CA 94086
(800) 346-5392; (408) 733-0745
Fax: (408) 733-2335
DocuComp II 1.34: Single-User List Price, $199.95; Network (Novell and 3-Com) List Price, $695 for a 5-user license; Street Price N/A

American Bar Association
750 North Lake Shore Drive
Chicago, IL 60611
(312) 988-5555
Fax: (312) 988-6281

ABA Technology Clearinghouse Information Packets (covering over 20 topics, from bankruptcy software to word processors for lawyers): List Price, $20 for one packet or $55 for three packets; ABA Member Price, $10 for one packet or $25 for three packets

Winning with Computers: Trial Practice in the 21st Century (edited by John Tredennick, Jr.): List Price, $99.95; Street Price N/A

Winning with Computers, Part 2: Trial Practice in the 21st Century (edited by John Tredennick, Jr. and James Eidelman): List price, $69.95; Street Price N/A

Jurisoft
(Division of Mead Data Central, Inc.)
763 Massachusetts Avenue
Cambridge, MA 02139
(800) 262-5656; (617) 864-6151
Fax: (617) 661-0630

CheckCite 3.1: Free to LEXIS subscribers

CiteRite II 4.0: List Price, $180; Street Price N/A

FullAuthority 3.0: List Price, $160; Street Price N/A

CompareRite 4.11: List Price, $160; Street Price N/A

Korenthal Associates, Inc.
511 Avenue of the Americas, #400
New York, NY 10011
(800) 527-7647; (212) 242-1790
Fax: (212) 242-2599

4Print 4.15: List Price, $69.95; via coupon near the back of this book, $39.95

LEXIS

Mead Data Central, Inc.
9393 Springboro Pike
P.O. Box 933
Dayton, OH 45342
(800) 227-4908; (513) 859-1608
Fax: (513) 865-1666

Charges $125 a month, plus $46 an hour, plus additional charges per search. Alternatively, charges $125 a month, plus $406 an hour. As third alternative, charges nothing for connect time, but charges significantly more per search. See also the ABA/net listing for the MVP plan.

Osborne/McGraw-Hill

2600 Tenth Street
Berkeley, CA 94710
(800) 227-0900; (510) 549-2805
Fax: (510) 549-6603

Dvorak's Guide to PC Telecommunications, Second Edition: List Price, $39.95; generally not discounted

Stenographic Legal Services

3000 Executive Parkway
Suite 530
San Ramon, CA 94583
(800) 443-8007; (510) 277-7955
Fax: (510) 277-7983

Discovery Pro 1.0 for Windows: List Price, $1,195; Street Price N/A

Summation Legal Technologies, Inc.

595 Market Street
Suite 2050
San Francisco, CA 94105
(800) 735-7866; (415) 442-0404
Fax: (415) 442-0403

SUMMATION II 3.1: List Price, $1,092; Street Price N/A

West Publishing Company

610 Opperman Drive
Eagan, MN 55123
(800) 328-9352; (612) 687-7000
Fax: (612) 687-7302

WESTLAW (online service): Charges $125 a month, plus $195 an hour for up to 50 hours of use, then $185 an hour for hours 51 through 100, then $175 an hour for hours 101 through 200, and then $160 an hour for hours 201 and up. In most cases, a "connection" charge of $35 to $50 an hour is added. Also, a minimum of three hours of use a month ($579) is charged. Alternatively, you can pay no monthly fee, but $240 an hour, plus a connection charge of about $30 to $40 an hour, and a minimum of 20 minutes of use a month ($80).

Document assembly programs: Coverage ranges from bankruptcy filings to jury instructions, at prices from $179 to $650; call for more information

Express Forms: Dozens of legal forms in electronic forms, priced at $49 a package (or less when you buy several packages at a time); call for more information

/FAST (Fast Access Searchable Text) Disks: Dozens of state and Federal code rule books on disk, at prices ranging from $115 to $150 a package; call for more information

CHAPTER
16

TOOLS FOR PHYSICIANS

The pen is mightier than the sword...the case for prescriptions rather than surgery.

—Marvin Kitman

Writing isn't an activity most people associate with the medical field. If you *are* a health professional, though, you know the job occasionally entails writing reports, journal articles, or at least correspondence to your peers, and so can be made easier with editing software designed to handle medical jargon. Specialized tasks, such as generating prescriptions and creating written directions for patients, can also largely be automated by software. And searching through medical literature, whether it's for a writing project or to determine the best treatment for a patient, can be enormously facilitated by electronic information sources. This chapter therefore covers medical editing tools, specialized tools, and research tools.

Editing Tools

The basic tools you need for medical writing are the same as those for any other kind of writing: a solid word processor and spelling checker.

There are some word processors written specifically for medical use, but your best bet remains WordPerfect for DOS. As Chapter 1 points out, WordPerfect is fast, comprehensive, offers legendary toll-free technical support, and is supported by more third-party products than any other program in the industry.

The latter is particularly relevant, because while WordPerfect has an excellent general-purpose spelling checker, it doesn't recognize most medical expressions. This deficiency is addressed by two competing products: Dorland's Electronic Medical Speller and Stedman's/25 Plus for WordPerfect.

Both of these packages are word lists that supplement WordPerfect's own spelling dictionary. Their job is to keep WordPerfect from flagging your correctly spelled medical terms—and, just as important, to allow Word-Perfect to provide appropriate suggestions when a medical term *is* misspelled.

Dorland's, from WordPerfect Corporation, adds over 140,000 medical words to the spelling dictionary of WordPerfect 5.0 or higher, and can be used with both the DOS and Windows versions of WordPerfect. The program draws its vocabulary from the W. B. Saunders books *Dorland's Illustrated Medical Dictionary* and *Dorland's Medical Speller*, and covers 58 medical and pharmacological specialties (including anatomy, anesthesiology, bacteriology, cardiology, dentistry, internal medicine, nursing, pediatrics, psychiatry, radiology, surgery, toxicology, and virology). The package costs $89, and comes out with annual updates to keep its terminology current.

Medicine (is) the only profession that labors incessantly to destroy the reason for its existence.

—James Bryce

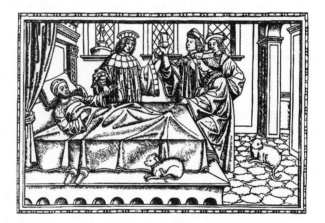

Stedman's/25 Plus, from Williams & Wilkins Electronic Media, adds 200,000 medical terms to WordPerfect 5.0 or higher for DOS or Windows. The package takes most of its words from the 25th anniversary edition of *Stedman's Medical Dictionary*; and additionally gets about 20,000 trade and generic drug names from such books as the *1992 United States Pharmacopeia Drug Index* and the *USAN/USP Dictionary of Drug Names*. Rather than simply integrate its word list with WordPerfect's, Stedman's sets up a medical "common word" list that's searched before the rest of the medical terms, thus speeding the spell-checking process. If you're using WordPerfect 5.1 or higher (as opposed to version 5.0), Stedman's will also identify capitalization errors in drug names, chemical symbols, and eponyms; for example, it will flag "thier" as a probable typo, rather than assume the word represents "Thier" in Weyers-Thier syndrome. Given its larger vocabulary, faster checking, and capitalization detection, Stedman's is—at least for the moment—the spelling checker add-on of choice. Its list price is $99. (By the way, if you don't use WordPerfect, take heart; a Microsoft Word for Windows edition of Stedman's is also available.)

If you also want support beyond spell-checking, you should consider William & Wilkins Electronic Media's Correct Grammar Medical. This program is based on the standard version of Correct Grammar (covered in Chapter 6, *Grammar and Style Checkers*), but adds to that package's general spelling dictionary most of the word list from Stedman's/25 Plus. It also appends to the 10 standard styles three medical ones: the American Medical Association's *Manual of Style*, which is used by doctors and transcription typists; Edward J. Huth's *Medical Style & Format* manual, which is used by medical writers and publishers; and the *Publication Manual of the American Psychological Association*, which is often used by nurses. Like standard Correct Grammar, the medical version works with a variety of word processors, and is available in both DOS and Windows editions. Correct Grammar Medical's list price is $199.

You can only cure retail but you can prevent wholesale.
—Brock Chisholm

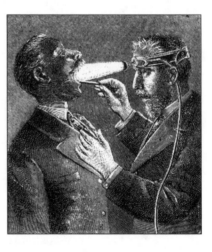

Lastly, if you'd like to look up the *meaning* of medical terms from your hard disk, the program to buy is Brody's Medical Dictionary from Inductel. Rather than a mere word list, this package is a full-fledged electronic version of the Brody book, containing more than 40,000 definitions. If you load the program as memory resident, it takes up as little as 12K, and displays the definition of the word your cursor is on at a keystroke. The program's list price is a low $59.95. However, an even better deal is to purchase Brody's along with Inductel's biology, physics, and chemistry dictionaries (called the Medical Library package) for a total of only $99.95!

When you look up a word, *all* the Inductel dictionaries you've installed are searched instantly (assuming you've set the program up a certain way), and all the definitions found are displayed on-screen. For more information about the Inductel product line, see Chapter 5, *Electronic Dictionaries and Thesauruses.*

Specialized Tools

If you diagnose patients, you know that the end of a session calls for some time-consuming paperwork—writing prescriptions, jotting down instructions, maybe even creating a note excusing the patient from work or school. You can speed patient discharge, and also improve the quality of the service you provide, by automating such tasks.

First, if your patient is already on medication, you'll want to check the possibility of adverse interactions with the new drugs you're prescribing. This can take a long time using books if many different drugs are involved; but it's a snap with a program such as Drug Master Plus from Rapha Group Software. This package, which contains data on the 3,300 most common medications, lets you select an array of drugs with a few keystrokes. It then displays a summary of potential interactions, and offers the option of providing more detailed messages about specific interactions. Drug Master Plus's price is $295.

As for writing the prescription itself, you'll get the most bang for the buck with the $195 EASY DOC Script. This menu-driven program lets you enter patient information (including a section for medication allergies); display the drugs available in the medication category you choose; select multiple drugs with a few keystrokes; and then print out your prescriptions, placing each drug on a separate sheet regardless of how many you selected. The program even gives you the option of transmitting your prescriptions to a pharmacy via modem! EASY DOC Script has no restrictions on the number of patients it handles, and can track information (such as addresses and DEA numbers) on up to 99 doctors who are using it.

Next, to ensure that your patient understands your diagnosis and prescribed treatment, a scribbled note is no substitute for a couple of pages of carefully prepared information. On the diagnostic end, there's Clinical Reference Systems' Adult Health Advisor, which contains over 500 handouts on medical and surgical topics, written by nine RNs and 18 MDs. You can select the diagnostic topic you want by typing its first few letters, and then print it by just pressing a function key. You can also revise a handout, or create one of your own. The program costs $395. (On the other hand, if your practice is more specialized, the company also publishes Pediatric Advisor and Ob/Gyn Advisor.)

As for your prescription, MedTeach from the American Society of Hospital Pharmacists provides 421 monographs, averaging one to two pages each, that cover thousands of common medications. You can search for appropriate monographs by drug brand name, drug generic name, or document number; and select and print up to 24 monographs at a time. You also have the option of personalizing the printouts by adding the patient's name, your name and number, and up to four lines of comments. You can even edit a monograph's contents (though you can't create new ones). MedTeach is, unfortunately, copy protected. It costs $435.

Of course, that's a lot of software to juggle around. With some practice, you can learn to quickly cycle through a variety of programs via a task-switching program such as Microsoft Windows (see Chapter 20, *Essential General-Purpose Tools*). However, you may prefer a more integrated approach.

God heals, and the doctor takes the fee.
—Benjamin Franklin

Script Consultant-DM, from Rapha Group Software, will store patient information, help you write and print prescriptions, and also provide patient handouts. For example, when you write a prescription, the program automatically checks to see if there's a record of your patient being allergic to the drug; if there is, it immediately tells you so. The package also does a great job of checking for potential drug interactions, because Drug Master Plus is built into it (hence the "-DM" after "Script Consultant"). The program can also print handouts for patients, though its monographs aren't carefully crafted in layman's language the way MedTeach's are, and it provides almost none of the diagnostic information Adult Health Advisor does. On the other hand, Script Consultant-DM can easily produce other documents, such as a list of all the medications a patient needs and the times each should be taken; and a "doctor's note" for the patient to take to work or school. This package's list price is $495.

Research Tools

While you can always conduct research in a library, you'll find it quicker and easier to at least begin by searching for your data electronically. There are two basic ways to do this: via an online service (as discussed in Chapter 10, *Online References*) or via CD-ROMs (as covered in Chapter 9, *CD-ROM References*).

The most popular online medical service is probably MEDLARS (Medical Literature Analysis and Retrieval Systems), which is run by the U.S. National Library of Medicine, or NLM. This system's main function is to let you to search through NLM's MEDLINE, which contains nearly seven million abstracts and citations on biomedical literature drawn from *Index MEDICUS*, *Index to Dental Literature*, and *International Nursing Index*. In addition, MEDLARS lets you access other bibliographic databases such as CANCERLIT (cancer topics), CHEMLINE (definitions of chemical substances), and TOXLINE (toxicological effects of drugs and chemicals). Connect charges are around $18 an hour, but they change frequently, so contact NLM to determine the current rates.

MEDLARS isn't the only route to MEDLINE. Another access service is PaperChase, developed by Boston's Beth Israel Hospital, which employs easy-to-use menus and plain language commands to guide you through various NLM databases. PaperChase is especially good at helping you construct efficient searches so you can reduce the amount of time you spend online. It also provides some unique options, such as a Fotocopy command that tells the service to locate the article you want, copy it, and then send it to you via first class mail, overnight delivery, or fax. PaperChase's connect charge is $23 an hour during the day, and $22 an hour after 7 P.M. Eastern time and on weekends.

Yet another alternative is the playfully named Grateful Med, a PC program developed by NLM. Like PaperChase, Grateful Med is based around a friendly menu system, and reduces wasted connect time by helping you build accurate search instructions. While this product doesn't provide as many options as PaperChase, it has the advantage of letting you construct all your search requests offline, so the time you spend with it doesn't cost you anything. When you're ready to conduct a search, Grateful Med automatically dials into MEDLARS, accesses the citations and abstracts you requested with your preset instructions, saves them to your floppy or hard disk, and logs off. You can buy the package from the National Technical Information Service for a mere $29.95.

Once you have your bibliographic information, you may opt to track down the actual articles at a nearby library. Again, however, you'll find it more efficient to retrieve the text online.

InfoPro Technologies' BRS Search Service lets you retrieve the full text of over 80 medical journals, including *The Journal of the American Medical Association*, *New England Journal of Medicine*, *Annals of Internal Medicine*, *British Medical Journal*, and *The Lancet*. It also carries the full text of more than 20 medical textbooks, such as *The Merck Manual* and *Gray's Anatomy*. The costs are an $80 annual subscription fee, plus $45 to $75 an hour (depending on the databases you access), and additional charges for the text you retrieve.

And if you're familiar with Mead Data Central's NEXIS or LEXIS services, you'll be comfortable using the same company's MEDIS service (which is actually a subset of NEXIS). MEDIS offers the full text of over 30 medical journals, as well as other data falling under the categories of drugs, cancer, administration of health care, emergency/poison information, and bibliographic information. This service is well-organized, but quite expensive, requiring $43 an hour plus substantial additional charges per search plus a monthly subscription fee of $50. If you plan to use NEXIS/MEDIS frequently, you may ultimately save money by signing on for a flat-fee membership; call Mead for specifics.

Perhaps the best online deal, however, comes from the new US Health-Link service, which operates through Oregon Health Sciences University, and is run by the former medical director of the now-defunct AMA/Net (a service that was affiliated with the American Medical Association). US HealthLink provides access to MEDLINE, EMPIRES (Excerpta Medica Physicians Information Retrieval and Education Service), DISEASE Synopsis Information, the Comtex Medical News Service, the DXplain Diagnostic Decision Support Service, the MEDICOM Drug Interaction Service, Patient Simulation Modules, an electronic mail system, forums for discussion with your peers, and more. This is all available for a flat fee of $35 a month for up to four hours of use, and then a mere $5.40 for each additional hour. With that kind of pricing, it's hard to go wrong. Premium services are also available for additional fees; call US HealthLink for details.

While online research is invaluable, it can also be a bit nerve-racking, since the meter is ticking for every minute you're connected. Therefore, if there are certain information sources you use frequently, you'll probably find it both more convenient and more cost-effective to access them via CD-ROMs.

For example, Macmillan New Media offers the full text from the past five years of the following publications: *New England Journal of Medicine*, *The Journal of the American Medical Association*, *British Medical Journal*, *The Lancet*, *Canadian Medical Association Journal*, *Annals of Internal Medicine*, and *Mortality and Morbidity Weekly Report*. Each journal collection is on a separate disc, and costs $295 (though Macmillan occasionally provides promotional discounts). Even if you have a complete paper collection of a particular journal, you won't be able to find information in it as quickly and consistently as you can with its CD-ROM version—and you won't enjoy the space savings a CD-ROM provides, either.

Never go to a doctor whose office plants have died.

—Erma Bombeck

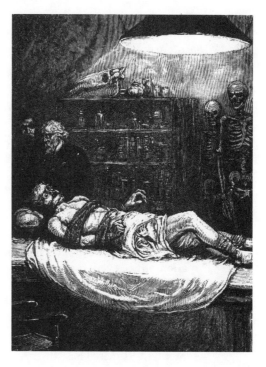

Similarly, if your field is internal medicine, you may benefit from Scientific American Medicine's well-regarded CONSULT disc, which contains the full text of *Scientific American Medicine* magazine, plus the DISCO-TEST library (over 45 patient management problems, available for CME credits), and sells for $395. And if you're tired of tediously leafing through your *Physicians' Desk Reference* for drug information and *The Merck Manual* for diagnosis and therapy data, you can get both of these fundamental references on a single disc for $895 from Medical Economics Data. (Alternatively, you can get the PDR by itself for $595.)

All the CD-ROMs I've mentioned so far provide you with complete text. The majority of medical CD-ROMs, however, are collections of abstracts and citations, such as MEDLINE, CANCERLIT, and AIDSLINE. While these types of discs offer only limited information, they'll sometimes be all you require to answer a research question. At other times, you can use them to prepare for an extremely efficient online session in which you access only the articles you need.

The desire to take medicine is perhaps the greatest feature which distinguishes man from the animals.
—William Osler

Not surprisingly, the most popular medical CD-ROM is MEDLINE, which is available from several publishers. For example, SilverPlatter Information offers a variety of purchase options, including the past 11 years of MEDLINE, updated monthly, for $1,795; and MEDLINE from 1966 to the present, updated monthly, for $2,475.

On the other hand, if you need MEDLINE data only on your particular specialty, you can save money with Macmillan New Media's MEDLINE subset CD-ROMs. These discs cost $195 each, and cover cardiology, critical care, emergency medicine, family practice, gastroenterology and hepatology, infectious diseases, obstetrics and gynecology, pediatrics, and general interest physician literature.

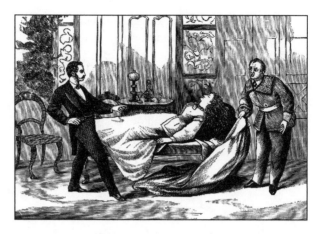

She got her good looks from her father—he's a plastic surgeon.

—Groucho Marx

There are scores of other CD-ROMs available, covering neurosciences, pathology, drugs and pharmacology, radiology, anesthesiology, psychiatry, nursing, health planning and administration, and many other areas of medicine. To learn what's out there for your specialty, you can get in touch with the publishers just mentioned—Compact Cambridge, Macmillan New Media, Medical Economics Data, and Scientific American Medicine —as well as such other publishers as Creative Multimedia Corporation; Healthcare Information Services; Little, Brown and Company; Micromedex; Oxford University Press; SilverPlatter Information; and Quanta Press. Contact information on all these publishers, plus brief notes about their respective product lines, appears at the end of this chapter.

Alternatively (or in addition), you may want to buy Meckler Publishing's CD-ROMs in Print to have available a comprehensive database of *all* types of existing CD-ROMs. More information about this useful $95 disc appears in Chapter 9, *CD-ROM References.*

Product Information

Note: Version numbers and prices may have changed by the time you read this.

American Society of Hospital Pharmacists
7272 Wisconsin Avenue
Bethesda, MD 20814
(301) 657-3000
Fax: (301) 657-8817

MedTeach 2.0: List Price, $435; generally not discounted; copy protected via software

Clinical Reference Systems
7100 East Belleview Avenue
Suite 305
Englewood, CO 80111-1636
(800) 237-8401; (303) 220-1661
Fax: (303) 220-1685

Adult Health Advisor 3.0: List Price, $395; discounted when purchased with other CRS programs

Pediatric Advisor 5.0: List Price, $395; discounted when purchased with other CRS programs

Ob/Gyn Advisor 2.2: List Price, $395; discounted when purchased with other CRS programs

Creative Multimedia Corporation
514 NW 11th Avenue
Suite 203
Portland, OR 97209
(800) 262-7668; (503) 241-4351
Fax: (503) 241-4370

CD-ROM titles include American Family Physician, Pediatrics on Disk, and Pediatric Infectious Disease Journal; call for free catalog

EASY DOC Corporation
P.O. Box 1474
Wilson, NC 27894
(919) 243-7246
Fax: (919) 243-7247

EASY DOC Script 2.1: List Price, $195; Street Price N/A

Healthcare Information Services, Inc.
2335 American River Drive
Suite 307
Sacramento, CA 95825
(800) 468-1128; (916) 648-8075
Fax: (916) 648-8078

CD-ROM titles include BiblioMed Cardiology Series, BiblioMed Citation Series, and BiblioMed Gastroenterology Series; call for free product literature

Inductel, Inc.
5339 Prospect Road
Suite 321
San Jose, CA 95129-5028
(800) 367-4497; (408) 866-8016
Fax: (408) 243-1762

Brody's Medical Dictionary: List Price, $59.95; generally not discounted

Medical Library (Brody's Medical Dictionary, McGraw-Hill Dictionary of Biology, McGraw-Hill Dictionary of Chemical Terms, and McGraw-Hill Dictionary of Physics): List Price, $99.95; generally not discounted

InfoPro Technologies
BRS Online Products
8000 Westpark Drive
McLean, VA 22102
(800) 955-0906; (703) 442-0900
Fax: (703) 893-0490

BRS (online) Search Service: Typically, $45 to $75 per hour (depending on the databases you access), plus additional charges for the text you retrieve, plus an $80 annual subscription fee; call for more information

Little, Brown and Company
34 Beacon Street
Boston, MA 02108
(800) 289-6299; (617) 227-0730
Fax: (617) 859-0629

Publishes the MAXX CD-ROM, which contains 21 popular Little, Brown medical references, including *The Manual of Medical Therapeutics, Interpretation of Diagnostic Tests, Manual of Neurology, A Practical Approach to Infectious Diseases,* and *Manual of Intensive Care Medicine*. List Price, $395 for three updates a year ($595 for institutions), $595 when the text of *U.S. Pharmacopeial Drug Information, Volume I* is included on the disk ($795 for institutions); generally not discounted

Macmillan New Media
124 Mount Auburn Street
Cambridge, MA 02138
(800) 342-1338; (617) 661-2955
Fax: (617) 868-7738

CD-ROMs containing the past five years of *The Journal of the American Medical Association, New England Journal of Medicine, British Medical Journal, The Lancet, Canadian Medical Association Journal, Annals of Internal Medicine,* and *Mortality and Morbidity Weekly Report*: List Price, $295 per disc ($495 for institutions); Street Price N/A, but promotional discounts *are* occasionally offered

Other CD-ROMs also available; call for free catalog

Mead Data Central
9393 Springboro Pike
P.O. Box 933
Dayton, OH 45342
(800) 227-4908; (513) 859-1608
Fax: (513) 865-1666

MEDIS (part of the NEXIS online service): $43 per hour plus additional charges per search plus monthly subscription fee of $50; a flat-fee option is available for frequent users; call for more information

Meckler Publishing
11 Ferry Lane West
Westport, CT 06880
(800) 632-5537; (203) 226-6967
Fax: (203) 454-5840

CD-ROMs in Print 1994: List Price, $95 (or $165 with book version included); generally not discounted

Medical Economics Data
Five Paragon Drive
Montvale, NJ 07645-1742
(800) 232-7379; (201) 358-7200
Fax: (201) 573-4956

Physicians' Desk Reference CD-ROM: List Price, $595 for three updates a year; generally not discounted

Physicians' Desk Reference/Merck Manual CD-ROM: List Price, $895 for three updates a year; generally not discounted

Micromedex, Inc.
600 Grant Street
Denver, CO 80203-3527
(800) 525-9083; (303) 831-1400
Fax: (303) 837-1717

CD-ROM titles include DRUGDEX (referenced drug information), EMERGINDEX (emergency and acute care), INDENTIDEX (tablet and capsule identification), and POISINDEX (poison identification and management); call for free product literature

National Library of Medicine
MEDLARS Management Section
8600 Rockville Pike
Bethesda, MD 20894
(800) 638-8480; (301) 496-6193
Fax: (310) 496-0822

MEDLARS online service: Around $18 per hour, but the prices change frequently, so call for the current rates

National Technical Information Service
5285 Port Royal Road
Springfield, VA 22161
(800) 553-6847; (703) 487-4650
Fax: (703) 321-8547

Grateful Med 6.0: List Price, $29.95; generally not discounted

Oxford University Press
200 Madison Avenue
New York, NY 10016
(800) 334-4249, ext. 7370; (212) 679-7300, ext. 7370
Fax: (212) 725-2972

Publishes Oxford Textbook of Medicine CD-ROM, as well as disk-based medical references such as Oxford Database of Perinatal Trials; call for more information

PaperChase
350 Longwood Avenue
Galleria Building
Boston, MA 02115
(800) 722-2075; (617) 278-3900
Fax: (617) 277-9792

PaperChase online service: $23 per hour during the day, $22 per hour after 7 P.M. Eastern time and on weekends; call for more information

Quanta Press, Inc.
1313 Fifth Street SE
Suite 208C
Minneapolis, MN 55414
(612) 379-3956
Fax: (612) 623-4570

Prescription Drugs—A Pharmacist's Guide CD-ROM: List Price, $79.95; Street Price N/A

Rapha Group Software
433 Carson Road
St. Louis, MO 63135
(314) 521-0808
Fax: (314) 521-0808 (same as voice number; RGS's machine automatically senses whether you're a person or a fax)

Drug Master Plus: List Price, $295; generally not discounted

Script Consultant-DM 2.5: List Price, $495; generally not discounted

Scientific American Medicine
415 Madison Avenue
New York, NY 10017
(800) 545-0554; (212) 754-0801
Fax: (212) 980-3062

CONSULT/Scientific American Medicine on CD-ROM: List Price, $395 for year of quarterly updated discs ($695 for institutional purchases); generally not discounted

SilverPlatter Information
100 River Ridge Drive
Norwood, MA 02062-5026
(800) 343-0064; (617) 769-2599
Fax: (617) 769-8763

One of the largest publishers of medical CD-ROMs, with titles ranging from CANCER-CD and HealthPLAN-CD to a series of Excerpta Medica discs; call for free catalog

US HealthLink
One Wheaton Center
Suite 1611
Wheaton, IL 60187
(800) 682-8770; (708) 682-8700
Fax: (708) 682-8740
Online information and signup: (800) 225-4652

For basic services, $35 a month for up to four hours of use, and then $5.40 for each additional hour. Premium services also available; call for more information

Williams & Wilkins Electronic Media
428 East Preston Street
Baltimore, MD 21202-3993
(800) 527-5597; (410) 528-4000
Fax: (410) 528-4422

Stedman's/25 Plus 2.1 (for both DOS and Windows versions of WordPerfect): List Price, $99; Street Price, about $65

Stedman's/25 Plus 2.1 (for Microsoft Word for Windows): List Price, $99; Street Price N/A

Correct Grammar Medical 1.0: List Price, $199; Street Price N/A

WordPerfect Corporation
1555 N. Technology Way
Orem, UT 84057
(800) 321-4566; (801) 225-5000
Fax: (801) 228-5377

Dorland's Electronic Medical Speller 1.0 (for both DOS and Windows versions of WordPerfect): List Price, $89; Street Price N/A

CHAPTER
17

TOOLS FOR SCIENTISTS
AND ENGINEERS

The writer is an engineer of the human soul.
—Joseph Stalin

Donald Knuth is famous in computer science circles for writing several classic volumes of computer algorithms. He's famous in the entire scientific and technical community, however, for being dissatisfied with the way his first volume looked when it was printed in the 1970s.

The problem was the programs running the typesetting machines did a poor job of handling technical symbols and complex mathematical formulas. After several years of study, Knuth came up with the typesetting language TeX (pronounced "tek"), which provides precise control over the way scientific characters and equations appear on a page. TeX has since become an extremely popular tool; a number of technical journals even accept submissions directly in the TeX format.

However, while TeX does a great job of talking to typesetters, it's not so great at communicating with humans. Like its mainstream cousin PostScript, TeX is fundamentally a programming language, and so requires you to enter a stream of esoteric programming commands. (For example, to produce the fraction x/y, you have to type the command $\frac {x} {y} $.) That's far from an ideal way of working; when you're composing a document, you should be concentrating on its content, not on which code sequence will generate a quadratic equation.

What TeX needed was an easy-to-use, visual front end—in other words, something akin to the function desktop publishing programs serve for PostScript. It took a while, but that missing link finally appeared in May 1992 in the form of a revolutionary Windows word processor called Scientific Word. That program is the focus of this chapter.

In addition, this chapter briefly discusses a DOS alternative for scientific word processing, a series of McGraw-Hill technical dictionaries, a technical desktop publishing package, and online and CD-ROM resources.

Scientific Word

Scientific Word, from Tools for Scientific Creativity Software Research, Inc. (which, mercifully, is also referred to as just TCI), provides support for special characters such as integrals and Greek letters; makes it easy to enter complicated, multi-line mathematical formulas; and uses TeX as its native file format. More specifically, it uses a "flavor" of TeX called LaTeX, which adds such advanced features as table of contents generation, cross-referencing, theorem numbering, bibliographies, and tables.

To a chemist, nothing on Earth is unclean. A writer must be as objective as a chemist; he must abandon the subjective line; he must know that dung-heaps play a very respectable part in a landscape.

—Anton Chekhov

Scientific Word is both visual and intuitive. For example, when you use a mouse to click on various icons near the top of the screen, you display drop-down palettes offering dozens of scientific operators, radicals, matrices, functions, brackets, and labels. With another click, the symbol you select is inserted into your document. Further, if the symbol normally has a number or variable near it, another click moves you to the appropriate spot for typing it in. Alternatively, if you don't care for using a mouse, Scientific Word also responds extremely well to keystrokes.

For example, to enter an integral with an *a* at the bottom and a *b* at the top (that is, $\int_a^b$), you can click on the integral icon to insert the symbol; click on an N_x icon to position your cursor at the bottom of the integral, and type *a*; click past the integral; and then click on an N^x icon to place your cursor at the top of the integral, and type *b*. Or, more simply, you can press Ctrl+I to insert the integral; type *a*; press Tab to move to the top of the integral; and type *b*. In both cases, to continue the formula or just resume normal typing, you can either click past the integral, or press Spacebar or End.

Similarly, to enter a fraction such as 1 divided by the square root of (5 + (x cubed))—that is, $\frac{1}{\sqrt{5+x^3}}$ —you'd do the following using the keyboard:

1. Press Ctrl+F to insert the division symbol; you're automatically positioned to enter the dividend

2. Type *1*

3. Press Down Arrow so you're positioned to enter the divisor

4. Type Ctrl+R to enter a square root symbol

5. Type *5+x*; the divisor is now the square root of (5+x)

6. Press Ctrl+H to place a superscripted number on the x

7. Type *3* to bring x to the third power; the divisor is now the square root of (5+(x cubed))

8. Press End to move from the fraction and resume normal typing.

At least as nice as the ease of entry is the ease with which you can make changes. For example, if you now decide you want the x variable raised to the fifth power, simply pressing Left Arrow once moves you back to the x superscript position; you can then press Backspace to delete the 3, type *5*, and press End to finish. Similarly, you can change the x variable to y by pressing Left Arrow twice, pressing Backspace, and typing *y*.

Another notable feature is Scientific Word's ability to automatically change the size and spacing of the elements of your formula as you make revisions. For example, if you have a summation sign in front of a fraction and you add elements to make the fraction grow vertically, the summation sign will automatically grow with it. Moreover, any limit numbers or variables on the summation operator will also be resized automatically.

The program's flexibility is evident in other ways, as well. For example, while you can insert the Greek alpha character by clicking on its icon, you can also do so by holding down the Ctrl key and typing *alpha*! And if you're a TeX expert, you can indirectly enter TeX code by composing your programming sequence in the Windows Clipboard and then using the Edit Paste command to insert it into your document, where it will instantly appear in its output form. (Similarly, Scientific Word can help you *learn* TeX. If you open the Windows Clipboard, highlight a formula in your document, and select the Edit Copy command, the Clipboard will display the formula's corresponding TeX code.)

Scientific Word offers other conveniences, such as italicizing mathematical sequences and displaying them in red on-screen so you can easily distinguish them from standard text. Further, it lets you change a selected section of your document from math formatting to text, and vice versa, with the press of a keystroke.

Scientific and humanist approaches are not competitive but supportive, and both are ultimately necessary.
—Robert C. Wood

You can also save any phrase, formula, or portion of a formula for future use, calling it up with a few keystrokes or mouse clicks whenever you need it. This feature lets you build a library of frequently used text and math that you can draw on both to save time and to ensure consistency.

Scientific Word structures your document with style sheets. The program provides more than 45 of them, including many for journal articles and technical books, and others for reports, memos, letters, exams, and even faxes. Unlike many Windows word processors, however, Scientific Word doesn't attempt to display on-screen precisely how your document will appear on paper; most significantly, it doesn't show where lines and pages actually break. Instead, it emphasizes ease of data entry and editing;

for example, it changes line breaks to accommodate the size of the window you're using. When you need to see an accurate display of what will be printed, you can select a Preview option.

In a nutshell, Scientific Word is a program that may forever change the way scientific and technical documents are created. It costs a steep $595 ($476 for academics), but if you use a lot of math in your writing, it's worth it.

Before Scientific Word, the technical word processor of choice was TCI's DOS-based graphical word processor T3. This product still has its uses. First, if your machine lacks the hardware essentials to run Windows, it will nonetheless be able to run T3. Second, T3 provides a wide array of chemical symbols that are not yet supported in Scientific Word. In addition, T3 allows you to create most of the same characters and math that Scientific Word does. On the other hand, the program is quirky in design, doesn't let you create equations nearly as easily and quickly as Scientific Word, doesn't produce printed pages that look as good, and doesn't save your files in anything resembling the TeX format. So although T3 rates a look, in most cases you'll be better off with Scientific Word, which in effect is the TCI upgrade of T3.

Politicians should read science fiction, not westerns and detective stories.
    —Arthur C. Clarke

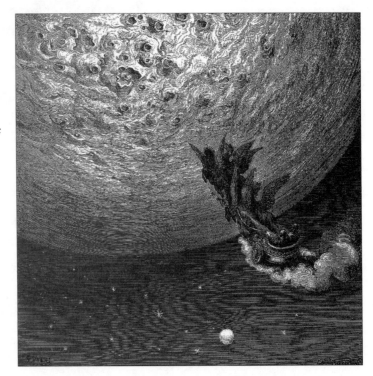

Other Tools and Resources

Like other professional fields, science and engineering have their share of jargon. When you run across an unfamiliar term, or when you simply need to double-check the spelling of a word, you'll probably find pressing a few keystrokes more convenient than leafing through a paper dictionary.

Inductel addresses this need with a PC version of the *McGraw-Hill Dictionary of Scientific and Technical Terms*. The book is broken down into six electronic dictionaries covering Biology, Chemical Terms, Computers, Electrical and Chemical Engineering, Mechanical and Design Engineering, and Physics. Together, they contain more than 120,000 definitions and take up about 9MB of your hard drive. If you're short on disk space, though, you can opt to install only the dictionaries you most require.

Scientists are Peeping Toms at the keyhole of eternity.

—Arthur Koestler

The universe is full of magical things patiently waiting for our wits to grow sharper.

—Eden Phillpots

Life is extinct on other planets because their scientists were more advanced than ours.

—Anonymous

Nothing in life is to be feared. It is only to be understood.

—Marie Curie

Had I been present at the creation of the world I would have proposed some improvements.
    —Alfonso X

The Inductel package also provides a program called KAS, which lacks an attractive display and intuitive operation, but searches through the dictionaries with lightning speed. If you load KAS as memory resident, it takes up as little as 12K, and displays the definition of the word your cursor is on at a keystroke. Further, you can set the program so that *all* the Inductel dictionaries you've installed are searched, and all the definitions found are displayed on your screen (with each definition preceded by the name of the dictionary it came from). At $149.95, The McGraw-Hill Technical Dictionaries package is an excellent deal. For more information about the Inductel product line, see Chapter 5, *Electronic Dictionaries and Thesauruses.*

On another front, if you need to lay out complex technical publications, the first program to consider is Frame Technology's FrameMaker for Windows. FrameMaker is a high-end desktop publishing package in the same league as PageMaker and QuarkXPress, but with powerful equation editors and other features that are tailored for scientific and technical publishing. The program is harder to learn than mainstream DTP packages, but you'll find the effort you expend more than justified if you produce numerous technical documents. More information about FrameMaker appears in Chapter 22, *Laying Out Your Work*.

Also, while they're beyond the scope of this book, you should be aware of the superb mathematical programs available, such as Gauss for math-oriented programming (Aptech Systems, (206) 432-7855), Mathcad for quick and easy calculating (Mathsoft, (800) 628-4223), TK Solver for equation/model solving (Universal Technical Systems, (800) 435-7887), and the stunningly powerful Mathematica for symbolic manipulation (Wolfram Research, (800) 441-6284). A nice summary of these tools, and several others, appears in author/scientist Barry Simon's "A Scientist's Software Toolbox" on pages 418 and 419 of the August 1992 issue of *PC Magazine*. If you belong to CompuServe (see Chapter 10, *Online References*), you can download the article in seconds from the Computer Database Plus service, which is accessed with the command GO CDP at the system prompt.

You should also take advantage of the scientific information available electronically. The best online resource is Internet, a worldwide computer service with millions of subscribers, many of whom work in universities or corporate R&D departments. If you aren't affiliated with an institution that's already on Internet, you can get access information from InterNIC, which is a nonprofit Internet support center.

Lastly, regarding CD-ROMs, there's too wide a range of products to list here, but Meckler Publishing's CD-ROMs in Print 1994 will provide you with a comprehensive, searchable database. For more information about this $95 disc, see Chapter 9, *CD-ROM References*.

Product Information

Note: Version numbers and prices may have changed by the time you read this.

CompuServe Information Service
5000 Arlington Center
Columbus, OH 43220
(800) 848-8199; (614) 457-0802
Fax: (614) 457-8149

Standard membership costs $8.95 a month and $8 an hour, and includes free access to about 35 basic services. Alternative "pay as you go" plan costs $2.50 a month and $12.80 an hour.

Frame Technology Corporation
1010 Rincon Circle
San Jose, CA 95131
(800) 843-7263; (408) 433-3311
Fax: (408) 433-1928

Framemaker 4.0 for Windows: List Price, $895; Street Price, about $525

Inductel, Inc.
5339 Prospect Road
Suite 321
San Jose, CA 95129-5028
(800) 367-4497; (408) 866-8016
Fax: (408) 243-1762

The McGraw-Hill Dictionaries (Biology, Chemical Terms, Computers, Electrical and Chemical Engineering, Mechanical and Design Engineering, and Physics): List Price, $149.95; generally not discounted

InterNIC
P.O. Box 85608
San Diego, CA 92186-9784
(800) 444-4345; (619) 455-4600
Fax: (619) 455-4640

Ask this nonprofit information clearinghouse for the free packet that identifies the companies or institutions providing Internet access in your area

Meckler Publishing
11 Ferry Lane West
Westport, CT 06880
(800) 632-5537; (203) 226-6967
Fax: (203) 454-5840

CD-ROMs in Print 1994: List Price, $95 (or $165 with book version included); generally not discounted

Tools for Scientific Creativity Software Research, Inc. (TCI)
1190 Foster Road
Las Cruces, NM 88001
(800) 874-2383; (505) 522-4600
Fax: (505) 522-0116

Scientific Word 1.1 (for Windows): List Price, $595; Academic Price, $476

T3 2.3 (for DOS): List Price, $495; Academic Price, $396

CHAPTER
18

TOOLS FOR
MULTILINGUAL WRITERS

Most of this book centers on tools to help you write better in English. However, our world is also home to hundreds of other rich languages, and you may be writing in one or more of them, as well.

If so, there are two categories of software you'll find helpful: multilingual word processors that allow you to enter, edit, and print foreign characters; and translation programs that convert your text from one language to another.

This chapter covers both of these product groups. Whether you're a New Yorker trying to learn Spanish, or a Chinese American writing to the folks back in Nanjing, or a Parisian translating technical manuals for clients in Berlin, there's something here for you.

Multilingual Word Processing

There are a surprisingly large—one might even say *bewildering*—number of ways to handle non-English text entry on a PC.

The first thing to realize is that if your needs are casual, and you only want to enter Roman-alphabet languages such as French, German, Italian, and Spanish, you can use *any* word processor, because letters such as É, è, â, Å, Ü, and Ñ are all standard PC characters. More specifically, they're part of the 256 letters and symbols in the American Standard Code for Information Exchange, or *ASCII*, that's built into DOS. (This group is also referred to as the ASCII *character set*.)

To enter a European letter, you can simply hold down the Alt key and type the character's ASCII code (which is listed in your DOS manual) on your numeric keypad; or use the DOS command KEYB (which is also covered in your DOS manual). However, both these methods quickly become tedious.

A better solution is a tiny (720-byte) memory-resident program called Euro KeyBoard, or EKB, which lets you use intuitive keystrokes to enter special characters. For example, when EKB is loaded and you're in any DOS-based program, Ctrl+Alt+E produces É, Ctrl+Alt+U produces Ü, Ctrl+Alt+2 produces ½, and Ctrl+Alt+e,^ produces ê. Thanks to the generosity of its programmer, Eric Meyer, EKB is entirely free. Using a modem, you can download it in a few seconds from a BBS or online service—for example, it's available in CompuServe's Foreign Language Forum library, which can be accessed by typing GO FLEFO at the system prompt. (If you aren't familiar with telecommunications, see Chapter 10, *Online References*.)

If you use Microsoft Windows, you should also try Foreigner, which pops up keypads displaying special ASCII and Windows characters. When you mouse-click on the character you want, it's instantly copied to the Windows Clipboard; selecting the Edit Paste command from your Windows program then inserts the character into your document. Foreigner can also be set to paste *directly* into many Windows programs, and then close or minimize itself automatically, which makes using it quick and unobtrusive. This handy utility comes from programmer Gordon Goldsborough and, like EKB, it's free and can be downloaded in under a minute from a BBS or online service.

EKB and Foreigner can only help you access DOS and Windows characters, though. To work with an alphabet not built into these operating systems, you have to install an electronic typeface family, or *font*, that's been specifically designed to represent your language's letters and symbols. (Actually, you need two sets of fonts: one to display the characters on-screen and another to print them onto paper.) Foreign language fonts are available from several companies, including Data-Cal and Linguist's Software.

Alternatively, you can obtain foreign character support directly from certain word processors. Most adept are two top-of-the-line DOS-based word processors recommended in Chapter 1: Nota Bene and WordPerfect.

Nota Bene gives you several ways to enter special characters, including Ctrl+Alt+letter combinations à la EKB, a pop-up menu à la Foreigner, and function key+letter sequences. Further, a supplementary program called

N.B. Lingua provides screen and printer fonts for Cyrillic, Greek, and Hebrew, giving you access to an impressive total of 3,000 characters. With N.B. Lingua installed, you can easily switch between "software keyboards" for different languages with a few keystrokes—for example, pressing Ctrl+ G sets you to Greek, pressing Ctrl+H,Ctrl+R selects Hebrew and right-to-left typing, and pressing Ctrl+E,Ctrl+L switches you back to English and left-to-right typing.

Nota Bene works exclusively in character mode, so text entry is always fast and smooth. (On the other hand, it can't display certain alphabets— such as Hebrew and Cyrillic—on screen simultaneously the way a graphics-mode word processor can; if that's an issue for you, see the description of Multi-Lingual Scholar later in this chapter.) The Nota Bene/N.B. Lingua combination lists for $748, but you can buy it for $299—a terrific bargain—via the Technology Group coupon near the back of this book.

In America only the successful writer is important, in France all writers are important, in England no writer is important, in Australia you have to explain what a writer is.

—Geoffrey Cotterell

WordPerfect is no slouch, either; it lets you enter French acute accents, German umlauts, European currency symbols, and other special characters via its Ctrl+V Compose feature—for example, the sequence Ctrl+V,E,' produces É, while Ctrl+Alt+e,^ produces ê. Using more complex number codes, you can also enter Cyrillic, Greek, Hebrew, Hiragana, and Katakana characters, plus such extras as mathematical and scientific symbols; altogether, a total of 1,500 characters. If topnotch print quality isn't required, you don't even have to buy special printer fonts to get these characters onto paper; WordPerfect can print them all by treating them as graphics.

Clearly, then, there are a variety of ways to enter and print non-English text. If you're going to spend a lot of time working in a foreign language, though, you'll also want additional tools, such as a spelling checker and thesaurus, and even program commands, that operate in that language. Fortunately, such powerhouse word processors as WordPerfect for DOS, Microsoft Word for Windows, and Lotus Ami Pro for Windows are all available in versions custom-tailored for foreign countries.

For example, fully translated editions of WordPerfect for DOS exist for 16 languages: Afrikaans, Danish, Dutch, Japanese, Finnish, French, French-Canadian, German, German-Swiss, Italian, Norwegian, Portuguese, Portuguese-Brazilian, Russian, Spanish, and Swedish. What "fully translated" means is that the documentation, program commands, spelling checker and thesaurus, hyphenation dictionary, keyboard driver and keycap decals, and screen and printer fonts were entirely redone for each language.

Language is an organism. To digest it one must be, paradoxically, swallowed up by it.

—Shemarya Levin

Languages are the magic forces of nature and of blood...a heritage of emotions, habits of thought, traditions of taste, inheritances of will—the imperative of the past.

—Shalom Spiegel

(WordPerfect also offers "partial translation" versions for six languages: Croatian, Czech, Greek, Hungarian, Polish, and Turkish. These give you the appropriate languages for screen display and printing; but their spelling checkers and thesauruses are in American or British English, and for some editions the program commands are also in English. Further, the documentation consists of standard English-language manuals, plus a small booklet in the foreign language which covers installation procedures and the main features of the program. These editions are therefore compromises, but you may find that they're good enough to suit your needs.)

For the idiom of words very little she heeded,
Provided the matter she drove at succeeded,
She took and gave languages just as she needed.

—Matthew Prior

A quiet, grave man, busied in charts, exact in
sums, master of the art of tactics...despising all
manner of éclat and eloquence...silent in seven
languages.

—Walter Bagehot

All these editions are complete versions of WordPerfect, and retail from $595 to $795. That's a justifiable cost if you plan to spend most of your writing time in a single non-English language; but it's too much if you're going to write in the language only occasionally, or must work in several languages. That's why WordPerfect Corp. sensibly also provides add-in programs called language modules. Costing only $99, a language module gives you a spelling checker, thesaurus, and hyphenation dictionary for your non-English language, plus a driver to redefine your keyboard and decals you can place over your keycaps; but it doesn't change the language of your program commands or include rewritten documentation. The module works in conjunction with a complete version of WordPerfect, which does *not* have to be the U.S. version; for example, if you own the French version of WordPerfect, you can buy a German language module to plug in for correspondence with your clients in Stuttgart, an Italian module to write to your buyers in Milan, and so on.

Modules are available for 23 languages: Afrikaans, Arabic, Australian-English, British-English, Catalan, Danish, Dutch, Finnish, French, French-Canadian, Galician, German, German-Swiss, Greek, Hebrew, Islandic, Italian, Norwegian, Portuguese, Portuguese-Brazilian, Russian, Spanish, and Swedish. The Arabic, Greek, Hebrew, and Russian modules additionally provide special screen and printer fonts; and the Arabic and Hebrew editions work right-to-left instead of left-to-right, and list for $149 instead of $99.

Microsoft Word for Windows is another strong contender for single-language editions, currently providing the following 14 localized versions: Australian-English, Dutch, Danish, Finnish, French, French-Canadian, German, Italian, Japanese, Korean, Norwegian, Portuguese, Spanish, and Swedish. While this lineup isn't as comprehensive as WordPerfect for DOS, it's in the graphics-based Windows environment where multilingual word processors really shine, because Windows can display any language's characters as easily as English letters. Thanks to this advantage and to aggressive marketing, Microsoft has actually managed to garner better sales than WordPerfect outside of the U.S.

Typically, each Word for Windows edition is a complete translation of the English version, meaning that it provides fully translated documentation and program commands, and a spelling checker, thesaurus, and even a *grammar checker* that works in the edition's language. However, it's a good idea to ask a few pointed questions before buying the edition you're interested in, since there'll be some variance among the different versions. Microsoft doesn't provide a central number for information on and sales of various editions, but you can use the number listed near the end of this chapter to locate the Microsoft foreign office handling the product you want.

Lotus Ami Pro also enjoys the advantages of being in a Windows environment, and it currently provides the following 13 localized editions: Australian-English, British-English, Canadian-English, Canadian-French, Danish, Finnish, French, German, Italian, Norwegian, Portuguese, Spanish, and Swedish. Each edition gives you fully translated documentation and program commands, and a spelling checker and thesaurus for the language (except for the Portuguese and Finnish editions, which don't include a thesaurus). However, only the British-English version currently includes a grammar checker. Like Microsoft, Lotus doesn't provide a central number for selling this software, but you can use the number listed near the end of this chapter to find the Lotus foreign office distributing the package you're after.

If you're already familiar with the standard version of a word processing program, you'll be quite comfortable using any of its non-English versions, since the basic command structure and features remain the same across all language editions. Therefore, if you frequently work in one or two non-English languages, and those languages are supported by a word processor you like, you're set.

If you'd prefer a more specialized approach, however, and especially if you need to work with many different languages, another word processor worth considering is Multi-Lingual Scholar from Gamma Productions.

This DOS-based program provides excellent screen and printer fonts for Latin (covering most English, European, and Scandinavian languages), Cyrillic (Russian, Bulgarian, and Ukrainian), Greek (classical and modern), Hebrew (Biblical, modern, and Yiddish), and Arabic/Persian. Fonts for additional point sizes and typestyles, as well as extra languages (such as Hindi, Bengali, and Tamil; Thai, Korean, and Lao; and the International Phonetic Alphabet) are available from $50 to $125 per set.

Multi-Lingual Scholar includes a spelling checker for one language of your choice; for $125 each, you can buy additional spelling dictionaries handling Danish, Dutch, Finnish, French, French-Canadian, German, German-Swiss, Italian, Norwegian, Portuguese, Spanish, Spanish-Latin American, Swedish, UK-English, and US-English. You can also change the English menu options and messages by buying an appropriate language module. As for your keyboard, you're provided with Mylar keycap labels for each language you purchase. Alternatively, Gamma Productions can sell you a keyboard designed for a particular language...or even a programmable LCD keyboard!

Multi-Lingual Scholar has some genuine problems, though—most notably, it's copy protected, requiring that a dongle be attached to your printer port. (See this book's Introduction on copy protection.) Also, the program works in graphics mode, so text entry and other operations are noticeably slow. Then again, the display is rock-solid; and graphics mode allows an unlimited number of alphabets and fonts to be displayed simultaneously, something that isn't possible for character-based programs such as Nota Bene. Also, the product is a capable word processor, with such features as headers and footers, footnotes, style sheets, the ability to work with up to eight documents at the same time, and page numbering (in multiple languages, of course). Overall, if you deal with lots of languages, Multi-Lingual Scholar is worth a look. The package's list price is $695, but you can get it for only $345 using the Gamma Productions coupon near the back of this book.

Lastly, you should know that for certain complicated languages, it's best to buy a word processor designed specifically for the language. For example, if you spend a lot of time writing in Chinese, the program to get is XinTianMa from Asia Communications, which provides ingenious keystroke shortcuts that spare you from having to tediously pop up a character menu and make a manual selection for each and every character. Similarly, if you want all the nuances done right for Arabic, the word processor of choice is AlKaatib International from Eastern Language Systems.

If you find all these different options a bit confusing...you should. The truth is, the foreign WP market has always been a bit of a mess. With any luck, life will get easier when ASCII, with its mere 256 characters, is replaced by a new standard called Unicode that supports a breathtaking 65,536 characters. Unicode is expected to encompass the characters of every major language (as well as a slew of other special symbols), which should greatly simplify international communication via PCs. If you're interested, you can get more information from The Unicode Consortium; or by buying the books *The Unicode Standard, Volume I* and *The Unicode Standard, Volume II* from Addison-Wesley Publishing.

Translation Software

Xerox recently ran an ad in the *Wall Street Journal* that virtually promised its UNIX program GlobalView would let you send a note through your PC and have it come out on a distant colleague's computer transformed perfectly into another language. (The copy begins: "Write it in English in London. Print it out...en español en Madrid.") This ad has produced lots of merriment among professional translators.

(Translating is) trying to pour yourself into an invisible glass so that you take the shape of your vessel, and transmit the author's light and flavor.
—Nevill Coghill

The truth is, there's no such thing as a black box that lets you push in English at one end and pull out accurate translations at the other. Languages are enormously complicated, and we're still many years away from the time when a program matches the work of a skilled flesh-and-blood translator.

What software *can* do, however, is make a human translator's work go faster and easier, and help to ensure consistent results. There are two basic approaches for providing this help: Computer-Assisted Translation (CAT) and Machine Translation (MT).

CAT Versus MT

Computer-Assisted Translation software typically waits in the background until you request help, and then supplies translations of the word or phrase your cursor is on. These programs are therefore similar to the electronic thesauruses discussed in Chapters 2 and 5, because they're useful for jogging your memory and coming up with synonyms you didn't know about. Some programs also let you add your own translations to their dictionaries, so that you don't forget a clever turn of phrase or risk interpreting a term inconsistently over the course of a long project. This chapter covers eight diverse CAT packages: The Concise Dictionary of 26 Languages, the Berlitz Interpreter, Lexica, Collins On-Line, MTX/MTX Reference, PC-Wörterbuch Englisch, Libraries of the World, and The Translator's Workbench.

To work through an interpreter is like hacking one's way through a forest with a feather.

—James Evans

Machine Translation programs, in contrast, can translate your entire document without your intervention. The quality of the translation won't be great, because the software will often miss nuances, and will also be monotonous in its unvarying translation of words without regard to repetition. Even worse, the resulting text will be riddled with errors, because words often have several meanings. Topnotch MT software is at best 95 percent accurate, which doesn't sound bad until you realize it means a substantive error on every other line of a typical page. More typical is a 90 percent accuracy level, and that results in an error on *every* line. You therefore have to very carefully edit the resulting text, ping-ponging back and forth between it and the source text. Machine Translation can therefore make your job *more* difficult, since it adds yet another layer of complication to the process. However, if you're working within a narrow range of specialty, and you make the effort of "training" your software by carefully adding preferred translations of words and phrases to its dictionaries, MT can indeed end up saving you much time and effort, and can ensure consistency over the course of long projects. The only PC-based MT program respected by the translators I've interviewed is the Globalink Translation System-Professional, and so GTS-Professional is covered in this chapter. In addition, MicroTac's inexpensive Language Assistant series is briefly discussed.

Casual Use Translators

If you're going to perform translations only occasionally and casually—for example, via your palmtop PC during a whirlwind world tour—then you may want to buy a program that's inexpensive and doesn't need much disk space. One candidate is Inductel's Concise Dictionary of 26 Languages, an electronic version of the book by Lyle Stuart. This $49 memory resident product handles Czech, Danish, Dutch, English, Esperanto, Finnish, French, German, Hungarian, Indonesian, Italian, Norwegian, Polish, Portuguese, Rumanian, Serbo-Croatian, Spanish, Swahili, Swedish, and Turkish; plus, transliterated into Roman-alphabet spellings, Arabic, Greek, Hebrew, Japanese, Russian, and Yiddish. The catch is, the program covers only the 1,000 most commonly used words in each language, while serious translation work demands around 50,000 words per language. However, the dictionary's ability to interpret terms from any language to any other language (as opposed to translating exclusively from, say, English to other languages) gives it great breadth—as its brochure points out, "650,000 translation combinations!"—and the whole package takes up just 1.5MB of your hard disk.

A small step up in word coverage is the $34.95 memory-resident Berlitz Interpreter from Microlytics, which translates between English, French, German, Italian, and Spanish, and provides 12,500 terms per language. Berlitz Interpreter for DOS takes up only 860K, so you can easily fit it on a single high-density floppy disk, a real convenience if you're a laptop or palmtop user. A Windows version is also available.

Yet another low-cost alternative is MicroTac's popular Language Assistant series, which has memory-resident English-French, English-German, English-Italian, and English-Spanish editions at a street price of about $50 each. These products translate in both directions; that is, from English to the second language and from the second language to English. They also provide 30,000 root terms, or *headwords*, per language, which wouldn't be bad if they didn't attempt to do actual sentence by-sentence machine translation using this relatively small word-base. Despite the hyperbole of

MicroTac's ads, these programs aren't of much use to professional translators; but they *can* prove helpful to students struggling to absorb a new language, since they provide lots of information on such things as verb conjugations, and syntactic and grammatical summaries. You might therefore find the Microtac programs to be fun and productive learning tools.

The Lexica Translating Thesaurus

Stepping up from the low end, the first product to consider is Lexica from the Writing Tools Group. Like the programs just covered, Lexica is a memory-resident multilingual thesaurus that you can pop up from any DOS-based word processor. However, Lexica offers a solid 50,000 headwords per language, and does an excellent job of providing appropriate synonyms. The full version covers Dutch, English, French, German, and Spanish, and can translate in any direction; that is, you can select any of the five languages to be your source language, and also any of the five as your target language. (If you choose the same language for both, Lexica just operates as a thesaurus for that language.) You can change your selections at any time with a few keystrokes or mouse clicks; for example, pressing F2 will instantly swap your source and target language selections.

(It's) like viewing a tapestry on the wrong side where, though the figures are distinguishable, yet there are so many ends and threads that the beauty and exactness of the work is obscured.

—Miguel De Cervantes

To use Lexica, you first load it into memory, where it takes up a mere 16K. You then run your word processor, bring up a document you're ready to translate, and start working normally. When you reach a word you're uncertain about, simply place your cursor on it and press the Lexica hotkey (the default being Ctrl+Alt+L). Lexica pops up a list of meanings for your word in the source language, and corresponding words or phrases in the target language.

"Out of sight, out of mind" when translated into Russian (by computer), then back again into English, became "invisible maniac."

—Arthur Calder-Marshall

To demonstrate, with English and French selected as my source and target languages, I've just placed my word processor's cursor on "eat" in the phrase "I like to eat" and pressed Ctrl+Alt+L to invoke Lexica. A screen comes up that first notes the word and the sentence fragment it appears in, and then lists target language meanings (grouped by concept) on the left and source language translations on the right. In this case, the English side offers three groups of synonyms: "consume, eat up, partake of, take"; "relish, enjoy, taste, savor, feast on/upon;" and (most interestingly) "affect, attack, corrode, damage, eat away at/into, erode, harm." On the French side, the term provided for the first group is "manger"; for the second group, the phrase "manger de bon appetit"; and for the third group, the synonyms "ronger, attaquer, corroder, entamer, éroder, manger, mordre." I now have a variety of options, including switching to a screen that more closely specifies which English and French terms correspond to each other; delving further by listing the synonyms of one of the terms, in *either* language, currently appearing on the screen; getting another set of translations by selecting a new target language; and looking up an entirely different word. However, the word I want is "manger," so I just move my cursor to it and press

Enter. Lexica instantly exits to the background again, I'm returned to my word processor, and "manger" is inserted in my document at the cursor position.

Lexica has two major drawbacks: it doesn't work with any other dictionaries, and it doesn't allow you to add words to its own dictionaries. If you can live with these limitations, though, you'll find Lexica to be a convenient, flexible, and even fun tool for supplementing your own translating skills.

The full version of Lexica lists for $149.95. However, if you don't need all five components, $49.95 will get you a two-language version that handles bidirectional translation of French-English, German-English, or Spanish-English.

Collins On-Line, MTX Reference, and MTX

If you want the option of customizing your dictionaries, and also want to avoid spending a lot, consider LinguaTech's Collins On-Line series (which derives its data from the European HarperCollins paper dictionaries).

Like Lexica, Collins On-Line can be run memory resident and invoked from your word processor when you need translation help. It normally takes up 120K, which lets it pop up without a moment's delay; but it can occupy only 10K if you direct it to swap data to your hard disk or a RAM disk.

The package's price is a low $89.95, which buys you the program and one dictionary *pair* (for example, English to Spanish and Spanish to English) that lets you translate in both directions. You can also purchase additional dictionary pairs handling English-French, English-German, English-Italian, English-Spanish, French-German, and French-Spanish for $39.95 each. The program lets you keep hooks into up to nine dictionaries simultaneously, so you can change your source and target language selections with a few keystrokes or mouse clicks.

Each Collins dictionary holds only 35,000 entries. However, you can create an associated annotation file for storing your own words and phrases, as well as usage notes and cross-references; so it's possible to customize each dictionary to meet your particular needs better than a larger, but unexpandable, dictionary would. Still, this product line will be more useful when its dictionaries are beefed up (which LinguaTech says will happen soon).

For heavy-duty translation work, a more appropriate choice is one of Collins On-Line's two big brothers: MTX Reference and MTX. (Yes, I know, they *are* awful names; but what can you do?) Both of these Lingua-Tech packages have all the capabilities of Collins On-Line. In addition, though, they work with a wide variety of bilingual dictionaries covering such fields as law, finance, banking, labor, and international trade; biology, chemistry, pharmaceuticals, computers, and solar technology; agriculture, aquaculture, fishery, food science, soil mechanics, and brewing; and metallurgy, textiles, paint, cement, and printing. These dictionaries come from a variety of sources, including Harrap's, NORTRANS, Eurolux, Elsevier, and Maison du Dictionnaire, and range in price from \$35 to \$500.

The best translations...are those that depart most widely from the originals—that is, if the translator is himself a good poet.

—George Moore

Aside from its ability to access these specialized dictionaries, and its higher list price of \$129.95 (which is for the program alone), MTX Reference looks and works almost identically to Collins On-Line. In fact, Collins On-Line is really a crippled version of MTX Reference, priced to sell to a broader audience.

MTX, on the other hand, has a different look and is a more complex tool. Most significantly, it lets you create and revise your *own* free-form dictionaries, which is especially useful for group projects where everyone needs to be working with the same terminology. Also, both MTX and MTX Reference let you load one of your own dictionaries together with a commercial dictionary, *plus* any annotation file you've created for the commercial dictionary; in other words, they let you use one static file and two types of customizable files simultaneously. When you look up a word, your own dictionary is always checked first, so placing your most frequently used terms in it can significantly speed things up. Your dictionary's higher priority also means you have the option of superseding translations in the commercial dictionary.

Because of its extra programming features, MTX lists for $325. In a workgroup situation, however, only those creating or revising dictionaries need MTX; everyone else in the group can use MTX Reference, which reads all dictionaries as readily as MTX does.

The broad customization features of MTX and MTX Reference, and the many specialized dictionaries that work with them, make these two programs powerful tools for manual translation work. LinguaTech doesn't sell its software directly, so for more information (and a free catalog listing all MTX-related products) contact the U.S. distributor, Wright & Associates.

The Translator's Workbench

Taking customization features even further is Trados' The Translator's Workbench, a suite of three programs that can be purchased separately but are most effective when used together.

The core product is MultiTerm, which—like MTX—lets you create free-form multilingual dictionaries. MultiTerm provides a number of powerful features, including the ability to enter up to 100 translation terms (for example, "tome, volume, arrest, collar, schedule, slate") per concept (for example, "book") in up to 16 languages; the ability to classify each term with up to 80 eight-letter codewords, or "attributes," of your own creation; automatic indexing of terms as soon as they're entered; flexible cross-referencing and search capabilities; and the option of setting filters that show you only terms having the attributes you specify.

The second program in the suite is Text Analyzer, which compares the terms in the text files you want to translate against the terms in your MultiTerm master dictionary. It then stores all matching terms, along with their translations, into a new file that in effect becomes a working dictionary for your translation project. This process is especially effective because the matches don't have to be exact; the program reduces words to their roots and so recognizes such deviations as plurals. Text Analyzer also creates a file containing terms that had matches in your original dictionary but for which you didn't provide translations; and another file containing the words for which there were no matches at all.

The final component of the Workbench is either Resident Ted or Ted (Ted being short for *t*ranslation *ed*itor). Resident Ted is a memory-resident utility that works in conjunction with your word processor, while Ted is a standalone word processor with special features for translators. The primary function of both programs is to highlight all the terms in your document that have translations available in the dictionary you're using (which will typically be the one you created using MultiTerm and Text Analyzer). When you move your cursor to a highlighted term, its translation is displayed on the bottom line of the screen, and you're given the option of instantly replacing the term with the translation. This way of working releases you from having to remember whether a term is already covered in your project dictionary. In addition, it saves you time and keystrokes, and helps ensure that your translations are consistent.

The earlier versions of the story of Cinderella have her wearing slippers of white squirrel fur ("vair" in old French). The story was rewritten by the French author, Charles Perrault, and in his version of Cendrillon, *published in 1679 in a collection of fairy tales, he mistook the word "vair" for "verre" (glass), and the error has remained in use since.*

—James Charlton and Lisbeth Mark,
The Writer's Home Companion

The Workbench collection can clearly be a valuable aid in performing translations. However, it demands that you put in a tremendous amount of time and effort building master dictionaries. It's also rather expensive, costing $1,295 with Ted or $1,095 with Resident Ted. The Workbench approach isn't for everyone; but if you regularly work on projects in a specialized field sharing a common terminology (for example, translating engineering manuals or tax statutes), it may be the ideal approach for you. The product's publisher, Trados, is based in Germany and doesn't handle U.S. sales. However, you can get more information from MCB Systems, which is the U.S. distributor.

Other Dictionaries

Systems like MTX and Translator's Workbench are great if you can justify the time it takes to customize them. However, if you translate only occasionally, or work with a wide variety of subjects, you may find it preferable to just buy a few high-quality dictionaries that don't require any tweaking.

One such product is the memory-resident PC-Wörterbuch Englisch, which translates from English to German and vice versa. The program doesn't have many fancy features; it simply offers over 80,000 words and excellent translations at a list price of $320. (Be warned, though—all the instructions are in German, including the program installation notes.) The publisher, Langenscheidt, plans to release a French-German dictionary shortly.

By the way, Langenscheidt has a small office in New York but, as you've probably guessed, the company is based in Germany. This brings up a noteworthy point—a lot of foreign software firms don't have *any* outside offices, but may nonetheless be the best source for the type of programs you need. It's therefore often a good idea to contact companies in the countries whose languages you're working in and order software directly from them.

You'll never really know what I mean and I'll never know exactly what you mean.
      —Mike Nichols

A thing well said will be wit in all languages.
      —John Dryden

If you'd rather do one-stop shopping, though, a product worth considering is a CD-ROM from NTC titled Languages of the World. This disc holds 18 complete monolingual and bilingual dictionaries (a total of seven million words!), including Brandsetters Science and Technology, Esselte Studium, Grupo Anaya's, Gyldendal, Harrap's Business, Harrap's Concise, Harrap's Science, Harrap's Shorter, Harrap's Data Processing, Kunnskaps

Forlaget, Nicola Zanichelli's, Werner, Wolters-Gendai's, and NTC's own Dictionary of American Idioms. (The package is also sold worldwide by the various other publishers involved; for example, in the UK it's Harrap's Multilingual CD-ROM Dictionary Database, and in Japan it's CD-Word 12+1.) The disc covers 12 languages: Chinese, Danish, Dutch, English, Finnish, French, German, Italian, Japanese, Norwegian, Spanish, and Swedish. It also lets you perform cross-searching among languages across the different dictionaries, providing for up to 132 language combinations. Its list price is a reasonable $249.95, and you may find it's the only multilingual product you need.

GTS-Professional

Finally, there's Globalink's GTS-Professional, the one high-end Machine Translation product covered in this chapter.

As I indicated previously, there's a magical quality to giving a program your text, going out for coffee, and coming back to a translated document; but getting a usable translation actually requires a great deal of both pre-editing work (primarily on your dictionaries, to ensure they hold as many pertinent translations as possible) and post-editing work (on the translated document, to fix the many inevitable errors that have been introduced, and to add nuance and style).

One quick 'n cruel way to test a bidirectional MT product is to generate a translation from English to the second language, and then have the program convert the resulting text back into English. No program will manage this task flawlessly, but you can nonetheless get a rough sense of what kind of the job your program is doing by observing just how garbled your final output is. (Needless to say, this test is also great at parties.)

There's no denying that I have a cruel streak, so I went ahead and applied the out-of-the-box English-Spanish version of GTS to the previous paragraph. After taking about 10 seconds to digest it, the program came up with the following translation:

"Uno rápido'nmanera fiera para probar un @@ bidirectional el producto DE TRADUCCIO'N AUTOMA'TICA está generar una traducción desde el Inglés a la segunda lengua, y entonces tener el programa convierte el dorso resultante de texto en el Inglés. No programa administrará esta tarea @@ flawlessly, pero Ud. puede conseguir sin embargo un sentido áspero de qué tipo del trabajo su programa hace por observador precisamente como mutiló su rendimiento final es. (No es preciso decir, esta prueba es también grandes en partidos.)"

Note that double "at" signs (@@) appear twice in the text, in front of "bidirectional" and "flawlessly." They indicate that those two words weren't in the general dictionary in any form, and so GTS couldn't even attempt to translate them. On the other hand, the dictionary not only recognized "MT," it expanded it to the full Spanish equivalent of Machine Translation.

To finish up, I fed the Spanish paragraph back to GTS, and the following English translation resulted:

"One ra'pido'nmanera cruel to prove a @@ @@ bidirectional the MACHINE TRANSLATION product is generated a translation from the English to the second language, and then to have the program converts the resulting text back into the English. Not program will administer this task @@ @@ flawlessly, but You can obtain however a rough sense of what type of the work their / its program makes by observant just how mutilated their / its final yield is. (Needless to say, this test is also large in parties.)"

"Also large in parties," indeed. The program also choked on retranslating "quick 'n cruel," and committed a number of subtler mistakes. Still, the gist of the original paragraph was preserved, and you can see how a quick post-edit would fix most of the problems. Of course, if I'd made the effort of adding some key terms to the 60,000-word dictionaries, the end result would have been markedly better. I also could've opted for the interactive mode, which pauses to display each source sentence in the top half of the screen and lets you revise the corresponding target sentence in the bottom half of the screen, greatly simplifying the error-correction process. Lastly, it should be noted that this is the most arduous test you can subject an MT program to, since the double-translation amplifies any initial inaccuracies.

GTS isn't a good choice for translating fiction or poetry, or for handling a wide range of text. However, like The Translator's Workbench, it's a fine tool for specialized documents using a common word-base. GTS offers several customization options, including the ability to add terms to its dictionaries and to create your own dictionaries. It also works with several small dictionaries, priced at $100 each, that cover such fields as law, business, finance, computers, cars, and petroleum/mining. If you're willing to invest the time required to "train" the program by steadily adding appropriate terms to its vocabulary, you may find GTS to be the ideal translation partner.

GTS-Professional comes in versions that translate between English and French, English and German, and English and Spanish, at a list price of $998 each. (There's also a Russian version, but at the time of this writing it translates only from Russian to English, and costs $1,495.) In addition, there's unfortunately a hassle-factor cost associated with GTS—it's copy protected, requiring a dongle that attaches to your parallel printer port (see the copy protection section in this book's Introduction).

Lastly, you should know that Globalink also sells a "crippled" version of its product line called GTS-Basic. This junior edition costs only $299 per language pair, but doesn't let you create your own dictionaries or access any of the add-on dictionaries, so its practical use is extremely limited. If money is tight, you're better off with a CAT program such as Lexica; or with a really good dictionary.

Product Information

Note: Version numbers and prices may have changed by the time you read this.

Addison-Wesley Publishing
Order Department
Route 128
Reading, MA 01867
(800) 447-2226; (617) 944-3700
Fax: (617) 942-1117

The Unicode Standard, Worldwide Character Encoding, Volume I
(softcover book, 682 pages): $32.95

The Unicode Standard, Worldwide Character Encoding, Volume II
(softcover book, 439 pages): $29.95

See also The Unicode Consortium, Inc. entry later in this section.

Asia Communications, Inc.
1117 Ste-Catherine West
Suite 606
Montreal, Quebec, Canada H3B 1H9
(514) 434-9373
Fax: (514) 434-9374

XinTianMa for Chinese 1.0: List Price, $695; generally not discounted (except for volume buyers, such as universities). Japanese and Korean modules may also be available by the time you read this.

Data-Cal Corporation
531 East Elliot Road
Suite 145
Chandler, AZ 85225
(800) 223-0123; (602) 545-1234
Fax: (602) 545-8090

Assorted Microsoft Windows screen and printer fonts for various languages, ranging in price from $99.95 to $249.95. Free catalog on request.

Eastern Language Systems
P.O. Box 502
Provo, UT 84606-0502
(800) 729-1254; (801) 377-4558
Fax: (801) 377-2200

AlKaatib International 2.0 (for Windows): List Price, $495; Street Price N/A;
copy protected via software

EKB
Eric Meyer
3541 Smuggler Way
Boulder, CO 80303
CompuServe mailbox 74415,1305

EKB (Euro Keyboard) 1.02: Free; can be downloaded from online services
such as CompuServe, or ordered on disk from mail-order shareware
distributors

Foreigner
Gordon Goldsborough
Brandon University
Brandon, Manitoba, Canada R7A 6A9
(204) 727-9786
Fax: (204) 726-4573

Foreigner 1.1 (for Windows): Free; can be downloaded from BBSs and online
services, or ordered on disk from mail-order shareware distributors

Gamma Productions, Inc.
710 Wilshire Boulevard
Suite 609
Santa Monica, CA 90401
(310) 394-8622
Fax: (310) 395-4214

Multi-Lingual Scholar 4.1: List Price, $695 for standard edition; via coupon
near the back of this book, $345

Globalink, Inc.
9302 Lee Highway
12th Floor
Fairfax, VA 22031
(800) 255-5660; (703) 273-5600
Fax: (703) 273-3866

Globalink Translation System Professional (GTS-Professional) 3.0: List Price,
$998 each for English-French, English-German, and English-Spanish

versions, and $1,495 for the Russian-to-English version (which, at the time of this writing, translates in one direction only); Street Price N/A; copy protected via a dongle that attaches to the parallel printer port

Globalink Translation System Basic (GTS-Basic) 2.0: List Price, $299 each for English-French, English-German, and English-Spanish versions; Street Price N/A; copy protected via a dongle that attaches to the parallel printer port

Add-on dictionaries are also available (varying with the language you're using) for $100 each.

Inductel, Inc.
5339 Prospect Road
Suite 321
San Jose, CA 95129-5028
(800) 367-4497; (408) 866-8016
Fax: (408) 243-1762

The Concise Dictionary of 26 Languages: List Price, $49; generally not discounted

Langenscheidt Publishers, Inc.
46-35 54th Road
Maspeth, NY 11378
(718) 784-0055
Fax: (718) 784-0640

PC-Wörterbuch Englisch 2.11: List Price, $320; generally not discounted

LinguaTech International
1113 South Orem Blvd.
Orem, UT 84058-0015
(801) 226-2525
Fax: (801) 226-7720

To order Collins On-Line, MTX and/or MTX Reference, see the entry for Wright & Associates (the U.S. distributor).

Linguist's Software, Inc.
P.O. Box 580
Edmonds, WA 98020-0580
(206) 775-1130
Fax: (206) 771-5911

Assorted Microsoft Windows screen and printer fonts for various languages, ranging in price from $59.95 to $149.95. Free catalog on request.

Lotus Development Corporation
55 Cambridge Parkway
Cambridge, MA 02142
(800) 343-5414; (617) 577-8500
Fax: (617) 253-9150

Lotus Ami Pro (for Windows), foreign editions: Prices vary from country to country

MCB Systems
3950 Mahaila Avenue
Suite H-34
San Diego, CA 92122-5727
(619) 457-7711
Fax: (619) 457-9613

MultiTerm 2.5: List Price, $795; Street Price N/A

MultiTerm 1.0 for Windows: List Price, $795; Street Price N/A

Text Analyzer 1.0: List Price, $295; Street Price N/A

Resident Ted 1.0: List Price, $295; Street Price N/A

Ted 2.0: List Price, $745; Street Price N/A

The Translator's Workbench (MultiTerm, Text Analyzer, and Resident Ted):
List Price, $1,095; Street Price N/A

The Translator's Workbench (MultiTerm, Text Analyzer, and Ted): List Price,
$1,295; Street Price N/A

Microlytics, Inc.
2 Tobey Village Office Park
Pittsford, NY 14534
(800) 828-6293; (716) 248-9150
Fax: (716) 248-3868

Berlitz Interpreter for DOS (English, French, German, Italian, and Spanish):
List Price, $34.95; Street Price N/A

Berlitz Interpreter for Windows (English, French, German, Italian, and
Spanish): List Price, $34.95; Street Price N/A

Microsoft Corporation
One Microsoft Way
Redmond, WA 98052
(206) 936-8661
Fax: No generic sales or information fax number

Microsoft Word for Windows, foreign editions: Prices vary from country to country

MicroTac Software
4655 Cass Street
Suite 214
San Diego, CA 92109
(800) 366-4170; (619) 272-5700
Fax: (619) 272-9734

Language Assistant 5.0 for French, German, Italian, or Spanish: List Price, $99.95 each; Street Price, about $50 each

NTC Publishing Group
4255 West Touhy Avenue
Lincolnwood, IL 60646
(800) 323-4900; (708) 679-5500
Fax: (708) 679 2494

Languages of the World (CD-ROM): List Price, $249.95; Street Price N/A

The Technology Group
36 South Charles Street
Suite 2200
Baltimore, MD 21201
(410) 576-2040
Fax: (410) 576-1968

Nota Bene 4.1: List Price, $449; via coupon near the back of this book, $179

N.B. Lingua 1.0: List Price, $299; Street Price N/A

Nota Bene/N.B. Lingua bundle: List Price, $748; via coupon near the back of this book, $299

Trados GmbH
Gutenbergstrasse 4b
70176 Stuttgart, Germany
+49 (711) 666 17-0
Fax: +49 (711) 666 17-50

To order The Translator's Workbench, see the entry for MCB Systems (U.S. distributor)

The Unicode Consortium, Inc.
1965 Charleston Road
Mountain View, CA 94043
(415) 961-4189
Fax: (415) 966-1637

The Unicode Standard, Worldwide Character Encoding, Volume I (softcover book, 682 pages): $32.95 alone, $37.50 when bundled with disk for Unicode programmers

The Unicode Standard, Worldwide Character Encoding, Volume II (softcover book, 439 pages): $29.95 alone, $33.95 when bundled with disk for Unicode programmers

WordPerfect Corporation
1555 N. Technology Way
Orem, UT 84057
(800) 321-4566; (801) 222-4200
Fax: (801) 228-5377

WordPerfect for DOS, complete foreign editions: List Price ranges from $595 to $795; Street Price N/A

WordPerfect for DOS, language modules: List Price is $99 each, except for the Hebrew and Arabic modules, which are $149 each; Street Price N/A

Wright & Associates
134 North Prospect Street
P.O. Box 994
Kent, OH 44240-0994
(216) 673-0043
Fax: (216) 673-0738

Collins On-Line 2.2 (including the program and one dictionary pair): List Price, $89.95; Street Price N/A

Collins On-Line Dictionaries for English-French, English-German, English-Italian, English-Spanish, French-German, and French-Spanish (each a dictionary *pair*, with one dictionary translating *from* the first language and the other *to* the first language): List Price, $39.95 each; Street Price N/A

MTX Reference 2.1: List Price, $129.95; Street Price N/A

MTX 2.16: List Price, $325; Street Price N/A

A wide range of electronic dictionaries are also available for MTX Reference and MTX, at prices ranging from $35 to $500; call for more information and free catalog.

Writing Tools Group
One Harbor Drive
Suite 111
Sausalito, CA 94965
(800) 523-3520; (415) 382-8000
Fax: (415) 883-1629

Lexica Translating Thesaurus 1.0, two-language version (French-English, German-English, or Spanish-English): List Price, $49.95; Street Price N/A

Lexica Translating Thesaurus 1.0, five-language version (English, Dutch, French, German, and Spanish): List Price, $149.95; Street Price N/A

One mail-vendor that carries many of the products covered in this chapter (plus a number of language-teaching programs) is:

Lingo Fun, Inc.
P.O. Box 486
Westerville, OH 43081
(800) 745-8258; (614) 882-8258
Fax: (614) 882-2390

Lastly, for more information about language translation, contact:

American Translators Association
1735 Jefferson Davis Highway
Suite 903
Arlington, VA 22202-3413
(703) 412-1500
Fax: (703) 412-1501

CHAPTER
19

TOOLS FOR STUDENTS
AND ACADEMICS

Being a writer is essentially a life full of homework...only it's impossible to write it the night before it's due.

—Fran Lebowitz

I'd like to think that you're *always* a student, so long as you maintain an active interest in learning about yourself and the world around you.

For the confines of this chapter, though, I'm defining *student* as, quite simply, someone who goes to school. And I'm defining *academic* as someone who performs research and writes for scholarly journals.

Those definitions still cover a broad range, so the chapter is divided into two parts. The first, "Tools for Young Students," is directed at parents, and discusses such kid-oriented software as low-end desktop publishing programs and electronic encyclopedias. The second, "Tools for Older Students and Academics," is for those doing college and graduate work, and talks about such software as bibliographic reference managers and text analyzers.

The programs I'll be covering aren't considered standard in most schools. (Actually, very little is, outside of a few foundation packages such as WordPerfect.) Don't let that stop you from exploring them, however. Instead, take the attitude of Mark Twain, who once proudly declared "I have never let my schooling interfere with my education."

Tools for Young Students

If you're a recent parent, you've probably been frustrated by the general dearth of information on children's software. While such programs never get as much press as business software, they *do* exist, and they merit your attention.

For example, if your child is four to seven years old, you might consider buying Kid Works 2 from Davidson and Associates. This package offers an elementary word processor, and the ability to make your PC "speak" the words that appear on the screen, thus providing a great way of reinforcing writing and spelling skills. It also includes a painting program and a symbol maker that work with the word processor, allowing your youngster to easily mix words and images together. Kid Works 2's street price is about $35.

If your offspring is in the seven to 12 age range, the program to look at is the Children's Writing and Publishing Center from The Learning Company. Recognizing that children take a more holistic approach to the learning process than adults do, this package bundles basic word processing and desktop publishing functions, making it a snap for kids to create their own printed stories, articles, and booklets.

The word processor component keeps things simple, providing only such fundamentals as the ability to enter and delete text, and cut and paste text. The desktop publishing component provides about 150 kid-related electronic pictures, which can readily be incorporated into the text; and also offers a few preset layouts to choose from, such as a multicolumn page, and a page with a large title across the top. The package's street price is about $45.

There are many other worthwhile programs targeted at children. Coverage of them is beyond the scope of this chapter, but you can learn more from three excellent books: *Pride's Guide to Educational Software* by Mary Pride (Good News Publishers/Crossway Books, 1992; $25); *Kids & Computers: A Parent's Handbook* by Judy Salpeter (SAMS, 1992; $12.95); and *Parents, Kids & Computers* by Robin Raskin and Carol Ellison (Random House, 1992; $20.00). All of these works are accessible, attractive, and smartly written...and miles above their competition.

Read over your compositions, and wherever you meet a passage which you think is particularly fine, strike it out.

—Samuel Johnson

At the same time, keep in mind that children's software can be outgrown quickly. If your kid becomes computer-savvy, don't hesitate to bring in business-oriented packages. One excellent choice is Microsoft Works, because it's easy to use, inexpensive, and allows smooth switching among its various program components. As noted in Chapter 1, those components include a full-featured word processor, which can be applied to such activities as writing to-do lists and school reports; and a database manager, which can keep track of such items as comic book collections and record collections. In addition, the DOS version provides a telecommunications program that can dial into inexpensive online services such as Prodigy and GEnie, allowing your child to look up a fact in an electronic encyclopedia, check the latest sports scores, or chat with other kids across the country. Microsoft Works for DOS has a street price of about $95, and Works for Windows has a street price of about $129.

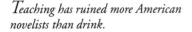

Teaching has ruined more American novelists than drink.

—Gore Vidal

Another fine value for a young student is The Writer's Toolkit from Systems Compatibility Corp. As detailed in Chapter 5, *Electronic Dictionaries and Thesauruses*, this product includes an excellent disk-based dictionary, an electronic thesaurus, a quotation collection, a grammar checker, a grammar and style guide, a factbook, and an abbreviation translator. Most of the components are only the *second* best on the market, and so might not be deemed good enough by a demanding adult writer; but they're more than sufficient for a child doing homework. Best of all, the package has a street price of only $35, which is a fraction of what you'd have to pay to obtain comparable editing and reference tools separately.

If your system includes a CD-ROM drive (see Chapter 9, *CD-ROM References*), you'll find an encyclopedia on disc a much better buy than a paper one. The electronic version will always be significantly cheaper; take up a whole lot less space; and give your child the handy option of searching for a word or phrase across all the encyclopedia's listings. One of the best CD-ROM encyclopedias is Microsoft's Encarta, which in addition to text and photographs offers such kid-pleasing features as sound and animation. Encarta has a street price of $249, and is discussed in more depth in Chapter 9.

If you can get past its "lazy substitute for reading the book" stigma, you might also consider buying the Bureau of Electronic Publishing's Monarch Notes on CD-ROM. This nifty product contains the text of every Monarch Notes booklet ever published...over 200 in all. It covers classics spanning the centuries, from Homer, Aristotle, and Plato to Franz Kafka, James Joyce, and Samuel Beckett. Contrary to popular belief, many of the book summaries are interesting and illuminating. Further, they're great as memory joggers and research tools. Because of its many uses—and its affordable $69.95 list price—Monarch Notes has become one of the most successful CD-ROMs in history, with over 100,000 copies sold. With appropriate parental guidance, you'll probably find that it serves to fuel, rather than diminish, your child's desire to read.

Of course, virtually any program can be a valuable learning tool if you get your kid to approach it in the right way. (In fact, it's a good idea to skim the other chapters in this book, keeping your child's interests in mind.) The key is to spend time with your young ones, and give them solid direction in how they can get the most out of the family PC.

Tools for Older Students and Academics

If you're performing college or graduate work, the first writing tool you'll need is a topnotch word processor. As noted in Chapter 1, *Choosing a Word Processor*, it's hard to go wrong with WordPerfect for DOS, which contains an awesome number of features, including powerful footnote, endnote, indexing, and foreign character capabilities. Further, the program is a virtual standard at many universities, because WordPerfect Corp. has for years provided students and faculty a greatly discounted price (typically, $125 a copy). If you opt for WordPerfect, you'll find that its popularity makes it easy to obtain help on how to learn and use it, reduces the risk of experiencing problems when exchanging document files with your peers, and allows you to choose among a wide variety of supplementary programs.

However, if you're willing to be a bit adventurous—or if you're at one of the universities that has adopted the package—you should also take a serious look at Nota Bene from The Technology Group. As explained in Chapter 1, Nota Bene is super-fast, powerful, and extremely flexible. On top of all that, it contains features and "hooks" for add-on products that are designed specifically for academics.

All of us learn to write in the second grade ...most of us go on to greater things.
—Basketball coach Bobby Knight

For example, if you work with languages that don't use the English alphabet, Nota Bene bundled with the add-on program N.B. Lingua provides screen and printer fonts for Cyrillic, Greek, and Hebrew, giving you access to an impressive total of *3,000* characters. The package also lets you easily switch between languages with a few keystrokes—for example, pressing Ctrl+G sets you to Greek, pressing Ctrl+H,Ctrl+R selects Hebrew and right-to-left typing, and pressing Ctrl+E,Ctrl+L switches you back to English and left-to-right typing. More information on Nota Bene's foreign language features appears in Chapter 18, *Tools for Multilingual Writers.*

If you have large amounts of text (source data, interviews, notes, papers, letters, and so on) scattered across thousands of files on your hard disk, you'll want the add-on program N.B. Orbis. This allows you to place your cursor on a word in a Nota Bene document, press a keystroke, and immediately find each occurrence of the word in your various text files. The files need not be marked in any way (though you can optionally insert classifying terms, or *keywords*, in them to facilitate pinpoint retrieval). Each Nota Bene file is displayed in its appropriate format, so you can readily see when an occurrence appears in, say, a footnote, or endnote, or snaking column.

Alternatively, you can open a window and type in the phrase you're seeking (which can be up to 100 words long). You can also narrow or widen your search using AND, OR, and NOT constructs ("Shakespeare AND iambic pentameter", "Shakespeare OR Milton"); and using the wildcard operator * (for example, "psych*" to match such occurrences as *psychology, psychohistory,* and *psychic*). A search will ordinarily proceed paragraph by paragraph, which means a "Shakespeare AND iambic pentameter" pattern will match the occurrence of any paragraph containing both of those terms. However, you can set the search to use any measure, including lines, sentences, pages, or entire files. N.B. Orbis can handle up to 16 million units of the measure you select, located in up to two million files.

Further, if you're also using N.B. Lingua, N.B. Orbis will do just as good a job locating Russian, Greek, Hebrew, and other foreign language text as it does finding English phrases. The program even allows you to set up links between related terms for future searches; so, for example, you can bring up such phrases as *fuzzball*, *mouser*, and *purr machine* when you enter *cat*.

Just as helpful for academic work is the specialized database manager N.B. Ibid. As you might guess from its name, this add-on product organizes the bibliographic references required for your theses, journal articles, and other scholarly papers. Specifically, it lets you enter, search, sort, cite, and print references.

From your parents you learn love and laughter, and how to put one foot in front of the other. But when books are opened, you discover that you have wings.

—Helen Hayes

For example, when you're writing a paper in Nota Bene, you can display any reference in your database by typing the author's last name, the date of the work, or the first word of the title, and then selecting the work you want from a list of matching entries. Each reference can contain up to 32,000 characters, giving you the option of entering voluminous notes about a work; and a database can hold up to 32,000 references. When you're ready to print, N.B. Ibid can format your citations in any of 12 major academic styles, including those of the *Chicago Manual of Style*, the *Modern Language Association Handbook*, the *Turabian Manual for Writers*, and styles specific to such fields as psychology, political science, anthropology, and medicine.

Nota Bene therefore offers you more than just a superb word processor; it provides the foundation of an integrated package fine-tuned to your needs as a student or academic. The Nota Bene/N.B. Lingua combination lists for $748, but you can buy it for $299—a terrific value—via The Technology Group coupon near the back of this book. Similarly, the Nota Bene/

N.B. Orbis/N.B. Ibid bundle lists for $847, but is available through the coupon for only $339. And if you want to have it all, Nota Bene combined with N.B. Lingua, N.B. Orbis, *and* N.B. Ibid has a list price of $1,146, but can be obtained via the coupon near the back of this book for an amazing $459! If you aren't wedded to WordPerfect, seriously consider taking advantage of these bargain prices; you may well find Nota Bene's suite of products to be the perfect one-stop solution for your scholarly needs.

Of course, you can always put together your own group of products —albeit at a steeper price. For multilingual work, you can buy foreign language versions of such standard word processors as WordPerfect and Microsoft Word; or a specialized package such as Multi-Lingual Scholar. More information on these products appears in Chapter 18, *Tools for Multilingual Writers*.

And for text retrieval, you can use a standalone product such as Zy-Index, which is comparable in features to N.B. Orbis; or you can opt for a more sophisticated, and more expensive, product such as Windows Personal Librarian. These programs are covered in Chapter 7, *Other Editing Tools*.

I know the answer! The answer lies within the heart of all mankind!—The answer is 12? I think I'm in the wrong building.

　　　—Charlie Brown (via Charles Schulz)

As for bibliographic reference managers, the best is ProCite from Personal Bibliographic Software. Like N.B. Ibid, this specialized database product organizes the citations for your articles, journals, books, plays, theses, and so on. Typically, areas are provided for the entry of such information as author name, title, publisher, date of publication, ISBN number, keywords, abstract, and notes. You don't have to work with a generic entry form, however; instead, you can select from among 20 predefined forms, each of which is tailored to a particular academic field (ranging from the arts and humanities to the hard sciences). In addition, you can design up to six entry forms of your own.

ProCite's capacity to handle data is, for most practical purposes, unlimited. It can store up to 16 pages per publication or, to use the database term, per *record*; up to 45 category headings, or *fields*; and up to two *billion* records per database—enough to satisfy any research center short of the Library of Congress. In addition, ProCite allows you to create an unlimited number of databases.

ProCite is very flexible, making it easy to search or reorganize data. It also gives you lots of formatting options; for example, it lets you enter and print a date as Jan. 1 1994, or January 1st, 1994, or 1/1/94, or even I/I/MC MLXXXXIV.

Perhaps best of all, though, is the way ProCite handles your citations. When you enter them into your document, the program inserts what amounts to a placeholder rather than the actual text. When you're ready to print, Procite lets you select which of 29 popular journal styles you want to use for your bibliography. Among the advantages of this approach is that if a journal passes on an article you've done, you can print out a copy formatted appropriately for a different journal with only a few keystrokes. ProCite has a street price of about $220, and I recommend it if you regularly deal with numerous reference works.

I was thrown out of college for cheating on the metaphysics exam; I looked into the soul of the boy next to me.

—Woody Allen

Copy from one, it's plagiarism; copy from two, it's research.

—Wilson Mizner

On the other hand, if your needs are more casual, you may want to consider a low-cost package. Two programs popular among students are Niles and Associates' Endnote, with a street price of about $80; and Endnote Plus, with a street price of about $145. Compared to ProCite, these products aren't as easy to use, handle only about half as much data per database, and provide only a third as many academic styles. Further, Endnote is weak on formatting, which means you're forced to do more work in creating your bibliographies; and offers few searching and sorting features, which is a major liability if you want to be able to use your databases as research tools. Still, if you aren't dealing with large amounts of data and/or don't anticipate using a bibliographic manager frequently, both Endnote and Endnote Plus do a solid job at a relatively low price.

A man ought to read just as inclination leads him; for what he reads as a task will do him little good.
—Samuel Johnson

A third package worth mentioning is Research Information Systems' Reference Manager, which is available in both student and professional versions. In most ways, Reference Manager is a fine program, with features that are comparable to ProCite's. However, because of marketing decisions made by its publisher, the program is most appropriate for either low-end use or workgroups.

Specifically, the student edition doesn't allow any database you create to store more than 400 references. If this isn't a significant limitation for you, the product is a very good buy at a list price of $79. However, you'll probably want the option of creating larger databases.

The professional version allows a database to store as many as 65,000 references, which doesn't approach ProCite's two *billion*-reference ceiling, but is nonetheless enough for most people's needs. The marketing twist here is that you're only allowed *one* large database; any other database you create is restricted to no more than *200* references! To make up for this limitation, Research Information Systems gives you permission to supply copies of the program and database for everyone in your workgroup at no extra cost. In effect, then, what you're buying with the professional version is a single database that can be used freely among your coworkers. If you want to create another large database, however, you have to buy another copy of the program...which has a list price of $299.

In addition to the base package, there are three utilities you can buy to enhance Reference Manager's usefulness. One helps you download citations from online services; the second provides more than 140 popular academic journal formats (the standard package includes only four); and the third lets you pop up Reference Manager while you're in your DOS word processor. If you own the student edition, you can buy the utilities for $59 each; while if you own the professional edition, you can either buy them separately for a slightly higher price, or buy all three bundled together with the main package for $499. Reference Manager is available in both DOS and Windows versions.

By academic freedom, I understand the right to search for truth, and to publish and teach what one holds to be true. This right implies also a duty: one must not conceal any part of what one has recognized to be true.

—Albert Einstein

Of course, a bibliographic reference manager isn't very useful without pertinent references to plug into it. The best sources for such information are online databases, which you can access with your phone line and a modem (as explained in Chapter 10, *Online References*). For example, in the field of education alone, you can access electronic versions of such fundamental works as the U.S. Department of Education's ERIC (Educational Resources Information Center), which contains over 700,000 citations; AgeLine; Dissertation Abstracts Online; Education Testing Service Test Collection; Exceptional Child Education Resources; Mental Measurement Yearbook; National College Databank; Resources in Vocational Education; Vocational Education Curriculum Materials; and the Wilson Education Index (covering 350 English language periodicals devoted to all areas of education).

You can access such databases from a variety of online services. For example, all the databases just mentioned are carried by InfoPro Technologies' BRS/After Dark, a relatively low-cost service for use during evenings and weekends; and by InfoPro Technologies' BRS Search Service, which is more expensive but operates during business hours.

An even more valuable online resource for academics is Internet, a worldwide computer service with millions of subscribers, many of whom work in universities or corporate R&D departments. If you aren't affiliated with an institution that's already on Internet, you can get access information from InterNIC, which is a nonprofit Internet information clearinghouse.

A man will turn over half a library to make one book.
          —Samuel Johnson

The chances are you'll occasionally want to get more than just citations and abstracts onto your hard disk. Fortunately, many online services also let you download the full text of various articles and books. You can also obtain electronic versions of complete works—say, the plays of Shakespeare, or the novels of Twain—through CD-ROM discs (see Chapter 9, *CD-ROM References*) and even standard floppy disks (see Chapter 8, *Disk-Based References*).

Further, if your work involves *analyzing* text, you probably ought to invest in Micro-OCP (Oxford Concordance Program), a PC version of the respected mainframe OCP program from Oxford University Press. Micro-OCP helps you produce concordances, word lists, and indexes from texts in a variety of languages and alphabets. It can also be used to probe such elements as writing style, vocabulary distribution, rhyme schemes, grammatical forms—almost anything that might be of academic interest. The package is designed to be accessible to novices, though it offers layers of depth for those with the computer knowledge to use them. It costs $295.

The great thing about writing: Stay with it ...ultimately you teach yourself something very important about yourself.
—Bernard Malamud

Finally, in addition to specialized academic tools, you should take advantage of the wide array of general-purpose writing tools available, such as computer dictionaries, grammar checkers, and electronic encyclopedias. It's therefore a good idea to skim through the rest of this book, paying special attention to Chapter 5, *Electronic Dictionaries and Thesauruses*; Chapter 6, *Grammar and Style Checkers*; and Chapter 8, *Disk-Based References*.

Product Information

Note: Version numbers and prices may have changed by the time you read this.

Bureau of Electronic Publishing
141 New Road
Parsippany, NJ 07054
(800) 828-4766; (201) 808-2700
Fax: (201) 808-2676

Monarch Notes CD-ROM: List Price, $69.95; Street Price N/A

Davidson and Associates, Inc.
P.O. Box 2961
Torrance, CA 90509
(800) 545-7677; (310) 793-0600
Fax: (310) 793-0601

Kid Works 2: List Price, $59.95; Street Price, about $35

GEnie Information Services
401 North Washington Street
Rockville, MD 20850
(800) 638-9636; (301) 251-6475
Fax: (301) 251-6421

During off-peak hours (6 P.M. to 8 A.M., and weekends), $8.95 a month for your first four hours, and $3 for each additional hour; during business hours, $12.50 an hour

InfoPro Technologies
BRS Online Products
8000 Westpark Drive
McLean, VA 22102
(800) 955-0906; (703) 442-0900
Fax: (703) 893-0490

BRS/After Dark online service: $80 one-time fee, plus minimum charge of $12 per month, plus additional charges depending on the databases you access (ranging from $10 to $50 an hour) and number of searches you conduct. This service is available only from 6 P.M. your time to 4 A.M. Eastern time, and most of the weekend; and doesn't allow access to all the databases BRS Search Service does.

BRS (online) Search Service: Typically, $45 to $75 per hour (depending on the databases you access), plus additional charges for the text you retrieve, plus an $80 annual subscription fee; call for more information

InterNIC
P.O. Box 85608
San Diego, CA 92186-9784
(800) 444-4345; (619) 455-4600
Fax: (619) 455-4640

Ask this nonprofit information clearinghouse for the free packet that identifies the companies or institutions providing Internet access in your area

The Learning Company
6493 Kaiser Drive
Fremont, CA 94555
(800) 852-2255; (510) 792-2101
Fax: (510) 792-9628

The Children's Writing and Publishing Center 1.5: List Price, $69.95; Street Price, about $45

Microsoft Corporation
One Microsoft Way
Redmond, WA 98052
(800) 426-9400; (206) 882-8080
Fax: No generic sales or information fax number

Microsoft Encarta 1.0 (CD-ROM for Windows): List Price, $395;
Street Price, about $249

Microsoft Works 3.0 for DOS: List Price, $149; Street Price, about $95

Microsoft Works 1.0 for Windows: List Price, $199; Street Price, about $129

Microsoft Works 2.0 (CD-ROM version): List Price, $199; Street Price N/A

Niles and Associates
2000 Hearst Street
Berkeley, CA 94709
(510) 655-6666
Fax: (510) 649-8179

Endnote 1.1: List Price, $149; Street Price, about $80

Endnote Plus 1.1: List Price, $249; Street Price, about $145

Oxford University Press
200 Madison Avenue
New York, NY 10016
(800) 334-4249, ext. 7370; (212) 679-7300, ext. 7370
Fax: (212) 725-2972

Micro-OCP 1.0: List Price, $295; generally not discounted

Personal Bibliographic Software
P.O. Box 4250
Ann Arbor, MI 48106
(313) 996-1580
Fax: (313) 996-4672

ProCite 2.2: List Price, $395; Street Price, about $220

Prodigy Services Company
445 Hamilton Avenue
White Plains, NY 10601
(800) 776-3449
Fax: N/A

Flat fee of $14.95 a month that covers virtually all services. Exceptions are about a dozen special sections, most of which involve interactive games; and electronic mail, which costs 25 cents per message *after* you've used up your allotment of 30 messages per month. Available seven days a week, 21 hours per day (the service closes for maintenance between 4 A.M. and 7 A.M. Eastern time daily).

Research Information Systems
Camino Vida Roble
Carlsbad, CA 92009
(800) 722-1227; (619) 438-5526
Fax: (619) 438-5573

Reference Manager Special Edition 5.07: List Price, $79; Street Price N/A

Reference Manager Professional Edition 5.07: List Price, $299;
Street Price N/A

Reference Manager add-on programs: Capture, $99 ($59 for Special
Edition); 100+ Journal Formats, $59 ($59 for Special Edition); Splicer, $99
($59 for Special Edition)

Reference Manager Complete Edition 5.07 (includes all three add-on
programs): List Price, $499; Street Price N/A

Reference Manager Complete Edition 5.51 for Windows (includes all three
add-on programs): List Price, $499; Street Price N/A

Systems Compatibility Corporation
401 North Wabash
Suite 600
Chicago, IL 60611
(800) 333-1395; (312) 329-0700
Fax: (312) 670-0820

The Writer's Toolkit 2.0 for DOS: List Price, $59.95; Street Price, about $35

The Writer's Toolkit 2.0 for Windows: List Price, $59.95; Street Price, about $35

The Technology Group
36 South Charles Street
Suite 2200
Baltimore, MD 21201
(410) 576-2040
Fax: (410) 576-1968

Nota Bene 4.1: List Price, $449; via coupon near the back of this book, $179

Nota Bene 4.1 *and* N.B. Lingua 1.0: List Price, $748; via coupon near the
back of this book, $299

Nota Bene 4.1, N.B. Orbis 1.0, *and* N.B. Ibid 1.1: List Price, $847; via
coupon near the back of this book, $339

Nota Bene 4.1, N.B. Lingua 1.0, N.B. Orbis 1.0, *and* N.B. Ibid 1.1: List Price,
$1,146; via coupon near the back of this book, $459

WordPerfect Corporation
1555 N. Technology Way
Orem, UT 84057
(800) 321-4566; (801) 225-5000
Fax: (801) 228-5377

WordPerfect 6.0 for DOS: List Price, $495; Street Price, about $269

WordPerfect 6.0 for Windows: List Price, $495; Street Price, about $279;
Competitive Upgrade (when offered), about $129

PART VI

HANDLING PC TASKS

The computer is no better than its program.
—Elting E. Morison

And now I see with eye serene
The very pulse of the machine.
—William Wordsworth

CHAPTER

20

ESSENTIAL GENERAL-PURPOSE TOOLS

Any sufficiently advanced technology is indistinguishable from magic.

—Arthur C. Clarke

Grammar checkers and rhyming dictionaries are great, but they won't speed up your system or manage your hard disk. For such computer-related tasks, you need to turn to general-purpose utilities.

At first blush, PC utilities may seem both boring and frighteningly technical. However, they can do more to enhance your productivity than a slew of specialized writing programs. While they're often more difficult to learn, the benefits PC utilities bring will reward your initial efforts many times over.

In this chapter, we'll look at software that doubles the space on your hard disk, provides more room in your PC's memory for running programs, makes your PC operate faster, protects and recovers your data from destructive accidents, lets you easily manipulate your files, and allows you to load multiple programs at the same time and quickly switch between them. We'll also cover a fun utility for saving your screen, and another for preserving your sanity.

Hey, these programs are *great*.

Stacker

Every once in a while, a program comes along that does magic. That's Stacker.

In a nutshell, this utility from Stac Electronics drastically increases your hard disk space. Typically, it doubles it—for example, if you had 40MB, it gives you 80MB; if you had 500MB, it gives you a gigabyte. This is great if you've been wanting to move a bunch of programs or data files onto your hard disk for easy access, but lacked the free space to do so. It's also useful if you have a machine with very limited disk space, such as a laptop.

Stacker performs its wizardry via sophisticated computer formulas that compress your data to take up less room. It's not unlike what cryptographers do to encode messages, except in this case the goal isn't to hide information, just shrink it.

More specifically, Stacker lurks in memory, constantly looking for operations involving data retrieval or storage. Whenever you access a file on your "stackerized" hard disk, Stacker automatically decompresses the data before passing it on to you; and when you save data to the disk, Stacker automatically compresses the data before storing it. The decompression and recompression occur so rapidly that they are effectively invisible—as far as you're concerned, you ask for data and boom, it's there, just the way things worked before Stacker. In fact, because there's less actual data to load from your hard disk, in some cases data retrieval is even *faster*, despite the time required for decompression. In addition, Stacker works with virtually *everything* (you can even Stackerize a RAM disk!), so you don't have to worry about conflicts with other programs.

Do not fold, spindle, or mutilate.
—Instructions on 1950s-era computer punch cards

Stacker does have a few limitations. For example, a Windows swap file must be stored on a noncompressed section of your drive; and if you want to defragment your disk (which ensures your file data is stored sequentially, instead of being scattered around the disk), you must use only the SDE-FRAG utility that's part of the Stacker package, as opposed to other company's defraggers. If you have an enormous hard disk, it's also noteworthy that you can't create a Stacker drive that handles more that 1,000MB of physical drive space. (However, you *can* create multiple Stacker drives—for example, a single-partition 1,500MB hard disk can be covered by two Stacker drives that each handle 750MB.) All these things are minor, though.

Stacker is one of the most exciting new pieces of technology to come out for the PC. Its compression formulas are already licensed for use in such cutting-edge software as Central Point Backup and Norton Backup, and in tape drives from such sharp companies as Colorado Memory Systems and Irwin Magnetic Systems. A version of Stacker was even slated to be included in DOS 6. (That deal broke down when Microsoft and Stac couldn't come to terms, and Microsoft ultimately bundled in a less effective compression program.)

No matter what size your hard disk is, you'll readily find ways to benefit from having twice as much of its free space available. Therefore, don't hesitate to buy and use Stacker. It may prove to be the most helpful utility you own.

QEMM-386

When DOS was first created in the early 1980s, Microsoft assumed that 640K of memory would be as much as any program would need to run. At the same time, Microsoft reserved an additional 384K of memory for various video and system operations, making the entire range of memory access 1,024K, or 1MB, long.

As it happened, though, RAM prices later plummeted, and programmers responded by writing software that was increasingly complex and memory-hungry. In addition, programmers created a new breed of software called terminate-and-stay-resident, or *TSR*, utilities that always stay in memory so you can access them instantly from within any program you're running. The problem is, if you have several TSRs loaded (say, a mouse driver, a grammar checker, the Stacker program described above, and the Super PC-Kwik cache described below), you may not have enough of your original 640K left to run any large programs—even if you have many megabytes of memory available in your system! This situation is called "hitting the 640K barrier."

To get around this dilemma, a good memory manager is essential. DOS 5 and DOS 6 include a memory manager called EMM386, which is better than nothing; but to take full advantage of your system's resources, you should buy Quarterdeck Office System's QEMM-386, which performs very sophisticated tricks to utilize every last byte of memory available on a 386 or better PC.

QEMM-386 can move your TSRs, device drivers, and other memory hogs into memory above the 1MB range, and then "fool" DOS into thinking those programs reside in free memory areas within your 384K range of reserved system space. This works because that 384K is seldom entirely used by system operations; on most PCs, there's usually 100K to 200K that's available for a clever memory manager to find and take advantage of. In addition, if you're not using graphics-based programs, QEMM-386 can —on *some* machines—get you up to 96K of additional memory by using the video area ordinarily devoted to EGA and VGA graphics. What this all amounts to is about 100K to 300K of freed up space in your precious 640K memory area. (On my system, for example, without using the graphics-quashing feature, and with TSRs and device drivers taking up about 200K, QEMM manages to leave me 610K of my original 640K.) The extra memory space gives you the freedom to load a *lot* of useful TSRs, and to run your large programs more efficiently as well.

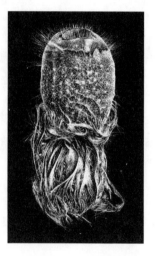

THE NATION THAT CONTROLS MAGNETISM CONTROLS THE UNIVERSE!

—Chester Gould (in his comic strip, *Dick Tracy*)

QEMM-386 also works fine with Microsoft Windows. Indeed, its memory savings really multiply under Windows, because they apply to *every* DOS program you open—for example, if QEMM-386 is giving you an extra 200K of program space and you run three DOS programs simultaneously under Windows, you'll in effect get an extra 600K of program space.

To supplement its state-of-the-art memory manager, Quarterdeck includes a state-of-the-art automation program called Optimize that first analyzes your system, then races through thousands of possible combinations before settling on the best memory placement for your various TSRs, and finally rewrites your system's CONFIG.SYS and AUTOEXEC.BAT files to put its organization scheme into effect. During certain sales periods, Quarterdeck also throws in the best system analysis/reporting program on the market, Manifest, which (among other things) allows you to manually check on how your memory is being allocated. For a street price of around $59, the QEMM-386 package is a bargain you can't afford to pass up (unless you buy the Quarterdeck DESQview-386 package, which will be covered shortly, and which bundles in QEMM-386).

The computer is down. I hope it's something serious.

—Stanton Deleplane

Of course, not everyone owns a 386 or better PC. If you have an 8088 or 286 system, the memory-management possibilities are more limited. However, if your machine meets the technical requirements of (take a deep breath) having an expanded memory board that can map more than 64K of memory at one time into the 640K to 1024K address range *and* uses EMS 4 or EEMS software; or if your PC is equipped with Chips & Technologies ShadowRAM; then (breath out now) you can try QRAM, which is also from Quarterdeck. QRAM typically gives you an additional 30K to 130K of memory for running TSRs and other programs that work with an expanded memory board, and even more extra room working with ShadowRAM hardware. Such memory management is especially tricky, though, so you might want to first check with your PC manufacturer or with Quarterdeck to make sure QRAM supports your particular machine. Alternatively, get hold of the free QTEST disk supplied by Quarterdeck, which tests your system and then tells you how effective QRAM will be on your PC.

PC-Kwik Power Pak

A computer's electronic memory is anywhere from 3 to 10 times faster than its mechanical hard disk. Therefore, one of the most effective ways to speed your PC's operation is to bypass your hard disk and retrieve data directly from memory. That's precisely what a *cache* does; it notes what data you request frequently, and keeps that data in memory so you can access it instantly instead of going to the hard disk. The cache does all this automatically, so the only operational difference you'll notice is that things happen a lot quicker.

A number of packages include cache programs, such as the very good SMARTDrive cache bundled with Microsoft Windows. The best cache on the market, however, is Super PC-Kwik, and if you're looking for optimal PC performance, that's the one to buy. (Super PC-Kwik is also a good choice if you use QEMM-386, since Quarterdeck and PC-Kwik Corp. cooperated to make sure their products work especially well together.)

Computers are useless. They can only give you answers.

—Pablo Picasso

You can buy Super PC-Kwik as a separate product. However, for just a little more money, I suggest you buy the PC-Kwik Power Pak, which bundles in several other wonderful utilities. Most notable is a print spooler, which places your printing jobs in memory and then sends them along to your printer from there. This allows you to continue using your program right after issuing a print command, instead of being forced to wait until printing is completed; the spooler takes over and executes your printing in the background while you continue working.

Other useful Power Pak tools are a DOS command editor that lets you quickly bring up and edit commands you previously entered at the DOS prompt; an accelerator that increases your keyboard repeat rate so that you can move around the screen more quickly; a screen enhancer that permits you to perform various tricks with your display; and a start-up program that allows you to choose which preset system setup you desire every time you turn on your machine.

Super PC-Kwik remains the real star of the package, but you'll probably find some of its companion programs to be of great use as well. PC-Kwik Power Pak is a fine value, and I highly recommend it.

The Norton Utilities and The Norton Desktops

When it comes to data accidents, the question isn't *if* but *when*. Accidentally erased files, prematurely formatted disks, media failures, and other disasters are an inevitable part of PC use. Since your data is the most valuable and irreplaceable part of your computer system, it's critical that you take steps to safeguard against serious data loss and have the tools available to quickly recover from data accidents.

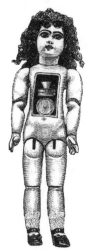

Civilization requires slaves...to do the ugly, horrible, uninteresting work...Human slavery is wrong, insecure, and demoralizing. On mechanical slavery, on the slavery of the machine, the future of the world depends.

—Oscar Wilde

Any of three somewhat overlapping products from Symantec will do the job: The Norton Utilities, The Norton Desktop for DOS, and The Norton Desktop for Windows. All three packages provide utilities that safeguard critical system information, keep track of deleted files, and ensure a formatted disk can be unformatted without data loss. They also all provide utilities for recovering deleted files and formatted disks, plus the invaluable Norton Disk Doctor, which can detect and correct a wide variety of disk-related problems. (Similar utilities are provided by the PC Tools package described shortly, but PC Tools' DiskFix isn't as smart and reliable as the Norton Disk Doctor.)

If your primary interest is in having high-level tools to fine-tune your system, The Norton Utilities is your best choice. This package provides such extras as a disk defragger that physically consolidates file data; a calibration program that rejuvenates aging hard disks; a specialized repair program that fixes spreadsheet and database files; and a DOS COMMAND .COM replacement that provides more flexible wildcard options, more powerful batch commands, the option to add descriptions to file names, and the ability to easily edit and recall commands from the DOS prompt.

On the other hand, if you're not especially technical and would appreciate some help in using arcane DOS commands, either The Norton Desktop for DOS or The Norton Desktop for Windows is more appropriate. Both products give you a beautifully designed Windows-like screen that contains icons representing your disk drives, menus containing all critical DOS commands (plus a number of commands DOS fails to provide), and the option to open multiple windows containing directory trees and file lists. The Norton Desktops make it a snap to view, move, copy, and delete files with a few mouse clicks. The Windows version also provides powerful options for organizing your icons in ways not readily achievable using the Windows Program Manager. In addition, both Desktops include such extras as a premium backup program (which is almost as good as the PC Tools program described below); a virus detector (see the virus section below); a scheduler that can pop up notes and run programs at scheduled times; and even some fun screen savers, which is especially nice for the DOS version (for Windows, nothing matches After Dark, which is discussed later in this chapter).

To sum up, if you're not afraid of technical tools, and you want a high degree of control over your system, buy The Norton Utilities. But if you want an intuitive, mouse-driven method for working with files and directories, buy either The Norton Desktop for DOS or The Norton Desktop for Windows, depending on which environment you spend most of your time in; versions of the most important data protection and recovery programs from The Norton Utilities are included in both packages.

Then again, if money's a bit tight, you might opt to skip all three and just go for the amazing PC Tools; so let's cover that option next.

PC Tools

PC Magazine says PC tools is "the most extraordinary bargain in the PC marketplace." *InfoWorld* says it's "one of the most capable, feature-laden packages to be found at any price." All the praise is due to the more than 20 powerful programs included in this low-priced package, many of which incorporate state-of-the-art technology.

One of the key components of PC Tools is CP Backup, which is the best backup program on the market. If you have a hard disk, it's inevitable that you'll occasionally experience accidents that destroy data. CP Backup furnishes a safety net by saving a highly compressed version of all your hard disk's data to either floppy disks or tape drive cartridges. Full-featured versions of the program for both DOS and Windows are provided.

PC Tools also offers a slew of data protection and recovery programs like those in The Norton Utilities, including software for undeleting files and unformatting disks.

Man seems to be a rickety poor sort of a thing, any way you take him ....A machine that was as unreliable as he is would have no market.

—Mark Twain

One machine can do the work of fifty ordinary men. No machine can do the work of one extraordinary man.

—Elbert Hubbard

An extremely powerful, flexible DOS shell is *also* included. This lets you perform all DOS commands, plus many commands not offered by DOS, through clearly organized menu options like those in The Norton Desktop for DOS.

But wait! (This is starting to sound like an ad for Ginsu knives.) You *also* get an integrated program, Desktop Manager, that provides nearly a dozen full-featured applications, including a simple word processor, a dBASE-compatible database, telecommunications programs for both modems and fax cards, simulations of Hewlett-Packard calculators, a macro editor, and an appointment scheduler. The whole program can be loaded as a TSR that takes up less than 40K of conventional memory, or can be loaded entirely into high memory (that is, above your first 1MB).

And if *that's* not enough, PC Tools also gives you utilities for data encryption, virus detection, disk optimization, and remote computing. The latter, Commute, lets you talk to, and even take over, another computer from your own keyboard via a modem or local area network connection, and is the best program of its kind available for the PC.

All these features made *InfoWorld* conclude that PC Tools "may be the only program some users need." I wouldn't go quite that far; but I would say that if you end up using even a fraction of its features, you'll find its street price of around $109 a bargain. CP Backup alone is virtually worth the price of the entire package.

A Virus Detector

You've probably heard about viruses—that is, software that invisibly attaches itself to programs and replicates itself, ultimately destroying part or all of the data on a hard disk. The virus threat is vastly overblown, and the odds of your being hit with one are tiny. However, the possibility *does* exist. More important, though, is that when something goes wrong with your system (and you can be sure that something will), it's useful to be able to rule out viruses as culprits right away so that you can concentrate on whatever is *really* causing the problem.

Both PC Tools and The Norton Utilities/Desktop products include pretty good virus detection programs. I personally use Virex, which is a very fast shareware program that can be downloaded from most on-line services and electronic bulletin boards. Whatever you use, it's a good idea to run your detector on any new software you're about to install on your system. It's also a good idea to use a backup program that has built-in virus detection (such as the topnotch CP Backup), and to check your entire system for viruses every month or two. The odds are small...but better safe than sorry.

A Task Switcher

It can be a hassle to have to constantly exit your word processor to run an idea generator, or a telecommunications program, or some other software you need to use before you can continue writing, and then have to reload your word processor to get back to where you started from. A better alternative is to use a *task switcher*, which lets you keep multiple programs active at the same time so that you can instantly switch to any of them with a keystroke.

Microsoft Windows 3.1 is the most popular program that performs task switching, keeping both Windows and DOS programs in memory simultaneously. If you're using Windows programs anyway, this is probably your best bet.

If you're using DOS programs exclusively, though, Quarterdeck's DESQview may be a preferable alternative. DESQview doesn't try to do all the many other things Windows does—virtually all it cares about is letting you switch among your programs quickly. As a result, it's a lot faster than Windows, and can run on almost any PC. Moreover, if you have a 386 or higher PC, you can buy DESQview 386, which includes the essential QEMM-386 memory manager as part of the package. (However, *don't* get the slow-running DESQview/X unless you have special need for networking, graphical, or UNIX features.)

(Technology) will make me Emperor of the Universe, of the planets, of all Creation!

—Ming the Merciless

Unfortunately, DOS programs were never written to run alongside each other, so you may encounter all sorts of quirky problems using either Windows or DESQview. You may even encounter flat-out system crashes, which are especially not fun if you haven't developed the habit of saving your work frequently.

If you run up against such difficulties, keep an eye peeled for Microsoft Windows 4.0, which is expected to excel at running multiple programs simultaneously. Microsoft is pushing hard for this program (and its corporation-oriented big brother, Windows NT) to be the operating system of the future, and Microsoft—unlike IBM, with its ill-fated OS/2—has a pretty good history of getting what it wants.

This is my prediction for the future: Whatever hasn't happened will happen! And no one will be safe from it!

—J. B. S. Haldane

After Dark

If you leave the same image on your monitor for many hours, there's a danger that the image will be permanently "burned" into the screen. You should therefore use a *screen saver* or *blanker*, which automatically changes what appears on your screen after your PC has been idle for a specified period (typically, five minutes). As soon as you press a key or move your mouse, your original screen image is restored.

Many blankers just turn the screen black. This does the job but, frankly, is *boring*. Fortunately, Berkeley Systems realized the graphic possibilities provided by screen savers running under Microsoft Windows, and thus was born After Dark, the MTV of PCs. With After Dark, you can turn your screen into an aquarium, a pinball machine, a kaleidoscope, a creature-infested cave, a haven for flying toasters (accompanied by floating toast), or any of 40 other exotic environments. You can even have sounds with your graphics—for example, spooky chirps and hoots from the creature-infested cave.

(Further, if you're a science fiction fan, check out Star Trek: The Screen Saver from Berkeley Systems. It features tribbles, hortas, Klingons, the Enterprise, and other ST icons; and can be used together with After Dark, or as an independent screen saver.)

After Dark won't save your data or make your word processor run faster, but it *will* add a little zest and humanity to your high-tech computer. I personally refuse to run Windows without it.

Super Tetris

Yeah, yeah, I *know* it's "just" a game. But it's the most addictive PC game ever!

Lookit, as a writer, you're going to procrastinate, anyway. You might as well do so using the best software available for the job. Super Tetris (and its siblings, such as "classic" Tetris and WordTris) are the premiere PC anti-productivity tools. When you find yourself getting too super-efficient using the utilities covered in this chapter, sit back and take out several dozen rows of bricks. Trust me; it's good for you.

Product Information

Note: Version numbers and prices may have changed by the time you read this.

Berkeley Systems
3261 Ash Street
Palo Alto, CA 94306-2240
(800) 877-5535; (510) 540-5535
Fax: (510) 540-5115

After Dark 2.0 for Windows: List Price, $49.95; Street Price, about $29

More After Dark 1.0 for Windows: List Price, $39.95; Street Price, about $25

Star Trek: The Screen Saver 1.0 for Windows: List Price, $59.95; Street Price, about $35

Central Point Software
15220 N.W. Greenbrier Parkway
Suite 200
Beaverton, OR 97006
(800) 445-4208; (503) 690-8090
Fax: (503) 690-8083

PC Tools 8.0 for DOS: List Price, $179; Street Price, around $109

Datawatch Corporation
P.O. Box 51489
Durham, NC 27717
(919) 490-1277
Fax: N/A

Virex 2.9: List Price, $49.95; Street Price, about $29

Microsoft Corporation

One Microsoft Way
Redmond, WA 98052
(800) 426-9400; (206) 882-8080
Fax: No generic sales or information fax number

Microsoft Windows 3.1: List Price, $150; Street Price, about $89

PC-Kwik Corporation

15100 SW Koll Parkway
Beaverton, OR 97006
(800) 234-5945; (503) 644-5644
Fax: (503) 646-8267

PC-Kwik Power Pak 3.1: List Price, $129.95; Street Price, about $45

Super PC-Kwik 5.1: List Price, $89.95; Street Price, about $35

Quarterdeck Office Systems

150 Pico Boulevard
Santa Monica, CA 90405
(800) 354-3222; (310) 392-9851
Fax: (310) 314-4219

DESQview 386 2.6: List Price, $149.95; Street Price, about $89

DESQview/X 1.2: List Price, $275; Street Price, about $169

QEMM-386 7.01: List Price, $99.95; Street Price, about $59

QRAM 2.0: List Price, $79.95; Street Price, about $49

Spectrum Holobyte

2061 Challenger Drive
Alameda, CA 94501
(800) 695-4263; (510) 522-3584
Fax: (510) 522-3587

Super Tetris 1.01 for DOS: List Price, $49.95; Street Price, about $29

Super Tetris 1.01 for Windows: List Price, $49.95; Street Price, about $29

Tetris Classic 1.0 for DOS: List Price, $44.95; Street Price, about $27

Tetris Classic 1.0 for Windows: List Price, $44.95; Street Price, about $27

Faces 1.0 (falling face segments): List Price, $19.95; generally not discounted

Wordtris 1.02 (falling letters): List Price, $44.95; Street Price, about $27

Welltris 1.02 (Tetris in 3-D): List Price, $34.95; Street Price, about $22

Stac Electronics
5993 Avenida Encinas
Carlsbad, CA 92008
(800) 522-7822; (619) 431-7474
Fax: (619) 431-9616

Stacker 3.1 for Windows & DOS: List Price, $149; Street Price, about $85

Symantec Corporation
10201 Torre Avenue
Cupertino, CA 95014-2132
(800) 441-7234; (408) 252-3570
Fax: (800) 554-4403

The Norton Utilities 7.0: List Price, $179; Street Price, about $115

The Norton Desktop 1.0 for DOS: List Price, $179; Street Price, about $115

The Norton Desktop 2.2 for Windows: List Price, $179; Street Price, about $115

PART VII

PRODUCING YOUR FINAL OUTPUT

For several days after my first book was published I carried it about in my pocket, and took surreptitious peeps at it to make sure the ink had not faded.

—Sir James M. Barrie

CHAPTER
21

CONVERTING FILE FORMATS

Convert: To change into another form, substance, state, or product; transform.

—The American Heritage Dictionary

I'll convert you

Into a stew!

—T. S. Eliot

After you've put the final editorial polish on your text, you're ready to make it presentable to your audience. If you're satisfied with the way your document looks, and all that's left to do is to get it onto paper, you're in good shape and can skip to Chapter 23, *Printing Your Work*.

However, if you need to import your document into another program, such as a desktop publishing package; or if you want to add graphics to your words; or if you're going to hand your file over to a colleague who has a different word processor, then you may run headlong into incompatibility problems. That's because, unfortunately, human languages aren't the only Tower of Babel we have to deal with nowadays; we also have to deal with computer formats.

This chapter discusses programs that help bring order to the chaos by translating file formats. Specifically, it covers Word for Word Professional, Software Bridge, and Outside In, which handle word processing files; HiJaak, which converts graphics files; and MacLinkPlus/PC, which allows you to move files between your PC and a Macintosh computer.

Converting Word Processing Files

As mentioned in Chapter 2, all PC word processing programs adhere to the ASCII format for representing plain text. However, they use ASCII only as a foundation; they then add special codes for underlining, boldfacing, font changes, margin settings, and a slew of other formatting information. Because no national committee has settled on a standard way to represent such formatting codes, each software company (in the purest spirit of laissez-faire) makes up its own, without much regard to the codes its competitors are using. As a result, word processors can't exchange documents directly; instead, they have to communicate through translation programs.

Some word processors (such as Ami Pro and Word for Windows) and layout programs (such as QuarkXPress and Ventura Publisher) have conversion software built in. If translations for the particular formats you need are included in your application program, *and* you don't need to perform many translations, *and* you're happy with the quality of the translation you're getting, then you're set.

Otherwise, though, you should consider purchasing a program devoted to word processing file translation. The best is Mastersoft's Word for Word Professional (or WFWP for short), which handles more than 90 file formats. These range from such popular word processors as WordPerfect for DOS and Word for Windows, to such fading programs as MultiMate, DisplayWrite, and Volkswriter.

More specifically, the PC word processors (and multipurpose programs that include word processing) that WFWP supports are Ami Pro, Display-Write, Enable, Framework, IBM Writing Assistant, Interleaf Publisher, Lotus Manuscript, Mass-11, Microsoft Word for DOS, Microsoft Word for Windows, MultiMate, OfficeWriter, PeachText 5000, PFS: First Choice, PFS: Write, Professional Write, Professional Write Plus, Q&A, Q&A Write, Samna Word, Signature, Total Word, Volkswriter, Wang PC, Windows Write, WordPerfect for DOS, WordPerfect for Windows, Word-Star for DOS, WordStar for Windows, WordStar 2000, and XyWrite.

Further, WFWP typically supports several formats for each word processor, providing a separate translation for every significant version of the program. For example, it contains four translators to handle WordPerfect for DOS versions 4.1, 4.2, 5.0, and 5.1; and seven translators for WordStar for DOS versions 3.3/3.31, 3.45, 4.0, 5.0, 5.5, 6.0, and 7.0. This is significant, because one edition of a program won't necessarily use the same codes for a feature as a previous edition.

Just because everything is different doesn't mean anything has changed.

—Irene Peter

The art of progress is to preserve order amid change and to preserve change amid order.

—Alfred North Whitehead

What we need is a flexible plan for an ever-changing world.

—Jerry Brown

WFWP also covers several ubiquitous spreadsheet and database formats, such as Lotus 1-2-3, Microsoft Excel, and dBASE, which is convenient if you need the data from such applications in a form that your word processor can understand. It even supports such Macintosh formats as MacWrite,

Microsoft Word for Macintosh, and WordPerfect for Macintosh, since it's now common for documents to be exchanged between PC and Macintosh computers. WFWP is available in both Windows and DOS versions (the latter designed to look Windows-like), but which one you buy is basically a matter of taste; both provide equal support for all file formats.

When you run WFWP, it displays two boxes: one for the directory containing the files you want to translate, or *source* files; and the other for the directory in which you want to save your translated copies, or *target* files. You can set these boxes to the appropriate directories for your session with a few keystrokes or mouse clicks. (At the same time, you can choose the three-letter extension to be appended to the names of your target files, or just accept the default of NEW.)

Next, if you're not certain a file contains a document you want converted, you can view the file's contents by simply selecting it and pressing a function key. WFWP automatically detects the format the document is in, and then displays it on-screen using the same "look" as the word processor that created it.

When you're ready, you can use either the Enter key or your mouse to mark each file you want translated. In contrast to the one-file-at-a-time translation process of a word processor, WFWP lets you mark as many files as you want, so that you can translate *scores* of documents in one fell swoop. If you have to deal with a lot of files, this feature can be an enormous time saver.

Next, pressing another function key displays a list of the supported formats available. As indicated previously, it's a long list, but you can jump around it quickly by pressing the first letter of the format you require. You can then use the Enter key or your mouse to select the format.

By the way, one notable option to use when selecting a source format is Automatic Recognition; if you choose this, WFWP will try to figure out the format of each of your selected files *automatically*. This feature is great if you aren't sure what format a file is in. It's also very convenient when you've selected multiple files created by several different word processors.

Finally, to execute the translation, you press yet another function key. Your source files remain unchanged, but in a short while (typically, a few seconds per document), copies of them in the new format you requested are saved to your target directory with the extension NEW (or whatever extension you specified). At this point, you should exit WFWP, run your target program, load each translated file, and clean up any problems that were created during the conversion. In most cases, the results will be quite good and there won't be much that requires fixing.

*A*ny change in whatever direction for whatever reason is strongly to be deprecated.

—Anonymous

*C*hange is not made without inconvenience, even from worse to better.

—Richard Hooker

*T*here is a certain relief in change, even though it be from bad to worse; as I have found in traveling in a stagecoach, that it is often a comfort to shift one's position and be bruised in a new place.

—Washington Irving

Word for Word Professional is terrific, but it's not the only word processing translation product on the market. Its main competition is Systems Compatibility Corporation's Software Bridge, which is significantly harder to learn how to use, doesn't provide as much support for different versions of word processors, takes a lot longer to perform translations, and doesn't offer a Windows version. Still, Software Bridge also does a solid translation job, and supports some word processors (such as DEC WPS-PLUS DX, Sprint, Smartware II, and WordMARC), spreadsheets (such as Quattro Pro and Microsoft Works), and databases (such as Paradox and R:BASE) that WFWP currently doesn't. If you need to translate from one of those formats, Software Bridge is worth a look.

Alternatively, if the way you work doesn't require the wholesale conversion of multiple files, but rather picking text out of one file, a graphic out of another, and a spreadsheet out of a third so you can combine them all into one document, you may prefer Systems Compatibility Corporation's Outside In for Windows. This product recognizes more than 120 word processing, spreadsheet, database, graphics, and compressed formats, and allows you to view the contents of a file in the format of the program that created it (especially handy if you don't happen to have that program on your system). It then enables you to select part or all of the file's contents, and to copy your selection to the Windows Clipboard while preserving the data's formatting information. This is particularly important for DOS-based word processing documents, which normally can be copied to the Clipboard only as ASCII text (that is, stripped of their formatting information). Lastly, you can paste the Clipboard data into your favorite Windows word processor. You can repeat this process over and over, until you've collected all the pieces you need from various files to complete the document you're working on.

The DOS and Windows versions of Word for Word Professional, and the DOS-based Software Bridge, each have a street price of about $85; while Outside In for Windows has a street price of about $65. If you use many different software packages, or must frequently exchange data files with other people, it's a good idea to have one of these programs on your hard disk at all times.

Converting Graphics Files

If word processing formats are a Tower of Babel, graphics formats are the Mount Everest of Babel.

For starters, there are two basic types of picture files: bitmap and vector. Bitmap graphics consist of numerous tiny dots (or *bits*) that collectively make up an image. They're what you get when you scan a picture, or draw one with a program such as Windows Paintbrush. They're relatively easy to create, but quickly take on a "jaggy" look when you try to resize or otherwise adjust them.

Vector graphics, on the other hand, are made up of objects, such as circles, rectangles, and curved lines. They can be created only by a high-end illustration program, such as CorelDRAW or Adobe Illustrator; or an auto-tracing program, such as Corel Trace or Adobe Streamline, that traces lines in a bitmapped image and translates them into geometric shapes. Vector graphics can easily be resized or otherwise adjusted, with no loss of image quality.

Two types of graphics aren't that hard to deal with. However, there's actually a multitude of formats for bitmap graphics, including:

- BMP (Bitmap): The standard for Windows graphics.
- DIB (Device Independent Bitmap): The standard for OS/2 graphics.
- FAX: The format in which PC fax boards save data.
- GIF (Graphics Interchange Format): The standard for both PC and Macintosh graphics files on the online service CompuServe.
- IMG (Image): A format used by old GEM-based programs, such as the original version of Ventura Publisher.
- JPG or JPEG (Joint Photographic Experts Group): A new format that supports a high level of data compression, thus enabling graphics to take up less room on your hard disk.

- PCX (PC piX): One of the oldest graphics formats, originating from the pioneering program PC Paintbrush.

- PIC (1-2-3 Picture): The format for Lotus 1-2-3 spreadsheet charts and graphs.

- PNT (Macintosh PaiNT): The oldest Macintosh graphics format, originating from the pioneering program MacPaint.

- TGA (Targa): A format for high-end color graphics.

- TIFF (Tagged Image File Format): Currently the most popular and versatile graphics format.

- WPG (WordPerfect Graphics): The format for WordPerfect and DrawPerfect pictures.

At this point, you've likely guessed the ugly truth: there are plenty of vector formats, as well. These include:

- CDR (CorelDRAW): The format for the excellent illustration program CorelDRAW.

- CGM (Computer Graphics Metafile): Currently the most popular vector format.

- DRW (Windows Draw): The format for the excellent programs Micrografx Designer and Windows Draw.

- DXF (AutoCAD 2-D): A standard for AutoCAD and other computer-aided design programs.

- EPS (Encapsulated PostScript): The format for PostScript output.

- IMA: The format for the high-end Mirage program by Zenographics.

- PICT (Macintosh Picture): The standard for Macintosh graphics.

- PLT (Plotter): A standard for pen plotters and line drawings.

And, I'm sorry to say, that's just the *beginning*. For one thing, certain formats (such as WPG and EPS) can handle both bitmap and vector graphics. Much worse, however, is that there are different "flavors" of formats; for example, TIFF comes in over 30 varieties, all of which are incompatible with each other! On top of that, many programs are very picky about which formats, and flavors of formats, they work with.

What all this means is that the odds of a graphics file you want to use being fully compatible with your word processor or desktop publishing package are slim. Even if your program is willing to read the graphic in, it may not display and print the picture properly. This can be a particularly unpleasant discovery to make when you're rushing to get a document out under deadline—which is, let's face it, the conditions under which most documents are created.

To the rescue comes HiJaak for Windows. This program from Inset Systems lets you freely convert from one bitmap format to another, from one vector format to another, and from vector format to bitmap. For example, it lets you translate virtually any of the 60+ graphics formats it recognizes to such popular bitmap formats as BMP, GIF, IMG, PCX, PNT, PICT, TIFF, TGA, and WPG.

Confusion is a word we have invented for an order which is not understood.

—Henry Miller

Further, HiJaak supports numerous flavors of key formats. Most notably, it can convert images into 34 different types of TIFF, many helpfully identified as being most appropriate for a particular application such as Ami Pro, Adobe Illustrator, CorelDRAW, Macintosh drawing programs,

Microsoft Word for DOS, PageMaker for Windows, PageMaker for Macintosh, QuarkXPress for Macintosh, Ventura Publisher, or WordPerfect for DOS. Even more impressive, if a program you're using isn't listed, HiJaak can analyze a TIFF file created by your application and then set up a *customized* TIFF format for you!

HiJaak can also handle such popular vector formats as CGM, EPS, DRW, WMF, and PLT, and can write out different versions of these formats, as well. For example, it can translate a vector graphic into any of 11 types of CGM, targeted at the illustration and presentation packages Applause, Arts & Letters, CALS, CorelDRAW, Draw Applause, Harvard Graphics, Lotus Freelance, Micrografx Designer, PageMaker for Windows, Pixie, and WordPerfect for DOS.

In addition to standard bitmap and vector formats, HiJaak understands the FAX formats of 24 popular PC fax cards. This means you can easily convert your FAX files into another format, such as TIFF, that an optical character recognition program can read and turn into editable text.

Actually, HiJaak for Windows does more than just translate graphics formats—it's an entire system for image handling. For example, it lets you view several pictures at a time; perform sophisticated color, shading, and scaling adjustments on your graphics; and print graphics with a click and drag of your mouse.

HiJaak even lets you capture DOS and Windows screens and save them as graphics files, which is an invaluable feature for software manual writers. In fact, there's also a DOS version of HiJaak, and about its only advantage over the Windows version is that it offers more options for capturing DOS screens. Unless that's a major issue for you, buy the Windows version, which is much more intuitive and interactive; for example, it lets you display a graphic and then watch as the image is converted from one format to another. The Windows version of HiJaak costs about $85, while the DOS version's street price is about $95.

Shuttling Data Between the PC and Mac

As if life isn't complicated enough, some of us have to move files between IBM-compatible PCs and Apple Macintosh computers. Because these machines use different floppy disk standards, there are actually two challenges involved: doing the translation, and transferring the data from one computer to the other.

The premiere product for handling both tasks is DataViz's MacLinkPlus/PC. On the transfer side, in case your Macintosh has a SuperDrive that can read PC disks, MacLinkPlus/PC supplies DOS Mounter software that lets you display and handle your PC disk as just another floppy on the Mac desktop. At the same time, in case you *don't* have a SuperDrive, MacLinkPlus/PC supplies cabling that lets you link any PC to any Macintosh via their serial ports (that is, the connections in the back normally used for communicating with a modem, printer, or mouse). The package also includes both PC and Mac software to complete the hookup and help you run your transfer session, which you can control from either machine.

On the translation side, MacLinkPlus/PC is even more impressive, offering hundreds of conversion combinations. These include translations between PC word processors such as Ami Pro, Microsoft Word, Microsoft Works, MultiMate, WordPerfect, and XyWrite, and Macintosh word processors such as MacWrite, Microsoft Word Mac, Microsoft Works Mac, WordPerfect Mac, and WriteNow. MacLinkPlus/PC also converts between the PC graphics formats BMP, CGM, DXF, IMG, PIC, PCX, TIF, WMF, and WPG and various flavors of the Macintosh PICT format (which is all that's necessary; when it comes to graphics formats, life is a lot easier on the Mac). The package also provides translations between various spreadsheet and database files, program files, and PostScript files.

The more the change, the more it is the same thing.
　　　　—Alphons

While MacLinkPlus/PC is a marvelous product, paying its $129 street price may be overkill. First, if you already have a means of moving your data between the PC and Mac—for example, via modems, or a Local Area

Network—then you can save money by buying MacLinkPlus/Translators, which provides only the translation software and has a street price of $109.

Second, you may not need MacLinkPlus at all if you already own other translation products. For example, Word for Word Professional will convert between PC word processor files and the MacWrite format, and virtually every Macintosh word processor recognizes MacWrite files. Similarly, HiJaak allows you to convert any PC graphic into the PICT format, which is the primary graphics standard on the Mac.

As an all-in-one solution for moving data between PCs and Macs, though, nothing beats MacLinkPlus/PC. If you have to perform such transfers frequently, it's a product well worth owning.

Product Information

Note: Version numbers and prices may have changed by the time you read this.

DataViz, Inc.
55 Corporate Drive
Trumbull, CT 06611
(800) 733-0030; (203) 268-0030
Fax: (203) 268-4345

MacLinkPlus/PC 7.0 (includes cables and DOS Mounter software): List Price, $199; Street Price, about $129

MacLinkPlus/Translators 7.0 (file translation software only): List Price, $169; Street Price, about $109

Inset Systems
71 Commerce Drive
Brookfield, CT 06804-3405
(800) 374-6738; (203) 740-2400
Fax: (203) 775-5634

HiJaak 2.1 for DOS: List Price, $189; Street Price, about $95

HiJaak Pro 2.0 for Windows: List Price, $169; Street Price, about $85

Mastersoft, Inc.
6991 East Camelback Road
Suite A320
Scottsdale, AZ 85251
(800) 624-6107; (602) 277-0900
Fax: (602) 970-0706

Word for Word Professional 5.2 for DOS: List Price, $149; Street Price, about $85

Word for Word Windows Edition 5.2: List Price, $149; Street Price, about $85

Systems Compatibility Corporation
401 North Wabash
Suite 600
Chicago, IL 60611
(800) 333-1395; (312) 329-0700
Fax: (312) 670-0820

Software Bridge 6.0: List Price, $99; Street Price, about $85

Outside In for Windows 2.1: List Price, $89; Street Price, about $65

CHAPTER
22

LAYING OUT YOUR WORK

Writing is a lonely business not just because you have to sit alone in a room with your machinery for hours and hours every day, month after month, year after year; but because after all the blood, sweat, toil, and tears, you still have to find somebody who respects what you have written enough to leave it alone and print it.

—Joseph Hansen

The content of your prose is important, but so is its appearance. If your words aren't presented in an attractive and professional manner, they may not be taken very seriously—if they get read at all. This is especially true in the 90's, when your writing must compete with such visually stimulating media as glossy magazines, broadcast television, cable, video, and film.

Fortunately, there are many tools available to help you create good-looking documents. These range from font managers to drawing software to full-blown layout, or *desktop publishing*, programs.

Covering the scores of fine DTP-related products available is beyond the scope of this book. However, this chapter briefly discusses the best packages, which include Microsoft Publisher, PageMaker for Windows, Quark-XPress for Windows, Ventura Publisher for Windows, FrameMaker for Windows, Adobe Type Manager, Lotus SmartPics for Windows, Windows Draw, and CorelDRAW. It also points you to sources for more information.

Entry Level Desktop Publishing

If the documents you're producing are relatively simple, you can lay them out effectively in a high-end word processor. For example, both Ami Pro and Word for Windows (which are discussed in Chapter 1, *Choosing a Word Processor*) require only a few mouse clicks and drags to perform such functions as changing tab settings, creating multiple columns, changing font sizes and styles, and integrating charts and graphics into your text. Best of all, they let you see the results of your formatting changes immediately on-screen. (In fact, they allow you to adjust the magnification of your screen from 10 percent to 400 percent, so you can study both formatting details and your overall layout.)

Further, if you're creating long technical or scholarly documents with uncomplicated designs, Ami Pro or Word for Windows may prove ideal, because both offer such sophisticated features as automatic numbering, annotations, table of contents and index generation, numerous header and footer options, complex footnote and endnote capabilities, the ability to open multiple documents simultaneously, and the ability to link files (such as book chapters) together when printing.

Freedom of the press is limited to those who own one.

—A. J. Liebling

However, if the particular word processor you're using doesn't offer adequate layout features, or if you need to perform complex design work, or if you'd simply prefer a dedicated layout tool that makes it especially easy to move around the various elements on a page, you should get a desktop publishing package.

For short documents of moderate complexity, such as business forms, flyers, and newsletters, an excellent choice is Microsoft Publisher for Windows. This program lets you place text and graphics in boxes, called *frames*, that you can move anywhere on the page using your mouse, and resize at any time by just clicking and dragging. MS Publisher also displays top and side ruler guides, and lets you set up nonprinting layout guides, to ensure that your positioning of the frames is precise and consistent. The layout guides are particularly helpful because when you move a frame near one, it "magnetizes" the frame to snap up right next to it, sparing you from having to fiddle around to make each frame line up perfectly.

MS Publisher has a number of other terrific features, including a 120,000 word spelling checker, a solid hyphenation dictionary, search and replace commands, remarkably strong support for imported graphics, an image library of over 120 of its own clip art graphics, a "pasteboard" for holding text and picture elements before inserting them into frames, a fun WordArt subprogram that lets you create special text effects (such as turning words upside down, or tilting them diagonally, or running them along a semicircle), and superb printing touches that produce exceptionally fine-looking output.

No author is a man of genius to his publisher.
—Heinrich Heine

What really sets the program apart, though, are its interactive document-building routines, which Microsoft calls Page Wizards. These amazing programs ask you questions about the kind of document you want to design, and as you supply each answer construct the design in front of you! Therefore, when you're done answering all the questions, you've not only learned a great deal about how to use MS Publisher, but have an expertly composed document template, customized to your specifications, that's ready for your immediate use. The Page Wizards will help you create newsletters, calendars, three-fold brochures, seven different types of business forms, greeting cards and invitations, and—just to show off—paper aeroplanes! There's nothing else like Microsoft's Wizards, even in high-end desktop publishing programs.

Books are the windows through which the soul looks out.
—Henry Ward Beecher

A person who publishes a book appears willfully in public with his pants down.
—Edna St. Vincent Millay

In short, MS Publisher is easy to learn and use, offers a number of excellent features, and is actually fun to work with. At a street price of about $89, it's a wonderful value.

Of course, MS Publisher also has some shortcomings. Most notably, it fails to support style sheets (a collection of formatting elements that can be applied uniformly to paragraphs—see the "Microsoft Word for DOS" section in Chapter 1 for more information). This means that if you change your mind about a formatting element, you can't just change it once on a style sheet, but have to manually change it everywhere it appears in your document. Therefore, if you typically produce long documents, a better program choice is PFS:Publisher for Windows from Spinnaker Software.

PFS:Publisher supports paragraph style sheets, a table of contents generator, an index generator, and other features that help you manage lengthy works. It also provides many useful extras, such as 50 design templates that can be used for a variety of documents; a built-in word processor, spelling checker, and thesaurus; and 100 clip art pictures. Its street price is about $95.

You may have noticed that all the products mentioned so far require Microsoft Windows. That's because Windows' graphical environment (which allows text and picture elements to be treated as movable objects) and its multitasking capabilities (which let you run a word processor, drawing program, and DTP package at the same time) are ideal for desktop publishing. However, if your PC is too slow for Windows, don't feel abandoned; you can still turn to Express Publisher from Power Up Software, which runs under DOS but has much of the pizzazz of its Windows competitors. In addition, Express Publisher sports ready-made templates and disk-based layout advice by respected designer Roger Parker, whose best-selling *Looking Good in Print* is one of the finest books available on desktop publishing. Express Publisher costs $79.95.

High-End Desktop Publishing

Programs such as Microsoft Publisher for Windows and PFS:Publisher for Windows are great for the type of quick layout work needed by individuals, small businesses, and even certain corporate departments. However, if you're creating design-intensive documents, or long and complex documents, you need more powerful tools.

A high-end desktop publishing package will give you fine control over such elements as point size (that is, the size of letters), leading (the spacing between lines), kerning (the spacing between two letters), and tracking (the spacing between *every* letter in a word or sentence). It will also provide you with the ability to flow text around an image, rotate text and graphics, and fully address commercial printing processes such as color separation.

There are four high-end products you should explore (with street prices ranging between $525 and $579): QuarkXPress for Windows from Quark Inc., PageMaker for Windows from Aldus Corp., Ventura Publisher for Windows from Ventura Software, and FrameMaker for Windows from Frame Technology. Each program is very powerful and flexible, and can handle a variety of tasks. However, each has strengths and weaknesses which make it best suited for a particular audience.

For example, if you're a graphic artist or designer who creates ads, color brochures, or glossy magazine pages, it's no contest: buy QuarkXPress. Nothing else touches this program's super-precise typographical and layout controls, or its four-color separation features. And nothing else allows you to deal with complex design projects so quickly and efficiently.

QuarkXPress lets you scale both type and leading in increments as astonishingly fine as 0.001 of a point (a point being 1/72 of an inch), and control kerning and tracking by 1/20,000 of an Em (an *Em* being approximately the size of the letter *m* in your current font). It also lets you rotate text and graphic frames up to 360 degrees in 0.001 degree increments.

Equally impressive is QuarkXPress' color capabilities. It can produce direct four-color separations from CYMK (Cyan-Yellow-Magenta-blacK) format graphics. Of course, it also supports spot colors; but alternatively, it can convert Focoltone, HSB, Pantone, RGB, or TruMatch values into

CYMK values. In addition, the program lets you specify exactly how color pairs will overlap to minimize problems with registration (that is, color alignment).

QuarkXPress also anticipates the daily needs of the designer in a variety of thoughtful ways. For example, it lets you save virtually any design element you've created to a "library" file for future use. And it lets you create up to 127 Master page layouts to hold repeating elements (as opposed to just two Master pages in PageMaker, and one in Ventura Publisher). This means that when you're hit with a complex rush job, you can construct it rather easily by pulling together pieces from your previous projects.

On the other hand, QuarkXPress falls short when it comes to long documents—it lacks such features as footnoting, indexing, and table of contents generation, and can't link separate files (though it *can* handle up to 2,000 pages in a single file). It also demands heavy-duty hardware: to take full advantage of it, you'll want a 486 PC and a PostScript printer. Nonetheless, for professional designers and art directors, it's a dream come true.

If your design needs aren't of the highest caliber, and you'd prefer something closer to a jack-of-all-trades, consider PageMaker. Like Microsoft Publisher, PageMaker provides a screen resembling a pasteboard, making it simple for you to set elements off to the side of your page until you need them, and rearrange text and graphics frames on the page easily with your mouse. Anyone who's performed physical cut-and-paste layout will quickly feel comfortable with PageMaker's way of doing things. The program doesn't match the precision and convenience features of QuarkXPress, but it usually comes close. Further, it provides a number of long-document features, and so is better able to tackle a wide variety of jobs.

When a book and a head collide and there is a hollow sound, is it always from the book?
—Georg Christoph Lichtenberg

Books are the most remarkable creation of man; nothing else that he builds ever lasts...Monuments fall...civilizations grow old and die out...but in the world of books are volumes that live on, still as young and fresh as the day they were written—still telling men's hearts of the hearts of men centuries dead.

—Clarence Day

Then again, if your *principle* activity is producing long and complicated documents (such as books, catalogs, and technical documentation), you should turn to either Ventura Publisher or FrameMaker. Both programs supply such important features as footnotes, dictionary-style headers and footers, cross-references, automatic numbering (for paragraphs, tables, figures, captions, lists, and so on), automatic table of contents and index generation, the ability to link different files together (for example, the separate chapters in a book), and conditional text (that is, sections of text which print only when you explicitly allow them to).

Ventura Publisher takes less time to learn, and some find it easier to use. Also, its color support is almost as good as QuarkXPress'. However, the program is plagued with a number of irritations, such as a "font width" calculating routine that needlessly increases the amount of time the software takes to load, a lack of standard support for the Windows Clipboard, and an inability to let you work with more than one Ventura document at a time.

FrameMaker is packed with powerful features, and requires significant training time before you can take advantage of them. However, for many people, it's worth the extra effort. Some advantages it enjoys over Ventura Publisher are the ability to open multiple documents; surprisingly strong built-in word processor and drawing programs; search and replace commands that offer rich formatting options; an equation editor that not only lets you type in equations, but can *solve* them for you; intelligent tables (that is, tables that dynamically move and reformat themselves depending on the text around them); and hypertext support, which lets you link a section of text in one document with related text in another file. Further, FrameMaker is totally compatible with its versions on the two other major families of computer systems, the Apple Macintosh line and Unix workstations (such as Sun), which is a big plus for corporations trying to standardize their operations. FrameMaker is most famous for its expertise in producing technical and scientific documentation, but you should give it serious consideration for handling any type of highly structured multi-chapter publication.

As I've said, each of these four high-end DTP programs is superb and, if you push hard enough, can tackle virtually any layout task. Therefore, you won't go terribly wrong buying any of them. However, if your production work ranges from design-intensive color posters to long, complicated catalogs, you might consider purchasing two of the packages (say, QuarkXPress and FrameMaker, or PageMaker and Ventura Publisher), so that you can always apply the most appropriate tool to the job at hand.

Other Layout Tools

While you'll be producing your overall layout with a word processor or DTP program, it's a good idea to also make use of some supplementary products. These include a font manager, clip art, a scanner, drawing software, and training materials.

The importance of fonts was expressed concisely in a recent *PC Magazine* article by its top reviewer, Edward Mendelson:

Type is the medium and vehicle of the printed word. When used effectively, it enhances communication by clarifying the structure and emphasis of your text, or by letting you forget its existence as you read hundreds of pages of unobtrusive printing without fatigue. When used badly, it can hinder communication by conveying a visual mood on the page that works against the verbal mood of the text, or by forcing you to notice the typographer's originality or ingenuity when you are trying to pay attention to the content of the words.

In other words, choose your fonts carefully, and mix them in the same document sparingly. That being said, the more fonts you have to choose from, the better.

A number of companies sell typefaces, including Adobe Systems and Microsoft. Also, desktop publishing and drawing packages often bundle in dozens of fonts as a premium (as demonstrated most overwhelming by the CorelDRAW package discussed later in this chapter).

The two principle font formats under Windows are TrueType and Type 1 (a subset of PostScript). TrueType was designed by Microsoft to work smoothly under Windows, so it doesn't require any extra software. However, most fonts are in the older Type 1 format and aren't supported by Windows, so you need a special program to properly scale, display, and print them. The program of choice is Adobe Type Manager, which is often included free in word processing and DTP-related packages. If a copy hasn't tumbled your way, though, don't hesitate to buy one at its street price of about $45, because ATM is an essential utility.

Another important element in your layout work is graphics. Unless you're a professional artist, you'll want to put together a library of ready-made images, or clip art, for jazzing up your words. The best clip art package is SmartPics for Windows from Lotus Development, which contains over 2,000 exceptionally high quality color images. All the pictures are in vector format (as opposed to bitmap), which means they'll print out great no matter how much you resize them. SmartPics also comes with a terrific graphics viewer which lets you see six images at a time, and copy any displayed picture to the Windows Clipboard with a single mouse click. (In fact, a good way to work with SmartPics is to expand the Clipboard to full screen size, and layer the viewer on top of it. Then when you copy an image to the Clipboard, you instantly see the image at full size.) I highly recommend SmartPics for Windows, which has an inexpensive street price of about $69.

Author's Prayer:
Our Father, who art in heaven,
And has also written a book...

Another popular art collection is Presentation Task Force from New Vision Technologies, which contains over 3,500 color vector pictures. Most of the images are drawn in a good-natured, cartoon-like style, and cover a broad range of subjects (with an emphasis on business topics). The package also provides around 20 small font families which, not surprisingly, *also* convey a playful, cheery mood; and a handy color to black and white graphics converter, in case you need to output high-contrast line art. If you like its somewhat eccentric drawing styles, you'll find Presentation Task Force to be a good value at its street price of about $119.

The writer writes in order to teach himself, to understand himself, to satisfy himself; the publishing of his ideas, though it brings gratification, is a curious anticlimax.

—Alfred Kazin

There are also an enormous number of images available on paper, many of which are in the public domain. You can get copies of these pictures into your computer by using a scanner. If all you care about are black and white graphics, nothing beats the outstanding Hewlett-Packard ScanJet IIp, which has a low street price of about $699. If you also need color, though, buy the larger and costlier HP ScanJet IIc, which has a street price of about $1,279.

After you've imported a clip art graphic or scanned in an image, you may notice a few aspects of it you want to change or enhance. Alternatively, you may decide to use the image as a springboard for your own original artwork. For such tasks, you need a drawing program.

Actually, drawing programs can be used for many diverse chores, such as inserting ovals and arrows to emphasize paragraphs in a direct mail piece; creating customized letterhead and logos for your business; drafting funny illustrations to liven up a newsletter; and designing professional-level artwork for ads, brochures, and posters.

The best entry-level product is Windows Draw from Micrografx, which is a cleanly designed program that's easy to learn and use, yet packs a lot of power under its hood. As you'd expect, the software allows you to create lines, boxes, ovals, and freehand curves. But it also makes it easy to create sophisticated Bezier curves; rotate, flip, duplicate, group, and ungroup objects; slant and stretch objects; create blends; and fill objects with gradually increasing shades of color, or gradients. Windows Draw is also great with text; for example, it imports a variety of word processor formats, lets you create impressive effects by flowing words around any curve, and bundles in over 50 outline fonts. Other features include support for 16 million colors, ruler and grid lines that make objects "snap" to them for easy placement, a fine library of over 2,600 clip art pictures, and strong printer support and excellent output. Windows Draw doesn't quite cut it as a professional designer's tool because it lacks a few key features, such as color separation options, and autotracing (which converts a bitmap graphic, such as a scanned image, into an vector graphic that's easier to manipulate). However, it's a marvelously powerful program for noncommercial artists and business users, and a bargain at its low street price of $85.

On the other hand, if you want what *PC Magazine* termed "the ultimate graphics bargain" and *Byte* called the "swiss army knife for illustrators," purchase CorelDRAW, a awesome Windows program from Corel Systems. The street price of CorelDRAW is $395, or over four times as much as Windows Draw. However, that extra $300 buys you software that would cost several *thousand* dollars if purchased separately.

*A*nd it does no harm to repeat, as often as you can, "Without me the
*literary industry would not exist; the publishers, the agents, the sub-agents,
the sub-sub-agents, the accountants, the libel lawyers, the departments of
literature, the professors, the theses, the books of criticism, the reviewers, the
book pages—all this vast and proliferating edifice is because of this small,
patronized, put-down, and underpaid person."*

—Doris Lessing

The heart of the package is its drawing program, which is one of the easiest to use, and yet also one of most powerful, on the market. For example, its text handling supports long paragraphs (up to 4,000 characters), long documents (up to 999 pages), automatic bullets, style sheets, spell-checking and thesaurus look-ups, the ability to flow text along a curve (and even perform kerning on the curve!), the ability to flow text around— or *within*—objects, and the ability to flow text from frame to frame (not unlike a desktop publishing program). Other features include color separation, 43 professionally designed layout templates, up to 99 levels of

UNDO (which allows you to back up from your previous actions), multi-layered drawing (with the option of making any layer nonprinting, invisible, and/or locked), the ability to rotate objects in three dimensions under a simulated light source, unusual object fills such as contour and multi-color fountain, and unusual drawing shapes such as wedge and teardrop (it can even simulate custom pressure strokes!).

Also bundled into the package is a photo-retouching and image-editing module (actually a version of the respected PhotoFinish program from ZSoft), which allows you to do such nifty things as imitate Van Gogh and Seurat painting styles; a charting module which supplies a wealth of chart types—including 3-D scatter, standard deviation, histrogram, and spectral —and can rotate charts in three dimensions; a screen-show module which lets you display sequential drawings and charts, and play animations, sounds, and videos, for your multimedia presentations; an autotracing module; and a picture manager that can quickly display and print your graphics files. Each of these modules is a substantial program in its own right, and holds up strongly against standalone programs on the market.

On top of all that, CorelDRAW provides two CD-ROM discs that contain an amazing 750 TrueType and Type 1 fonts (650 of which come from the respected font publishers Bitstream and ITC); and a jaw-dropping 18,000 clip art images and symbols! Still not satisfied, Corel Systems *also* includes libraries of animations and sounds.

In short, CorelDRAW is one of the most incredible values ever offered for the PC. If you have need for even a portion of its features, snap it up.

Of course, even the best desktop publishing tools are of little help unless you understand how to use them effectively. Therefore, the most important thing you can do to improve the appearance of your documents is teach yourself basic desktop publishing principles.

For starters, read a few good books. You can get the basics from *The Desktop Style Guide* by James Felici (Bantam Books, 1991; $11.95). Then, to learn how to deal with fonts, buy *Desktop Typography* by David Collier (Addison-Wesley Publishing, 1991; $16.25) and *How to Get Great Type Out of Your Computer* by James Felici (North Light Books, 1992; $22.95). Lastly, for excellent design advice, plus loads of fine examples, purchase the acclaimed *Looking Good in Print, Third Edition* by Roger C. Parker (Ventana Press, 1993; $24.95).

There's also one inexpensive periodical that's essential reading: *Publish*, which is the premium magazine on desktop publishing for both PC and Macintosh owners. A year's subscription (12 issues) costs $29.95.

If you plan to devote a lot of time and energy to DTP work, you might also think about joining the National Association of Desktop Publishers. For a $95 annual membership fee, you get a monthly subscription to the informative *Desktop Publishers Journal*; money-saving discounts on hardware and software products, DTP-related books and magazines, trade shows, DTP training classes, and high-resolution output services; a job bank for locating designers or for offering your own services; and an 800 number you can call to get answers to your technical questions about DTP products.

Whether you intend to become a hard-core desktop publisher or not, though, I recommend that you explore at least a few of the products covered in this chapter. Even if you have someone else laying out your words, you'll be in a much better position when requesting special printing effects or asking for changes on page proofs if you understand the production process.

On the other hand, all good things should be used with moderation. So if your main job is supposed to be writing, and you're suddenly tempted to spend hours messing around with the fonts and leading on an office memo, try hard to not lose sight of what's of *paramount* importance—the content of your message, and your precious time.

Product Information

Note: Version numbers and prices may have changed by the time you read this.

Addison-Wesley Publishing
Order Department
Route 128
Reading, MA 01867
(800) 447-2226; (617) 944-3700
Fax: (617) 942-1117

Desktop Typography by David Collier (1991 softcover book): $16.25

Adobe Systems, Inc.
P.O. Box 7900
1585 Charleston Road
Mountain View, CA 94039-7900
(800) 833-6687; (415) 961-4400
Fax: (415) 961-3769 (main number); (408) 562-6775 (sales)

Adobe Type Manager 2.5 (for Windows): List Price, $99; Street Price, about $45; often bundled in for free with word processing and desktop publishing packages

Many high-quality fonts are also available for sale; call for details. Also, be sure to ask for Adobe's terrific free font catalog.

Aldus Corporation
411 First Avenue South
Seattle, WA 98104-2871
(800) 627-8880; (206) 628-2320
Fax: (206) 628-5737 (automated info center); (206) 343-3360 (customer service)
PageMaker 5.0 for Windows: List Price, $895; Street Price, about $579

Corel Systems Corporation
1600 Carling Avenue
Ottawa, Ontario, Canada K1Z 8R7
(800) 836-3729; (613) 728-8200
Fax: (613) 761-9176
CorelDRAW 4.0 (for Windows): List Price, $595; Street Price, about $395

Frame Technology
1010 Rincon Circle
San Jose, CA 95131
(800) 843-7263; (408) 433-3311
Fax: (408) 433-1928
FrameMaker 4.0 for Windows: List Price, $895; Street Price, about $525

Hewlett-Packard Company
P.O. Box 58059
Santa Clara, CA 95051-8059
(800) 752-0900; (408) 246-4300
Fax: (208) 344-4809
ScanJet IIp (generates black and white images only): List Price, $879; Street Price, about $699
ScanJet IIc (can generate either black and white or color images): List Price, $1,599; Street Price, about $1,279

Lotus Development Corporation
55 Cambridge Parkway
Cambridge, MA 02142
(800) 343-5414; (617) 577-8500
Fax: (617) 253-9150
Lotus Ami Pro 3.0: List Price, $495; Street Price, about $249; Competitive Upgrade (when offered), about $95
SmartPics 1.0 for Windows: List Price, $89; Street Price, about $69

Micrografx, Inc.
1303 Arapaho
Richardson, TX 75081
(800) 733-3729; (214) 234-1769
Fax: (214) 234-2410

Windows Draw 3.0 (for Windows): List Price, $149; Street Price, about $85

Microsoft Corporation
One Microsoft Way
Redmond, WA 98052
(800) 426-9400; (206) 882-8080
Fax: No generic sales or information fax number

Microsoft Word 2.0 for Windows: List Price, $495; Street Price, about $299; Competitive Upgrade (when offered), about $129

Microsoft Publisher 2.0 for Windows: List Price, $139; Street Price, about $89

TrueType Font Pack 1 for Windows (44 fonts): List Price, $69.95; Street Price, about $45

TrueType Font Pack 2 for Windows (44 fonts): List Price, $69.95; Street Price, about $45

National Association of Desktop Publishers
462 Old Boston Street
Topsfield, MA 01983
(800) 874-4113; (508) 887-7900
Fax: (508) 887-6117

NADTP Annual membership: $95 a year, which includes a monthly subscription to *The Desktop Publishers Journal*; discounts on hardware, software, publications, trade shows, training, imagesetting, and other products and services related to desktop publishing; a job bank for locating designers or for offering your own services; and an 800 technical information and support number

New Vision Technologies, Inc.
38 Auriga Drive
Unit 13
Nepean, Ontario, Canada K2E 8A5
(613) 727-8184
Fax: (613) 727-8190

Presentation Task Force 4.0: List price, $199; Street Price, about $119

North Light Books
1507 Dana Avenue
Cincinnati, Ohio 45207
(800) 289-0963; (513) 531-2222
Fax: (513) 531-4082

How to Get Great Type Out of Your Computer by James Felici (1992 softcover book): $22.95

Power Up Software Corporation
929 Campus Drive
San Mateo, CA 94403
(800) 851-2917; (203) 268-0030
Fax: (203) 268-4345

Express Publisher 3.0 for DOS: List Price, $79.95; Street Price N/A

Express Publisher 1.0 for Windows: List Price, $79.95; Street Price N/A

Publish
(Division of International Data Group)
Subscriber Services
P.O. Box 5039
Brentwood, TN 37024
(800) 685-3435; (615) 377-3322
Fax: (615) 377-0525

Publish (monthly magazine): $29.95 for 12-issue subscription, $47.90 for 24-issue subscription

Quark, Inc.
1800 Grant Street
Denver, CO 80203
(800) 788-7835; (303) 894-8888
Fax: (303) 343-2086

QuarkXPress 3.2 for Windows: List Price, $895; Street Price, about $579

Random House, Inc.
400 Hahn Road
West Minister, MD 21157
(800) 733-3000; (410) 848-1900
Fax: (800) 659-2436

The Desktop Style Guide by James Felici (1991 softcover book): $11.95

Spinnaker Software Corporation
201 Broadway
Cambridge, MA 02139-1901
(800) 826-0706; (617) 494-1200
Fax: (617) 494-1219

PFS:Publisher 1.1 for Windows: List Price, $149; Street Price, about $95

Ventana Press
P.O. Box 2468
Chapel Hill, NC 27515
(800) 743-5369; (919) 942-0220
Fax: (800) 877-7955

Looking Good in Print, Third Edition by Roger C. Parker (1993 softcover book): $24.95

Ventura Software, Inc.
15175 Innovation Drive
San Diego, CA 92128
(800) 833-0525; (619) 673-0172
Fax: (619) 673-7777

Ventura Publisher 4.1 for Windows: List Price, $795; Street Price, about $549

CHAPTER
23

PRINTING YOUR WORK

Your manuscript is both good and original; but the part that is good is not original, and the part that is original is not good.
—Samuel Johnson

The covers of this book are too far apart.
—Ambrose Bierce

This is not a novel to be tossed aside lightly. It should be thrown with great force.
—Dorothy Parker

Tonstant Weader fwowed up.
—Dorothy Parker, under her *New Yorker* alias "Constant Reader," reviewing *The House at Pooh Corner*

The focus of this book has been on *software* tools. However, when you've finished composing, polishing, and laying out your words, you'll need to deal with a number of issues concerning hardware. Therefore, this final chapter provides some down-to-earth advice about such items as printers, paper, and PostScript cards—and discusses a few software packages in the bargain.

Printers

Life is full of tough decisions, but every now and then it tosses us some easy ones. Happily, that's the case with printers, where the main thing you have to remember is one name: Hewlett-Packard.

Hewlett-Packard has dominated the PC printer market for most of the past decade, and deservedly so. The company has consistently come out with products that offer high quality and tremendous reliability at remarkably low prices.

If you're looking for an inexpensive printer, your best bet is an HP Desk-Jet, which is small, light, and whisper quiet. The latter attribute may not seem very important unless, like me, you once had your nerves (and your neighbor's nerves) shattered daily by the jackhammer clanking of a dot matrix or daisy wheel printer, which pounds ink into paper. In contrast, the DeskJet is an inkjet printer, which means it silently sprays fast-drying ink onto your pages. In addition to avoiding noise pollution, this approach helps reduce the number of moving parts in the printer and so extends its problem-free operation. I can offer a real-life testimonial on that score— I've used the same DeskJet printer for five years, and it's still going strong.

The HP DeskJet 500 yields a text print quality nearly as good as that of a laser printer. It prints about two pages a minute, which is fast enough for many home and small business uses, and it virtually never jams or stalls. Indeed, the machine is so well designed that you'll even have fun replacing its ink cartridges. Basically, the DeskJet 500 is a honey, and at a street price of around $309, a terrific bargain.

If you need to be able to generate color documents—say, for business presentations, or for recreational art, or for your kid's school project—another excellent machine is the HP DeskJet 550C. This printer can do everything the DeskJet 500 can when you use a black ink cartridge. In addition, it can print attractive color images using a cartridge containing cyan, yellow, and magenta ink that it mixes in various subtle ways. (Of course, you also need to use a program that supports the printer; but most modern painting, desktop publishing, and word processing packages do so.) The HP DeskJet 550C has an affordable street price of $575.

On the other hand, if you need to generate pages that look good enough to be reproduced in a newsletter, or if you want a "draft" machine that closely approximates how your work will look after it's sent to a high-resolution printer service, or if you simply need a machine that churns out pages quickly, then you really ought to buy a laser printer.

The HP LaserJet IIIP is nearly as compact, quiet, and problem-free as a DeskJet. However, its print quality is finer, which is especially noticeable with text and line art. It also has a slot into which you can insert a PostScript cartridge, which is a virtual necessity if you plan to use an output service for a high-resolution final printout (typically, 1,270 dots per inch, versus the 300 dpi of the IIIP). Further, the IIIP can print up to four text pages a minute, which is double the speed of the DeskJet; and it can print graphics at triple or quadruple the speed of the DeskJet. The HP LaserJet IIIP's street price is about $879.

An even better bargain, though, is the HP LaserJet 4. This product's biggest advantages are that it prints eight pages a minute, versus the four pages of the IIIP; and it offers a printing resolution of 600 by 600 dpi, which is four times as many dots as the IIIP's 300 by 300 dpi (360,000 versus 90,000), and so provides enormously better print quality. The LaserJet 4 also has subtler advantages, such as a paper tray that holds 250 pages, versus the IIIP's 70; a relatively straightforward paper path, versus the IIIP's somewhat cumbersome one that has trouble accommodating stock heavier than 28 pound; a superior parallel port connection that can accept data more quickly and supports more fluid communications with your PC than the IIIP's; 45 high-quality built-in fonts, including 10 TrueType fonts, which means it can typically print documents from Microsoft Windows faster than the IIIP; and a superior PostScript add-on option that lets you print PostScript documents more quickly. Further, despite the LaserJet 4's power, it's about as light and compact as the IIIP. The HP LaserJet 4's street price is a fantastically low $1,369—only $490 more than the IIIP—and is the ideal printer for handling heavy-duty needs. (Indeed, it's the machine I turned to when I needed to churn out this book.)

Selecting a printer doesn't end your purchase decisions, though. After all, a printer doesn't live on love and electricity alone; you also have to "feed" it. Hence, the next section.

Paper and Ink

The one nuisance about HP DeskJet printers is that they're finicky about paper. If you don't use a brand that jibes well with their ink-spraying technique, your output will look faded and unattractive. For best results, I recommend Hammermill Xero/Lasercopy paper, which costs about $3.50 a ream (500 sheets).

Laser printers are less picky about paper, and so provide room for diversity. For example, if you're printing mostly draft copies and in-house work, stock up on the popular Hammermill Copy Plus, which produces attractive output for around $2.50 a ream. If your work goes out to others, though, you may prefer the more expensive Hammermill Xero/Lasercopy paper for a higher quality look.

For important reports and presentations, and for knock-em-dead letterhead, turn from standard 20 pound paper to 24 pound. Two excellent brands are Hammermill Laser Print, which provides a smooth surface and high brightness, and costs about $5.50 a ream; and Hammermill Laser Bond, which has 25 percent cotton fiber content, is watermarked and acid-free, and costs about $10 a ream.

Two great mail-order sources for paper—and loads of other supplies—are Quill and Elek-Tek. Quill is the best one-stop-shopping source, because it carries everything you can think of for office work, from paper clips to chairs to fax machines, and all at excellent prices. For many computer-related supplies, however, Elek-Tek's prices are even better.

For example, Elek-Tek's price for Copy Plus paper is $2.69 a ream, while Quill's is $3.99; Elek-Tek's charge for Xero/Lasercopy paper is $3.25 a ream, while Quill's is $4.68; and Elek-Tek's rate for Laser Bond paper is $7.99 a ream, while Quill's is $11.98. Naturally, both vendors also provide discounts for volume. For example, if you buy a case of 10 reams of Xero/Lasercopy paper, Elek-Tek will charge $3.10 a ream for a carton for 10 reams, and Quill will ask for $4.39 a ream.

Of course, you can put more in your laser printer than plain white paper. If you have specialized needs, or simply want to have more fun with your printer, turn to Paper Direct. This mail-order house offers gorgeously designed paper in a wide variety of colors, styles, shapes, and weights. In addition, it carries such novelties as colored foil that transfers itself to your pages (including holographic foil!), and LaserKleen paper that removes dust build-up and toner deposits when you run it through your machine. The company even sells a delightful sample kit that includes hundreds of different types of 8 1/2 inch by 11 inch paper, so you can conveniently try before you buy (and the $19.95 price of the kit is refunded with your first order over $30!). The only downside to Paper Direct is that it's not cheap; for example, its designer colored papers are typically priced at $20 per 100 sheets (that is, $100 a ream). However, if you're doing direct mail solicitations, or sending out party invitations, or performing some other activity that demands pizazz, the chances are you'll be glad these nifty papers are available and cheerfully pay the extra bucks for them.

Of course, even the best paper won't do you much good without ink. For the HP DeskJet, there are two kinds of black ink cartridges—the standard version that can print 500,000 characters, and the more economical double-capacity model that can output one million characters. If you own a DeskJet 550C, you'll also need a color ink cartridge, which can produce 250 pages. Again, Elek-Tek has the lowest prices, selling the standard black cartridge for $15.99, the double-capacity for $23.99, and the color for $25.99.

I fell asleep reading a dull book, and I dreamed that I was reading on, so I awoke from sheer boredom.

—Heinrich Heine

From the moment I picked up your book until I laid it down I was convulsed with laughter. Someday I intend reading it.

—Groucho Marx

People who like this sort of thing will find this the sort of thing they like.

—Abraham Lincoln, reviewing a book diplomatically

My dear fellow, I may perhaps be dead from the neck up, but rack my brains as I may I can't see why a chap should need 30 pages to describe how he turns over in bed before going to sleep.

—Editor rejecting Marcel Proust's *Swann's Way*
    (Remembrance of Things Past)

Considerably more economical are toner cartridges for laser printers. While they have a high initial cost—typically, $80 to $100, depending on the printer model—they can tackle thousands of sheets of paper before running dry, giving you lower cost-per-page expenses than any other type of printer. In fact, these savings should be a factor in considering the purchase of a laser printer, since they help to offset the higher price of the machine.

For even more savings, you can recycle your cartridges. For example, Quill sells a kit for $8.99 that lets you mail in a used DeskJet cartridge and get back a filled one. It also offers a Xerox/Diablo product consisting of ink-filled plastic bottles you can use to twice refill a DeskJet cartridge yourself. Be careful with the latter, however; I've found the bottles always contain more ink than needed, and this flawed design once resulted in my accidentally spraying a wall with unremovable black ink. If you like living dangerously, Quill sells this kit for $15.98.

You can also recycle your laser toner cartridges. Aside from ecological considerations, you can save quite a bit of money this way. For example, Quill will refill a $100 toner cartridge for $44.99, and can do so up to three times before the cartridge wears out. (In many cases, you'll even get superior print quality, since the toner refills often produce darker printouts than the toner used in new cartridges.) Toner cartridge recycling is a standard practice at many large companies, because when several heavily used laser printers are involved, the savings add up rapidly.

Of course, there's also a simpler way to reduce costs, and that's to cut down on the amount of paper and ink used. You don't even have to exercise self-restraint to accomplish this worthy goal; you just need to use one of the two helpful software packages covered in the next section.

4Print and Treesaver

If you're a programmer dealing with reams of code listings; or if you're an accountant wishing you could see more of a spreadsheet's columns at a time; or if you're a court reporter buried under piles of transcripts; or if you're in any other profession where you'd benefit from squeezing more information onto a sheet a paper, then you ought to know about 4Print from Korenthal Associates and TreeSaver from Discoversoft.

If you own an HP DeskJet or LaserJet, 4Print allows you to print two, three, or four pages of text on a single sheet. Further, it makes it simple for you to use both sides of your paper by printing the front side of your pages on the first run-through, and then the back side of your pages after you flip over your sheets and reinsert them into the printer. If you then place your printout in, say, a three-ring binder, you'll be able to view up to eight pages at once, because when you open the binder, you'll see the back of one sheet and the front of the next.

4Print accomplishes its page-shrinking by using a set of small but easily readable fonts. The pages are printed across the 11 inch length of an 8 1/2 inch by 11 inch sheet using your printer's horizontal, or *landscape*, mode (as opposed to its usual vertical, or *portrait*, mode). For example, if you chose to print three pages of text on one side of a sheet, you'd get a page on the left, a page in the middle, and a page on the right running across the sheet's 11 inch length.

4Print works only with ASCII files, so if you want it to print, say, your WordPerfect document or FoxPro database, you first have to save the data in ASCII from your application. On the other hand, 4Print is perfect for handling program code, on-disk documentation, electronic mail, and other data that exists only in ASCII form.

Under DOS, the program works using command line switches...and it has a slew of them. For example, when you're at the DOS prompt, typing *4PRINT -np* tells it to number each page; typing *4PRINT -p#-#* instructs it to print the specified range of pages, which is especially useful if some pages get crunched during your print-run; and typing *4PRINT -1 -tiny -sq* causes it to print one long page using a "tiny, squeezed" font, for when you need to fit up to 242 characters per line onto a single sheet (a handy way of viewing long spreadsheets). There are also switches for centering text, inserting titles and borders, numbering lines, replacing multiple blank lines with a single line, and some 40 other formatting commands. If you find all these options confusing, however, you can ignore them and simply type *4PRINT* followed by your filename to get four pages printed on each sheet, with two pages per side.

Another component of the package is 4Book, a small gem of a program that lets you create 5 1/2 inch by 8 1/2 inch booklets in two simple steps: printing four pages to a sheet, and then folding all the sheets in half. If you want to get fancy, 4Book provides dozens of formatting options, such as cover styles (including *sunrise, sunburst,* and *eclipse*), large title fonts, boilerplate text that can be selectively included, and even randomly generated quotations that print out differently every time a booklet is printed. You can make these booklets serve a variety of roles, from catalogs to promotional literature to custom briefing books for corporate meetings.

Finally, in case you use Microsoft Windows, the package includes a Windows program that lets you select options from menus in lieu of typing dash-letter combinations at the DOS prompt.

4Print is a terrific package that gets you up and running quickly, but offers sophisticated printing control if you desire it. It also has the keen distinction of being described by famed *PC Magazine* columnist Bill Machrone as "way cool." 4Print has a list price of $69.95, but you can purchase it for only $39.95 using the Korenthal Associates coupon near the back of this book.

Another useful page-squeezing utility is TreeSaver. Like 4Print, this program lets you print up to four pages on a single sheet of paper, or perform double-sided printing to fit up to eight pages on a sheet. Unlike 4Print, however, TreeSaver doesn't package its LaserJet and DeskJet programs together, and it doesn't offer a Windows version at all. It also lacks the many small touches for controlling print formatting that 4Print provides. However, TreeSaver has its own charms.

First, when you're running the program by itself, TreeSaver lets you select options from menus, which is more intuitive than using DOS control switches.

The girl doesn't, it seems to me, have a special perception or feeling which would lift that book above the "curiosity" level.

—Editor rejecting *The Diary of Anne Frank*

I am only one, only one, only. Only one being, one at the same time. Not two, not three, only one. Only one life to live, only sixty minutes in one hour. Only one pair of eyes. Only one brain. Only one being. Being only one, having only one pair of eyes, having only one time, having only one life, I cannot read your MS three or four times. Not even one time. Only one look, only one look is enough. Hardly one copy would sell here. Hardly one. Hardly one.

—Editor rejecting Gertrude Stein's *Ida: A Novel*

Why don't you write books people can read?

—Nora Joyce, to her husband James

The House Beautiful *is the play lousy.*

—Dorothy Parker

Second, TreeSaver has a memory-resident version that you can control with Alt keystrokes. This means that you can use it from within your word processor, or spreadsheet, or database, without having to go through the interim step of creating an ASCII file. Even better, TreeSaver will preserve your program's formatting codes, as well as any graphics in your document, in effect acting like a software photo-reduction machine. Therefore, if you prefer to print reduced documents directly from an application program, TreeSaver is the way to go. Its LaserJet version has a list price of $49.95, and its DeskJet version, TreeSaver DJ, has a list price of $29.95.

Other Printing Accessories

There's a wide range of other software and hardware products you'll find helpful when printing. Among the most useful are PrintCache, SuperPrint, the HP PostScript SIMM, and the WinJet/1200. These, and a few other items, are covered in this final section.

One of the simplest ways to boost your productivity is to use a print spooler. Such a program automatically directs all the data from your print job to your computer's memory, or to your hard disk, thus freeing the program you're using from waiting for your printer. It then transfers the data to your printer in the background as you work.

There are numerous print spooler programs—for example, the PC-Kwik Power Pak software recommended in Chapter 20, *Essential General-Purpose Tools*, includes a fine spooler. If you want the very best, though, buy PrintCache from LaserTools. In addition to the basics, PrintCache offers such features as control of your printer's settings from your keyboard, extra fast printing of graphics files, extra fast printing under Microsoft Windows, and an icon under Windows that displays the amount of memory PrintCache is using and changes colors to reflect the status of your print job. It's these bells and whistles that make PrintCache tops in its category. The program's street price is about $55.

If you use Microsoft Windows, another software package to consider is SuperPrint from Zenographics, which packs three utilities in one: a print spooler almost as good as PrintCache; an on-the-fly font scaler, which functions similarly to Adobe Type Manager (see Chapter 22, *Laying Out Your Work*) and can work in conjunction with ATM; and a set of replacement programs for communicating with your printer that significantly improves the speed with which graphics are printed under Windows. Further, if you own a dot matrix printer, you'll find SuperPrint especially effective because it's better than virtually any other program at producing crisp, professional-looking dot matrix output. SuperPrint has a list price of $99.

For sophisticated layout work, or for work you eventually need printed on a high-resolution machine (such as a Linotronic), you'll want to use PostScript, which functions as a universal language for high-end printers. You'll get the most bang for the buck by combining an HP LaserJet 4 with an HP Postscript SIMM board, which prints significantly faster than the PostScript cartridges made for previous LaserJets (such as the IIIP), and costs about $259. If you want to print PostScript documents at 600 dpi, you'll also need to buy an extra 4MB of LaserJet memory (for about $149), to be added to the 2MB already present in the printer.

If you will only take the precaution to go in long enough after it commences and to come out long enough before it is over, you will not find it wearisome.

—George Bernard Shaw reviewing the play *Redemption*

When I saw Annie *(at a date's insistence), I had to hit myself on the head afterward with a small hammer to get that stupid "Tomorrow" song out of my head.*

—Ian Shoales

Very nice, but there are dull stretches.

—Comte De Rivarol, on a two-line poem

We have read your manuscript with boundless delight. If we were to publish your paper, it would be impossible for us to publish any work of lower standard; and as it is unthinkable that in the next thousand years we shall see its equal, we are, to our regret, compelled to return your divine composition, and to beg you a thousand times to overlook our short sight and timidity.

—Rejection slip from a Chinese economic journal
(according to a columnist in the *London Financial Times*)

If I'm a lousy writer, a helluva lot of people have got lousy taste.

—Grace Metalious, author of *Peyton Place*

Alternatively, if you haven't made your printer purchase yet, go for an HP LaserJet 4M, which is identical to the LaserJet 4 except that it comes packaged with the PostScript SIMM, a full 6MB of memory, *and* an Appletalk connection for communicating with Apple Macintosh computers. The LaserJet 4M has a street price of about $1,929, approximately $550 more than the LaserJet 4.

Another PostScript option is LaserMaster's WinJet1200 (for the LaserJet 4) and WinJet800 (for all other HP LaserJets). These combination software/hardware packages provide you with PostScript, 50 Type 1 PostScript fonts and 50 TrueType fonts, much faster PostScript printing, and higher dpi resolutions (though not quite as high as the numbers indicate; for example, the WinJet1200 provides 1200 dpi horizontally but a somewhat lower resolution vertically that is "fudged" by the software to simulate 1200 dpi). The products operate exclusively under Microsoft Windows, but that's not a huge constraint because they'll work with any DOS program that you're running in a window.

I am sitting in the smallest room in the house. I have your review in front of me. Soon it will be behind me.

— Max Reger

*T*he point of good writing is knowing when to stop.

— Lucy M. Montgomery

One nice aspect of the WinJet series is that they don't require you to add memory to your printer, because they perform their work through your PC. (Indeed, the faster your computer is, the faster your printing will be.) They may force you to upgrade your *PC*, though—the WinJet800 requires that your computer have at least 8MB of memory, and the WinJet1200 requires 16MB. Otherwise, the WinJet products are quite affordable; the WinJet800 has a list price of only $495, and the WinJet1200 has a list price of $995.

Finally, to keep up-to-date on how to get the most from your HP printer, consider subscribing to a periodical that covers new products, and tips and tricks. I recommend the *LaserJet Journal*, a respected monthly 16-page newsletter that costs $49 a year.

Printing can be the most satisfying part of any writing project. After all your hard work, you just press a button, sit back, and watch your finely honed words and polished layout magically appear on paper.

Maybe, as the philosophers say, the journey *is* the goal. Still, it feels good to finally arrive at your destination.

Product Information

Note: Version numbers and prices may have changed by the time you read this.

Discoversoft
1516 Oak Street
Alameda, CA 94501
(510) 769-2902
Fax: (510) 769-0149

TreeSaver 3.2: List Price, $49.95; Street Price N/A

TreeSaver DJ 1.0: List Price, $29.95; Street Price N/A

Elek-Tek, Inc.
7350 North Linder Avenue
Skokie, IL 60077
(800) 395-1000; (708) 677-7660
Fax: (708) 677-7168

Carries wide range of low-priced computer supplies, including printer cartridges and paper; call for free catalog

Hewlett-Packard Co.
P.O. Box 58059
Santa Clara, CA 95051-8059
(800) 752-0900; (408) 246-4300
Fax: (208) 344-4809

HP DeskJet 500: List Price, $365; Street Price, about $309

HP DeskJet 550C: List Price, $719; Street Price, about $575

HP LaserJet IIIP: List Price, $1,099; Street Price, about $879

PostScript Level II Cartridge (for LaserJet IIIP): List Price, $495;
Street Price N/A

HP LaserJet 4: List Price, $1,759; Street Price, about $1,369

PostScript SIMM for LaserJet 4: List Price, $499; Street Price, about $259

4MB SIMM memory for LaserJet 4: List Price, $279; Street Price, about
$149

HP LaserJet 4M: List Price, $2,399; Street Price, about $1,929

Korenthal Associates, Inc.
511 Avenue of the Americas, #400
New York, NY 10011
(800) 527-7647; (212) 242-1790
Fax: (212) 242-2599

4Print 4.15: List Price, $69.95; via coupon near the back of this book,
$39.95

LaserJet Journal
1945 Techny Road
Suite 14
Northbrook, IL 60062
(800) 323-2686; (708) 498-0920
Fax: (708) 498-3277

LaserJet Journal (monthly 16-page newsletter): $49 for one year subscription;
$98 for two year subscription, and a premium (at the time of this writing,
Lotus SmartPics)

LaserMaster Corporation
9955 West 69th Street
Eden Prairie, MN 55344
(800) 365-4646; (612) 943-8286
Fax: (612) 944-9519

WinJet800: List Price, $495; Street Price N/A

WinJet1200: List Price, $995; Street Price N/A

LaserTools Corporation
1250 45th Street
Suite 100
Emeryville, CA 94608
(800) 767-8004; (510) 420-8777
Fax: (510) 420-1150

PrintCache 3.1: List Price, $99.95; Street Price, about $55

Paper Direct
205 Chubb Avenue
Lyndhurst, NJ 07071
(800) 272-7377; (201) 507-5488
Fax: (201) 507-0817

Carries beautifully designed laser printer paper in a wide variety of colors, styles, shapes, and weights; call for free catalog

Quill Corporation
P.O. Box 1450
Lebanon, PA 17042-1450
Northeast: (717) 272-6100; Southeast: (404) 479-6100; Midwest: (708) 634-4800; West: (714) 988-3200
Fax: (708) 634-5708

Carries comprehensive line of low-priced office supplies, including printer cartridges and paper; call for voluminous free catalog

Zenographics
Four Executive Circle
Irvine, CA 92714
(800) 366-7494; (714) 851-6352
Fax: (708) 634-5708

SuperPrint 3.0: List Price, $99; Street Price N/A

PART VIII

APPENDICES

APPENDIX

A

GLOSSARY

I've tried to avoid computer jargon while writing this book. However, for the sake of clarity and conciseness, there were certain terms I felt had to be included. This section is provided in case you hit one of these peculiar terms and haven't a clue as to what it means.

For considerably more (and considerably more complete) definitions, refer to a computer dictionary, either in book form or on disk. Recommendations for the latter are covered near the end of Chapter 5, *Electronic Dictionaries and Thesauruses*.

286 Short for 80286 chip, and for the PC based around this chip. The 286 is faster than the 8088, but not as fast as the 386 or 486.

386 Short for 80386 chip, and for the PC based around this chip. The 386 is faster than the 8088 and 286, but not as fast as the 486. If you want to comfortably run cutting edge software like Microsoft Windows, you should buy a 386 or 486 PC.

486 Short for 80486 chip, and for the PC based around this chip. The 486 is currently the fastest chip designed to run PC software, so if you can afford it, you'll want to buy a 486 PC.

8088 Refers to the first chip created for the PC, and to a machine based around the chip. These PCs are inexpensive, and they'll run super-fast word processors such as XyWrite tolerably, but they're too slow and dumb to handle most modern software.

Alt key Short for Alternate key. Changes the meanings of other keys when pressed in combination with them; for example, Alt+F might open a program's File menu, and Alt+P might tell a program to print your document.

arrow keys The keys that move a program's cursor one position to the left or right, or one line up or down. Also called **cursor keys**.

ASCII Short for American Standard Code for Information. Interchange, and pronounced *ask-ee*. ASCII is a universal format for PC data. Its shortcoming is that it can't include formatting information such as underlining, boldface, fonts, and margins.

batch file A text file with the extension BAT that contains a series of commands you'd otherwise specify one at a time at the DOS prompt. A batch file allows you to automate the executing of a series of DOS instructions and programs. The most important batch file is AUTOEXEC.BAT, which is run automatically every time you turn on your PC.

BBS Short for electronic Bulletin Board Service, a BBS is a computer system that's typically operated by an enthusiastic hobbyist as a free service, and offers such basics as a message board for trading information and gossip, a program section that contains hundreds of **shareware** programs you can download, and (buried somewhere) a file with the phone numbers of other BBSs in your area. You access a BBS using a **modem**.

bit Either a one or a zero in the binary number system. Eight bits make up a byte.

bitmap graphic An image that's made up of dots, and that may lose its quality when resized. In contrast, a **vector graphic** is an image that's made up of lines, arcs, and other geometric shapes, and that fully maintains its quality when resized.

byte A fundamental unit of computer data. For example, a single letter (such as *A*) or digit (such as *9*) is stored in one byte. As another example, a 3.5 inch high-density floppy disk holds over 1.44 million bytes.

board A board that holds chips and other electronic components. The main board in your PC is called the *motherboard*. The devices you place in the slots on your motherboard to increase your PC's capabilities are also called boards, though they may alternatively be referred to as **cards**.

cache A program that notes what data you request frequently, and keeps that data in memory so you can access it instantly instead of going to the hard disk. The best cache available is Super PC-Kwik from PC-Kwik Corporation.

card A board that holds chips and other electronic components, and that you can place in one of the slots in your PC to enhance your system's capabilities. For example, a modem card allows your PC to dial into other computers, and a sound card (in conjunction with speakers and the proper software) lets your PC produce high quality music and sound effects.

CD-ROM Short for Compact Disc Read-Only Memory, a CD-ROM is a shiny disc that looks identical to a music CD, but in addition to sound can "play" text, pictures, animation, video, and programs. A CD-ROM can hold up to 630MB of information, which is the equivalent of 275,000 pages of text, or 1,800 double-density floppy disks, or thousands of images, or 74 minutes of music.

clip art Typically, professionally designed pictures that are either in the public domain or that customers of a clip art package are granted permission to use. Such canned graphics can prove very handy when you're seeking an image to clarify a point or liven up a document.

Control Panel A program in Microsoft Windows that controls Windows settings such as window colors, the keyboard repeat rate, the mouse speed, and the pattern or picture used for the Desktop background.

conventional memory The first 640K of your PC's memory, which is a critical area for programs running under DOS (as opposed to Windows). A memory manager such as QEMM-386 (see Chapter 20, *Essential General-Purpose Tools*) can optimize the use of your conventional memory space.

Ctrl key Short for Control key. Changes the meanings of other keys when pressed in combination with them; for example, Ctrl+S might tell a program to save your document, and Ctrl+P might tell the program to print it.

cursor Typically, a blinking underline or rectangle that moves as you work, and indicates the spot on your screen where you're set to enter or edit data.

cursor keys The keys that move a program's cursor one position to the left or right, or one line up or down. Also called **arrow keys**.

database A electronic collection of structured information.

database manager A program that stores data in a structured fashion, and can retrieve, sort, and print information you specify from the database.

defragment To physically reorganize the data on a disk so that each file's information is stored sequentially, instead of being scattered around (or *fragmented*). Defragmentation can speed your PC's operation, because it takes less time to retrieve file data stored in the same disk area.

desktop computer A standard (that is, large and heavy) PC that you keep on your desk. Alternatives include a portable machine, such as a **laptop** or **palmtop**.

desktop publishing A category of software that helps you lay out your documents attractively, often with the goal of producing high-resolution output for commercial printing. Abbreviated as **DTP**.

device driver Software that lets you use a computer device, such as a printer, mouse, or CD-ROM drive.

dialog box A box with a text message, and one or more options you're prompted to select.

directory The DOS equivalent of a file folder. Directories allow you to organize your files into distinct groups (and near-infinite sub-groups), so that you might have some chance of locating a particular file amidst the thousands on your hard disk. (If you can't, though, consider using a File Find utility like the ones discussed in Chapter 7, *Other Editing Tools*.)

disk The primary PC data storage device. A hard disk can hold from 20MB to over 1,000MB, but it typically isn't removable; while a floppy disk holds only about 1MB, but it *is* removable. A hard drive operates about five times faster than a floppy drive.

download To receive data from another computer using a **modem**.

driver See **device driver.**

DTP See **Desktop Publishing.**

DOS Short for Disk Operating System, and pronounced "dahss." An operating system runs in the background and in effect acts as your PC's brain. DOS, which was created by Microsoft, is the first operating system for the PC, and still the most widely used. **Windows**, which was also created by Microsoft, is an increasingly popular operating system that works in conjunction with DOS. For more information, see the Introduction.

EGA Short for Enhanced Graphics Adapter, EGA represents a collection of specifications for a low-resolution PC display. EGA is a relatively old standard that has effectively been replaced by **VGA.**

EEMS See **EMS.**

EMS Short for Expanded Memory Specification, this refers to a method for creating a special memory area, called **expanded memory**, using the RAM above the first 1MB in your PC. The current specification is named EMS 4, and can handle up to 32MB of RAM. It incorporates the best of earlier EMS techniques including Enhanced EMS, or **EEMS**, and can be used on all PCs (though in slower machines requires a special card to work). An alternative, and more popular, memory management technique is **extended memory**, which works with only 286 and higher PCs.

Enter key Also called the Return key, Enter is typically a large key on the right side of the keyboard with an arrow drawn on it. In word processing, you should press Enter to end paragraphs and create blank lines; and in all programs, you generally press Enter to execute a selection or command.

expanded memory A special memory area above a PC's first 1MB. For more information, see **EMS.**

export To convert data in the program you're using to a different format and saving the data to a disk file. The file can then be loaded into a program that supports the second format.

extended memory Refers to both a specification for handling the memory area above 1MB in your 286, 386, or 486 PC, and the memory itself. Most modern programs, including Microsoft Windows, support extended memory, which is a more efficient memory management technique than **expanded memory.**

floppy disk A thin magnetic platter, housed in a plastic jacket, that stores your PC data. A floppy disk operates slower and holds much less data than a hard disk. However, it's removable, so you can use a floppy disk drive to store data on an unlimited number of floppy disks.

font A family of characters designed in a particular typeface. For more information, see Chapter 22, *Laying Out Your Work*.

format 1) In the term *file format*, the way data is arranged in a file. 2) Adjusting the look of a document by setting margins, applying boldfacing and underlining, and so on. 3) Preparing a new disk for use, or wiping the information from a disk you want to reuse, via the DOS FORMAT command.

Function key The set of keyboard keys labelled F1, F2, and so on through F10 (or, on most modern PCs, through F12). The action of a function key will vary from program to program, though F1 is typically defined as the Help key. Certain programs, such as WordPerfect, assign a meaning to the function keys by themselves *and* in combination with Shift, Ctrl, and Alt, for a total of 40 commands.

GB See **gigabyte**.

gigabyte Approximately one billion bytes. (Specifically, it's 1,000MB, or 1,0240,000,000 bytes.) Abbreviated as **GB**.

graphics Electronic pictures, as opposed to text. The two basic types of graphics are **bitmap** and **vector**.

gray-scale A series of shades from white to black. Generally, the more gray-scale an image has, the more realistic it will look.

hard disk One or more metallic platters used to store your PC data. A hard disk operates faster and holds much more information than a floppy disk, but it's typically not removable.

hardware Computer equipment you can touch (such as chips, boards, cables, drives, and disks), as opposed to software, which is intangible.

high memory The area between the first 640K and first 1MB of memory in your PC. When the PC was designed, this area was reserved for non-program use (such screen display storage), but modern memory managers have come up with ways of using this space to increase your **conventional memory**.

icon A small on-screen picture that can represent anything from a command to a program to one of your disk drives.

import To load data into an existing document, typically from a disk file created by a program other than the one you're currently using.

K See **kilobyte**.

kilobyte Approximately one thousand bytes. (Specifically, it's 1,024 bytes, or two to the tenth power, which is an important value for PCs since they operate on a base 2 number system.) Abbreviated as **K**.

LAN See **Local Area Network**.

laptop A PC that's small enough to hold in your lap as your work. Laptops are popular with people who travel frequently or have long train commutes. They're easier to type on than **palmtop** PCs, but they're also significantly heavier.

LaserJet The brand name of laser printers manufactured by the Hewlett-Packard Company. For more information, see Chapter 23, *Printing Your Work*.

Local Area Network Typically consists of a central computer, called a *server*, and other computers in the same building that are linked together. A Local Area Network allows everyone in a company to access a common base of data, and makes it easy for coworkers to communicate electronically. Abbreviated as **LAN**.

macro A routine that runs a sequence of keystrokes. Macros are great for automating repetitive tasks, which both saves time and ensures consistency.

mail merge A process that combines, or merges, a list of addresses with a template document to produce form letters or mailing labels.

MB See **megabyte**.

megabyte Approximately one million bytes. (Specifically, it's 1,000K, or 1,0240,000 bytes.) Abbreviated as **MB**.

megahertz Abbreviated as **MHz**, and representing one million cycles per second. MHz is the unit of measure of a PC's clock speed, and provides a rough indication of how fast a PC with a particular chip runs. For example, a 33MHz 386 is faster than a 20MHz 386 (but is slower than a 33MHz 486).

memory resident A program that lurks hidden in memory, and either performs some function in the background, or simply waits for you to pop it up on your screen with a designated keystroke when you need it. An example is an electronic dictionary you can invoke from whatever program you're using when you need to check the definition of a word. Also called a **TSR**.

menu A rectangular list that's usually accessed from a line, or *menu bar*, near the top of the screen, and that organizes commands under a particular category (for example, File, Edit, or Help). You can open a menu by clicking on its name with your mouse. If you then click on one of the displayed menu options, that command is executed.

MHz See **megahertz**.

Microsoft Windows See **Windows.**

modem A device that converts data from your PC into audio tones that can be transmitted over phone lines, and converts similar tones from other computers into data your PC can understand. These processes are called *modulation* and *demodulation*, and it's from the first few letters of these two terms that we get "modem." You need a modem to dial into **BBSs** and online services.

monitor The high-resolution TV-like device that displays your computer data.

mouse A device resembling a bar of soap, with two or three large buttons at its top (though most programs pay attention only to the left button), and a ball underneath it that tracks its movements. A mouse lets you move a pointer anywhere on your screen quickly and easily, and is especially effective at selecting menu commands and dialog box options. A mouse is a virtual necessity when you're running Microsoft Windows programs.

multitasker Software that allows you to run two or more programs at the same time. In addition to letting you switch from program to program (see **task switcher**), a multitasker lets you start a process in one program (say, a long spreadsheet calculation, or an online download) and leave it running in the background while you work in other programs.

network See **Local Area Network.**

online The state of being connected to other computers via a modem. (This word has other meanings—for example, your printer must be "online" before you can print—but the telecommunications meaning is the only one used in this book.)

PC Short for personal computer; or, more narrowly, for IBM-compatible or DOS-compatible personal computers. This book uses PC in the latter sense, and tells you explicitly when it's discussing other types of computers, such as the Apple Macintosh line.

palmtop A PC small enough to hold in your hand. Palmtops are especially useful for people on the go, because they're compact and light. However, they're more difficult to type on than a **laptop** or **desktop** PC.

parallel port A plug on the back of your PC that lets you connect a printer or other parallel device to your computer via a parallel cable.

partition Before your hard disk is formatted by the DOS FORMAT command, you (or the vendor who sold you the drive) must specify how many partitions it will divided into. For example, a 400MB hard drive can be defined as a single- partition drive C, or as a 200MB drive C and a 200MB drive D. You can generally ignore partitioning unless your partition table data becomes damaged, in which case you can try to repair the data using a program such as The Norton Utilities or PC Tools; or give up and run the DOS FDISK command to repartition your drive, and the DOS FORMAT command to reformat it. (This frightening scenario, by the way, is yet another reason to back up your data frequently to floppy disks or tape.)

port A plug at the back of your PC that lets you attach various devices to your system via cables. For example, the parallel port lets you attach a printer, the serial lets you hook up a modem or scanner, the mouse port lets you connect a mouse, and so on.

PostScript A page description language from Adobe Systems, PostScript provides a way of defining how text and graphics should look both on-screen and on paper. PostScript is supported in all high-end PC desktop publishing programs, is available as an option for virtually every brand of laser printer, and is a standard feature in several high-resolution (1,270 dpi and 2,540 dpi) printers. PostScript therefore allows you to lay out a document on your PC, print draft copies on your laser printer, and then have an output service generate high-resolution final pages.

print spooler A program that automatically directs all the data from your print job to your computer's memory, or to your hard disk, thus freeing the program you're using from waiting for your printer. It then transfers the data to your printer in the background as you work.

program A series of computer instructions that performs a particular task on your PC. Also called **software**.

Program Manager The portion of Microsoft Windows that manages your program icons, and lets you run a program by double-clicking on its icon.

RAM Short for Random Access Memory, this is the memory your PC uses to perform all its activities. For example, your computer can't run a program until it loads it from your hard or floppy disk into RAM. The PC also performs all its calculations in RAM, keeps DOS and memory resident programs in RAM, and so on. When you turn your machine off, all the data in RAM is instantly erased, which is why it's necessary to save your work to a permanent storage medium such as a hard or floppy disk.

resolution The degree of sharpness of an image displayed on your screen or printed on paper. Resolution is typically represented by the number of dots across and lines along a screen, or by the number of dots per inch (dpi) on a page.

serial port A plug on the back of your PC that lets you connect a modem, scanner, or other serial device to your computer via a serial cable.

shareware A category of software that you're encouraged to obtain from friends, BBSs, online services, or low-priced shareware disk vendors. After a trial period (say, 30 days) during which you use a program for free, you're honor-bound to pay for it if you intend to keep using it.

Shift key Changes the meanings of other keys when pressed in combination with them. Like its typewriter equivalent, the Shift key is most often used to capitalize a letter (for example, inserting *A* instead of *a*) or to select the character at the top half of a key (for example, inserting ? instead of /).

slot A receptacle on your motherboard into which you can insert a card to enhance your PC's capabilities. For more information, see **card**.

software A series of computer instructions that performs a particular task on your PC. Also called a **program**.

spooler See **print spooler**.

spreadsheet A program that simulates a paper worksheet by letting you enter numbers, text, or formulas into cells that are organized into rows and columns. The spreadsheet lets you perform a variety of calculations on the cells, generate graphs from your data, and print attractively formatted reports.

status line An information line that's typically displayed near the bottom of your screen, and that provides data on the state of various program elements and activities.

style sheet A collection of formatting elements such as underlining, bold-facing, and type size that can be applied uniformly to sections of text. Style sheets are a powerful tool for making formatting changes quickly and consistently.

swap file A disk file used by certain programs as a temporary storage area. Under Windows, a swap file can speed your PC's operation, because it allows Windows to save to disk portions of a program in memory that you're not accessing frequently, and to allocate more memory to programs that you *are* accessing frequently.

task switcher Software that lets you keep several programs (say, a word processor, a drawing program, and a desktop publishing package) in memory at the same time, and switch from one to the other with a few keystrokes or mouse clicks. Working this way can be much easier than having to always exit a program before running another one.

telecommunications A field centered around going **online** to communicate with other computer systems using a **modem**.

TSR Short for *terminate-and-stay-resident*. For more information, see **memory resident**.

TrueType A recent font format created by Microsoft for use in Windows 3.1. Unlike PostScript/Type 1 fonts, TrueType fonts can be scaled, displayed, and printed properly through Windows without the help of additional software.

Type 1 A highly popular font format created by Adobe Systems that's a subset of Adobe's PostScript format. To properly scale, display, and print Type 1 fonts under Windows, you should use the Adobe Type Manager program (see Chapter 22, *Laying Out Your Work*).

utility A program that helps your system run more safely or efficiently, or helps you get better use out of your application programs (that is, your word processor, electronic spreadsheet, database manager, and so on). Typical utilities include data compressors, memory managers, caches, disk defraggers, file recovery software, file location software, file translators, print spoolers, virus detectors, and screen blankers.

vector graphic An image that's made up of lines, arcs, and other geometric shapes, and that fully maintains its quality when resized. In contrast, a **bitmap graphic** is an image that's made up of dots, and that may lose its quality when resized.

VGA Short for Video Graphics Array, VGA represents a collection of specifications for a medium-resolution PC display. VGA is currently the minimum standard for PC displays. More advanced standards include Super VGA.

Windows An operating system created by Microsoft that works in conjunction with DOS and takes over many of DOS' functions. Windows is based around dynamic images rather than static text, and so allows for a more flexible and colorful display. In addition, it provides such technical advantages as better management of your PC's memory and the ability to run multiple programs at the same time. However, it requires significant computing power to run smoothly; at minimum, you'll want a 12 MHz 286 and 4MB of memory.

Windows Control Panel See **Control Panel**.

Windows Program Manager See **Program Manager**.

word processor Fundamentally, a program that lets you enter, edit, format, and print text. High-end word processors—such as WordPerfect, Ami Pro, and Microsoft Word—pack in many extra features, such as spell-checking, thesaurus look-ups, grammar checking, file translation, outlining, document notation, revision tracking, and rudimentary desktop publishing.

workgroup A group of people who share data and are typically working on similar projects. A workgroup is often linked by a **Local Area Network**, making it easy for multiple users to access the same electronic data simultaneously.

writer "And it does no harm to repeat, as often as you can, 'Without me the literary industry would not exist; the publishers, the agents, the sub-agents, the sub-sub-agents, the accountants, the libel lawyers, the departments of literature, the professors, the theses, the books of criticism, the reviewers, the book pages—all this vast and proliferating edifice is because of this small, patronized, put-down, and underpaid person.'"—Doris Lessing

APPENDIX

B

RESOURCES

This book was created primarily to "open doors" by discussing software writing tools you may not have known existed. Therefore, there's a great deal about PCs and PC products that it hasn't covered. This appendix offers some suggestions on where to seek further information.

First, of course, there are other books. Most titles are devoted to narrow subjects, such as a single business program (or, occasionally, a single game). However, an entertaining tome that furnishes an overview of all types of PC products is *The Personal Computer Book* by Peter McWilliams. Besides supplying down-to-earth advice, this book is crammed with humorous photographs, movie stills, and—yes—Dover clip art. It costs $19.95, and you can order it by calling (800) 543-3101 or (213) 650-9571; or by writing Prelude Press, 8159 Santa Monica Boulevard, Los Angeles, CA 90046.

While books are great at providing breadth and depth, they can't stay on top of fast-breaking products. Therefore, you also ought to read a computer magazine. Specifically, you should subscribe to *PC Magazine*, which is by far the best of its breed. *PC Mag* (as its editors affectionately call it) assumes that its readers have a high level of computer knowledge, so it can be tough going at first. However, the consistently crisp, clear writing it publishes will help even beginners muddle through. (Besides, after you read it for a few months, you'll start comprehending its freely tossed-off jargon through sheer osmosis.) For your efforts, you'll be rewarded with stories about hot new products, extraordinarily intelligent reviews, and incisive analysis (including two sharp-tongued, addictive pages per issue by industry curmudgeon John Dvorak). *PC Magazine* costs $29.97 for 22 biweekly issues. To order it, call (800) 289-0429, or write PC Magazine, P.O. Box 51524, Boulder, CO 80321-1524.

If you need even more product news, and need it on a weekly basis, you should also subscribe to *InfoWorld*, a tabloid-sized newspaper. This one is tougher to get hold of, because it's a controlled circulation magazine. What that means is it's *free*, but only if the answers you give on an application form indicate you're the sort of high-volume buyer *InfoWorld* advertisers want to reach. Otherwise, you can still subscribe, but only at the high price of $130 a year. To get the application form, call (800) 457-7866 or (708) 647-7925; or write InfoWorld, P.O. Box 1172, Skokie, IL 60076.

There's more to a publication than its editorial material. If you're in a shopping mood, what you really want is lots of advertisements from low-priced mail order vendors. The magazine that delivers such stuff in spades is *Computer Shopper*, which gives you over 800 tabloid-sized pages of newsprint a month bound within full-color glossy covers. *Computer Shopper's* articles are more filler than filling, but its ads feature bargains galore. A subscription costs $19.97 for 12 issues, and can be ordered by calling

(800) 274-6384, or by writing Computer Shopper, P.O. Box 51021, Boulder, CO 80321-1021.

Moving from print to people, another invaluable information resource is a users group. There's just no substitute for talking to folks who can offer firsthand accounts of what nightmares ensue when you run software *x* and software *y* together, or who know of a little shop off of Main Street that performs excellent PC repairs, or who are trying to get a bunch of people together to buy CD-ROMs at a volume discount. User group meetings offer great opportunities for learning, establishing business contacts, and making friends.

Computer Shopper publishes a list of user groups in every issue, including some obscure ones you may not hear about elsewhere. However, this guide is far from comprehensive. For example, the October 1993 issue failed to include the Boston Computer Society (617/252-0600), Houston's HAL-PC (713/623-4425), the Capital PC Users Group in Maryland (301/762-9372), NYPC in New York (212/533-6972), and the Sacramento PCUG in California (916/386-9865), which are the five largest PC groups in the country.

A surer method way of finding a club is to call the User Group Locator at (914) 876-6678. This is an automated telephone system run by the Association of PC User Groups (APCUG), which represents a loose affiliation of over 350 nonprofit computer societies. The Locator allows you to search by area code, state, or zip code using a push-button phone, and is your best bet for uncovering PC meetings taking place near your neighborhood.

Then again, if you're stuck at home, a great way of chatting with people is via a local BBS, or through an online service such as CompuServe or GEnie. For more information on these terrific resources, see Chapter 10, *Online References*.

On a more personal note, in case you're curious about the resources *I* tapped to create this book (and to give credit where credit is due):

For the computer stuff, most of the material came from the products themselves, and from interviews with the programs' publishers. However, I also leaned heavily on articles and ads I clipped from my magazine collection, which includes *PC Magazine, PC Sources, InfoWorld, PC Week, Byte, PC/Computing, PC World,* and *Publish*. In addition, I was helped enormously by Computer Select, a CD-ROM disc that contains a year's worth of full-text articles from 75 major computer magazines. More information about Computer Select appears in Chapter 9, *CD-ROM References*.

As for the scores of wise sayings about writing, they were culled from the following quotation collections:

Bartlett's Familiar Quotations, The Concise Columbia Dictionary of Quotations, The Great Quotations, The Movie Quote Book, The Oxford Dictionary of Quotations, Peter's Quotations, The Portable Curmudgeon, The Quotable Quote Book, The Quotable Woman, Rotten Rejections, This is Really A Great City (I Don't Care What Anybody Says), Webster's New World Dictionary of Quotable Definitions, Whole Grains, The Writer's Home Companion, The Writer's Quotation Book, The 637 Best Things Anybody Ever Said, The Other 637 Best Things Anybody Ever Said, and *The Third and Possibly the Best 637 Best Things Anybody Ever Said.*

Finally, the illustrations accompanying the quotes came from over two dozen books in the wonderful Dover Pictorial Archive series (Dover Publications, Inc., 31 East 2nd Street, Mineola, NY 11501). Collect them all!

APPENDIX
C

DISCOUNT COUPONS

This section contains discount coupons for some of the best software discussed in this book. The coupons are organized alphabetically by company name.

Please note that the discount offers apply only when you mail in the *original* coupons on the following pages. No phone orders or photocopies of the coupons will be accepted.

All of the publishers represented here have promised to honor their coupons until at least January 1, 1995, and apply them to whatever are the most current versions of their software. After that time, some publishers may continue to honor their coupons, while others may not. Therefore, past January 1, 1995, it's recommended that you not mail in your order until you've called the company carrying the product you're interested in and confirmed that its coupon is still being honored.

Every discount that follows is not only well below the list price, but below the *street* price. Therefore, these coupons offer you bargains you're unlikely to find anywhere else.

In a nutshell, the coupons give you the opportunity to purchase great products at great prices. Buy and enjoy!

Please send me Idegen++ 2.3 for DOS at the discounted price of $99 (66% off the list price), plus $5 for shipping and handling. (California residents, please add sales tax.)

Name _____

Company _____

Address _____

City _____ State _____ Zip _____

Daytime Phone ( ) _____

Method of Payment: ☐ Check *(Payable to Finntrade, Inc.)*

☐ American Express ☐ Visa ☐ MasterCard

Card Number _____ Expiration Date _____

Cardholder's Signature _____ Date _____

Mail to: Finntrade, Inc., 2000 Powell Street, Suite 1200, Emeryville, CA 94608

Offer good with original coupon only

Please send me Multi-Lingual Scholar 4.1 for DOS at the discounted price of $345 (50% off the list price), plus $5 for shipping and handling. (California residents, please add sales tax.)

Name _____

Company _____

Address _____

City _____ State ____ Zip _____

Daytime Phone ( ) _____

Method of Payment: ☐ Check *(Payable to Gamma Productions, Inc.)* ☐ MasterCard

☐ Visa ☐ American Express Preferred Disk Size: ☐ 3 ¹/₂ ☐ 5 ¹/₄

Card Number _____ Expiration Date _____

Cardholder's Signature _____ Date _____

Mail to: Gamma Productions, Inc.
710 Wilshire Boulevard, Suite 609, Santa Monica, CA 90401

Offer good with original coupon only

IdeaFisher Systems, Inc. • 2222 Martin St., #110 • Irvine, CA 92715 USA
(800) 289-4332 • (714) 474-8111 • (714) 757-2896 Fax

Please process my order for the ❏ DOS 5 1/4 ❏ DOS 3 1/2 Version 4.0 of *IdeaFisher*. Included is $99.00 + $9.00 shipping and handling. CA residents please add sales tax. International customers please add $75.00 for shipping and handling.

Name: _____ Title: _____

Company: _____ Phone: _____

Address (No P.O. Boxes): _____

City/State/Code/Country: _____

❏ Check ❏ VISA/MC/Discover/AMEX #: _____ Exp. : _____

Cardholder's Signature: _____

This original coupon must be presented with order.

☑ **YES! I want to be creative with Babble!**

Regularly $35

Special offer for readers of this book: Only $25!

Mail your order to: Korenthal Associates, Inc.
511 Ave. of the Americas #400
New York NY 10011

Babble! plus Best of Babble! $35.00
$25.00*

Payment ❏ Check (U.S. funds drawn on a U.S. bank)
❏ MC ❏ Visa ❏ Amex

Shipping & Handling $_____
$5 U.S./Canada, $10 Foreign

Card #_____ Exp._____

Signature_____

NYS Residents add sales tax $_____

Name_____

Total $_____

Company_____

*Special offer good only with original coupon from this book.

Address_____

60-day money-back guarantee.

_____

_____

Disk Size ❏ 5¼" ❏ 3½"

Daytime Phone_____

☑ **YES! I want to save paper with 4Print!**

Regularly $69.95

Special offer for readers of this book: Only $39.95!

Mail your order to: Korenthal Associates, Inc.
511 Ave. of the Americas #400
New York NY 10011

4Print for DOS & Windows $~~69.95~~
$39.95*

Shipping & Handling $_____
$5 U.S./Canada, $10 Foreign

NYS Residents add sales tax $_____

Total $_____

*Special offer good only with
original coupon from this book.

60-day money-back guarantee.

Disk Size   ☐ 5¼"   ☐ 3½"

Payment   ☐ Check (U.S. funds drawn on a U.S. bank)
☐ MC   ☐ Visa   ☐ Amex

Card #_____ Exp._____

Signature_____

Name_____

Company_____

Address_____

_____

_____

Daytime Phone_____

Please send me Info Select 1.0 for Windows or Info Select 2.0 for DOS at the discounted
price of $79.95 (46% off the list price), plus $5 for shipping and handling.
(New Jersey residents, please add sales tax.)

Name _____

Company _____   Daytime Phone (   ) _____

Address _____

City _____   State _____   Zip _____

Method of Payment: ☐ Check *(Payable to Micro Logic)*   ☐ MasterCard

☐ Visa   ☐ American Express   ☐ Preferred Disk Size: ☐ 3½   ☐ 5¼

☐ Windows Version   ☐ DOS Version

Card Number _____   Expiration Date_____

Cardholder's Signature _____   Date _____

Micro Logic

Mail to: Micro Logic, P.O. Box 70, Dept. 510, Hackensack, NJ 07602

Offer good with original coupon only

Please send me MindLink Problem Solver 2.2 for Windows at the discounted price of $99 (66% off the list price), plus $5 for shipping and handling. (Vermont residents, please add sales tax.)

Name _____

Company _____   **MindLink**

Address _____

City _____ State _____ Zip _____

Daytime Phone ( ) _____

Method of Payment: ☐ Check *(Payable to MindLink, Inc.)*   ☐ MasterCard

☐ Visa   ☐ American Express

Card Number _____ Expiration Date _____

Cardholder's Signature _____ Date _____

Mail to: MindLink, Inc., Box 247, King's Highway, North Pomfret, VT 05053

Offer good with original coupon only

Please send me Corporate Voice 1.0 for DOS at the discounted price of $125 (50% off the list price), plus $7 for shipping within the U.S. and Canada. (Louisiana and Maryland residents, please add sales tax.)

Name _____

Company _____ Daytime Phone ( ) _____

Address _____

City _____ State _____ Zip _____

Method of Payment: ☐ Check *(Payable to Scandinavian PC Systems)*

☐ Visa   ☐ MasterCard

Card Number _____ Expiration Date _____

Cardholder's Signature _____ Date _____

Mail to: Scandinavian PC Systems, P.O. Box 3156, Baton Rouge, LA 70821-3156

Offer good with original coupon only

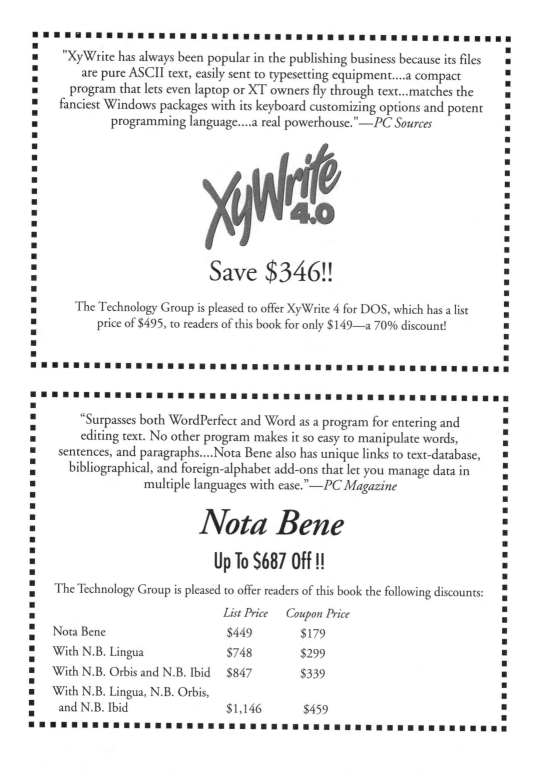

XyWrite 4.0

Yes, I want the word processor of choice for writers and publishing professionals! Send me XyWrite 4 for DOS at the discounted price of $149, plus $10 shipping and handling. (Maryland residents, please add sales tax. Customers outside the U.S. or Canada, please call for shipping charge information.)

Name _____

Company_____ Daytime Phone ( )_____

Address_____

City_____ State_____ Zip_____

Method of Payment: ☐ Check *(Payable to The Technology Group)*

☐ Visa ☐ MasterCard Preferred Disk Size: ☐ 3 ¹/₂ ☐ 5 ¹/₄

Card Number_____ Expiration Date_____

Cardholder's Signature_____ Date_____

Mail to: The Technology Group, 36 S. Charles St., Suite 2200, Baltimore, MD 21201

Offer good with original coupon only

Please send me the following:

☐ Nota Bene $179
☐ Nota Bene and N.B. Lingua $299
☐ Nota Bene, N.B. Orbis, and N.B. Ibid $339
☐ Nota Bene, N.B. Lingua, N.B. Orbis, and N.B. Ibid $459

Name _____

Company _____ Daytime Phone ( ) _____

Address _____

City _____ State _____ Zip _____

Method of Payment: ☐ Check *(Payable to The Technology Group)*

☐ Visa ☐ MasterCard Preferred Disk Size: ☐ 3 ¹/₂ ☐ 5 ¹/₄

Card Number _____ Expiration Date _____

Cardholder's Signature _____ Date _____

Mail to: The Technology Group, 36 South Charles St., Suite 2200, Baltimore, MD 21201

Offer good with original coupon only

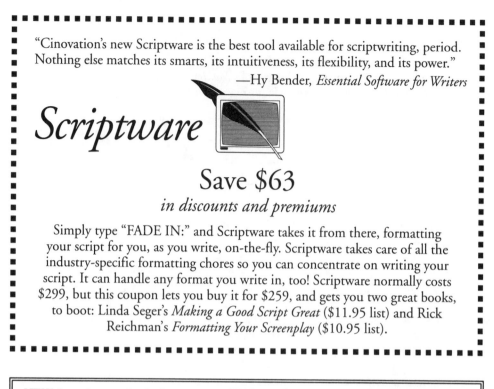

INDEX

Index of Authors Quoted